THE GOVERNMENT AND POLITICS OF ONTARIO
Fifth Edition

Edited by Graham White

Now in its fifth edition, this textbook is the standard authority on the government and politics of Ontario. Ideal for undergraduate students, it provides general background information, discusses government institutions, and covers key issues on the political scene such as the role of the media, women in politics, and the North. Extensively revised and updated to reflect the experiences of the NDP government and the early Harris era, this edition also features a new section on change and continuity in the Ontario political system.

GRAHAM WHITE is Professor of Political Science, University of Toronto.

The Government and Politics of Ontario

FIFTH EDITION

Edited by Graham White

UNIVERSITY OF TORONTO PRESS
Toronto Buffalo London

Fifth edition

© University of Toronto Press Incorporated 1997
Toronto Buffalo London
Printed in Canada
Reprinted 2001
ISBN 0-8020-0890-9 (cloth)
ISBN 0-8020-7873-7 (paper)

Printed on acid-free paper

Canadian Cataloguing in Publication Data

Main entry under title:

The government and politics of Ontario

5th ed.
ISBN 0-8020-0890-9 (bound)   ISBN 0-8020-7873-7 (pbk.)

1. Ontario – Politics and government.   I. White, Graham,
1948–   .

JL276.G68 1997   320.9713   C97-930756-2

University of Toronto Press acknowledges the financial assistance to its
publishing program of the Canada Council and the Ontario Arts Council.

Contents

Preface

When the previous edition of this book was published in early 1990, it seemed the eternal verities of Ontario politics continued to hold sway. The Liberals may have ended four decades of Tory reign, but their policies and their style had increasingly come to resemble those of the deposed Conservatives. Indeed, having adopted the Tories' centrist, 'progressive conservative' approach, the Liberals seemed set for a prolonged stay in office.

Yet within a few months, the NDP under Bob Rae had, astonishingly, won its first provincial election victory and had set out on an ambitious reform agenda. When the New Democrats lost power five years later, the victors were the Conservatives under Mike Harris, whom all but the staunchest Tory true believers had dismissed as serious contenders for office, seeing them as far to the right of 'mainstream Ontario.' In short order, the Conservatives began to fundamentally restructure Ontario society through a program unmatched in Ontario history (and possibly in Canadian history) for its radicalism, its scope, and its speed of implementation.

Accordingly, a principal concern of this book is the identification and evaluation of these remarkable changes. Have Ontario political culture and politics shifted in fundamental ways? Is the 'Common Sense Revolution' really all that revolutionary? Are the province's political and governmental institutions and its political processes changing in irreversible ways?

I am grateful to the authors of the chapters in this book for their efforts at coming to grips with such difficult yet essential questions as they have described and analysed Ontario politics and government on the cusp of the millennium. One significant consequence of these efforts is that returning authors did not simply revise their chapters from the fourth edition; in most cases they all but completely rewrote them.

As with the fourth edition, I am pleased to acknowledge my debt to Donald C. MacDonald, who developed the book and edited its first three editions, for entrusting his cherished progeny to me. Donald continues to offer advice and encouragement without looking over my shoulder. Readers familiar with previous editions will recognize that I continue to rely heavily on the basic structure Donald established and on the authors he recruited.

At the same time, I am pleased to welcome several new authors to the fold: Sid Noel, David Cameron, Bob MacDermid, Cheryl Collier, Rose Sottile, David Wolfe, Chuck Rachlis, Peter Woolstencroft, Tom Walkom, Nelson Wiseman, and Jim Suderman.

Thanks are also due to Virgil Duff at the University of Toronto Press for his enthusiasm for the book. Virgil has a long-standing association with this enterprise, having been responsible for the first edition while at Macmillan in the 1970s. Thanks also to John St James for the myriad improvements his unobtrusive copy-editing brought to the manuscript.

And, finally, my love and gratitude to Cathy and to Kate, Heather, and Patrick for putting up with a husband-father/editor preoccupied with overdue chapters, baulky disks, missing manuscript pages, and the like.

Graham White
February 1997

PART I

Introduction

ONE

Sic Permanet: Ontario People and Their Politics

Desmond Morton

In 1885, the Ontario government finally tore down the old lunatic asylum in Queen's Park and began building Canada's ugliest legislative building. It stands there still, recently renovated: a huge, asymmetrical red toad, squinting past the trees, statues, and a couple of flagpoles at the traffic on Toronto's University Avenue.

Like the provincial motto, *Ut incepit sic permanet fidelis*, 'as it began, so it remains, faithful,' the legislative building symbolizes Ontario's official allegiance to tradition. The ponderous sandstone monument that most Ontarians call Queen's Park is a museum for a theory of parliamentary government long since eroded by one-party dominance, bureaucratic growth, public apathy, cabinet dominance, and powerful interest groups. Annually thousands of students are bused to the legislature to surge up its wide stairways and through the corridors and to listen dutifully to lectures on constitutional history. They would be only a little farther from reality at Upper Canada Village or Old Fort William.

Permanent displays at Queen's Park carefully instruct visitors that Ontario is heir to the British parliamentary tradition. Since many students and some journalists regularly confuse that form of government with the constitutional principles of the neighbouring United States, the differences are worth mentioning. In the British model, the executive, legislature, and judiciary are not separate but tightly integrated. All power resides in a sovereign, symbolized a little feebly on the provincial scene by a federally appointed lieutenant governor. The sovereign, however, may act only through or on the advice of an executive – the premier and cabinet – which, in turn, holds office only so long as it retains the confidence of a majority of elected members in the legislature. The judiciary serves as 'lions under the throne,' immune from partisan meddling but upholding the sovereign's laws. Such are the principles of constitutional government in Ontario, moderated by time, circumstances, a young Charter of Rights and Freedoms, and the working of a federal system that distributes the authority of an omnipotent sovereign between Ottawa, the ten provinces of Canada, the two (three after 1999) territories, and, under assorted arrangements, over six hundred 'First Nations.'

When the building in Queen's Park was finally completed in 1893, its legislative function mattered rather more than at present. After all, there were fewer than seven provincial employees for each of the ninety elected members, and most of them owed their jobs to party patronage or a politician's favour. Even in a two-month session, members of the legislative assembly could scrutinize every penny of public spending: one early scandal was provoked by the corkscrews a profligate government had purchased for a political junket to the north. The legislative building itself was praised as a monument to prudent control of taxpayers' money. Oliver Mowat, the provincial premier, boasted that construction had cost less than the estimated $1.25 million. True to a long parliamentary tradition, Mowat was less than frank. In 1880, the 'Christian Statesman,' as Mowat loved to be called, had promised that the government's new home would cost no more than half a million dollars. No matter. Well aware that similar projects in the United States had inspired prodigies of graft and extravagance, Ontarians could rejoice in still more evidence that God and a British constitution had made them better than their neighbours.

In Canadian constitutional history, Mowat has been celebrated for expanding the trivial status originally envisaged for Canada's provinces under the British North America Act. This was not because Mowat had an expansive view of government. Even some contemporaries complained of the cheese-paring style of his Liberalism. Mowat's constitutional struggles with Ottawa were motivated as much by partisanship as by principle. The core issue in several struggles, control of liquor licensing, mattered because booze was the best known lubricant for loosening a vote. Mowat's eventual triumph in the courts meant that taverns would henceforth be in the hands of fellow Liberals – at least until a change of government.

On the whole, though, Oliver Mowat offered Ontarians cheap, efficient administration. The province's entire executive machinery, as well as the legislative assembly, could be comfortably housed under a single roof. Indeed, when Queen's Park opened, Mowat was reported as wondering how all the rooms could ever be used. In 1893, a million dollars in statutory grants from the federal government and two million more in revenues from the province's forests met almost all the cost of Ontario's government. The most conspicuous form of provincial taxation, licence fees, yielded only $294,757. The corporation of the City of Toronto spent almost as much each year to meet the demands of its 120,000 citizens as did the entire provincial government.

A century later, the government of Ontario confessed to employing over 90,000 people. A far larger army, from child-care workers to university professors, depended for the bulk of their income on provincial grants. Hardly a soul in the province could contrive to escape entirely from some share in the provincial revenues from provincial income, corporation, and retail sales taxes, to say nothing of a host of sophisticated and obscure revenue sources. A toddler shoving a sticky coin across a counter for some candy is a provincial taxpayer. Reluctant lodgers in the province's jails have their prison wages docked for their room and board.

The Fathers of Confederation in 1864 had lacked prophetic skill. Who among them could have imagined that education, roads, or 'hospitals, asylums, charities and eleemosynary institutions' would ever matter more than federal responsibility for railways, canals, and promissory notes. A century later, Ontario citizens insisted that schooling and medical care be available to them free of charge, wrote Fred Schindeler, and 'that public funds be used to sustain them and assist them when they fall prey to the inescapable hardships of life.' Ontarians had become more specialized and less self-sufficient.

The growth in public expectations was only one of a host of transformations in Ontario since Confederation. In 1867, the province was overwhelmingly agricultural. Toronto, the provincial metropolis, had only 59,000 people of a total population of 1,621,000. As late as 1941, 23.2 per cent of Ontarians were gainfully employed in agriculture, almost as many as in manufacturing. By 1991, agriculture found work for only 2.2 per cent of Ontario's working population of 5.7 million. Indeed, an ancient rural nightmare had come true. The 226,750 Ontario men, women, and children who lived on farms were far outnumbered by the province's chartered accountants, financial officers, and auditors.

Ontario has experienced other population changes that, in political terms, might well have been as traumatic as the movement from farm to city. In 1871, the quarrelsome races of the British Isles – the Irish, English, Scots, and Welsh – virtually had Ontario to themselves with 82 per cent of the population. By 1991, people of British origin had dwindled to a mere 34.9 per cent, while Italians, whom census-takers had ignored in 1871, had surpassed the Germans to achieve third place behind Franco-Ontarians. There were more Ontarians born in Asia (434,000) than in the United Kingdom (408,000). Of 9,977,000 million Ontarians, 8,594,000 spoke English only, 54,425 were unilingual francophones, 1,136,240 claimed to be bilingual, and 192,930 spoke neither of Canada's official languages.

At Confederation, Catholics formed a small and sometimes nervous minority of 17 per cent in a sea of determined Protestants. Even in 1941, Catholics were only 22.5 per cent of the population, a shade ahead of the Anglicans and far behind the United Church. In 1991, 35.5 per cent of Ontarians were Roman Catholics, easily outnumbering Anglican and United Church supporters combined. Unbelievers (icily dismissed as 'pagans' in 1871) had numbered only a couple of thousand wayward souls. In 1991, 1,247,640 people insisted that they had no religious affiliation at all.

Since Ontario politics have frequently revolved around issues of language, religion, and urban-rural friction, the political landscape might have been as changeable as demography and popular passions. At moments, this has seemed true. A visitor to the province's legislative chamber may note, among the plaster tracery in the ceiling, a cruciform device. Spotted over a century ago by a vigilant Protestant, it was solemnly offered as proof that Oliver Mowat had secretly sold Ontario's soul to the Pope. Such allegations helped win six seats for the Protestant Protective Association in the 1894 election. In 1919, resentment at rural depopulation helped sweep the United Farmers of Ontario (and a clutch of labour allies) out of nowhere to capture 34 per cent of the popular vote and fifty-five seats in the legislature. In 1943, on equally short notice, the Co-operative Commonwealth Federation shot up from 5 to 32 per cent of the vote. With thirty-four seats, the CCF had almost enough strength to give Ontario a socialist government, an achievement actually deferred for another forty-seven years.

In practice, political turbulence has been exceptional. Despite remarkable changes in the province's economy, the religious and ethnic composition of its people, and the size and role of its government, Ontarians have generally earned a reputation for political immobility. In only nine of thirty-six general elections between Confederation and 1997 have voters forced a change of government, though three of those changes have occurred between 1985 and 1995. From 1872 until 1905, the Liberals were in office. With interruptions only for Ernest Drury's United Farmers in 1919–23 and for Mitchell F. Hepburn's Liberals from 1934 to 1943, the Conservatives remained in charge until 1985. The non-stop hegemony of the Progressive Conservatives from 1943 to 1985 would be the envy of any totalitarian regime in its duration and its massive legislative majorities. The ten-year interregnum, almost evenly shared between the Liberals under David Peterson and the New Democrats under Bob Rae, ended with a renewed Conservative majority on 10 June 1995.

Any explanation of the durability of Ontario governments must be cautious, multifaceted, and undoubtedly flattering to the dominant regime. The most important single reason is that, for most of its history, Ontario has been relatively easy to govern. As the chief beneficiary of Confederation, Ontario's industrial development was secured in the nineteenth century by tariff protection and, for much of the twentieth century, by low-cost energy. Toronto gradually overtook Montreal as Canada's financial capital. Since 1867, Ontario has shared all the booms and only some of the busts of Canada's roller-coaster economy. Whenever Ontario cabinets have contemplated costly reform, ideology has usually been a bigger obstacle than an empty treasury. In 1959, before a major wave of social reform swept Canada, even the do-nothing Duplessis government was spending 9.5 per cent of the province's personal income, while Ontario, far better endowed with public institutions and services, was absorbing only 7.4 per cent. When Ontario voters demanded new hospitals, multi-lane highways, instant universities, a network of community colleges, and universal medicare, the province could afford them with little apparent risk to its triple A credit rating. In 1971, after well-organized pressure groups persuaded voters that urban expressways were an unquestionable evil, Premier William Davis wrote off tens of millions of dollars his government had lavished on a Toronto ditch and won a handsome harvest of support. How many other governments in Canada or abroad would have been rewarded for such prodigality?

Even in the recessionary times of the 1991 census, Ontario had the highest per capita incomes in Canada: $33,036 for men, $19,303 for women on average, and $57,227 for families. As owners and custodians of wealth, Ontarians are not politically adventurous. Davis himself insisted that Ontarians were immensely preoccupied by a government's ability to 'manage the store.' That skill includes getting rid of such unwanted merchandise as the Spadina Expressway or, in 1995, racial and gender equity in hiring practices. In his recent study of Ontario's political culture, John Wilson has attributed Ontario's current electoral skittishness to a desperate search for a leader who could claim government of managerial efficiency.

On its own, prosperity is not enough to guarantee re-election, though it would have been a blessing for George Henry's Tories in Depression-ridden 1934 or for Bob Rae's New Democrats in the early 1990s. In a province notable for electoral stability, government longevity owes a lot, paradoxically, to the high degree of competitiveness in Ontario's party system. For all their frustrations, Ontario's opposition parties have maintained a surprising vitality. One reason is that they are never totally out of sight of victory. In five of the eight provincial elections in which Oliver Mowat and his Liberal successors held power, a bare percentage point separated the popular vote of winner and loser. Conservative triumphs after 1905 were usually more clear-cut, but not since 1929 has any party won more than a minority of Ontario's votes. From 1943 to 1985, the Conservatives retained power largely because the discontented majority divided itself between Ontario's opposition parties, the Liberals and the CCF (after 1961, the New Democratic Party). Between 1985 and 1995, Liberals and New Democrats each had a turn at government and neither party was annihilated in the subsequent defeat.

A divided opposition enhances the notorious tendency of a 'first-past-the-post' electoral system to give the victors more seats than they deserve. In 1967, John Robarts won 69 of 117 constituencies with only 42 per cent of the vote, and in 1990, Bob Rae held 74 of 130 seats with only 38 per cent support. On the whole, Liberals have offered voters an alternative version of the current Progressive Conservative ideology, while the NDP defended the interests of organized workers and farmers and proposed some of the kitchen-tested reforms its social-democratic counterparts had applied in western Canada. Real competition for votes has meant that few Ontario governments have been left to the complacent enjoyment of power. Deceptively fat majorities in the legislature could vanish at the next contest with the defection of only a small share of a fickle electorate. All three of Ontario's parties have now had the chastening experience of defeat.

A century ago, Oliver Mowat provided Ontario with a useful recipe for government survival: bustling half-measures of reform plus scapegoating of the federal government. In the 1960s, Premier John Robarts demonstrated the technique as his government resisted universal health insurance. Robarts began, like most of the province's doctors, with a rooted opposition to Medicare, passed through several reports and two phases of compromise, and concluded with a faithful adoption of the national blueprint. Change comes most easily in Ontario if it is almost imperceptibly achieved by incessant nudges and prods. Enthusiasts for national unity have demanded that Ontario proclaim official bilingualism. Political wisdom moved, instead, to make it a functional reality. Innovators succeed when they perform as reluctant dragons. The NDP seemed much more successful in implementing its policies when they were imposed on a minority Liberal government in 1985–87 than when the party itself was in power between 1990 and 1995.

One can move too fast, of course, and too slowly. A province-wide sense that reform was out of control helped defeat both William Hearst's Conservatives in 1919 and the farmer-labour government of Ernest Drury that replaced them. A sense that Mitch Hepburn's Liberal successors were hopeless reactionaries helped beat them in 1943. The victor that year, George Drew, had borrowed some of his more popular ideas from the CCF.

A further explanation for the twentieth-century longevity of the Conservatives is that they rarely depended on a single durable leader. Sir Oliver Mowat bestrode his party and his province for so long that his departure for Ottawa in 1896 left his party gravely weakened. Mowat's two successors, Arthur S. Hardie and George Ross, could only postpone a collapse to 1905. The Tories have been wiser or more fortunate. Death, retirement, or transfer to the federal arena ended the provincial careers of James Whitney, Howard Ferguson, George Drew, Leslie Frost, and John Robarts at moments when their political stars may have begun to wane. The three Conservative defeats in this century have occurred under leaders who may have been kept in cold storage too long: William Hearst, George Henry, and Frank Miller. Changing leaders is a risky business; reluctance to do so is even more dangerous.

Prosperity, the pressure of competition, and a collegial rather than an individual approach to survival may help to explain why Ontario governments, particularly the Progressive Conservative administrations between 1943 and 1985, survived so long. The explanations say little about the consequences. One outcome, described by Schindeler in 1969 and increasingly apparent afterwards, is the close identification between the party in power and the provincial administration. 'Members of the civil service,' Schindeler observed, 'are found equating the Government with the majority party and seeing themselves as the servants of the party instead of as servants of the administration. Publications concerned with various aspects of Ontario government seem as a matter of course to become vehicles for expounding the virtues of the Government of the day. In a thousand little ways, it becomes evident that civil servants see their prime loyalty to be to a particular party instead of to the general public they are meant to serve.'

A thousand-and-first little way was illustrated in several Ontario elections when Premier Davis used the services and prestige of Treasury Board officials to evaluate the cost of Liberal and New Democrat promises. No comparable expert evaluation was made of what the Conservative government preferred to call its 'commitments.'

Any institution has pride and a stake in the status quo. Even its most discontented members understand its procedures and their justification better than the most informed outsider. Civil servants may privately sympathize with an opposition party's philosophy and program, but they bridle at apparently captious and ill-informed criticism of their efforts. Disaffected officials use photocopiers and plain brown envelopes to leak embarrassing documents to the opposition parties or the media, but they are a small minority. At the depth of the Depression, Mitch Hepburn delighted taxpayers by firing thousands of civil servants and auctioning off government limousines. No subsequent change of government has seen anything like such a slaughter, but Liberals, and especially the NDP after 1990, wondered whether they could count on their officials. Those doubts, freely expressed and compounded by inexperienced ministerial staff, probably did deprive an inexperienced government of help it desperately needed.

Stability had virtues no less real than change. Free from radical political change, Ontario's public officials could devote more time than counterparts elsewhere to achieving managerial efficiency. Through long service, the more competent ministers learned the potential and limitations of cabinet government and department organization from practical experience rather than as external critics or academic theorists. At the same time, entrenched bureaucracies can become more skilful at protecting themselves than at safeguarding the people who pay their salaries. Trust-company scandals in the early 1980s surfaced because the tide of prosperity had gone out, not because government watchdog agencies had done their job. A series of miscalculations on engineering technology as well failures in the more conjectural business of forecasting demand turned Ontario Hydro from a provincial asset to a crushing financial incubus. 'The system worked,' boasted Mr Justice Grange, after inquiries into why children had died under suspicious circumstances at Toronto's

Hospital for Sick Children, echoing the complacency of a medical, legal, and police system that had apparently failed almost everyone else.

One important consequence of one-party dominance in Ontario has been the absence of mass participation in government. For most people, democracy is a mildly boring spectator sport. Political activity is the preoccupation of an elite, increasingly ranged in single-issue pressure groups. Provincially, voter turnout has almost consistently been 10 per cent lower than in federal contests. In the mid-winter 1981 election, only 57 per cent of eligible voters managed to go to the polls; on a warm spring day in 1985, participation was only 3 per cent higher. In June 1995, 62.9 per cent of the voters turned up to support or oppose Mike Harris's 'Common Sense Revolution,' fewer than voted for or against Bob Rae in 1990. Considering the ease of voter registration and the simplicity of voting, Ontarians have no reason to be proud of their democratic enthusiasm. Civics, as taught in the province's schools, reinforces a view that involvement stops at the ballot box. Activism is for others.

The lure of public funds make politics a regulated activity. Officially registered parties, including Greens, Libertarians, Northern Heritage, and something called the Unparty, have variously won and lost the privilege of offering tax relief to their contributors. Others struggle vainly beyond the fringes of a modest registration requirement. Occasionally Conservatives and Liberals boast of huge lists of members, but the names turn out to be all those who have ever been bused to a nomination meeting. More over, party officials confess that no one knows how many true Grits or Tories the province boasts. New Democrats, who cultivate formal membership with more zeal, currently claim only 27,000 active members out of Ontario's 6,500,000 adults. Official financial reports, part of the price imposed for modest provincial subsidies and tax relief, reveal the extent of donations to the parties. The Conservative party, as the party of government, as well as of business and wealth, claims the largest income, though it remembers years of paralysing debt. Until it offended unions and militant members by the compromises of office, the NDP had the most donors.

Ontarians pay more attention than other Canadians to national affairs. Federal politics form their frame of reference on those occasions when they judge provincial politicians. This sometimes fosters the myth that Ontario voters consciously elect opposing parties in Toronto and Ottawa. Studies in the 1960s and 1970s suggested that different results were chiefly due to a higher turnout in federal than in provincial elections. Certainly Ontarians visit the sins of federal governments on their provincial parties. The long federal reign of the Liberals in the twentieth century has been as convenient to Conservatives as Sir John A. Macdonald's government was for Oliver Mowat. Federal elections often occur when provincial governments are at the mid-term nadir of their popularity and vice versa. However, when the Conservatives were defeated in 1985, Brian Mulroney's government was still popular. So was Jean Chrétien in 1995, but that was no apparent help to the Liberals' Ontario leader, Lyn McLeod.

Ontario's Ottawa fixation does exact a price. Provincial politicians, government and opposition alike, wrestle with profound public indifference. The press gallery at Queen's Park shares their frustration and, often, seeks a livelier assignment. The daily struggle for attention may explain the raucous and indecorous mood of the legislature. Governments use their majorities and end-of-session deadlines to shove through massive omnibus bills; opposition parties perform unarmed guerilla tactics to attract attention. Even governments have felt occasional twinges of conscience about the insignificance and ineffectiveness of the legislative assembly. Before similar reforms were adopted in Ottawa, John Robarts extended some modest research assistance to the opposition parties and to his own backbenchers. However, any visitor to the crush of little offices occupied by private members of the provincial parliament at Queen's Park soon appreciates that the problem of insignificance persists. Except on those rare occasions when they have the power to defeat the government or affect its intentions, provincial opposition parties can claim little attention from the media or the public. The exceptions are those MPPs whose well-practised exhibitionism grabs the attention of a bored press gallery.

This is not unique to Ontario. Traditional theories of popular sovereignty and responsible government seem irrelevant in a global economy where the most important decisions seem to be made in the financial markets of New York, London, or Tokyo. The squabbles of elected politicians seem more irrelevant than offensive. Public indifference is deeply frustrating to those who believe in classical democracy.

Ontario experience once suggested that substantive political action now lies outside the legislature. This is not new. From time to time during the political year, throngs of students, trade unionists, farmers, or, on one occasion in the NDP years, young business people gather on the parking lot in front of Queen's Park to articulate their grievances. The legislative building is conveniently accessible by public transit and it is a recognizable backdrop for the television cameras. The rugged façade gives a pleasing resonance to amplifiers as leaders and sympathetic politicians bellow their speeches into the wind. Only the ugly metal fencing, put in place by the Harris government, spoils the ambience. It also gives the only visible evidence that demonstrations might, some day, make a difference. So did the use of club-wielding riot police to clear a path for government MPPs through a throng of resentful public employees in 1996. Ontarians expect civility as well as stability from their rulers.

The politically significant have usually shunned vulgar and chilly displays outside the legislature, and make their way easily through corridors and tunnels to the government office buildings east of Queen's Park Crescent. It is there that people who really make decisions may be found. If there is a power centre in the Ontario government, it is the cabinet, where ministers with or without departmental responsibilities (or 'portfolios') gather under the benign guidance of the person who chose them for their jobs, the provincial premier. Ontario cabinets have grown. When the province first came into being in 1867, only five cabinet officers were authorized. By the time J.P. Whitney took office in 1905, he could appoint seven departmental ministers and three more without portfolio. By 1988, Premier David Peterson was joined by twenty-seven ministers heading thirty-five 'ministries,' as departments had come to be called. Two ministers without portfolio awaited more secure positions in the cabinet hierarchy, while outside the cabinet two dozen 'parliamentary assistants' awaited ambition's call.

Like its counterpart in Ottawa and the other provinces, Ontario's cabinet (or Executive Council) matters a great deal because it represents the highest level at which policy and political decisions are amalgamated. Admittedly, most of the issues reach the cabinet only after lengthy processing through ministries and committees, after public hearings and private consultations with those most affected, and after cautious scrutiny by lawyers and legislative drafters. Otherwise, cabinet business would be utterly error-prone and hopelessly bogged down. For many decisions, however, the Executive Council is the court of last resort and, in a litigious age, there is pressure to make it function in a more judicial way. This ignores the fact that its primary drive is to do that which is politic, not always that which is just.

Also like its federal counterpart, the Ontario cabinet performs an informal but important representative function. Without any necessary regard for talent, ministers may be included because they can speak for regions, for religious and ethnic groups, and for economic interests.

Roman Catholics, Franco-Ontarians, women, and Northern Ontarians can be expected to scrutinize the balance of cabinet membership and to protest absence or even relative weakness. Bob Rae took pride in his array of women ministers; Mike Harris takes equal pride in his self-made millionaires.

The cabinet is always the expression of its first minister. Canadian politics did not wait for television to accept the importance of personal leadership. Lacking more than a part-time monarchy, Canada and its provinces moved to a presidential version of prime ministership faster and earlier than did their British exemplars. Ontario has been no exception. If few of its premiers have imitated the dictatorial manner of a Mitch Hepburn or his flamboyant private life, all of them, from the time of John Sandfield Macdonald to the present, have been more than first among equals. Ontario premiers have been identified as the symbols of their period of government, lightning rods for public acclaim or condemnation. They have usually felt free to make policy with or without consulting cabinet colleagues. In 1984, William Davis decided to equalize funding for Catholic public schools, reversing a policy that had helped win him the 1971 election. He felt no need to consult his minister of education. Nor did David Peterson feel qualms about endorsing the Meech Lake Accord in 1987, though it was conspicuously at odds with some of his party's policies.

As in so much else, Oliver Mowat set the pattern. In addition to his constitutional battles with Ottawa to keep the saloons safe for Liberal licence-holders, Mowat took a well-informed interest in the adjustment of constituency boundaries, using the electoral map to cling to power as his party's rural base began to shrink. Once many Ontario farmers had turned to the Tories, rural overrepresentation and oleaginous flattery of farmers became a bipartisan Ontario tradition. Ontario premiers, however urbane, have almost always cultivated a small-town image, as though honour and statesmanship were foreign to the metropolises where most Ontarians now live. The crafty and sophisticated Leslie Frost purported to rely on the 'Law of Killaloe.' Bill Davis kept his home in Brampton, proclaiming its small-town virtues long after it had been swallowed up by Greater Toronto. Mike Harris brings his wisdom from North Bay. The only premier to make no claim on small-town virtue, York South's Bob Rae, represented as ethnically diverse a riding as Toronto can boast. He lasted one term.

Mowat's Grit backers professed to be sturdy yeomen, uninterested in pelf and plunder from the public treasury. In fact, Ontarians shared an appetite for the politics of patronage that remains unsatiated, if trans-formed. At least until 1943, changes of government were accompanied by the wholesale dismissal of provincial employees. A wartime shortage of manpower and George Drew's minority status curbed the traditional slaughter; so did Drew's personal memory of being a Liberal victim in 1934. With time and patience, Drew and his successors found alternative ways of rewarding the local notables on whom their party depended. The growth of government in Ontario included a lush proliferation of agencies, boards, commissions, and crown corporations, from the Sol-diers' Aid Commission, founded in 1915, to the more contemporary Ontario Council on the Status of Women. Some, like the Workers' Com-pensation Board, are household names; others, like the Wolf Damage Assessment Board or Thunder Bay Ski Jumps Ltd., have a more local following. Almost all such organizations provide honourable and some-times lucrative rewards for government supporters and occasionally even for opposition members whose early departure from the legislature might be helpful to the party in power. Outside the sprawling realm of government is a host of other positions at the government's disposal, as directors of marketing boards, governors of universities and hospitals, and regents in the community-college system. Many agencies, boards, and commissions have died under the 'Common Sense Revolution,' but political common sense will doubtless see others emerge.

Since nomination to these important bodies constitutes one of the most important ways that the people of Ontario gain a voice in the institutions and agencies of government, it is fair to add that party allegiance is neither the only, nor always the more important, consideration in filling vacancies. The representative principles so familiar to Canadian public life must be kept in mind. If business is represented, there will often be a token trade unionist. Region, religion, and youth must all be served. Someone will almost certainly remind the government that over half the population is female. The north, perennially disaffected by the concen-tration of wealth and influence in the south, is acutely sensitive to its interests, particularly since public spending is a major source of income for the region. The north itself is monolithic only from a distance. No one survives long in Ontario politics without realizing that a nominee from Timmins arouses little gratitude from Thunder Bay, Sudbury, or even Kirkland Lake. Similar sensitivities can be found in eastern and western Ontario, as among francophones and newer Canadians. Resentment and frustration can be held in check only by reminders that fresh vacancies will occur and that new agencies emerge in almost every session, even when governments are most determined to 'down-size,' 'privatize,' and generally diminish their own functions.

Government appointments are more than sinecures for the party faithful; they also provide an infusion of the ideas, values, and priorities of the dominant party and of other citizens. Vigilant and hard-working appointees can assert the public interest or promote the virtues of businesslike management among entrenched and complacent bureaucrats. Appointees who interest themselves in their work and do it well can give friends in government advice and warnings long before the vibrations of discontent are recorded by the party's official pollsters.

How efficient is government in Ontario? On public platforms, Conservative and even Liberal politicians routinely proclaim the superiority of private enterprise over public administration. An innocent might wonder why people who despise government should so regularly be entrusted with its management.

Speeches may be deceiving. In the 1960s, Ontario's Tories helped transform the top layers of the Ontario public service into a modern, talented institution. New blood was introduced, salaries and training were improved, and modern administrative techniques were adopted. The reforms were opportune. The new energy and sophistication of Ontario's senior officials helped the province implement major social programs in the 1960s and helped Canada survive a period of acute federal-provincial conflict in the 1970s. Modernization led to the restructuring of a century-old system of municipal government, the reform of social services, and aggressive expansion of public housing, transit systems, land-use planning and servicing, and other developments that rapid urbanization demanded. Indeed, the rapid pace of reform and the simmering discontents it engendered cost the Davis government its majority in 1975. In the ensuing period of minority governments, the Conservatives could blame Liberals and New Democrats for bothersome innovations while harvesting the underlying satisfaction.

It may be that the old rules of Ontario politics have changed, and that further, wrenching changes lie ahead. The Free Trade Agreement of 1989, opposed by the Peterson government and by half of Ontario's voters, reflected a conclusion that the old national economic strategies had already failed or had little future. By the 1970s, some of the traditional pillars of Ontario prosperity – low-cost energy close at hand, an excellent public education system, an attraction for highly skilled immigrants, a location next to some of the richest American states – had begun to sag. Ontario, once again, is a major energy importer. Few would boast of present-day Ontario education, and the skilled workers who flooded into postwar Ontario have retired. The former 'Iron Triangle' of wealthy industrial states like Ohio, Michigan, and Pennsylvania is now the 'Rust Belt,' deserted for the cheap labour and warmer temperatures of the South and Southwest. Protected from these brutal realities for a generation by its ability to raise credit, Ontario is confronted by brutal changes. It is more than doctrinaire neo-conservatism to insist that a political community cannot live for long beyond its means, and it is a reality of contemporary communications technology that those means are largely independent of local legislative fiat.

Moreover, as the central core province of Canada, Ontario has a major stake in the survival of Confederation. No region contributes more to equalization and no province gains more from the resulting economic, political, and social unit. Ontarians instinctively recognized their stake when, by the narrowest of margins, they defied the national trend and supported the Charlottetown Accord in 1992. Their premiers have consistently reflected a yearning for a stronger national identity.

Whether or not Canada survives as a whole, the politics and government of its biggest province will change. But the habits and achievements of 130 years are not quickly set aside. More than any other region of Canada, Ontario possesses a diversified economy, a well-developed infrastructure, a tolerable climate, and, above all, an earned reputation for political stability and justice. For the people of the province these are valid assets in an uncertain and difficult future.

Further Reading

Ontario's federal fixation is reflected in many ways, not least in the relative lack of writing about Ontario's own politics. The situation was so embarrassing that, in typical Ontario fashion, the government tried to fill the gap with an official program of Ontario Historical Studies. OHSS has produced some solid biographies of provincial premiers, a general history of the province, Joseph Schull's *Ontario since 1867* (Toronto, 1978) and some useful monographs. Among the most relevant biographies are Peter Oliver's *G. Howard Ferguson: Ontario Tory* (Toronto, 1977), Roger Graham's *Old Man Ontario: Leslie M. Frost* (Toronto, 1990), and Alan K. McDougall's *John P. Robarts: His Life and Government* (Toronto, 1986). Not part of OHSS is Graham White's *The Ontario Legislature: A Political Analysis* (Toronto, 1989), a work of solid and informed scholarship.

Journalists and political practitioners have provided more lively interpretations of Ontario provincial politics. Jonathan Manthorpe's *The Power and the Tories* (Toronto, 1974) explained the longevity of the Progressive Conservatives; the *Toronto Star*'s Rosemary Speirs, in *Out of the Blue: The Fall of the Tory Dynasty in Ontario* (Toronto, 1986), gave the end of the story. Claire Hoy's highly critical biography *William Davis: A Biography* (Toronto, 1985) added a little to the story. Two Liberal party staffers left their own account of David Peterson's defeat: Georgette Gagnon and Dan Rath, *Not without Cause: David Peterson's Fall from Grace* (Toronto, 1991). The New Democrat's one-term government will doubtless attract scholars. The best account is probably Thomas L. Walkom's *Rae Days* (Toronto, 1995), followed by Patrick Monahan, *Storming the Pink Palace – The NDP in Power: A Cautionary Tale* (Toronto, 1995). A somewhat premature account of the Harris victory in 1995 is Christina Blizzard's *Right Turn: How the Tories Took Ontario* (Toronto, 1995).

Among the more lively personal accounts are Donald C. Macdonald's *Happy Warrior: Political Memoirs* (Toronto, 1988), by the man who led the CCF-NDP and produced the first editions of this book. Another insider account, by a technician of the 'Big Blue Machine,' is E.A. Goodman's *Life of the Party: The Memoirs of Eddie Goodman* (Toronto, 1988).

TWO

The Socio-Economic Setting of Ontario Politics

Rand Dyck

In the course of governing Ontario, authorities encounter demands from many different interests. This chapter sketches the basic socio-economic setting of the Ontario political system, including its geography, its economy, its class structure, and its demographic background. In the process, it seeks to identify typical demands raised in the politics of the province.

Geography

PHYSIOGRAPHY

Ontario is just over one million square kilometres in area, making it about one-third smaller than Quebec. It is actually the third largest province in terms of land, but because it contains so much water, it is slightly bigger than British Columbia in total area. If Ontario were an American state, it would be second in size to Alaska, and if it were a separate country, it would rank close to South Africa, Bolivia, Egypt, or Peru, being twice as large as Spain or France, and four times larger than Britain. It stretches 1690 kilometres from eastern to western tip and 1730 km from northern to southern extremities.

Apart from the Hudson Bay Lowlands immediately adjacent to that body of water, Ontario has two major physiographic regions. The northern two-thirds of the province is part of the geological formation known as the Canadian or Precambrian Shield, characterized by rugged bare rock, rivers, lakes, trees, and a harsh winter climate. The Shield extends from the northern limits of the province as far south as an imaginary line drawn roughly between the tip of Georgian Bay and Renfrew. Below this, the fertile Great Lakes and St Lawrence Lowlands constitute the largest amount of prime agricultural land in the country. Unfortunately, it is disappearing rapidly owing to the pressures of urbanization.

The Canadian-U.S. border extends through the middle of Lakes Superior, Huron, Erie, and Ontario, accounting for a large portion of Ontario's aquatic area. Leaving that aside, however, Northern Ontario especially is replete with lakes and rivers that are conducive to recreational use and the tourist industry.

REGIONALISM

Except for the Precambrian Shield, geology does not dictate any natural regional divisions within Ontario. Instead, its regions reflect the province's vast distances, as well as certain regional distinctions in natural resources, demography, and economic development. The provincial government recognizes five economic regions – North, Central, Eastern, and Southwestern, and the Greater Toronto Area – but many government departments divide the province differently. Although the regional designations and specific boundaries are therefore rather arbitrary, it would seem best to employ something close to the five mentioned, six if the north is considered as two rather than one.

Only the northern region has been officially recognized in law. This region used to include all territory north of the French River and Lake Nipissing, but in 1988 Northern Ontario was redefined to include all of the Parry Sound and Nipissing Districts. This allows a slightly larger territory to benefit from special government programs oriented to northern needs, and it is the only region to have a ministry (Northern Development and Mines) unto itself. The provincial government also operates the Northern Ontario Development Corporation, the Northern Ontario Regional Economic Development Program, and the Northern Ontario Heritage Fund, while FEDNOR is the federal government's economic-development agency for Northern Ontario. In addition, the north until recently received special consideration in the distribution of seats in the legislature. The terms of reference of the 1986 Electoral Boundaries Commission established that there should be a minimum of fifteen constituencies in Northern Ontario, even if the population of the region did not really justify them. (The Harris government eliminated this overrepresentation in 1996.) Northern constituencies are also distinguished by special election-expenses rules and MPPs' allowances.

The population of Northern Ontario is spread over a huge territory and such distances sometimes require the recognition of a subdivision between the northwest, centred on Thunder Bay, and the northeast, containing the urban centres of Sault Ste Marie, Sudbury, Timmins, and North Bay. But whether it is considered to be one region or two, the north can be identified in fairly specific geological and geographic terms, as well as in the peculiarities of its ethnic mix, its natural resources, its political culture, and its social and economic problems. In particular, the provision of health services in the north is a constant challenge, and special educational and social services are also inadequate. The north's settlement pattern is characterized by isolated resource-based single-industry communities subject to great variations in economic prosperity. In response to this problem, the Peterson government initiated the Northern Ontario Relocation Project, involving the transfer of a number of government operations from Queen's Park to supplement resource-industry employment in the region.

Where to draw the lines between the various regions of southern Ontario is a more difficult proposition. The Toronto region is primarily identifiable, of course, as heavily urbanized, but its actual boundaries vary. For some purposes, the region corresponds with the Municipality of Metropolitan Toronto. For others, it is the labour-market area stretching from Oakville to Ajax. But increasingly, the regional municipalities of Peel, Halton, Durham, and York are lumped with Toronto under the designation 'Greater Toronto Area.'

Eastern Ontario, centred on Ottawa, Kingston, and Pembroke, is also a widely recognized region. Apart from the north, the east is generally the most economically depressed region of the province – even its farmland is inferior to that in the southwest – and it benefits from the Eastern Ontario Development Corporation. The fact that the east contains the national capital gives it a more federal orientation than the rest of the province.

Most observers would designate a central region immediately north, east, and west of the Greater Toronto Area, including Barrie, Muskoka, and Peterborough to the northeast, the Kitchener-Waterloo and Guelph area to the northwest, and Hamilton and the Niagara peninsula to the southwest. This area is probably the least well defined and, in a sense, consists of what is left after the other more distinct regional boundaries have been drawn.

The last region is the southwest. Again, there is no question of its existence, only some variation in where the dividing line should be drawn. The southwest contains such large urban centres as London, Sarnia, and Windsor, as well as Ontario's largest stretch of first-class agricultural land, from the Bruce Peninsula down to the southwestern tip of the province.

Thus, although universal agreement on the actual regional divisions within the province is regrettably absent, there is no doubt that Ontario is marked by regional cleavages. Distinctive demands arise from different regions, varied voting patterns are often apparent, and governments are acutely aware of the necessity to distribute cabinet posts and other appointments, public works, and public finances on a reasonably equitable regional basis.

TRANSPORTATION AND COMMUNICATIONS SYSTEMS

Given the fact that such a large proportion of the Ontario population lives along the Windsor-to-Cornwall corridor, this part of the province is particularly well served by transportation systems. Highway 401, or the Macdonald-Cartier Freeway, provides a speedy connection here, as does the VIA Rail passenger service and a variety of airlines. In addition, the provincially owned GO Transit system is designed for commuters working in Toronto. It spans out in seven directions from Union Station, with a terminus in each of Oshawa, Hamilton, Milton, Georgetown, Stouffville, Bradford, and Richmond Hill, and is supplemented by GO buses.

Southern Ontario also possesses a great matrix of smaller highways, and is linked to the northeast by highways from Ottawa and Toronto to North Bay and Sudbury and the summer ferry link from Tobermory to Manitoulin Island. In turn, the northeast is linked to the northwest by highways north from Sudbury, Sault Ste Marie, and North Bay, all eventually ending up in Thunder Bay. All the highways are heavily used by truck and bus transport (including the Greyhound and Voyageur bus lines), as well as by private cars.

Besides its lakeshore run, VIA Rail used to provide daily passenger services beginning in Montreal and Toronto and consolidating in Sudbury before the long progression to Thunder Bay and beyond. In 1989, however, the federal government announced a reduced Lakeshore operation, elimination of the Montreal–Sudbury train, and the bypassing of Thunder Bay on the route west from Toronto. A provincial crown corporation, Ontario Northland, connects Toronto by rail to North Bay, Cochrane, and

Moosonee on James Bay, and serves other northern communities by bus, while the Algoma Central Railway links Sault Ste Marie and Hearst. CN, CP, and other freight trains traverse these same routes.

Toronto's Pearson International is by far the biggest airport in Canada. Other busy Ontario airports in terms of passengers served in 1994 are as follows (with national ranking): Ottawa (5), Thunder Bay (16), London (18), Sudbury (24), Windsor (27), Sault Ste Marie (29), Timmins (30), and Toronto Island (31). In terms of air cargo, Pearson is first in the country, with other Ontario airports having the following ranking: Ottawa (9), Hamilton (13), Trenton (18), Thunder Bay (20), and London (34). With airline deregulation in recent years, the number of airlines operating in the province has increased dramatically, and as Air Canada concentrates on larger markets, many outlying centres are now being served by smaller planes and companies. As a cost-cutting move, the Harris government closed the government-owned NorOntair in early 1996.

Marine transportation in the province is centred on the St Lawrence Seaway, the world's largest canal system, including the Welland Canal that bypasses Niagara Falls. The Seaway has converted Thunder Bay into a port for ocean-going vessels – it is Canada's eighth largest port – as well as increasing business to most of the ports along the way. Ranked nationally in terms of 1994 tonnage, they are as follows: Hamilton (10), Nanticoke (12), Sault Ste Marie (16), and Windsor (19).

Distances and divisions within the province are also overcome by various forms of communications, especially radio, television (including the government's own TVOntario), telephones, faxes, and the Internet. Bell Canada carries most of the telephone calls, but Thunder Bay and several smaller communities still maintain publicly owned phone systems.

While many aspects of transportation and communication are under federal jurisdiction, numerous demands on the provincial government arise from this field as well. Concern about wider and better highways has been a constant of Ontario political life, as it has been in other provinces, and it continues to be regularly expressed, especially in the north. Demands for the expansion of the GO Transit system and for the continuation of the Ontario Northland system and TVOntario are also common.

POPULATION DISTRIBUTION

The Ontario population was 10.1 million at the time of the 1991 census,

TABLE 1
Metropolitan areas in Ontario over 50,000 (1991)

Toronto	3,893,046
Ottawa	683,900
Hamilton	599,760
London	381,522
St Catharines–Niagara	364,552
Kitchener	356,421
Windsor	262,075
Oshawa	240,104
Sudbury	157,613
Kingston	136,401
Thunder Bay	124,427
Peterborough	98,060
Guelph	97,213
Brantford	97,106
Belleville	95,000
Barrie	92,165
Sarnia	87,870
Sault Ste Marie	85,008
North Bay	63,285
Total	7,969,973

Source: Statistics Canada, 1991 Census, cat. no.
93-303, adapted by author; reproduced with
permission of the Minister of Supply and Services
Canada, 1996

and reached 11,103,300 by 1 July 1995. Ontario thus contains about 37.5 per cent of the total Canadian population. The 1991 census determined that 81.8 per cent of the Ontario population was urban and only 18.2 per cent rural, making it the most urbanized province in the country. In fact, 78.9 per cent of the province's population lived in the nineteen urban areas of over 50,000 people, including the largest metropolis in Canada, Toronto. These centres are listed in table 1 (which uses labour-market-area figures rather than those of municipal boundaries). Clearly, several were on the verge of exceeding the 100,000 mark in 1991.

Although four of these urban centres are in the north, that region contains only about 8 per cent of the province's population, compared to 80 per cent of its area. In contrast, the Toronto labour-market area includes 38.5 per cent of the provincial population. Toronto and, even more so, the Greater Toronto Area rank first in almost every aspect of economic life in Canada: labour force, manufacturing, finance, retail sales, services, real estate, and so forth. It is therefore not surprising that 'Toronto' dominates the economic and political life of the province. The core of the Ottawa economy, of course, is the federal government, but especially as it downsizes its operations, the national capital area is becoming more dependent on the private sector.

Needless to say, each of these urban communities and the others listed in table 1 does its best to attract new industry to boost its tax base and employment. They also seek federal and provincial government favours, such as special grants and the establishment of government offices, and put pressure on private firms to locate in their area. Municipal politicians spend a great deal of their time at Queen's Park and even in Ottawa; this is probably the most obvious evidence of regional demands being made on federal and provincial authorities.

Economy

The estimated total value of all goods and services produced in Ontario in 1996, the Gross Domestic Product (at factor cost, 1986$), was $218.5 billion, or about 39.1 per cent of Canada's GDP ($558.3 billion). In other words, Ontario's economy was nearly twice as large as that of Quebec (21.8 per cent of the Canadian GDP), and compares favourably with that of many sovereign countries. Economies are typically divided into three sectors by statisticians and economists: the primary and secondary, which together constitute the 'goods producing' sector, and the tertiary or 'services' portion. These different industries can be examined in terms either of the employment they provide or of the value of their production, as illustrated in table 2 (p. 26).

Statistics clearly indicate that the historical pattern of Ontario's economic development has been from primary resources to manufacturing, and now increasingly to a 'post-industrial' society where services are the most important part. Almost four million Ontarians work in the tertiary sector, such that the community, business, and personal-services sphere constitutes the largest part of the labour force and virtually the only part that is growing, while the manufacturing and trade sectors are tied for second place. The changing nature of the Ontario economy from an industrial to a post-industrial one has important political ramifications, requiring different education and training, diminishing the prospects for class-consciousness and unionization, and altering political values to some extent, all to the detriment of traditional social-democratic appeals. Let us examine some of these subdivisions in more detail, beginning with the primary sector.

TABLE 2
Ontario employment (1991) and Gross Domestic Product
(at factor cost) by industry (1996)

	Employment		GDP (1986$)	
	Number	%	Value	%
Primary industries	190,180	3.5	5,311	2.4
Agriculture	139,885	2.6	2,608	1.2
Forestry	13,970	0.3	469	0.2
Fishing/trapping	1,965	–	37	–
Mining	34,360	0.6	2,197	1.0
Secondary industries	1,301,890	25.2	72,042	33.0
Manufacturing	942,995	17.4	55,812	25.5
Construction	358,895	6.6	10,337	4.7
Utilities	66,160	1.2	5,893	2.7
Services	3,943,780	72.5	140,886	64.5
Transportation, storage, & communications	310,295	5.8	16,760	7.7
Trade	934,830	17.2	28,230	12.9
Finance, insurance, & real estate	353,225	6.5	34,657	15.9
Community, business, & personal services	1,867,810	34.3	49,356	22.6
Government services	411,455	7.6	11,883	5.4
Total	5,435,850		218,489	

Sources: Statistics Canada, 1991 Census, cat. nos. 93-326 and 95-338, and Conference Board of Canada, Provincial Outlook, Economic Forecast, Ottawa: Autumn 1995, vol. 10, no. 4, calculations by author and used with permission. See also Statistics Canada, *Provincial Gross Domestic Product by Industry, 1994–95,* cat. no. 15-203-XPB (May 1996). The statistics above on the agriculture, forestry, mining, and manufacturing components of GDP are approximately half the size of those reported in tables 4–6 on these four industries. That is primarily because the figures used in this table refer to 'value added,' whereas those cited below for these industries (tables 4, 5, and 6) are for 'gross output.' Economists generally prefer the use of the value-added figures, since gross output involves considerable double-counting.

AGRICULTURE

In recent years, Ontario has consistently led the other provinces in the total value of farm cash receipts, and agriculture is the leading Ontario primary industry. Most of the farming is done in the south, where the moderate climate and fertile soil are particularly congenial, but the 'clay

TABLE 3
Leading Ontario agricultural products, 1994

Product	Farm cash receipts	National ranking
Dairy	$1,151,435,000	2
Cattle & calves	929,560,000	2
Hogs	537,646,000	2
Soybeans	470,713,000	1
Poultry	454,811,000	1
Floriculture & nursery	421,307,000	1
Vegetables	411,117,000	1
Tobacco	344,613,000	1
Corn	332,853,000	1
Eggs	201,257,000	1

Source: Statistics Canada, Agriculture Economic Statistics, cat. no.
21-603E (30 Nov. 1995); reproduced with permission of the Minister of
Supply and Services Canada, 1996

belt' around New Liskeard in the north is also conducive to agriculture, especially silage corn, hay, barley, and potatoes.

Ontario had 68,633 census farms in 1991; with a total acreage of 13,470,700 (down 3.5 per cent from 1986), the average farm was just under two hundred acres in size. In 1994, Ontario farm cash receipts amounted to $5.9 billion, or slightly over $6 billion if government subsidies were included. About 60 per cent of these receipts came from livestock and 40 per cent from crops. Within the former category, as table 3 indicates, dairy products and cattle vied for first place, with hogs third. Ontario was the second-largest producer of each of these three types of livestock, but the national leader in poultry, eggs, sheep, and lambs. Within the crops category, Ontario led the other provinces in soybeans, floriculture and nursery, vegetables, tobacco, and corn, as well as in most fruits. The largest acreage was occupied by hay, grain corn, and soybeans.

When agricultural products are processed, they pass from the primary to the secondary sector. Among the leading agriculture-based manufactured products are beer, liquor, and soft drinks, canned and preserved fruit and vegetables, milk and dairy products, meat products, flour mixes and cereals, and bread and bakery products. Thunder Bay has the world's largest grain-handling facility, but it is western grain that is transferred there from trains to ships.

Although Ontario contains some of the country's most prosperous farms, many other farmers in the province face economic difficulty. The provincial government therefore regularly hears demands from farmers for better and more stable prices, easier credit, cheaper machinery, and more marketing assistance. New farmers in particular seek help to get established. In addition, environmentalists demand a slowdown of the urban development of prime agricultural land, while the health-conscious demand a conversion of tobacco farms to some other crop.

MINING

If petroleum is excluded, Ontario ranks first among the Canadian provinces in the value of mineral production, nearly $5 billion in 1994. As table 4 indicates, Ontario comes first or second in many important mineral products.

Most of the mining takes place in the Canadian Shield in Northern Ontario. Nickel and copper are found primarily in the Sudbury area, the largest mining centre in Canada. The INCO and Falconbridge operations there also produce several precious metals such as gold, silver, cobalt, and platinum. The gold mines are basically concentrated in the Timmins, Red Lake, Kirkland Lake, and Hemlo areas, with other sites including Wawa, Detour Lake, and Virginia Town. The Kidd Creek mine in Timmins produces zinc, copper, and silver. Elliot Lake used to be the centre of the uranium industry, but the last mine closed in 1996, as Saskatchewan has taken over as Canada's uranium producer. Iron ore was also once a leading Northern Ontario product, but this industry has declined through depletion of the resource and reduced demand. Algoma Steel's mine at Wawa is the principal remaining source.

These minerals move from the primary to the secondary sector when they are smelted and refined. Sudbury is also the site of much smelting and refining, as is Port Colborne, but some of this activity is done outside the province, a practice that is a continuing point of contention. Several other manufacturing industries, including fabricated metals and machinery, are also derivatives of mining.

In addition, Ontario is blessed with such structural materials as lime, clay, stone, cement, and sand and gravel, leading the country in every one. These are mainly found in the southern part of the province.

Generally speaking, the mining industry has been in decline in recent years, primarily because of reductions in demand and increases in international competition. These factors, along with technological advances, have caused a severe decline in the number of workers in this industry. Many northern mining towns have endured a boom-and-bust existence,

TABLE 4
Leading Ontario mineral products, 1994

Mineral	Value	National ranking
Gold	$1,154,706,000	1
Nickel	947,140,000	1
Copper	697,958,000	2
Sand & gravel	349,922,000	1
Cement	289,294,000	1
Stone	215,649,000	1
Zinc	212,531,000	2
Lime	114,379,000	1
Cobalt	113,115,000	1
Clay products	91,214,000	1
Silver	44,834,000	1
Total: Metals	$3,468,193,000	
Non-metals	263,931,000	
Fuels	73,559,000	
Structural materials	1,060,458,000	
Total	$4,866,141,000	

Source: Statistics Canada, Canada's Mineral Production, Preliminary estimates 1994, cat. no. 26-202 (March 1995); reproduced with the permission of the Minister of Supply and Services Canada, 1996.

none more so than Elliot Lake, for the uranium market has been particularly volatile. Nickel, copper, and gold prices go up and down and it is difficult to predict future trends in these fields, but the discovery of vast quantities of nickel and copper at Voisey's Bay in Labrador is unlikely to bode well for the future of Sudbury.

Mining is a risky and expensive business, so producers and investors continually demand incentives, tax breaks, and other financial concessions in order to start up or keep going. At the same time, people outside the industry demand that more refining be done in the province and that mining companies reduce their pollution of the environment.

FORESTRY

About 80 per cent of the province is covered by trees, with the forestry industry also located primarily in the northern Canadian Shield. Ontario ranks third among the provinces in forestry, after British Columbia and Quebec, whether in area of forest land, area of productive forest land,

TABLE 5
Value of Ontario forestry industry, 1993

Logging		$1,154,500,000
Wood		
Sawmills	$ 956,000,000	
Other wood	$1,743,600,000	
Total wood		$2,699,600,000
Paper		
Pulp & paper	$3,569,400,000	
Other paper	$3,020,400,000	
Total paper		$6,589,800,000
Total		$10,443,900,000

Source: Statistics Canada, Canadian Forestry Statistics, 1993,
cat. no. 25-202-XPB (February 1996); reproduced with permission of the Minister of Supply and Services Canada, 1996

wood volume, or total value of forestry production. Nearly 85 per cent of the forested area is owned and controlled by the provincial government, so that logging is done mostly by private firms on Crown land, under the authority of timber licences and forest-management agreements. The leading companies include Abitibi-Price, Canadian Pacific Forest Products, Domtar, E.B. Eddy, and Mallette. The boreal forest of Northern Ontario is primarily characterized by softwoods – mainly black and white spruce and jack pine, with lesser amounts of balsam fir, tamarack, and white cedar. The deciduous forest region of the south is made up of oak, beech, poplar, birch, and maple.

Trees pass into the secondary sector when they are sawn into lumber or further processed and their value is increased, as noted in table 5. Ontario contains some five hundred sawmills and many pulp-and-paper mills, veneer mills, and panel-board mills. Some of the largest sawmills are in Thunder Bay, Nairn Centre, Cochrane, Hearst, Timmins, and Dryden, while the principal pulp-and-paper mills are in Thunder Bay, Sault Ste Marie, Espanola, Sturgeon Falls, Iroquois Falls, Kapuskasing, Marathon, Dryden, Kenora, Fort Frances, Red Rock, Terrace Bay, North Bay, and Smooth Rock Falls. Ontario actually ranks in second place among the provinces in pulp-and-paper production, and within that category, to first place in 'other paper products.'

The forestry industry is also volatile, depending heavily on demands from other countries, especially the United States. This regularly leads forestry companies and communities to request financial and export assistance from the provincial government. Whether through the fault of companies or of government policy, forest management and renewal efforts were not impressive in the past, but it is generally agreed that they are improving. Other recent influences have been restrictions on Canadian softwood-lumber exports imposed by the United States. This problem partly inspired the Canada-U.S. Free Trade Agreement in the first place, but that agreement did not resolve the issue. Also complicating the picture are environmental concerns and native land claims, especially the protracted and continuing dispute in the Temagami area. In addition, the gypsy moth and jackpine and spruce budworms have become cyclical threats to the forest, leading to controversy over whether to spray the forests with insecticide.

FUR AND FISH

Ontario ranks first among the provinces in the value of wild fur pelts (especially marten and beaver), as well as in fur farm production, principally mink, but it is near the bottom as far as the fishing industry is concerned. With no salt water fishing, the province's commercial freshwater fishing industry is located primarily in the Great Lakes, but the pollution of these lakes, and others, has been a major constraint on the industry.

ENERGY

With only a tiny amount of petroleum in the province (found in the Sarnia area), Ontario has specialized in electricity as a form of energy. Ontario was an early leader in the production of hydroelectricity and the first province to establish a Crown corporation (Ontario Hydro) to provide it. The largest hydroelectric stations are located at Niagara Falls and on the St Lawrence, Ottawa, and Madawaska Rivers, but many Northern Ontario rivers have been developed for the production of electricity, including the Abitibi, English, Mississagi, Mattagami, Montreal, and Nipigon. Others such as the Severn, Winisk, Attawapiskat, and Albany have not, and in this respect Northern Ontario is not as productive as is Northern Quebec. The portion of Ontario Hydro's electricity generated by hydraulic sources fell to 25.1 per cent in 1995. The portion produced from burning fossil fuels (mostly coal) was 10.6 per cent, the four largest plants of this kind being in Nanticoke, Mississauga, Sarnia, and Kingston. The Crown corporation thus depends increasingly on nuclear-powered generating stations (64.3 per cent in 1995), with the major stations being Bruce (Kincardine), Pickering, and Darlington (Bowmanville). Ontario Hydro has been the leading customer for Atomic Energy of Canada's Candu reactors, as well as for the uranium formerly produced at Elliot Lake.

The energy industry has been a source of great controversy in recent years, primarily because of its heavy reliance on nuclear power. The nuclear plants have far exceeded their construction budgets and many fear that a malfunction within an operating plant could have disastrous consequences. Moreover, no solution is in sight for the problem of disposing of nuclear waste. Other observers, however, see little alternative to taking the nuclear route.

MANUFACTURING

Ontario annually produces about 53 per cent of all the manufactured goods in Canada, and leads other provinces in every manufacturing sector except paper and paper products, wood products, clothing, and textiles. Ontario's advantages in this respect include raw materials, cheap and abundant electricity, a pool of skilled workers, good transportation facilities, close proximity to the U.S. automobile-production industry, and, until recently, the protection of the national tariff. At its height, in 1989, 16,103 Ontario manufacturing establishments employed 770,547 people in production and related activities, and over a million workers in total. By 1993, however, the number of establishments had fallen to 12,837 and the production workforce to 609,197. In other words, Ontario lost some 200,000 manufacturing jobs over that four-year period. The principal causes of this traumatic downturn were the global restructuring that began about 1990, the recession, and the Canada-U.S. Free Trade Agreement. Table 6 shows the composition of the production side of Ontario manufacturing in 1993.

The automobile industry is the backbone of Ontario's manufacturing sector, if not the province's whole economy. In addition to the principal car-assembly plants (see table 7, p. 34), hundreds of smaller firms spread throughout southern Ontario manufacture auto parts. The industry has remained generally stable and prosperous since the Auto Pact was signed between Canada and the United States in 1965, although economic recession has sometimes caused a serious downturn in both countries. That agreement provided that automobiles and auto parts could flow freely

TABLE 6
Manufacturing production in Ontario, 1993

Sector	Establish-ments	Workers	Salaries & wages	Value of shipments
			(millions of dollars)	
Transportation equipment	643	124,245	$5,037.1	$53,538.4
Food & beverages	972	60,270	1,891.2	19,700.3
Chemicals & chemical products	545	30,174	1,056.0	12,141.0
Electronics & electrical products	696	48,616	1,533.4	11,656.1
Primary metals	201	38,067	1,743.1	10,709.7
Fabricated metals	2,494	61,993	1,887.9	9,005.6
Refined petroleum & coal products	68	2,786	140.2	6,625.6
Paper & paper products	289	27,268	1,061.1	6,589.8
Printing & publishing	1,842	34,434	1,182.7	6,399.1
Machinery	855	30,364	1,003.8	5,529.9
Plastic	556	24,359	615.1	3,596.6
Wood	657	18,185	502.6	2,699.6
Non-metallic minerals	533	15,784	548.9	2,898.1
Primary textiles & textile products	303	13,922	354.0	2,126.9
Furniture & fixtures	516	18,803	458.8	2,058.7
Rubber	81	8,166	255.8	1,522.7
Clothing	405	20,686	383.7	1,512.8
Other	1,181	31,065	782.6	4,937.2
Total	12,837	609,197	$20,438.0	$163,248.1

Source: Statistics Canada, Manufacturing Industries of Canada, 1993, cat. no. 31-203 (December 1995), calculations by author; reproduced with permission of the Minister of Supply and Services Canada, 1996

across the Canada-U.S. border subject to meeting certain Canadian value-added requirements. It is no wonder that the Ontario government was sensitive to changes in the Auto Pact during the Canada-U.S. Free Trade and NAFTA negotiations.

Other than the auto industry, the most notable aspect of Ontario manufacturing currently is the new emphasis on high technology. Although Canada is generally behind other industrialized countries in this respect, all recent Ontario governments have given this sector encouragement.

Beyond the auto industry, Metro Toronto encompasses manufacturing firms of almost every imaginable kind, but these do not contribute as much to the local economy now as in the past. It is increasingly in the area immediately beyond Toronto's actual boundaries that much of the province's manufacturing is done. Many new industrial operations are

TABLE 7
Location of principal auto plants in Ontario

Company	Location	Employment	Product
Chrysler	Windsor	2,000	Ram vans
		5,600	Chrysler minivans
Chrysler	Bramalea	3,200	Dodge Intrepid, Chrysler Concorde, Eagle Vision
Ford	St Thomas	2,700	Crown Victoria / Grand Marquis
Ford	Oakville	3,600	Ford Windstar
		1,000	F-series pick-up trucks
GM	Oshawa	3,250	C/K pick-up trucks
		7,050	Chevrolet Lumina, Monte Carlo, Buick Regal
Cami	Ingersoll	2,200	Geo Metro, Tracker, Suzuki Swift, Sidekick
Toyota	Cambridge	800	Corolla
Honda	Alliston	1,800	Civic

Source: *Globe and Mail*, 2 March 1996; reproduced with permission

being established to the west, such as in Mississauga, Brampton, and the Region of Peel. Further west, but still part of the Toronto labour market, is Oakville in Halton Region. Many new, large plants have also been established immediately north of Metro Toronto, in York Region, including Markham. Some facilities, like Volkswagen's, are going farther north to Barrie, or east to Durham Region.

Hamilton has historically been dependent on the primary and fabricated metal industries (especially steel), represented by Stelco and Dofasco, but the wire, electrical, and heavy-machinery industries are also important. St Catharines–Niagara is well known for its food and beverage firms, but nowadays it is really a more important producer of transportation equipment and auto parts. London, Kitchener-Waterloo, and Guelph are increasingly concentrating on technology, communications, and electronics. Ottawa has become the 'Silicon Valley' of Canada, and is now home to some seven hundred firms in the advanced technology field, such as Newbridge, Mitel, Digital Equipment, Bell Northern Research / Northern Telecom, Corel, Lumonics, Cognos, and Gandalf.

Manufacturing constitutes the great bulk of Ontario's exports. The United States was the destination for 91 per cent of Ontario's (foreign) exports in 1994; at the same time, some 76 per cent of Ontario's (foreign) imports came from the United States. While the verdict on the Canada-U.S. Free Trade Agreement and NAFTA is not yet in, the province has experienced more shutdowns and lay-offs than usual since the agreements came into effect in 1989 and 1994 respectively. While Ontario has an unfavourable balance of trade with the rest of the world, it exports more goods and services to each other province than it imports.

SERVICES

Among the prominent parts of the service sector in Ontario are banking, insurance, investment, trade, education, computer technology, hospitals and health care, tourism and recreation, and government. Toronto houses outstanding educational, health, and recreation facilities, is home to the main production facilities of the national English-language radio and television networks (CBC and CTV), is a key wholesale and retail distribution centre for both domestic and imported goods, and its many cultural, athletic, and recreational activities attract millions of tourists annually. It is estimated that almost 10 per cent of the Metro Toronto labour force is directly or indirectly involved in cultural industries.

Toronto is also the financial capital of Canada. While three of the five main chartered banks (Canadian Imperial Bank of Commerce, Toronto-Dominion, and Nova Scotia) have their official headquarters there, the other two (Royal and Montreal) also perform their executive functions in Toronto. Furthermore, almost all of the foreign-owned banks operating in Canada have head offices in the Ontario capital. This is also true of the largest Canadian investment dealers, such as RBC Dominion Securities, Midland Walwyn, Burns Fry, and Nesbitt Thomson. They are largely gathered around the Toronto Stock Exchange, which carries out over 80 per cent of Canada's total value of share-trading activity. Trust and insurance companies and other financial institutions such as CT Financial, Canada Trustco, National Trustco, Manulife Financial, Sun Life, Canada Life, Mutual Life, London Insurance and London Life, Metropolitan Life, Zurich Canada, Royal Insurance, General Accident Assurance, and Co-operators are also headquartered in Toronto or elsewhere in the province – Waterloo, London, Guelph, or Ottawa.

As mentioned, tourism constitutes a major portion of the services sector, and virtually all parts of the province have something to offer in this regard. Beyond the well-known attractions of Toronto and Ottawa, tourist highlights include historic Kingston, theatrical Stratford and Niagara-on-the-Lake, new casinos in Windsor, Orillia, and Niagara Falls, and a host of northern wilderness areas.

The services sector also includes the government, without which no account of the Ontario economy would be complete. At the time the

New Democratic Party brought in its social-contract legislation in 1993 and applied it to the entire public sector, the latter was seen to be composed of the following categories of employment: provincial public service, 90,000; provincial agencies, boards, commissions and Crown corporations, 50,000; municipalities and school boards, 300,000; colleges and universities, 80,000; and health and community services, 370,000. Alternatively, Statistics Canada reports provincial-government employment of 340,641; local governments, 192,078; school boards, 210,796; and public hospitals, 175,496.* In either case, the total number of public-sector employees is about 900,000. In fact, in almost every community, public or semi-public bodies are among the largest employers – federal, provincial, and municipal governments, school boards, hospitals, community colleges, and universities. In 1994–5, the provincial government spent about $60 billion, while local governments spent $32.7 billion, just over half of the provincial figure. Thus, in employment and monetary terms alone, it can be seen that the government portion of the Ontario economy is a large one. Such government activities are essentially the accumulated responses to demands from the different regional and economic interests outlined above and other class and demographic interests discussed below.

The Mike Harris government elected in 1995 was determined to reduce the public payroll, whether by cutting jobs in the provincial public service, privatizing government agencies, or reducing grants to municipalities, universities and colleges, school boards, and hospitals. This provoked a five-week Ontario Public Service Employees Union (OPSEU) strike in early 1996, and in its wake the government laid off some 10,600 public servants. Combined with downsizing at the federal level, the role of government in Ontario will definitely shrink in the near future.

Class

An analysis of social class in Ontario society is not as clear-cut and straightforward as that of the other three main characteristics examined in this chapter – geography, economy, and demography. One approach to this question would be to divide Ontario residents into the corporate elite or upper class, the upper middle class (small business, affluent farmers, and self-employed professionals), the new middle class (salaried profes-

*Statistics Canada, *Public Sector Employment and Wages and Salaries, 1994,* cat. 72–209 (October 1995)

sionals), the working class, and the poor. Other approaches come up with other combinations and permutations of these groupings, such as dividing the working class into public- and private-sector components, but individuals often behave according to the interests of the class they think they belong to – usually the middle class – rather than the one into which social scientists would place them.

. DISTRIBUTION OF INCOME

Given its immense resources and other assets, Ontario ranks with Alberta and British Columbia as one of the three provinces with the highest per capita income in the country. Ontario's was $23,593 in 1992, about $1000 above the other two. However, such average figures disguise great income disparities among individuals, families, communities, and regions within the province. Since income disparities are to some extent related to education, it is useful to examine the educational attainments of Ontarians. The 1991 census revealed that of a population of 7,922,920 over fifteen years of age, 38.7 per cent had less than a high-school graduation certificate, while another 24.7 per cent had stopped at that level. Those with a trade certificate accounted for 9.7 per cent, 13.9 per cent had other training short of a university degree, and 13.0 per cent possessed such a degree.

The level and distribution of personal income is also related to the question of unemployment. From 1986 to 1990, Ontario had the lowest unemployment rate in the country, in the range of 5 to 6 per cent. But the recession that began about 1990 hit Ontario harder than most other provinces, and since then its unemployment rate has generally been higher than that of the four western provinces (1991, 9.6%; 1992, 10.8%; 1993, 10.6%; 1994, 9.6%; 1995, 8.7%), although still below the national rate. Moreover, unemployment has now struck the middle class and those who consider themselves to be middle class, so that it is not just the traditional lower classes that are affected. Most studies show that the income disparities between rich and poor in Ontario are once again starting to increase.

THE CORPORATE ELITE

Ontario is home to some of the richest entrepreneurs and families in the world. In January 1996, the *Financial Post* found that five Ontario-based families were in the billionaire category (with national rankings and net worth as follows): Ken Thomson (1), $8.2 billion; the Eatons (4), $1.7 billion; Ted Rogers (5), $1.4 billion; Galen Weston (6), $1.3 billion; and the McCains (7), $1.2 billion. Thomson owns Thomson newspapers, the Hudson's Bay Company, Zellers, and many other firms in the information-services and publishing fields. The Eaton family are proprietors of the department-store chain, the Eaton Centre in Toronto, and CFTO-TV and the Baton chain of television stations. Ted Rogers began in cable television and then purchased the giant Maclean-Hunter empire, including magazines and newspapers. Weston controls several firms with the family name, as well as Holt Renfrew, Eddy Paper, Loblaws, and many others. Wallace McCain, originally from New Brunswick, fought with his brother there and then moved to Ontario to take over Maple Leaf Foods.

The next echelons of the corporate elite include those with a net worth over $700 million – Terry Matthews and Michael DeGrotte; over $500 million – the Bata family; over $400 million – Hal Jackman and Ron Joyce; over $300 million – Peter and Edward Bronfman; over $200 million – Joseph Burnett, Michael Cowpland, the Southam/Fisher families, and Paul Pheland; and over $145 million – Joseph Rotman, Seymour Schulich, Peter Munk, the Blackburn family, Allan Slaight, George Gardiner, and Charles Rathgeb. Among the largest annual compensation packages received by corporate chief executive officers in 1995 were the following: Gerald Pencer (Cott Corp.), $13 million; Stephen Hudson (Newcourt Credit Group), $4.2 million; Richard Thomson (TD Bank), $3.3 million; Lawrence Bloomberg (First Marathon), $3.3 million; Gerald Schwartz (Onex), $3.2 million; William Holland (United Dominion Industries), $3.1 million; Brian Steck (Nesbitt Thomson), $2.5 million; Richard Currie (Loblaws), $2.4 million; and Anthony Fell (RBC Dominion Securities), $2 million.

Toronto has already been identified as the financial capital of Canada, and while the non-financial Canadian corporate sector is not quite so geographically concentrated in Ontario, twenty-three out of fifty of the *Financial Post*'s five hundred leading firms (ranked by 1994 sales) have headquarters in the province. These are as follows: GM (1), Ford (3), Chrysler (4), George Weston (5), Ontario Hydro (7), Thomson Corp. (8), IBM Canada (9), Imperial Oil (11), Noranda (16), Brascan (18), Oshawa Group (19), Hudson's Bay Co. (21), Canada Post (28), Sears Canada (30), Canadian Tire (36), Magna International (37), Onex Corp. (38), INCO (39), Horsham Corp. (40), Moore Corp. (43), Maple Leaf Foods (44), Laidlaw (48), and Mitsui (50).

Even though many of the large corporations with headquarters in the Toronto region are national and transnational in scope, there is no question that they press the Ontario government to adopt policies at the provincial level that are most favourable to them. They, along with hundreds of other companies with their headquarters at a stone's throw from Queen's Park, are well situated – geographically, economically, and socially – to do so.

THE MIDDLE CLASS

The middle class, in objective social-science terms, includes self-employed and salaried professionals and small-scale entrepreneurs. This class was reared on the assumptions that working hard and getting a good education would produce economic security. Members of the middle class may have paid a disproportionate amount of taxes, but they benefited from public education and health-care programs, and had money left over for considerable consumption.

In the 1990s, however, many members of the middle class were rudely awakened. Technology, globalization, downsizing, recession, and concern with government debt have significantly reduced employment opportunities, whether for those who previously had good jobs or for those newly trained to pursue them. A high level of education was still the best route to a good job, but no longer a guarantee.

In these new economic circumstances, the middle class began to shrink, as well as to divide between its secure and insecure components. The former generally supported government cutbacks and tax cuts, while the latter began to protest reductions in public education, health care, and other programs, cutbacks that frequently cost them their own jobs.

THE WORKING CLASS

The working class – at least the self-conscious element thereof – has always faced economic insecurity, and that which confronts it in the 1990s is more severe than ever. More and more members of the working class can find only part-time, short-term, or contract jobs. Those most conscious of their class position generally believe that the most appropriate way to address working-class employment concerns has been to form or join a union.

As a result of the economic trend from primary and secondary to tertiary industry, the largest labour unions in the province are no longer industrial, but rather reside in the public sector. The three largest are CUPE (the Canadian Union of Public Employees), the National Union of Provincial Government Employees (which includes the Ontario Public

Service Employees Union), and the Public Service Alliance of Canada, followed by the United Steelworkers of America, United Food and Commercial Workers, Canadian Auto Workers, and Teamsters. Many of these (and others) have joined forces in the Ontario Federation of Labour, the provincial branch of the Canadian Labour Congress, giving the OFL a membership of about 650,000.

Of a labour force of about 4.3 million in 1992, total union membership in Ontario was 1,369,100, or 31.6 per cent, somewhat below the national average of 34.9 per cent. The highest rates of unionization were in educational services (68.7%), public administration (67.0%), primary metals (61.9%), construction (61.6%), and paper (60.9%). By contrast, manufacturing had a unionization rate of only 34.3 per cent; mining, only 29.5 per cent; and forestry, only 23.2 per cent.

Besides the growth of public-sector unions, two other developments demand attention here. First, and related to the shift in employment towards the public- and general-services sectors, an increased proportion of unionized workers are women – forty per cent in 1992. The second development is the Canadianization of the union movement, which began with the dramatic breaking away of the Canadian Auto Workers from the U.S.-based UAW, moving this major group from the international to the national category. By 1992, 501,000 unionists in Ontario belonged to international unions, compared to 675,300 in national (private sector) unions, and 192,800 in government unions.

The labour movement is never short of political issues in which it has an interest. It achieved several legislative successes in the 1985–7 Liberal minority-government period, such as an act to facilitate acquisition of a new union's first contract and improvements to the occupational health and safety law. The NDP government was even more receptive to labour's demands, as with Bill 40, which made it easier to form a union and unlawful to hire replacement workers during a legal strike. On the other hand, the NDP's social-contract legislation, which overrode collective agreements to roll back public-sector wages, alienated much of the labour movement. Sitting out the 1995 election worked out to their detriment, however, as the new Harris government repealed Bill 40, laid off public servants, and diluted safety and compensation legislation. After the election, organized labour resorted to mobilizing anti-Harris rallies in several Ontario cities.

THE POOR

At the far end of the income spectrum are the poor. The 1991 census reported that among Ontarians 11 per cent of families and 31 per cent of unattached individuals (for a total of 13 per cent) fell into the 'low income' category. The Ontario Social Development Council calculates that the average poor family in Ontario has an income $7500 below the poverty line; in January 1996, some 617,000 Ontarians received social assistance. The three main identifiable categories of recipients were the disabled, sole-support parents (mostly women), and the employable unemployed, although children constituted the single largest group. The stratum immediately above those on social assistance is made up of the 'working poor,' whose reliance on the minimum wage leaves them below the poverty line.

The poverty problem in Ontario was impressively addressed by the 1988 Thompson Report, entitled *Transitions*, which called for an immediate increase in social benefits, an income-supplementation program for the working poor, and the provision of incentives for those on social assistance to seek employment. The Peterson and Rae governments addressed some of these recommendations, but the Harris government undid most of the progress made, cut all social-assistance programs, and developed plans for a 'workfare' (work for welfare) system instead. To some extent, Premier Harris was encouraged to do so by the repeal of the Canada Assistance Plan by the federal Chrétien government and the resultant cut in federal funding for the poor. The new provincial government was proud of the decline of the number of Ontarians on social assistance, but while some ex-recipients undoubtedly found jobs, others turned to food banks and other charitable organizations to avoid the hassles of the welfare system. The Harris government also made many cuts to other programs, such as legal aid, under which the poor benefited more than any other social group.

Demography

Besides the class cleavage, the other demographic variables that are usually most politically relevant in Ontario are ethnicity and language, religion, gender, and age.

ETHNICITY AND LANGUAGE

Statistics Canada collects data on three main questions relating to ethnicity: ethnic background, mother tongue, and language used at home. The three measures are related, but present quite different pictures of ethnicity in Ontario.

TABLE 8

Languages in Ontario, 1991: mother tongue, home language, and ability to speak

Mother tongue	Home language	Able to speak
English 74.6%	English 85.2%	English 97.5%
French 5.0%	French 3.2%	French 11.9%
Other 20.3%	Other 11.6%	Other 24.1%

Source: Statistics Canada, 1991 Census, cat. no. 96-313E, adapted by author; reproduced with permission of the Minister of Supply and Services Canada, 1996

Specific figures on ethnic background are difficult to use because census respondents increasingly possess mixed backgrounds and can also call themselves 'Canadians.' Nevertheless, in terms of single, unmixed, origins, it is clear that the top five groups in Ontario are British, French, Italian, German, and Chinese.

The question of language is more easily measured, and table 8 reveals the groups ranking highest in these measures. Obviously, many of the immigrants have assimilated into the 'English' culture, as have some of the French, pushing the English 'home language' figure about 10 per cent higher than that of English 'mother tongue.' Indeed, 97.5 per cent reported themselves capable of speaking English.

These statistics allow us to approach the subject of ethnic cleavage in Ontario, including the questions of bilingualism and multiculturalism. The French-English cleavage has been a prominent generator of political activity, in relation first to schools and, more recently, to the question of other government services. From the late 1960s onward, the Conservative government encouraged the development of French-language high schools, and in the early 1980s expanded the range of French-language provincial services, especially in the courts. In 1988, the Peterson government passed Bill 8 (French Language Services Act) to guarantee provincial-government services in French on a regional basis, that is, in any community that had at least 5000 francophones, or in which 10 per cent of the population was French-speaking. The principal areas involved are listed in table 9, the City of London having recently been added. Municipalities within designated areas had the option of providing services in French if they chose, but instead several took the unnecessary step of declaring themselves to be officially unilingual English.

Although this regional approach to French-language services is prob-

TABLE 9
Designated areas under French Language Services Act

Municipality of Metropolitan Toronto
Regional Municipalities: Ottawa-Carleton and Sudbury
Cities: Hamilton, Port Colborne, Welland, Mississauga, Windsor (and surrounding towns and townships), Pembroke, and London
Towns: Tilbury, Penetanguishene, Geraldton, Longlac, and Marathon
Counties: Glengarry, Prescott, Russell, and Stormont
Districts: Algoma, Cochrane, Nipissing, Sudbury, and Timiskaming
Townships: Winchester, Dover, Tilbury East, Stafford, Westmeath, Tiny, Essa, Ignace, Manitouwadge, Beardmore, Nakina, and Terrace Bay

ably less controversial than a general declaration of official bilingualism would be, it has sparked heated disputes in some of the areas where it has been applied. The government now faces demands for both more and less bilingualism in the province. Peterson and Rae established unilingual francophone colleges, whereas the Harris government has generally reduced support for French-language programs.

According to the 1991 census, 65.5 per cent of Ontarians were born in the province, 10.4 per cent were born elsewhere in Canada, and 24.1 per cent were born abroad. Of the ten million residents in 1991, about 670,000 were post-1981 immigrants. Of all the post-1981 immigrants to Canada, 59 per cent of those came to Ontario and 39 per cent settled in Metro Toronto. Such groups come increasingly from the Caribbean and Asia, along with Central and South America and Africa, so that 'visible minorities' represent about 70 per cent of recent arrivals and 30 per cent of the total Metro population. Some projections suggest that this figure could exceed 50 per cent by 2001. Table 10 (p. 44) indicates the leading sources of Ontario immigrants from 1983 to 1992.

This large number of 'visible' immigrants has transformed Metro Toronto into a highly diversified ethno-racial community. Such a development has obvious implications for public services, the educational system, and public finance, as well as for Ontario's political culture, political parties, and elections. All political parties, for example, now scramble to attract the support of various new ethnic groups in the province. The debate over multiculturalism is increasingly controversial, especially in the Toronto region where entire communities and neighbourhoods are

TABLE 10
Immigrants to Ontario by place of birth, 1983–92

1	Hong Kong	72,121
2	Poland	66,706
3	India	51,017
4	China	44,338
5	Philippines	42,883
6	Jamaica	36,687
7	Britain	34,765
8	Vietnam	34,755
9	Portugal	32,629
10	Guyana	29,024
11	Sri Lanka	27,282
12	U.S.A.	27,236
13	Iran	20,137
14	Lebanon	16,368
15	Trinidad	16,176
16	El Salvador	15,920

Source: Public Works and Government Services
Canada, Immigration Statistics, cat. no. MP22-1
reproduced with permission of the Minister of
Supply and Services Canada, 1996

primarily Italian, Chinese, Greek, Portuguese, Black, or South Asian. Multiculturalism raises such issues as the adequate representation of such groups in public employment (for example, police forces) and discrimination in the private sector. Since roughly 40 per cent of recent immigrants speak neither English nor French, the 'new' Toronto faces many linguistic issues. Starting in September 1989, for example, school boards in the province were required to provide Heritage Language classes when a request to teach a particular language was made by the parents of at least twenty-five students of that board. Such classes could be offered after school, in the evenings, or on weekends, and principally included Italian, Portuguese, Chinese, Greek, Polish, Ukrainian, German, Spanish, Korean, Punjabi, and Hindi students.

The Bob Rae government enacted the most comprehensive employment-equity legislation in the country, providing preferential employment access for women, aboriginals, visible minorities, and the disabled, but the law ignited a backlash in the 1995 election campaign and the new Harris government quickly repealed it. The most overt racism problem in the province probably affects the black community in Toronto. On the

TABLE 11
Aboriginal Ontarians

	Aboriginal origins	Aboriginal identity
North American Indian	220,140	102,925
Métis	26,905	12,050
Inuit	5,245	785
Total	243,555	115,760

Source: Statistics Canada, 1991 Census, cat. nos. 94-325 and 89-533, adapted by author; reproduced with permission of the Minister of Supply and Services Canada, 1996

one hand, a small number of blacks have been involved in high-profile criminal acts, which have generated racial tension, while on the other, the black community has accused members of Toronto-area police forces of being racist.

In the 1991 census, 243,555 Ontarians (2.4 per cent) declared themselves to have aboriginal origins, but in a supplementary survey, only 115,760 claimed to have an aboriginal identity, as indicated in table 11. This discrepancy can be explained in part by the fact that many in the first category had non-aboriginal origins as well, and had therefore lost their aboriginal identity. In 1993, the Department of Indian Affairs and Northern Development reported that 125,743 registered Indians abided in Ontario, approximately the same number as possessed a North American Indian identity, and about half of these, 64,787, resided on reserves.

The native population of the province is outnumbered by many other ethnic groups and is generally subject to federal rather than provincial jurisdiction. Nevertheless, native issues increasingly require the attention of provincial politicians, particularly with respect to native land claims, on which little progress has been made. The NDP and aboriginal leaders signed a statement of political relationship in 1991 that recognized the first nations' inherent right to self-government within the Canadian constitutional framework. Other small advances have included the teaching of native languages in certain public schools and the establishment of a native health centre, but the aboriginal peoples of the province continue to suffer from dismal economic prospects, poor government services, and widespread discrimination. One native was killed in a skirmish with police at Ipperwash in 1995, though a more positive development is the new native-owned Rama casino near Orillia.

TABLE 12
Religious background of Ontarians

Protestant			4,428,305	(44.4%)
United Church	1,410,535	(14.1%)		
Anglican	1,059,910	(10.6%)		
Presbyterian	422,160	(4.2%)		
Baptist	264,625	(2.7%)		
Lutheran	227,915	(2.3%)		
Other Protestant	1,043,160	(10.5%)		
Roman Catholic			3,544,515	(35.5%)
No religious affiliation			1,247,640	(12.5%)
Eastern Non-Christian			379,625	(3.8%)
Eastern Orthodox			187,910	(1.9%)
Jewish			175,640	(1.8%)
Other			13,415	(0.1%)

Source: Statistics Canada, 1991 Census, cat. no. 93-319, calculations by author; reproduced with permission of the Minister of Supply and Services Canada, 1996

RELIGION

The 1991 census results on the religious background of Ontarians are displayed in table 12. The main implications of this religious distribution relate to the educational system. The Constitution Act, 1867, guaranteed a Roman Catholic separate-school system in Ontario. Until the 1980s, after Grade 10, Roman Catholics could attend public or private high schools, but were required to pay taxes to the public system regardless. In 1984, however, Premier Bill Davis responded to Catholic demands to extend full public support to that system starting in 1985, a controversial move that had major electoral consequences for the Conservative party. Later, when the law was challenged as being discriminatory against other religions, the Supreme Court of Canada recognized that the Charter of Rights allowed the continuation of such pre-Charter constitutional protection for the Ontario Roman Catholic separate-school system. This issue has taken many years to settle at the local school-board level.

Certain other religions have tried without success to gain the right to mount their own publicly supported school systems; failing that, they can at least try to ensure that the public system is genuinely non-discriminatory. Through court action, for example, they have forced changes in opening and closing exercises that formerly included the Lord's Prayer. Now a variety of religious expressions are reflected in such exercises. Sunday shopping is another issue related to religion, and changes have been made in this policy to reflect the fact that to the extent Sunday remains a 'pause' day, this is no longer based on the Christian Lord's Day.

GENDER

The 1991 census revealed that females outnumbered males in Ontario by 5,131,805 to 4,953,080, although this negligible difference is of little political significance in itself. On the other hand, such gender-related issues as day care, abortion, pay equity, and employment-equity programs for hiring and promotion in the public and private sectors *are* of increasing importance. These have, in fact, become leading items on the provincial political agenda in recent years, and politicians have been paying far more attention to the female portion of the population than ever before. The overall rate of female employment and their rate of participation in the labour market have declined since 1990 in Canada, but Ontario has one of the highest proportions of women in the labour force of any province: in 1995, 54 per cent of Ontario women aged fifteen and over were employed, and the participation rate was 58.7 per cent. In an effort to reduce the residual wage gap between men and women, the Pay Equity Act was proclaimed in 1988. It is overseen by the Pay Equity Commission. By 1994, the median earnings of Ontario women working full time were 73.8 per cent of men's, and the median income of all female earners was 59.2 per cent of men's. The NDP established new women's health centres and abortion policies, but many programs of primary interest to women were among the casualties of the Harris government cutbacks.

At the same time, sexual orientation has become a political issue in recent years. A clause was added to the Ontario Human Rights Code in 1988, during the minority-government period, to protect homosexuals from discrimination. The Rae government extended spousal employment benefits within the public service to same-sex partners, but its attempt to pass a general law extending same-sex benefits to all employees was defeated in a free vote.

AGE

The mean age of Ontarians in 1991 was 33.6 years, with some 3,475,405 residents (34.5%) under the age of 25, and 1,183,475 (11.7%) over 65. The varied needs of different age groups have always been reflected in demands on government. In the future, however, the most striking change in this area will be the aging of the population – to an estimated median of 39.6 years by 2016. By that year, Statistics Canada estimates, those under 25 will form 29.6 per cent of the population, while the proportion of those over 65 will have increased to 15.1 per cent. Such figures reveal that Ontario residents are not only living longer, but they are also reproducing less. This trend has given added significance to the pension issue, which has become a leading public concern in the province. It also has many implications for health care and social services for the elderly, including pressure to supply adequate nursing-home and home-support services. At the other end of the age spectrum, however, young people – including new university graduates – are increasingly desperate for employment.

Conclusion

For many years it was commonly said that Ontario was an easy province to govern. That was largely because it was a relatively homogeneous province, at least in terms of the demands articulated by its residents, and because its prosperity readily provided the means to satisfy them. In the 1990s, however, Ontario is extremely diverse in its social composition and its economy is in the doldrums. Among the salient political issues as Ontario approaches the turn of the century are persistent regional disparities within the province, the unemployment caused by adjusting to a more technological society and to various international trading agreements, and a more visible and vehement expression of class, ethnic, religious, and women's concerns. The authorities in the second half of the 1990s will be challenged as never before, especially given the predominant view that their financial resources are severely limited. Precisely because of this factor, on the other hand, the party elected in 1995 deliberately chose to ignore many such social demands in an effort to reduce the size and significance of government.

THREE

The Ontario Political Culture: An Interpretation

Sid Noel

Ontario differs from the other provinces of Canada in two important respects. First, there are differences of scale that reflect Ontario's disproportionate size: with more than eleven million people, no other province approaches it in population, in the size and diversity of its economy, in accumulated wealth, or in the amount of financial, corporate, and media power concentrated in its capital city. Second, there are differences of political culture that reflect Ontario's unique historical experience, its economic preoccupations, and the evolution of its social, cultural, and political institutions. While these two sets of differences are closely connected, the focus of this chapter is primarily upon the latter. Its aim is to identify the distinctive characteristics of the Ontario political culture, trace their origins, and assess their influence on the province's political life. It also seeks to identify the points at which change is taking place or appears to be imminent.

Since the term *political culture* is used analytically in several different senses and is variously applied to both present and past societies, it is necessary to offer a brief definition. As used here, it refers to a set of widely shared outlooks, beliefs, and sentiments that a people holds over some extended period of time and that broadly conditions their political behaviour. In contrast to public opinion, which is oriented to the issues or personalities of the moment and tends to be as changeable as the weather, political culture is long-term and oriented to values and habits of mind. Like the climate, it tends to change gradually, but when change does take place the consequences are likely to be profound.

A further distinction should be made between what may be termed the *ideational* and the *operative* elements of political culture. Ideational elements are the ideologies, principles, and theories about government and politics that are present in the intellectual discourse of a society; they include such ideals as freedom and equality, doctrines of 'left' and 'right,' and visions of 'national sovereignty.' Operative elements are the generally unarticulated assumptions, expectations, and understandings of people – the norms they quietly hold – about the way their politics ought ordinarily to be conducted, what they can reasonably expect of government, and their sense of their society's proper place in relation to other societies and the world at large. These two types of elements are of course related and all political cultures contain both, but the particular mix and the emphasis placed on one or the other type often varies strikingly from one society to another. Ideational elements are more likely to inspire fundamental conflicts involving *principles* or *rights*, and for that reason they tend to dominate the rhetoric of political debate and attract serious media and scholarly attention. Operative elements, by contrast, are generally not matters of open contention. For the most part, they are rooted in everyday political life and manifested in broadly shared norms about the *ordinary means* and *attainable goals* of politics – such as the expectation of managerial competence in government or the understanding that democracy in practice requires a balancing of interests. They tend to be closely related to non-political community values and identities and to be matters of habitual response rather than the products of deliberation. Since they also tend not to be consciously promulgated by anyone, they rarely attract media or scholarly attention. Nevertheless, their underlying influence is pervasive.

The links between political culture and political behaviour and between political culture and political institutions, moreover, are complex and interactive rather than demonstrably causal. Ideational concepts, such as beliefs about democracy, are commonly absorbed by institutions from the society at large, sometimes after being initially resisted, and are then actively perpetuated by them. Operative norms are commonly influenced by longstanding institutions such as the legislature and cabinet, by unusually influential or 'formative' leaders, and by political parties; and these in turn are influenced by the way people normally expect them to behave. Political culture, then, should not be conceived as a single independent variable that by itself is capable of explaining specific political events, such as the outcome of an election; rather, it should be conceived as a set of interrelated cultural and psychological variables that can be used to explain, and trace changes in, the broad contours of political behaviour.

Finally, it should be understood that the political culture of a society as old and multilayered as Ontario is far from being a uniform construct. While at any given time more remains the same than changes, the political culture is also prone to display divergent or even totally contradictory tendencies. In small Ontario communities, for example, it is not unusual to find customary 'Old Ontario' political patterns coexisting, sometimes uneasily, with others of more recent origin – the result of economic change, suburbanization, the influence of television, or some mixture of all of these. By contrast, in the large cities, and particularly in Toronto, a state of constant flux is more or less the norm. There are also pronounced regional differences (most strikingly in the case of Northern Ontario, which contains marked subregions of its own and is an exception to most generalizations about the province as a whole) and innumerable fissures based on conflicting economic interests and group rivalries.

Since there is no obvious overarching ideology to subsume these real and potential cleavages, nor any unifying identity built around a shared consciousness of language or ethnicity, it might easily be assumed – as indeed it often is assumed, even in scholarly writing on the subject – that the Ontario political culture could not be other than weakly defined or even indiscernible. Yet, paradoxically, despite its multifold diversities and its endemic if generally superficial style of partisan fractiousness, Ontario has never been a deeply fragmented or divided society. While generally suspicious of ideology, and oblivious to questions of identity, in circumstances that count its people have always shown a clear appreciation of their common interests and a well-developed capacity for social cohesion. In other words, to look only at the tenuous *ideational* elements of the Ontario political culture is to miss the greater part of it, for its main distinguishing features have always been above all *operative*. To look at those elements is to see a political culture that is undeniably complex, but also resilient, adaptive, and powerfully integrative. For more than two hundred years it has been consistently sustained.

The Upper Canadian Origins

Historical starting points do not dictate the subsequent evolution of a society any more than the circumstances of birth dictate the fate of an individual; yet few would deny that both societies and individuals are profoundly influenced by their origins. Any attempt to interpret the political culture of Ontario must therefore come to grips with the meaning of its foundation and early development in the Province of Upper Canada between 1791 and 1841.

That province was founded in the aftermath of the American revolution by United Empire Loyalists, political refugees who had trekked north into British-held territory and established a thin band of settlement along the upper St Lawrence River and in the Niagara region. From these beginnings, over the following half-century it grew into a substantial agrarian society of approximately half a million people, spread mainly across the broad fertile southwestern peninsula between the Great Lakes, and increasingly centred, politically and economically, on its capital city of Toronto. The original Loyalists probably numbered fewer than ten thousand, and they were soon swamped by succeeding waves of later settlers, but no account of Upper Canada's history can fail to acknowledge their formative and ultimately mythic role in its creation. Like the Puritans of New England and the original habitants of Quebec, the Upper Canadian Loyalists must be accorded a primacy that extends beyond their number, not merely because of the timing of their arrival, which was largely adventitious, or because of the covenantal symbolism of their exodus and eventual triumphant renewal, powerful though that was, but because of the distinctive imprint they placed on the province's emerging political (and economic) culture.

Like other political refugees, the Loyalists were presumably the bearers of whatever ideological precepts happened to be current in their time and place. But they also appear to have been little disposed to reflect upon them, or if they were, the surviving written testimony of their reflection is scant. They were in any case largely an illiterate people – farmers, frontiersmen, and artisans, veterans of the King's loyal American regiments – who had thrown themselves into the backbreaking work of land clearing, with political ideology being probably the subject furthest from their minds. The literate elite who were their leaders – members of the officer class and the professions – were also overwhelmingly preoccupied with immediate practical concerns, though some would on occasion espouse a conventional public rhetoric of 'toryism,' consisting of fervent expressions of faith in the monarchy and the British connection and an abhorence of the evils of republicanism. These beliefs were no doubt genuinely and deeply held, and were ultimately consequential: when challenged *in extremis*, by invasion in 1812 and by armed rebellion in 1837, the Upper Canadian elite rallied to their defence with considerable ferocity and no little popular support. But these same views were also notably unhelpful in most ordinary political situations: Upper Canadian elections, for example, could be hotly and expensively contested, but it was not unusual for all candidates to espouse identical Loyalist and anti-republican sentiments, competing only in the ardour of their expressions. It is doubtful whether such ritualized ideology exerted much influence on everyday political behaviour or on the political culture that was emerging. These were more profoundly influenced by what the Loyalists actually experienced in Upper Canada, and in particular by their experience of three distinctive relationships which in Upper Canadian life were practically unavoidable: (1) their relationship with their new physical environment, and specifically with the land itself, on whose productivity, as an agrarian people, they had staked their future; (2) their relationship with government in the multifold endeavours of building a new society; and (3) their relationship with a locally rooted system of clientelism, involving both commercial and political patronage, that formed the key linkage between ordinary citizens and local elites and between local and provincial elites.

The result was a society with its own peculiar political outlook and its own peculiar mix of values, operative norms, and expectations. These developed early, but were never absolutely fixed and continued to evolve more or less in step with changing economic and political circumstances. They were sometimes a source of conflict, as different combinations and weightings of norms produced different and sometimes opposed subcultures. But they also broadly set the parameters of the political future – like a kind of genetic code whose traces may still be found in the body politic of modern Ontario.

The Operative Norms

In the discussion that follows five key norms derived from Ontario's past are identified and related to the present. These are: (1) the imperative pursuit of economic success; (2) the assumption of pre-eminence; (3) the requirement of managerial efficiency in government; (4) the expectation of reciprocity in political relationships; and (5) the balancing of interests. No single one of these is entirely unique in and of itself – which could hardly be otherwise, given that Ontario is an open society and has always had close cultural and economic ties with the wider world. What is *sui generis* to Ontario is the particular mix or combination of the above norms, their reflection in the workings of the province's political institutions, and their deep historical resonance. The ordering given here is not meant to indicate either the sequence of their development or their contemporary salience; for the norms developed together and their salience is relative to several other factors, including the goals of the party in power and the impact upon Ontario of external trends and forces. Rather, the aim here is to show that the Ontario political culture displays both continuity and change and that the points of change are of special significance. At these points political conflict tends to take on a heightened intensity – it is definitely not 'politics as usual' – and the decisions taken are likely to influence future generations.

1. THE IMPERATIVE PURSUIT OF ECONOMIC SUCCESS

All people must pursue economic success to some extent if they are to survive at all, but some people define success more exclusively in economic terms than others and pursue it more single-mindedly, and some simply have better luck. The original Upper Canadians were possessed of single-mindedness and luck in about equal measure – though they naturally preferred to see the one as a badge of industry and the other as a mark of divine favour. Like many later migrants, they knew the meaning of loss and dispossession, and it gave a certain edge to their endeavours: the vindication they sought was not merely survival but visible material success, in terms that would be well understood, and to that end they accumulated land – Upper Canada's chief source and symbol of wealth – with what can only be described as compulsive avidity. They were also doubly fortunate. Through a happy accident of geography and climate, Upper Canada turned out to contain a vast expanse of some of the continent's finest agricultural land, a renewable natural resource of incalculable value and a prodigious long-term generator of wealth. And through another happy accident, their first government (1791–6), led by Lieutenant Governor John Graves Simcoe, turned out to be far-sighted, energetic, and completely supportive of their ambitions.

Simcoe believed that the new province would ultimately stand or fall on the performance of its agricultural economy, and he favoured systematic government intervention on a massive scale to promote its growth: offering attractive inducements to new settlers, improving transportation, facilitating exports, assisting in the formation of capital, discouraging competition for investment from the fur trade, drawing the leading merchants into his plans as advisers and recipients of his patronage, and even seeing through the legislature a bill abolishing slavery (a progressive humanitarian act that also cut off the possibility that a plantation-

based economy might develop). 'Perhaps no maxim will bear less examination,' he wrote, 'than that Trade should be left to itself. It is not true in
theory nor in practice, unless on a limited scale and in petty operations.'
Upper Canada, he believed, was destined to support 'a numerous and
Agricultural people.' To establish the security of the people on a foundation of economic success was thus the first and ultimate Upper Canadian
goal, an official as well as a popular imperative, and the role of government was to serve as a constructive partner in this pursuit.

The experience of government as a positive and beneficent force was
an exceedingly rare thing in the eighteenth century, when governments
generally, and perhaps especially colonial governments, were most often
experienced by their subjects as neglectful, incompetent, or predatory.
None of the imperial governors who came after Simcoe matched his
capacity for constructive governance or shared his rapport with Upper
Canadians, and their lasting influence was slight; it was Simcoe's bril-
liant formative administration that defined the norm. In effect, Simcoe
set the standard by which the others would be judged, and for the next
two hundred years no successful Ontario administration ever perceived
its role in terms that were essentially different from his.

At a later critical juncture in the late nineteenth century, when Ontario
faced the prospect of dire economic dislocation as a result of changing
conditions of international trade, the government of Premier Oliver Mowat
(1872–96) responded with a far-reaching program of modernization. Its
aim was to anticipate and adjust to the inevitable loss of Ontario's once-
paramount role as a wheat producer by promoting specialization in a
variety of more profitable crops and food products. It included measures
to support research and training in horticulture, animal husbandry, and
food-processing technology and to encourage efficient land use and conservation. In related areas, the Mowat government acted decisively to
ensure that the province as a whole would benefit from industrialization,
which was then just getting under way, and from important new sources
of wealth (and tax revenue) that the mining and forestry industries were
beginning to develop in Northern Ontario. These policies were expertly
conceived and administered, and the Ontario economy emerged more
highly productive and competitive than ever.

In the twentieth century, the long Progressive Conservative dynasty
from 1943 to 1985, under various premiers, played a role similar to the
Mowat government's, promoting and smoothing the transition to a modern urban and industrial economy through massive public investment in
infrastructure such as new highways and electrical power-generating

plants; measures designed to attract investment in manufacturing; and the development of social programs to serve a rapidly increasing population. Like other successful governments before it, the PC dynasty's clear and overriding purpose was the pursuit of economic success.

Underlying that pursuit had always been an implicit understanding that economic success should be measured above all by the success of individuals in increasing their private prosperity, but an important secondary measure was the success of Ontario as a whole in increasing its public prosperity. When, under the government of Frank Miller (1985), the Tory dynasty seemed no longer to have any realistic sense of how to assist Ontarians in pursuit of the first, and to be ideologically ill disposed towards the second, it finally went down to electoral defeat. The Liberals under David Peterson (1985–90) fared no better. They talked in general terms about the need to manage the transition to an information-based economy, but never developed a clear idea of what they might usefully do, and in the end seemed less interested in pursuing economic success than in pursuing an agenda of rights creation and national unity. They too went down to defeat. The New Democratic Party under Bob Rae (1990–5) perhaps had a clearer sense than the Liberals of the Ontario norm. Its intentions in regard to the private sphere were suspect, however, since it also favoured measures that would redistribute income without necessarily increasing it, while in regard to the public sphere it could do little to stem the erosion of civic amenities in the face of a relentless economic recession.

The Progressive Conservative government of Mike Harris (1995–) that replaced the NDP came to power expressly committed to the resumption of Ontario's historic quest for economic success – which, it argued, had been lost sight of and hindered by previous governments in their misguided pursuit of goals such as 'employment equity.' But at the same time it also expressly rejected the idea that government might legitimately play a useful instrumental role in the economy. During a decade in opposition the PC party had been recast as an ideological party of the right and emerged bearing less resemblance to its former namesake (with the exception of the Miller government) than to the federal Reform and U.S. Republican parties, whose 'neo-conservative' anti-statist assertions it now stridently echoed: the opening words of its election platform, *The Common Sense Revolution*, were 'The people of Ontario have a message for their politicians – government isn't working anymore.' In its preferred model of society, economic success would be a matter of individual competition in the market place, with government involvement kept to a minimum. Like the NDP, therefore, in regard to the private sphere its intentions are suspect, because it too is implicitly redistributive in its leanings (though in the opposite direction of the NDP) and, like the Miller government, it is ideologically ill disposed to the public sphere.

The question that is at issue, and is reflected in the repeated turnover of governments since 1985, is whether a basic norm of the Ontario political culture is finally, after two centuries, undergoing fundamental change. The Harris government, which is unusual in the clarity and frankness of its ideology, is obviously betting that it is. If it also happens to be right, a new understanding of the meaning of economic success, and of the role of the government of Ontario in its pursuit, is in the process of being born. In the new understanding, the pursuit of economic success will be reconceived as a singularly individualistic activity, unfettered by illusions of partnership between public and private interests or of wealth held and enjoyed in common; and government will be reconceived as at best a neutral referee, at worst an enemy. Such perceptions, however, cut so squarely across the grain of Ontario's historic political culture that they are unlikely to be achieved without substantial dissent, or without consequences for the practice of politics, including the likely reconfiguration of the party system and perhaps a testing of the boundaries of legitimate political protest.

2. THE ASSUMPTION OF PRE-EMINENCE

One of the more curious norms of the Ontario outlook, so widely assumed for so long as to be generally a matter of no conscious awareness or interest, is that Ontario is naturally entitled to a position of preeminence in any Canadian economic or political context of importance, and often in other contexts as well.

This norm is partly a reflection of Ontario's sheer size and economic power, but its psychological roots lie deeply imbedded in the province's Upper Canadian past. The Loyalist founders were a people uniquely favoured by the British government with both material support in their resettlement and honorific recognition of their service and loyalty to the Empire. And they were not long in Upper Canada before they came to see themselves as well as 'a people highly favoured of God.' Governor Simcoe's view of their future was grandly ambitious, his high regard for them flattering, and the patronage he heaped upon them, mainly in gifts of land, astounding. After their undeniably vital role in the defence of Upper Canada in the War of 1812, which they later proudly embellished and mythologized, the Loyalists began to see themselves as the pre-eminent colonists of the British Empire, which in their eyes they had defended as no others. Their elite, especially, tended to identify themselves as an 'imperial' rather than a 'colonial' people, which probably accounts for their extraordinary and quite unconscious arrogance. The formidable Chief Justice of Upper Canada, John Beverley Robinson, for example, apparently saw nothing odd or presumptuous in thunderously lecturing even members of the British government when he felt they needed instruction in the duties of empire.

By the time of Confederation the Upper Canadian elite, whatever their political stripe, were of one mind in their assumption of Upper Canada's pre-eminence in British North America and would support no federal union that would not acknowledge it. Thus, the west had to be included because it would bring Upper Canada an empire of its own. In the revealing words of George Brown's *Globe*: 'The wealth of 400,000 square miles of territory will flow through our waters and be gathered by our merchants, manufacturers and agriculturalists. Our sons will occupy the chief places of this vast territory, we will form its institutions, supply its rulers, teach its schools, fill its stores, run its mills, navigate its streams. Every article of European manufacture, every pound of tropical produce will pass through our stores. Our seminaries of learning will be filled by its people. Our cities will be the centres of its business and education, its health and refinement.' Westerners themselves, of course, would later have a few choice words of their own to say about these presumptions, but the outlook nevertheless lingered.

In the 1880s, when the early constitution of Confederation proved too confining for Ontario's liking, the Mowat government's reaction was automatic: either Confederation would have to change, or it would have to go. Under Mowat's aegis, Ontario rejected the idea that it might accept the status of a mere secondary jurisdiction in Canada and instead aggressively reasserted its longstanding interests. What it demanded was nothing less than a huge increase in its legislative powers, restoration of its supremacy over its own resources and economic development, and a huge addition to its territory in the shape of what is now Northern Ontario. These demands – for autonomy, for land – resonated from the very core of the Upper Canadian consciousness, and in the end both proved irresistible. The Mowat government won a stunning victory in 1884, when the Judicial Committee of the Privy Council awarded Ontario virtually the whole of the northern territory it claimed, at one stroke more than tripling the province's land area and enclosing within its borders the entire Canadian portion of the Great Lakes system. With their province's pre-eminence in Canada assured, Ontarians thereafter preferred to see their interests and Ottawa's as basically compatible. Not surprisingly, to this day, of all the people of Canada, they are the least inclined to see fundamental conflict between them. And as an additional unanticipated benefit, Ontarians soon found they could sidestep potentially troubling issues of divided identity by simply dropping the 'Upper' part of their name and unambiguously asserting the 'Canadian' part. Again, to this day Ontarians are the Canadians who feel the least dissonance between their national and provincial identities: they solved the problem by simply projecting their own identity onto Canada's – which unfortunately did nothing to lessen their legendary reputation for presumptuousness.

Most twentieth-century Ontario premiers, with the exception of Mitchell Hepburn (1934–42), have at least tried not to offend the sensibilities of the federal government and the other provinces, but the assumption of Ontario's pre-eminence is hard to escape. It dictates the large role that Ontario premiers are expected to play in federal-provincial and interprovincial affairs, for example, even though this carries with it much attendant risk and is probably the major reason why it is generally considered impossible for a premier of Ontario to become prime minister of Canada. Over the past decade of constitutional crises, especially, the role of Ontario's premiers in the province's external relations has been a major source of their domestic political troubles: despite good intentions, they irritate Canadians in other provinces if they appear to be appropriating the mantle of 'Captain Canada'; if they support an unpopular federal prime minister they suffer damage by association; and when constitutional negotiations fail they are blamed in Ontario for their failure. No premier since John Robarts (1961–71) has achieved any positive gains by venturing onto the national stage, while two recent premiers have suffered major setbacks: David Peterson's prospects were seriously diminished by the failure of the Meech Lake Accord in 1990 and Bob Rae's by the defeat of the Charlottetown Accord in 1992. It is no wonder the Harris government has tried to avoid national involvement, apart from some minor sparring over fiscal issues. However, sooner or later Premier Harris will have to represent Ontario in the full unforgiving glare of the national stage, possibly in the midst of a dire constitutional and financial crisis in the event that Quebec votes to secede. But without

Quebec, Ontario's disproportionate size will be all the greater and its assumed pre-eminence all the harder for the rest of Canada to accept with equanimity.

3. THE REQUIREMENT OF MANAGERIAL EFFICIENCY

Managerial efficiency in government, variously conceived and interpreted, has always been one of the core norms of Ontario's operative political culture. In the eighteenth century the prevailing notion of efficiency was, like so much else, drawn from the military; Governor Simcoe's ideal administration, for example, was one modelled on a well-run regiment: firm and fair in its authority, clear in its objectives, and paternalistic in its concern for the welfare of all ranks. Later, Oliver Mowat defined a new model of efficiency drawn from agriculture. Efficient administration, in his view, was akin to expert 'husbandry' in the management of a farm: that is, it should be economical in operation, modern in its methods, progressive in outlook, and constant in its attention to the betterment of the whole estate. Later still, the PC dynasty of 1943–85 drew its model of efficiency from the world of business. Under Leslie Frost (1949–61), the ideal model was a prosperous family-run firm that was managed cautiously, invested wisely in future expansion, and paid close personal attention to details. 'Government,' Frost would say, 'is business, the people's business,' and good government is 'a matter of common sense' – but it must always be understood as 'a partnership between the two philosophies of economic advance and human betterment.' Under John Robarts ('I'm a management man myself') the ideal model was a corporation run by a dynamic CEO (the premier) with an experienced board of directors (the cabinet), employing the very best managers and technicians (the public service), and serving the interests of its shareholders (the people of Ontario).

Ontario governments, moreover, have been held to an unusually high and exacting standard of performance. As John Wilson has convincingly demonstrated, the Ontario electorate will forgive some failings, but it will not tolerate demonstrable incompetence. This attitude probably derived originally from Mowat, who governed for so long and with such consistent excellence that the electorate simply came to expect a high level of performance from its leaders.

Hence, more than the people of any other province, and perhaps more than any people anywhere, Ontarians tend to define political leadership in terms of managerial capability rather than other qualities such as personal charisma, and to award or withhold their electoral support accordingly.

One of the reasons governments in Ontario have been turned out with such regularity since 1985 is their seeming inability to realize that there is an operative norm of managerial efficiency in the province that they must observe, and that if they do not, neither style nor charisma nor good intentions – nor ideological commitment – will save them.

The Harris government will almost certainly find itself judged by that same norm. Some of its policies and approaches seem to clearly recognize this. Ballooning annual deficits, ever-increasing taxes, and the pursuit of controversial and costly social goals while the economy shrinks are the opposite of the Ontario idea of efficiency. Hence, if the Harris government succeeds in putting the province's public finances in order and generally demonstrates a steady hand in administering public business, it can be expected to earn a large measure of popular approval.

The most revealing test for the PCs will come if the norm of efficiency and their professed right-wing ideology end up conflicting – for example, if in some cases privatization appears to be less rather than more efficient, or if some cases of deregulation appear to entail hidden environmental or other costs. Governor Simcoe too had a strong ideological disposition and was fond of rhetoric; but when push came to shove, he never let either stand in the way of efficient government.

4. THE EXPECTATION OF RECIPROCITY

The most subtly generalized of the Ontario operative norms is the expectation of reciprocity in the processes and relationships of politics. That expectation grew naturally in the social and economic environment of Upper Canada, where both the system of land settlement and the type of agriculture necessitated complex reciprocal transactions of exchange, typically involving a relationship between a patron and a client. Personal alliances of this type – that is, between individuals of unequal status and resources but mutual interests (a system of clientelism) – thus came to form the basis of early political life and became absorbed into the political culture. As Ontario's political parties developed, they incorporated clientelistic norms of reciprocity into their structure and outlook, as exemplified by their extensive use of patronage to build local organizations and to link local and provincial elites. In Oliver Mowat's Liberal

Party, the great prototypical party organization of the nineteenth century, these norms were refined into what became known as 'the Ontario system.'

That system rested on the understanding that parties were a necessary part of democratic politics, and that those who worked for them should therefore legitimately expect to receive some reward, however modest, for their effort. The key was that the effort should be genuine, the reward fitting, and the recipient deserving. But beyond that it was assumed that a web of reciprocal obligation served as an essential link between government and local communities, involving large numbers of ordinary citizens. Under Mowat the system was carefully and scrupulously administered and extremely effective.

In a later era, the Tory dynasty from George Drew (1943–8) to Bill Davis (1971–85) pragmatically adapted Mowat's approach to fit the needs of its time; for example, by greatly expanding Ontario's system of agencies, boards, and commissions and creating numerous Crown corporations. These became major new sources of reward for those who served the PC party, but the entire Tory network was far wider, its positions and rewards generally modest, and its partisanship generally restrained. As in Mowat's time, scrupulous attention was paid to the network's maintenance: no one who worked within it was supposed to labour without recognition, even if that involved only some small honour or a personal letter of thanks from the leader. One of the great strengths of the dynasty, which perhaps as much as anything accounts for its longevity, was that in every community there were respected citizens who were connected to it, spoke well of it, and who expected in return to have its ear on matters of local concern.

After about 1980, however, there were increasing signs that the norm of reciprocity was falling into abeyance. It is possible that the norm itself was weakening, but it is equally likely that a party too long in power was becoming careless and out of touch with its grass roots. Patronage was being awarded to those who had performed no appreciable service, for reasons that were not readily discernible; local elites were being ignored, to their puzzlement and annoyance, even on issues directly affecting their communities; and for many, Queen's Park was beginning to feel somehow much further away.

Since 1985 the norm of reciprocity has been differently interpreted by the Liberals and the NDP during their respective terms in office. The Liberals, after forty-three years in the political wilderness, had lost touch with the old Ontario tradition and never set out to build the kind of local elite network that had been associated with the Tory dynasty. Instead, believing they had won election through modern media-oriented (and extremely expensive) campaign methods, they opted to use patronage to pursue what were seemingly two more modern approaches: first, to reward key fund-raisers and those presumed to have influence with the media; and second, more innovatively, to reward selected individuals, many of whom had done nothing for the party, but who were symbolically representative of various ethnic, minority, or social groups – whose members, supposedly, would then feel a sense of reciprocal obligation to the party because one of their own had been selected for preferment. The whole scheme went disastrously wrong. The first approach ended in charges of corruption that reached into the Premier's Office and the successful criminal prosecution of a Liberal fund-raiser; and the second approach, operating like a patronage lottery machine gone berserk, caused only astonishment. Both contributed to the government's ignominious demise.

The Rae government tried a different tack, reverting to something closer to the PC understanding of the norm but substituting an elite of mainly Toronto-centred labour and interest-group leaders for local business and professional elites. Again, the result was disastrous. The NDP's clients were showered with rewards, but showed no inclination to reciprocate. Instead, under pressure from their members, they made impossible group demands upon their NDP patrons. And when not satisfied, they turned upon them with a vengeance and withdrew their financial and electoral support.

There is no reason to conclude, however, that the norm of reciprocity has ceased to be generally operative. The spectacle of Bob Rae, who was generally seen as a moderate and capable premier, being viciously attacked by his party's own client groups was widely regarded as a breach of the Ontario way of doing things, and was one of the factors that brought the Harris government to power. If it is to avoid the NDP's fate, it will have to keep its own strident supporters at bay; and it will have to ensure that its patronage is honestly earned and used to build the kind of modest, low-partisan system of links with local communities that Ontarians have long favoured.

5. THE BALANCING OF INTERESTS

In September 1792, in his inaugural Speech from the Throne, Governor Simcoe assured the newly elected members of the first Legislature of

Upper Canada that the people they represented were 'singularly blessed ... with a Constitution which has stood the test of experience' and which would enable them to enjoy above all the inestimable value of 'balance.' In this he was propounding the theory, common in his day, that a system of parliamentary government in which power was shared among different interests – according to the classical model, among Crown, aristocracy, and people – offered the best guarantee of individual freedom and the surest defence against tyranny. In practice, this meant merely that government should try to strike a balance in its policies and not allow itself to be controlled by any one interest.

As Simcoe soon discovered, however, that was easier said than done. Initially, he had distrusted the merchant oligarchy, whom he found 'justly obnoxious' but in whose hands the economy of Upper Canada very largely rested, believing that they had no conception of the public interest and would always try to use the government for their own selfish ends. Hence, to remove their influence, he abolished their positions of local power and extended the scope of his central administration, whose officials were for the most part Loyalist ex-officers. But when that too produced imbalance, Simcoe took precisely the opposite tack, bringing the merchants back into government positions and vigorously promoting their commercial interests. Those interests, he could now see, were vital to the prosperity of the province. Agriculture was already producing surpluses for export and the signs of its future potential were clear; but it could fully prosper only if backed by a well-financed, profit-driven commercial trading system. The pursuit of economic success, from the very beginning, required the continuous pragmatic balancing and rebalancing of interests.

Over time, the general understanding of the idea of balanced government grew to include the corollary that all legitimate interests were *entitled* to be included in the process of balancing. Also, that *process* became more elaborate and formal. One of the important innovations of the Mowat government, for example, was to encourage the creation of organized interest groups, in some cases with the government's financial assistance, in order to ensure that no significant interest would be unconsulted on matters affecting it or left out of the government's calculations. Later governments were rarely as adept as Mowat's, at least until the Tory dynasty, which followed the same basic approach and enjoyed a similar level of success.

In the modern era, however, the balancing of interests has become progressively more difficult and problematical and the traditional norm more frequently challenged. The *general* expectation that all interests will be consulted and included in the balance is as strong, if not stronger, than ever; but over many *specific* issues there is much contestation of the right to be included and there are no clear criteria for determining which interests are legitimate 'stakeholders.' Even such traditional major interests as business and labour are no longer as clearly defined as they once were; and in areas of social policy such as education, health, and social welfare, the groups claiming legitimacy and demanding inclusion are legion, their rhetoric often extreme, and their posture often uncompromising. The Rae government, apparently believing that these groups had played a valuable role in the NDP election victory in 1990 and were potentially an important new source of future political support, was at first inclined to grant them inclusion; but it quickly backed away when their specific demands conflicted with NDP policies or the interests of traditional NDP client groups. Some within the NDP argued that these groups could and should have been accommodated. But in fact they were not, and during the 1995 election campaign they were as relentlessly hostile to the NDP as they had been to the Liberals in 1990.

The norm of balance requires that governments at least make a serious attempt to consult and accommodate divergent interests, however difficult that may be. The Harris government may not be enamoured with those it defines as 'special interests,' but interests considered 'special' or even 'justly obnoxious' by the government of the day are not exactly new. They have been around for at least two hundred years, and wise governments have always come to the conclusion that the province as a whole is best served when they are included in the balance.

Conclusion

The argument presented here is that the Ontario political culture is defined above all by strong operative norms about the goals and conduct of government. All of these have roots that stretch far back into Ontario's history; but they have never 'congealed' into the sort of codified formulaic abstractions that are characteristic of more ideationally based political cultures. Rather, they have continued to evolve more or less in parallel with the various stages of the province's economic growth and development, and hence retain their relevance in the present. To a striking degree, the Ontario norms reflect at their core a double helix–like intertwining of political and economic aspirations. Indeed, there are few societies where this particular trait is so prominent a feature of the political culture; and while the explanation for this may be largely historical, there seem as well to be sociopsychological and demographic factors involved whose effects need to be explored further.

The effects of immigration are particularly intriguing and need to be considered afresh. Many societies that experience mass immigration find that their historic political cultures are ineffectual agents of integration, and that this gives rise to the development of parallel immigrant subcultures; but in Ontario, which has received immigration on a scale matched by few other societies, the political culture tends on the whole to be strongly integrative in that the great bulk of new immigrants readily absorb it. Indeed, most seem to find it very much to their liking. Whatever the reasons may be, the Ontario political culture thus appears to be one of the very few historic political cultures to be effectively strengthened by mass immigration rather than weakened or disrupted by it. If that is true, the human appeal and power of essentially operative norms may be very much underestimated.

The effects of economic insecurity must also be considered, for it is unlikely that a political culture as economically intertwined with economic aspirations as Ontario's can remain unaffected by the changes that are taking place in its economic environment. In the late twentieth century – very much as in the late nineteenth century – Ontario is undergoing a difficult period of economic restructuring; now, however, the combined effects of changing investment patterns, new technology, and the globalization of production are more complex than ever and the impact on local communities more severe. It is not by accident that the Ontario political culture is under greatest pressure to change at precisely those points where it is most at odds with external economic forces – and with the powerful currents of anti-government ideology that are allied to them.

The broad general direction in which the political culture is being pushed is clear: towards a more purely private conception of economic success and a corresponding reduction in the role of government. But it is by no means clear that it has as yet actually moved very far in that direction. The economy has always been a matter of both pride and concern for Ontarians: pride in their achievement in building it into one of the world's foremost wealth-creating machines, and concern whenever it appears that the machine is not being properly managed. Their manifest dissatisfaction, which over the past decade has produced a string of short-lived governments, is therefore easily misread. It could mean that the political culture is in the process of reinventing itself – that

Ontarians are in fact becoming more ideological in their core perspectives, more individualistic, more competitive, more attuned to global forces – and therefore only a government that embraces and reflects these new orientations will be permitted to enjoy anything more than a brief moment of success. Equally, however, it could mean only that the political culture is adapting gradually to new circumstances, resiliently bending before the ideological winds as it has done so many times before, but that its core operative norms are as strong as ever. On this view, no one should be surprised that Ontarians gave a string of governments what amounted to a probationary term in office, found their performance unsatisfactory, and – as is their democratic right – fired each of them in turn. The proper lesson, therefore, may be that unless a government shows that it understands the norms and can meet the requisite standard of performance it is unlikely to win the public's favour.

Political cultures change, but they do not change overnight. New impositions take time to become accepted, whether through consensus or because resistance to them seems futile. And in a democracy, time is rarely on the side of those in power. In Ontario, when a government butts heads against the political culture, it is usually the government that gets changed.

Further Reading

Craig, Gerald M. *Upper Canada: The Formative Years, 1784–1841*. Toronto: McClelland and Stewart, 1963.

Errington, Jane. *The Lion, the Eagle and Upper Canada: A Developing Colonial Ideology*. Kingston and Montreal: McGill-Queens University Press, 1987.

Evans, A. Margaret. *Sir Oliver Mowat*. Toronto: University of Toronto Press, 1992.

Graham, Roger. *Old Man Ontario: Leslie M. Frost*. Toronto: University of Toronto Press, 1990.

MacDonald, Donald C. 'Ontario's Political Culture: Conservatism with a Progressive Component.' *Ontario History* 86, no. 4 (December 1994): 297–317.

MacDougall, A.K. *John P. Robarts: His Life and Government*. Toronto: University of Toronto Press, 1986.

McKenty, Neil. *Mitch Hepburn*. Toronto: McClelland and Stewart, 1967.

Manthorpe, Jonathan. *The Power and the Tories: Ontario Politics – 1943 to the Present*. Toronto: Macmillan, 1974.

Noel, S.J.R. *Patrons, Clients, Brokers: Ontario Society and Politics, 1791–1896.*
Toronto: University of Toronto Press, 1990.

Stewart, Ian. 'All the King's Horses: The Study of Canadian Political Culture.'
In James P. Bickerton and Alain-G. Gagnon, eds, *Canadian Politics*, 2nd ed.
Peterborough: Broadview Press, 1994.

Vipond, Robert C. *Liberty and Community.* Albany: State University of New York
Press, 1991.

Wilson, John. 'The Red Tory Province: Reflections on the Character of the
Ontario Political Culture.' In Donald C. MacDonald, ed., *The Government and
Politics of Ontario*, 2nd ed., 210–33. Toronto: Van Nostrand Reinhold, 1980.

Wise, S.F. 'The Ontario Political Culture: A Study in Complexities.' In Graham
White, ed., *The Government and Politics of Ontario*, 4th ed., 44–59. Toronto:
Nelson, 1990.

PART II

Governmental Institutions

FOUR

The Legislature: Central Symbol of Ontario Democracy

Graham White

The legislature – Queen's Park – is perhaps Ontario's most central politi-cal symbol. It stands as the embodiment of the province's democratic values – the people's representatives making laws in accordance with democratically expressed public opinion. As with most highly symbolic institutions, the reality of what transpires at the legislature does not correspond very closely to the symbolism. Indeed, much of the popula-tion harbours highly inaccurate views of the role played by the legisla-ture in Ontario politics, about its power, and about the influence wielded by its members. The natural expectation of an institution called a 'legisla-ture' is that it makes laws, but for the most part the Ontario Legislature is better understood as a law-passing rather than a lawmaking body. In Ontario, as in other parliamentary systems, for most practical purposes the cabinet and the bureaucracy makes the laws. From time to time, the legislature does significantly influence policy, but this influence tends to be subtle and indirect rather than operating through formal amendments to the bills going through the House.

If the legislature's prime function is not making laws, what does it do? Among the important functions it does perform are representing the people, holding the government accountable, debating important issues, recruiting and training political leaders, and legitimizing and building support for government policies. The representation function includes not only voicing the views and concerns of various groups and commu-nities, but also assisting constituents in their dealings with government (sometimes called the members' 'ombudsman function'). Accountability

means that the legislature requires the government – both elected ministers and their bureaucratic officials – to explain and defend its policies
and their administration. In debating the issues of the day, the legislature
brings new problems to public attention, educates the public about those
problems and possible solutions to them, and permits the voters to assess
the positions of the various political parties on the issues. Although
many powerful and important government policy makers are to be
found in the bureaucracy or in ministers' offices rather than in the legislature, all ministers must be (by convention, if not by law) MPPs, and the
House acts as both a training ground for potential cabinet ministers and a
proving ground for those in cabinet. Finally, the legislature legitimizes
government policy in the formal sense of providing legal authorization
for laws and for government spending, but in a much more fundamental
sense it encourages people to accept government measures that they
dislike because they believe that the decisions were made by their elected
representatives and that public opinion and public involvement are central elements behind the decisions these representatives make.

This chapter cannot evaluate in any detail how successfully the legislature performs these functions, but they should be kept in mind as various
aspects of the legislature are discussed. The chapter begins with an
overview of the legislature's basic structure; subsequent sections examine the characteristics and the situations of the MPPs, the organization
and influence of parties, the increasingly unpleasant atmosphere of the
House, some basic features of legislative operations, and the role and
activities of legislative committees.

Structure

Fundamental to the understanding of the Ontario Legislature is the
recognition that, like the House of Commons in Ottawa and all Canadian
provincial legislatures, it is premised on the British model of cabinet-
parliamentary government. Such familiar principles as ministerial responsibility, the adversarial government-opposition division, and the
requirement that the cabinet retain the confidence of the House represent
the essential constitutional underpinning of the legislature.

The legislature is (in 1996) composed of 130 MPPs (Members of Provincial Parliament), each elected from a geographic district called a
constituency or riding. The Harris government has reduced the number
of MPPs to 103 for subsequent legislatures.[1] This commitment is rooted
in ideology and symbolism – reducing the scope of the state and demon-

strating the Conservatives' dedication to cost-cutting – for the financial savings will be marginal and a substantially smaller house may well be a substantially less-effective house.[2]

In its formal structure, the Ontario Legislature has changed little since Confederation. It has grown slowly in size (from eighty-two members in 1867). Only occasionally, most recently in the 1920s, have members been elected other than in single-member districts (a handful of two- and three-member districts existed in the larger cities). Ontario is unique among the original Canadian provinces in that its legislature has always been unicameral, that is, without an upper house. This continuity in basic structure should not, however, be equated with lack of change, for in many ways the legislature has changed profoundly, particularly over the past two or three decades.

One of the most significant long-term changes in the Ontario Legislature has been the emergence of a permanent three-party house. All other Canadian provincial assemblies are essentially two-party houses; either third parties are very small in number (often only one or two members) or episodes marked by substantial representation of three parties, as in Manitoba and Alberta, prove transitory. The Ontario Legislature is unique among provincial houses by virtue of its strong permanent three-party system.

In terms of electoral following, Ontario's current three-party system dates from the Second World War, but particularly during the 1950s and early 1960s the peculiarities of the electoral system distorted the number of seats won by the parties so that the CCF (the precursor of the NDP) elected only a handful of members despite attracting nearly 20 per cent of the vote and the third of the vote that went to the Liberals translated into well less than a quarter of the seats. Since 1967, however, whichever party has been in third place (which all three parties have been) has held at least 16 seats. The fact that all three parties have formed the government within the last decade attests to the intense three-party competition in the legislature.

Parliaments with three substantial parties are qualitatively different from those with only two parties. In three-party houses, the primal division between government and opposition may not correspond to ideological divisions. For most of the postwar period, by way of illustration, no matter who formed the government, the principal ideological division lay between the CCF-NDP and the two older parties (in the era of the 'Common Sense Revolution,' the central ideological division appears to be between the Conservatives on one side and the Liberals and

the NDP on the other). Moreover, the presence of three parties compli-
cates the political calculus in the House, mainly through the competition
between the two opposition parties to prove which is 'the real opposition.' One of the keys to the long Conservative period in office (1943–85)
was the government's success in ensuring that the Liberals and New
Democrats in the House spent as much time and energy fighting one
another as they did attacking the government. On an everyday level, in
devising tactics for question period and for committee meetings, opposition strategists must try to anticipate not only how the government will
respond, but also the questions and tactics employed by the other opposition party.

For all this, however, the most important consequence of a three-party
house is the possibility of minority government, in which the government party holds fewer seats than the opposition parties combined. And
indeed, three of the last seven governments have been minorities: 1975–
7, 1977–81, and 1985–7. These minority situations not only greatly enhanced the power of the legislature with respect to the government and
to the policy process, but also left a lasting legacy in terms of procedural
reforms and members' attitudes towards the House.

The MPPs

Public cynicism about the political process is evident in frequent complaints that MPPs receive extravagant pay and perks for an 'easy' job (the
House sits no more than about a hundred days a year) that likely leads to
a cushy patronage plum. Such criticisms are quite unfair to the great
majority of MPPs. In 1996, MPPs were paid $78,007 a year. The Speaker,
ministers, and party leaders earned substantially more. Committee chairs,
whips, house leaders, and parliamentary assistants received a few thousand dollars above the basic indemnity. Members also received a host of
other benefits, such as allowances for non-Toronto MPPs to pay for
accommodation in the capital and transportation costs between Queen's
Park and their homes. The Harris government scrapped the MPPs' generous pension plan. By comparison with most of their constituents, MPPs
are well paid, though if the basis for comparison is either the upper levels
of the bureaucracy or middle-range positions in the private sector, members do not fare very well. Indeed, business people and professionals
elected to the legislature are often faced with a dramatic decline in
income, and with job security that lasts only until the next election
(unlike a quarter-century ago, almost all current members are full-time

MPPs and maintain no outside employment). As for the accusation that MPPs can routinely look forward to well-paying patronage jobs when they leave the legislature, it is certainly true that some former MPPs are rewarded with appointments to various federal and provincial government bodies. Yet many have considerable difficulty adjusting to life after politics, including finding jobs; one former Liberal MPP who was defeated in the 1995 election was unable, despite good political connections, to find work, and ultimately committed suicide.

Financial concerns, however, are not nearly so important as the personal sacrifices members are called upon to make. Members face unrelenting demands on their time; not only do they work long weekday hours, but they are expected to attend all manner of local meetings and social events in their ridings on weekends. The House, as noted above, may only sit for four or five months a year, but committee activity fills in many of the gaps and the press of constituency business never lets up. The time pressures, the lack of privacy (members, especially those from ridings outside large urban centres, are often besieged by constituents' calls to their homes), and the need to be away from home for extended periods are highly destructive of family life. Coupled with the frustrations that most members, both government and opposition, encounter over their inability to affect policy significantly, these demands can make the lot of the MPP a trying one indeed.

MPPs have significant, though by no means excessive, staff and logistical support in carrying out their duties. Members are provided with offices at the legislature and in their ridings and funding for three or four full-time staff members. Each party caucus also has a research bureau and other facilities and staff to assist members with media relations, political organizing, and other needs. A sizeable contingent of professional, non-partisan legislative workers, such as the reference specialists and research staff of the legislative library, are also available to members. Almost none of these services and facilities existed before the early 1970s.

Members of the Ontario Legislature bring a wide range of backgrounds and experiences to their tasks. In certain respects, MPPs mirror the social composition of the province, but in other ways they are quite unrepresentative of Ontario's population. Members are on balance much better educated and older than their electors. They are disproportionately drawn from small business and professional occupations (particularly teaching and law); relatively few Ontario MPPs have backgrounds in working-class or lower-middle-class (sales and clerical) jobs. In terms of their religious affiliation and their national origins, MPPs are generally representative of the provincial population, with one glaring exception: whereas at least 10 per cent of Ontario residents are of non-European origin – a great many in the 'visible minority' groups – in 1996 only two of 130 members of the legislature did not trace their origins to Europe. Only 15 per cent of the MPPs are women.

The Speaker occupies a unique position in the legislature. He – no woman has ever been Speaker – is elected as a party politician in a riding, but once chosen to be Speaker must be completely neutral in presiding over the rough-and-tumble of the House, treating all members with complete fairness. He does not take part in legislative debates or in his party's caucus activities and votes only in the exceedingly rare event of a tie. A strong, independent speakership is essential to a mature, effective parliament, and although the Office of Speaker in Ontario has increased substantially in prestige and power in recent years, the Speaker remains hamstrung both by a lack of formal powers and by the members' lack of respect. For example, Ontario was one of the last jurisdictions in Canada to permit the Speaker's decisions to be overturned by a vote in the House. Until 1990, the Speaker was chosen by the premier, which naturally compromised perceptions of his neutrality; the last two Speakers have been elected by secret ballot of all MPPs, as is done in the House of Commons. Unfortunately, this has not substantially enhanced members' respect for the office; opposition suspicions about the Speaker's neutrality continue to undermine his authority. In recent years, the Speaker has assumed a wide range of administrative duties as head of the large legislative bureaucracy; in this respect, his position is analogous to that of a minister.

The budget for the legislature in 1996–7 was approximately $101 million, a decline of about 9 per cent over the previous year.[3] A substantial professional bureaucracy serves the legislature, but these officials differ from civil servants in that they serve members of all parties with equal diligence. Civil servants in the ministries are often helpful to opposition MPPs, but they are clearly working for the government (though not the government party), whereas the staff of the Legislative Assembly work for and answer to all members. The Clerk of the House is the Speaker's chief procedural adviser as well as the administrative head of the legislative bureaucracy.

Similarly, several important offices report directly to the legislature rather than to the government. These include the Office of the Provincial Auditor, the Office of the Ombudsman, the Information and Privacy Commission, the Election Office, the Environmental Commissioner, and the Commission on Election Finances. The functions performed by these organizations – overseeing the electoral process, investigating government decisions, auditing public expenditures, adjudicating disputes over government release of information, and the like – require them to be independent of government direction. Thus, their responsibility is to all members of the legislature rather than to government ministers, as is the case with the civil service.

Parties

The important number in the Ontario Legislature is not 130 but three. Almost without exception, MPPs belong to one of the three main Ontario parties; the one independent elected in 1995 was the first to win office in decades (very occasionally MPPs break with their parties to sit as independents). More significantly, party discipline is strong and pervasive, so that what count are the positions of the three parties rather than the views of the 130 members. The opinions of individual members may have an important bearing in formulating party positions, but to the extent that this occurs it is largely a behind-the-scenes process that has little bearing on the operation of the House and its committees. In all three parties, tension exists between the ordinary MPPs and the party leadership over questions of political strategy and policy instances, but it is especially acute on the government side. Government MPPs, particularly during majority governments, are often frustrated by their lack of influence in policy making but lack the opposition members' compensation in being able to vent their frustration through vigourous public criticism of the government in question period and elsewhere.

Each party caucus is highly organized, with well-defined leadership. Party leaders enjoy a dominant position and in most cases are able to impose their will on the caucus, though, paradoxically, effective leadership makes sparing use of such power. The collectivist ideology of the NDP and the party's commitment to internal party democracy restrict the NDP leader's power in comparison to the other party leaders, but even he is clearly in charge. Party leaders have far more extensive staff support than do other members. They are the prime focus of media attention and are given special treatment in many other ways, both formal and informal; by way of illustration, the first four questions during question period are reserved for party leaders, and leaders are permitted more supplementary questions than other MPPs.

The other key figures in the parties' legislative apparatus are the house leaders and the whips. The house leader is responsible for developing strategy in the House and for coordinating house tactics, and is the key figure in the extensive interparty consultations and negotiations that are necessary for the smooth running of the House. The whips work closely with the house leaders but are not considered as important; their prime tasks are promoting members' attendance in the House and in committees, ensuring that all members are available for votes (and that they actually do vote), maintaining party morale and enthusiasm, and, when necessary, enforcing party discipline on wayward members. Although the possibility of coercion of MPPs by the whips or by the party leaders is an element in party discipline, it is generally less important than the pressure exerted on members by their peers to be team players. Moreover, members genuinely believe in their parties and their programs and think that 'the system' works best with strong, cohesive parties. Accordingly, the whips spend a good deal of their time cajoling and bullying members to improve their attendance records, but they are not often called upon to deal with members publicly critical of their parties, let alone contemplating voting against them in the House.

Not surprisingly, party organizations differ substantially from government to opposition. Being larger, and by virtue of just being the government, the government caucus is more complex and more hierarchical. Premiers and their ministers are so much more powerful than other government members that in important respects the position of government backbencher (that is, non-minister) is more akin to that of opposition member than to minister. The premier appoints some MPPs as 'parliamentary assistants' to ministers to lighten their loads, but they are not junior ministers; their duties, which are typically set at the whim of the ministers they serve, are often fairly minimal and, with rare exception, they wield nothing like the power and influence of ministers. Still, they rank slightly ahead of the ordinary backbencher in the pecking order of the government caucus. On the opposition side, the distinction found in some British-style parliaments between frontbencher and backbencher is absent. All opposition members are appointed by the party leader as 'critics' responsible for taking the lead in attacking the government and developing policy alternatives in specific fields; usually each ministry and major government agency will have opposition critics assigned to 'shadow' it. To be sure, some critic 'portfolios' (for example, treasury, health and education, and labour in the NDP) are more important than others, but the pecking order is not nearly so sharply defined in the opposition caucuses as it is on the government side.

All parties have various forms of caucus committees, but generally they are not important. The Liberals, the NDP, and most recently the Conservatives have all developed a substantial array of caucus policy committees for backbenchers, but their overall influence has been limited. In part because their caucuses have been much smaller, such committees have either been altogether lacking or essentially hollow shells on the opposition side. An important exception to this generalization have been the so-called task forces mounted by the opposition parties. These consist of three or four MPPs who travel the province holding public meetings and developing policy proposals on specific topics such as energy, workers' compensation, forestry, Sunday shopping, liquor marketing, health care, and youth unemployment.

Almost nothing that occurs in the legislature can be understood except through the prism of party. The fundamental attitudes determining MPPs' behaviour and the ways in which issues or proposals are presented, debated, and resolved are premised on parties rather than individuals as the key elements in the legislature. Even the rules of the House (the *Standing Orders*) emphasize the parties' predominance. Far more than those of the House of Commons or of other provincial legislatures, the Ontario assembly's procedures presume that all MPPs' interests and views are subsumed in their parties. The allocation of questions in Question Period, the distribution of committee chairs, the determination of which issues are to be dealt with in what committees and other important procedural questions are stipulated in the rules as matters to be decided by the parties. Little or no provision is found in the *Standing Orders* for independent MPPs or for members who might wish a different course of action from that chosen by their party leaders (at least with respect to house business). Any evaluation of the legislature's effectiveness, as any prescription for remedying its shortcomings, must take as a starting point the overwhelming importance of party.

The Atmosphere in the House

The past decade has witnessed important, if largely intangible, changes in the culture and atmosphere of the legislature. During the long Conservative reign, in many ways the legislature operated like a club. MPPs certainly disagreed politically with their opponents, but they also exhibited a strong sense of camaraderie based on shared experiences and common problems. A good deal of the outrage exhibited in the House was essentially theatrical and the bantering and heckling there were generally more good-natured than vitriolic; cross-party friendships among members were common. The club-like atmosphere was fostered by the fact that virtually all MPPs and senior legislative staff members were men.[4] The essentially moderate tone of debate and the relative civility that underlay the apparently raucous behaviour of MPPs made for a House that operated fairly smoothly and conducted its business with reasonable dispatch and cooperation among parties.

In the late 1990s, however, moderation, reasonableness, and civility are in short supply at the legislature. The bitter, politically charged atmosphere that has come to characterize house proceedings has notably adverse effects on the capacity of the House to conduct its business. This is not to suggest that the club has been entirely disbanded, for much of what transpires in the legislature continues to be better understood as theatre than as reality, and MPPs continue to adhere to important unspoken codes of behaviour, for example, refraining from seeking political advantage by bringing to public attention aspects of other members' personal lives. Nor should the Frost-Robarts-Davis era be romanticized as one of sweetness and reason at Queen's Park; tough, nasty, protracted catfights were hardly unknown in the legislature. On balance, however, long-time observers agree that genuine rancour between the parties is far more pronounced now than in the 1970s and 1980s, that brutal, give-no-quarter legislative tactics have become routine, and that the legislature is less effective for these changes.

Several factors have contributed to the sea-change in the atmosphere, and thus the operation, of the legislature. The end of evening sittings in 1986 significantly reduced the amount of time MPPs spent in and around the chamber in relaxed conditions conducive to developing respect and friendship among members of all parties. The advent of extensive television coverage of the House about the same time had similarly adverse affects on the interpersonal dynamics of the legislature. Not only could members now follow house proceedings on television in their offices (thus obviating the need to come to the chamber, where they would have personal contact with MPPs from other parties), but television also encourages dramatic confrontation.

More fundamental, though, has been the larger political changes that have transformed Ontario since the end of the Davis government in 1985. For most of the postwar Tory hegemony, opposition Liberals and New Democrats might have talked bravely in public about ending the Conservative dynasty, but privately many never believed it would really happen, so that for the opposition a good deal of legislative politics

meant going through the motions. Now that all three parties have recently tasted power, however, the stakes at Queen's Park are much
higher; conceivably any issue before the House might hold the potential
to shift the political balance sufficiently to produce a change in government. Accordingly, parties are more aggressive and intransigent in the
House.

As well, first with the NDP government and even more strikingly with
the Harris Conservatives, the middle-of-the-road politics of moderation
that marked the Davis and Peterson governments have been replaced by
strongly ideological politics emphasizing the psychological gulf between
government and opposition. Moreover, measures brought to the legislature by NDP and Conservative governments in the 1990s (on such matters as labour relations, employment equity, and massive government
cutbacks) are inherently controversial and highly ideological, and have
inflamed members' political passions. In the House the passage of these
centrepiece bills has been notable for opposition obstructionism and
increasingly draconian government attempts at overcoming opposition.
(Faced with unprecedented opposition-mounted delays in passing even
its routine bills, the NDP government resorted to significantly more
extensive use of procedures to limit house debate than previous governments had required; it also brought in a tough set of rule changes to
reduce opposition opportunities to hold up passage of government measures. Early in their mandate, the Conservatives attempted to secure
quick passage of perhaps the most far-reaching legislation in Ontario
history – the notorious 'omnibus' Bill 26, with minimal public involvement, provoking what amounted to an opposition occupation of the
legislative chamber.)

These inherently conflictual developments have been exacerbated by
the extensive turnover in house membership resulting from the dramatic
turnaround in all three parties' fortunes in the last three elections. In the
wake of the 1995 election, only a dozen MPPs had experience dating back
even as far as the previous Conservative government in 1985. More
significantly, when the NDP took office in 1990 and the Conservatives
replaced them in 1995, all but a handful of their large backbench contin-
gents were brand-new MPPs, with little understanding of the traditions
or the complexities of the legislature (having never been in opposition,
for example, they exhibited little sympathy with or understanding of the
opposition's legitimate right to criticize and delay government measures). And with very few experienced government backbench MPPs to
act as mentors (since most experienced, talented members became minis-

ters), an important potential leavening of the hostility between government backbench and opposition was lost.

The Legislature in Operation

The *Standing Orders* stipulate that the House is to sit from about mid-March until late June and again from late September until mid-December, with a 'constituency week' off each spring and fall. This provides just over ninety sitting days a year. The government can override the legislative calendar by extending the session or by delaying the recall of the House. The months when the House is not in session are usually characterized by extensive committee activity; it is quite common for three or four committees to meet simultaneously during such periods. During the extended breaks in and between sessions, committees often travel throughout the province holding public hearings on proposed legislation and on other policy issues, or, much less frequently, venture outside Ontario on fact-finding missions. When in session, the House meets Monday to Thursday at 1:30 p.m. and adjourns at 6:00 p.m., with an extra sitting from 10:00 a.m. to 12:00 noon on Thursdays for private members' business. In unusual circumstances, and routinely towards the end of June and December, the House may meet in the evenings.

Legislative proceedings are divided into two distinct components: routine proceedings and orders of the day. As the term implies, routine proceedings follow the same format every day. Whereas the government has little control over the content of routine proceedings, during orders of the day, which begin once routine proceedings have been completed (usually about 3:00 p.m.), the government chooses the items for debate. This is the time when government bills, spending proposals, and policy papers are debated. Although the opposition may delay the passage of bills or government business, it has no procedural means of forcing the government to bring forward for debate bills the government does not wish to proceed with. The opposition may be able to force the government's hand through political pressure, but in effect the government retains virtually complete procedural control over this crucial part of the legislative agenda. (Up to ten times a year, on 'opposition days,' the opposition parties choose the subject for debate in the House, but the rules do not permit them to use these opportunities to debate legislation.)

Save on Thursdays, when private members' business is taken up in the morning, the legislative day begins with ten minutes of members' statements. Any member other than a minister or a party leader is permitted to speak for ninety seconds on any topic; some MPPs prefer to address local riding concerns and others focus their statements on larger issues of government policy. MPPs like making these statements, in part because no direct rebuttal is allowed, but they generally attract little media attention. The next routine proceeding is statements by the ministry, during which ministers make policy announcements and other official statements. Major government initiatives are often announced at this time, though there is no rule against ministers making important statements outside the legislature before informing the House about them. Each opposition party has five minutes to reply to ministry statements, but since the opposition seldom knows beforehand what is coming these replies tend to be vague and unfocused.

Following ministry statements is the highlight of the legislative day: question period. For an hour each sitting day, the government is subjected to tough questioning on the entire range of its policies and its administrative operations by its principal political opponents. Ministers have no formal warning of what questions they will be asked, though many questions can be predicted from a quick reading of the morning's *Globe and Mail* or *Toronto Star*. Still, question period is a key element in keeping the government accountable: not only must ministers answer publicly for their actions, but in making decisions they and their officials must anticipate possible questions that could cause serious political embarrassment. In this way, the effectiveness of question period, along with other accountability mechanisms such as the Public Accounts Committee, may lie more in the threats they pose for potential damage than in the actual questions that are asked. Government backbenchers' questions are almost invariably innocuous or congratulatory of the government. Once question period is over, most MPPs and virtually all reporters in the press gallery leave, and on most days the remaining routine proceedings are completed quickly.

Since the late 1980s, opposition obstruction has become a prominent element of legislative life in Ontario. A full-fledged 'bells incident' in 1989 saw the opposition bring the House to a standstill for eight days by keeping the division bells (which call MPPs into the chamber to vote) ringing. In 1991, Mike Harris tied up House proceedings for several days by introducing bills purporting to deal with zebra-mussel infestations in specified Ontario bodies of water, which permitted him to spend hours at a time reading the names of Ontario lakes, streams, bays, rivers, and the like. The Liberal and New Democratic opposition to the Conservatives' omnibus bill late in 1995 caused an unusual disruption of the

House when they physically refused to allow the Speaker to have a Liberal MPP ejected for a minor rule transgression on a vote related to the proceedings on the bill. In a last-ditch stalling manoeuvre against the Tories' 'megacity' legislation the opposition parties forced the House to sit around the clock for ten days early in 1997 to deal with more than 10,000 amendments to the bill (none passed).

These dramatic episodes, and other, more mundane delaying tactics reflect the increasingly acrimonious atmosphere in the House, the high political stakes at issue, and the opposition's essentially powerless position in the face of a determined majority government. The escalation of obstructionist opposition tactics is also a function of government-instigated rule changes closing loopholes and restricting the opposition's ability to delay government measures through more conventional means. Under the Liberals, the rules were changed in 1989 to limit division bells to thirty minutes; the NDP government changed the *Standing Orders* in 1992 to prevent a repeat of Harris's zebra-mussel gambit. As well, time limits have been placed on MPPs' speeches in most circumstances, and governments of all political stripes have increasingly come to rely on time-allocation mechanisms to limit debate on important or controversial measures.

None of this, it should be emphasized, is unique to the Ontario Legislature; indeed, compared to other Canadian legislatures (particularly the House of Commons), the Ontario House came relatively late to extensive time limits on members' speeches and frequent recourse to government action cutting off debate. The more acrimonious atmosphere in the House does, however, mark a noteworthy change from the way the Ontario Legislature functioned barely a decade ago.

As is the case in Westminster-style parliaments, the most significant steps in the lawmaking process are pre-parliamentary; in other words, the most important decisions on any government bill are made by the cabinet and the bureaucracy before the bill's first reading in the House. First reading is little more than a formality, though it is important in that the bill becomes a public document that is officially placed on the *Order Paper*, the legislature's agenda. After several weeks, during which the opposition parties have an opportunity to analyse the bill and determine their stances, the bill is 'called' by the government for second reading. This debate on the principle of the bill usually takes only an hour or two, and almost never exceeds two days. Straightforward, uncontroversial bills then proceed directly to third reading, which in many cases is a formality, though substantive, and sometimes time-consuming, debates at third reading, which were once all but unknown, have become common in recent years. Bills that require amendment or detailed study must pass through a committee stage before third reading. A single MPP can force the committee stage on a bill. The less significant bills are usually referred for consideration to the Committee of the Whole – simply the House sitting in the chamber as a committee; the rules of debate are somewhat relaxed and the Deputy Speaker presides. The government retains the authority to decide the scheduling of matters that come before the Committee of the Whole.

Approximately a quarter of government bills – invariably the more complex and controversial – are referred to standing committees for study. Procedurally, this route is equivalent to Committee of the Whole treatment, but in political terms the differences are substantial. The committees themselves, rather than the government, decide the order in which the business before them is to be taken up; with a majority government this power matters little, but in minority times it means that the government effectively loses control over the scheduling of business before standing committees. Furthermore, unlike the Committee of the Whole, a standing committee can hold public hearings, meet with expert witnesses, and travel to gather information relevant to the bill before it. These processes can have important political consequences: public attention can be focused on the bill and significant political forces mobilized in support or in opposition to it. A particularly contentious or important bill may be before a standing committee for weeks or months. Amendments to the detailed provisions of a bill are often made in committee, but major changes are not common. Even during minority governments, most important amendments either originate with or are acceptable to the government.

The *Standing Orders* permit twenty members to force a government bill to standing committee, but the opposition rarely has to resort to this device since the parties, through their house leaders, usually agree before second reading on whether to send bills to a standing committee or the Committee of the Whole.

When the committee has completed its work, the bill is referred back to the House; under the rules, debates may occur at this stage, but almost never do. Bills considered in standing committee may be referred to the Committee of the Whole before third reading. Following third reading, bills receive royal assent from the lieutenant governor; the lieutenant governor has the constitutional authority to withhold royal assent (either out of personal choice or on instructions from the federal government), but the conditions under which this might actually occur are very difficult to imagine. Most bills 'come into force' – that is, become law – as soon as they receive royal assent; others come into force on a specific date named in the bill; and a few others do not become law until the cabinet issues a proclamation authorizing them. The government is under no legal requirement ever to proclaim the latter, and though unusual it is not unknown for bills, or parts of bills, to pass all other stages of the process but never be proclaimed into law.

Almost all government bills contain an often overlooked but crucial provision authorizing the government to make 'regulations' for the administration of the policy established in the bill. This gives the government enormous power to issue legally binding directives (also called delegated legislation) setting out details of the policy without requiring any approval from the legislature. Although it is true that the legislature has neither the time nor the expertise to review the thousands of pages of regulations passed every year, the consequence is that vast areas of government policy making escape scrutiny by the elected members (although all regulations, once passed, are referred to a legislative committee, this committee lacks the authority to deal with anything beyond the legal technicalities of the regulation). This is a serious weakness in the legislature's ability to hold the government accountable.

Private members' business can take the form of bills or resolutions. Even if passed, resolutions are simply expressions of the House's opinions ('that, in the opinion of this House, the government should ...'), which carry no legal force. By contrast, if private members' bills are passed, they become the law of the land. Private members' business provides a certain scope for members to pursue pet projects and to have a palpable, albeit minor, impact on the policy process. The significance of private members' business arises not from the prospects of bills passing into law, for these are slim: in the two decades after the new rules, from 1976 to 1996, only about thirty private members' bills passed (about thirty more than passed in the two decades before 1976), and none has brought about major policy changes.[5] Rather, private members' bills and resolutions can sometimes generate substantial public interest and support for a policy proposal, they can be useful as trial balloons for government, and they can serve as levers for pressuring the government to act. At the end of the debate on an item of private members' business, a vote must be held. Hence, embarrassing bills and resolutions cannot simply be talked out as is the case in most provincial legislatures; MPPs (most notably government members) must indicate publicly their support or rejection of the proposed measure.

Private members' bills are often confused with private bills, but the two are very different. Whereas private members' bills deal with any matter of public policy (with the restriction that they can neither impose taxes nor directly allocate government payments), private bills are concerned with specific, one-time-only (and usually minor) legislative requests from individual corporations, charitable institutions, municipalities, and the like. A good illustration was a private bill, introduced in 1996, to exempt the National Ballet of Canada from municipal taxes on a property it owned in Toronto. Generally private bills are non-controversial and pass with little difficulty.

Committees

Members of the legislature devote substantial time and energy to their committee work, for they recognize that committees offer much greater scope than does the House for delving into, and indeed influencing, policy. In turn, work carried out by committees often carries considerable political and policy significance.

Committees' effectiveness reflects their small size – usually about a dozen MPPs – their concentration on specific issues for extended periods, their staff support, and their less-partisan atmosphere (which in turn often reflects the lack of media interest in their work). For all this, it should not be thought that legislative committees possess anything like the power and influence of committees in American legislatures, that they don't engage in a good deal of futile make-work, or that partisanship is ever far below the surface.

As is generally the case in Westminster-style parliaments, membership on committees reflects the party standings in the House. In the Conservative majority government following the 1995 election, for example, each committee had eight Conservatives, three Liberals, two NDP members, and a non-voting chair. More generally, in times of minority government the government has fewer members on each committee than do the opposition parties combined, whereas during majorities the government has numerical control. Placement of MPPs on specific committees is rigidly controlled by party leadership so that troublesome or maverick members can be removed from committees if their activities are not to the liking of their leaders. Committee chairs possess limited formal powers, although an astute chairperson can exercise substantial influence over committee activities. The Ontario Legislature is unusual in Canada for guaranteeing in its rules that opposition MPPs chair a number of committees, including the Estimates Committee and the Public Accounts Committee.

Committees engage in three types of activity. First, they review and amend legislation, as described above. Second, as in the case of one committees, the Standing Committee on Estimates, they also consider some of the government's annual spending estimates. While this exercise has some utility as a forum for discussing government policy, its accountability value is minimal; much of the money is already spent before the committee discusses it, and the likelihood of the committee actually *controlling* (as opposed to reviewing) government spending is nil. Even during minority governments, when the opposition outnumbered government members on estimates committees, virtually no attempts were ever made to reduce specific items of spending; furthermore, committees lack the constitutional authority to propose spending increases, a power reserved to the cabinet. Finally, committees conduct special enquiries, that is, studies of government administration and of proposed policy changes that are not associated with any bill or estimate before the House. It is in these special studies, when the government is genuinely interested in receiving advice from a committee, that their influence is greatest.

Committees are designated as 'standing' or 'select,' but for most practical purposes this is not an important distinction. Select committees examine specific policy issues or sets of issues, such as Sunday shopping, constitutional reform, or education, and disband once their task is completed, whereas standing committees are permanent. The same rules apply to both, however, and in their approaches, operations, and effectiveness, they are indistinguishable. A more useful distinction is between the generalist policy field committees – social development, resources development, administration of justice, and general government – and the specialist committees. Virtually all legislation referred to standing committees is handled by the policy field committees, which also conduct special studies into policy issues in the fashion of select committees. They are the workhorses of the committee system.

The specialist standing committees are active within more restricted realms. The Government Agencies Committee reviews the operations of the province's myriad semi-independent agencies, boards, and commissions and can review (but not veto) the appointment of those proposed by the government as members of these boards and agencies. The Regulations and Private Bills Committee performs a cursory review of delegated legislation, which is largely confined to legal technicalities and does not include the substantive policy behind regulations. It also serves as the committee that reviews private legislation. The Finance and Economic Affairs Committee conducts pre-budget hearings and deals with bills arising out of the budget and related issues of macroeconomic policy. The Legislative Assembly Committee is principally concerned with the House's rules and procedures and with services to members. The Public Accounts Committee scrutinizes government spending for waste and mismanagement; it has consistently been the most partisan and most politically significant of the specialist committees. The Standing Committee on the Ombudsman is unique in Canada in that it not only serves as liaison between the legislature and the ombudsman, but also reviews in detail and reports to the House on individual cases where the government has rejected the recommendations of the Ombudsman. As mentioned above, the Standing Committee on Estimates is charged with examining the details of proposed government spending.

Over the course of a year, a committee may meet dozens of times and sit for hundreds of hours. Committees are entitled, if they wish, to exclude the public and the press from their meetings (this is referred to as sitting 'in camera'), but do so only rarely. Most committee meetings take the form of public hearings on bills and policy studies. Although they may do so, individual citizens rarely take part in these meetings; most of the witnesses appearing before committees are representatives of organized interest groups.

Each committee has a clerk to see to its administrative and procedural needs, and committees typically have one or two researchers from the Legislative Library's research unit working for them; they may also hire their own consultants or legal counsel. Committees often depend heavily on the government for information, but no longer engage in the once common practice of seconding ministry staff to work for them.

Committee meetings tend to be far less formal than House sittings: MPPs remain seated while speaking, consume endless cups of coffee, and engage in real discussions among themselves and with witnesses; the atmosphere in committees is usually much more collegial and relaxed than in the chamber. This relative informality should not, however, obscure the formidable powers committees can exercise should occasion so demand. For example, if the persons or documents a committee wishes to examine are not produced, it can request the Speaker to issue a warrant (similar to a subpoena) forcing virtually any person in Ontario to appear before the committee and to bring whatever documents the committee demands (cabinet documents are important exceptions).

Committees produce large numbers of routine reports on estimates and legislation, and a smaller number of substantive reports often containing far-reaching recommendations on policy and administration. The government is under no legal obligation to accept these reports, but may encounter political difficulty in rejecting them, especially if recommendations are made with all-party agreement. Committee impact on policy depends on the extent to which the government is open to advice and on the degree to which committee members set aside partisan differences in favour of developing and improving policy rather than scoring political points. Even in areas characterized by strident partisanship and sharp political divisions, however, committees may have influence, although through very different mechanisms. Committee attention to an issue often raises public awareness and concern, which may force the government to modify a policy or publicly justify to hostile interest groups its refusal to do so; it also offers the opposition good opportunities to put forward its alternatives.

Conclusions

The legislature stands as the centrepiece of democracy in Ontario, and yet its capacities as a decision-making or policy-formulating body are limited. The fact that it serves as the focal point of public and press attention to Ontario politics is only one reason why its lack of direct power over the policy-making process should not be the cause for dismissing it as insignificant. As detailed throughout this chapter, the legislature is a complex and subtle institution, and the functions it performs in the Ontario political system are important.

This is not to suggest that these functions are always performed well, or even adequately; for example, the legislature's record in keeping the government accountable for its policies and administration is spotty at best. Nor is the Ontario Legislature a static institution; the picture of the legislature in the mid-1960s painted by F.F. Schindeler in his book *Responsible Government in Ontario* seems scarcely recognizable to the observer of the current House. Even since the end of the Davis era in 1985, the House has changed substantially, both in formal rules and in intangibles of culture and atmosphere. Some elements of the legislature, however, remain unchanged. It continues as the prime target of those with complaints against government, whether they maintain solitary vigils camped out on the front lawn or gather in their thousands in protest rallies; in other words, the legislature's symbolism remains potent. And, indeed, underlying this enduring, powerful symbolism is the important reality that an understanding of the legislature – its failures as well as its successes, its complexities as well as its obvious features – is central to any evaluation of the health of democracy in Ontario.

Notes

1 The Common Sense Revolution promised a reduction to 99 seats. However, since this was premised on the savings possible from simply adopting the federal riding boundaries, and since the number of Ontario seats in the House of Commons was raised in 1996 from 99 to 103, the government adopted the latter target.
2 For a discussion of how size affects legislative operations, see Graham White, 'Big Is Different from Little: On Taking Size Seriously in the Analysis of Canadian Governmental Institutions,' *Canadian Public Administration* 33 (Winter 1990): 527–34.
3 These are routine operating expenditures and exclude the cost of a major renovation to the century-old legislative building (roughly $7 million in 1995–6 and $0.6 million in 1996–7).
4 For an insightful account of the culture of the legislature in the mid-1980s, see Carolyn Thomson, '"This Place": The Culture of Queen's Park,' in Graham White, ed., *Inside the Pink Palace: Ontario Legislature Internship Essays* (Toronto: OLIP/CPSA, 1993), 1–20.
5 In the 1993–4 session an astonishing 18 private members' bills passed, more than had passed in the previous four decades. This seems to have been an anomaly rather than the beginning of a new era of private members' legislative activism.

Further Readings

'Committee Systems in Quebec and Ontario,' *Canadian Parliamentary Review* Part 1 (Spring 1996): 25–30; Part 2 (Summer 1996): 20–6. A useful practical review of the central features of the Ontario committee system, with extensive statistical data on committee operations in 1993–4.
Lyon, Vaughan. 'Minority Government in Ontario, 1975–1981: An Assessment,' *Canadian Journal of Political Science* 27 (December 1984): 685–706. Examines the political and policy consequences of minority government in the Davis era.
White, Graham. *The Ontario Legislature: A Political Analysis.* Toronto: University

of Toronto Press, 1989. A detailed account of the structure and operation of the legislature. Several formal and informal changes have occurred since the book's publication, but the essentials are unchanged.

- *Inside the Pink Palace: Ontario Legislature Internship Essays*. Toronto: Ontario Legislature Internship Programme / Canadian Political Science Association, 1993. Essays by legislative interns, drawing on their first-hand experiences at Queen's Park; includes several detailed case studies of Question Period, private members' bills, and legislative committees.

FIVE

Making and Implementing the Decisions: Issues of Public Administration in the Ontario Government

Richard A. Loreto

The purpose of this chapter is to describe and analyse the institutional context and issues affecting the role, organization, and management processes of the Ontario Public Service (OPS) within the ministry sector of government. The analysis focuses exclusively on developments since 1990, encompassing the term of office of the New Democratic Party (NDP) government and the Progressive Conservative government elected in 1995. The analysis expands, rather than reiterates, the body of knowledge on the OPS and its institutional context established in the four prior editions of this book. In particular, readers are directed to the chapter on 'The Bureaucracy' in the fourth edition of this book, which contains useful information on the historical, legal, and organizational foundations of the OPS.[1]

The chapter is organized in three parts. The first part examines the evolution of the cabinet system under Premier Rae and Premier Harris, respectively. The focus is on the policy-approval process, and a distinction is made between the institutionalized system that flourished between the early 1970s and mid-1990s and the significant reforms undertaken by Premier Harris. The second part looks at changing approaches to the expenditure budget process, with particular emphasis on the different responses of the NDP and Progressive Conservative governments to the fiscal crisis that has plagued governments across Canada during this decade. The third part discusses three broad issues facing the OPS both currently and in the foreseeable future: the relationship between public servants and the political process, labour relations, and organizational change, with an emphasis on the implications of 'downsizing' and demographic trends.

The emphasis in the first two parts on the institutional context provides a broad frame of reference for the discussion of the selected issues in the third part of the chapter. Moreover, the approval processes for policy and expenditure represent the main theatre of interaction between the political executive and the 'bureaucracy.'

An Overview of the Organization of the OPS

The organization of the OPS reflects the well-known features of bureaucracy identified several decades ago by German social theorist Max Weber (for example, hierarchy and specialization). Its bureaucratic character can be analysed from two perspectives. From a macro perspective, the key structural components are line ministries and central agencies, both of which are under the direct control of ministers. Line ministries are responsible for the delivery of goods and services to the residents of Ontario, while central agencies support line operations through the performance of staff or support functions. The second perspective is a micro one. Its focus is on the arrangement of the internal elements of government organizations, whatever their functional orientation.

Excluding the Crown agency sector, the macro organization of the Ontario government consists of eighteen line ministries or offices and six central agencies. This configuration illustrates the substantial restructuring of portfolios initiated under the former NDP government and continued by the current Progressive Conservative government. The line ministries serve Ontario's residents directly in areas such as health, education, and correctional services. Central agencies have government-wide mandates and their clients are internal. Although they account for a small proportion of classified employees, central agencies exercise substantial authority and influence in governmental decision-making processes. The six central agencies are the Premier's Office, Cabinet Office, Ministry of Intergovernmental Affairs, Civil Service Commission, Management Board Secretariat, and Ministry of Finance.

The organization of the OPS can also be viewed from a micro perspective. In Ontario, a typical government portfolio contains a ministry, which is under the direct control and supervision of a minister, and a number of agencies that report either directly to the minister or through the minister to the legislature. The minister is the political head of the ministry; the administrative head is the deputy minister. Both are appointed by the premier. In a ministry, the bureaucratic strata below the deputy minister follow a fairly common pattern with respect to the terminology used to indicate the scale of operations and the level of hierarchy. Divisions are normally the largest internal components of a ministry's headquarters structure (the need for field units reflects both functional and political considerations). Divisions are subdivided into branches, and branches, in turn, into sections. In hierarchical terms, divisions are supervised by either an assistant deputy minister or an executive director, depending on the scale of operations. Branches are headed by directors, and sections are under the direction of either managers or section heads. Both line and staff functions are evident at these various administrative levels.

The Cabinet System

OVERVIEW: FROM ROBARTS TO RAE

When Premier John Robarts appointed the Committee on Government Productivity (COGP) in late 1969, he gave impetus to the 'institutionalization' of cabinet government in Ontario, a process that would culminate with the creation of a new Treasury Board in 1991 by the government of Premier Rae. Institutionalization emphasized the modernization of decision making at the 'apex of government' in response to the increasing complexity of public policy issues and to expansion of the state's role.

One feature of the system nurtured from Robarts to Rae was functional specialization. Coordinating and policy committees of cabinet proliferated. Typically, there were ten or more committees and ministers could expect to allocate their scarce time to two or three of them. Cabinet posts also proliferated, reaching a record high of thirty-three in 1985 under Conservative Premier Frank Miller and acquiring a degree of ambiguity when, in February 1993, Premier Rae appointed seven ministers without portfolio in an effort to reduce the size of cabinet during a period of fiscal crisis. The ministers without portfolio neither attended cabinet nor cabinet committee meetings and their nominal role was to lighten the ministerial burdens of their colleagues with portfolio (usually the responsibility of a parliamentary assistant, a government MPP assigned by the premier to assist a minister). In the opinion of more critical observers of Ontario politics, the position allowed Premier Rae to demote former ministers gracefully while maintaining the illusion of a more streamlined government.

Coordination and consultation were hallmarks of the institutionalized system. Central agencies such as the Cabinet Office, Management Board Secretariat, and Treasury Board Division of the Ministry of Finance were entrusted with the coordination role and their complement expanded accordingly, reaching a zenith under the NDP government. Formal cabinet-submission procedures were introduced in 1973 by Premier Davis, completely revised by Premier Peterson in the late 1980s, and changed incrementally by Premier Rae during the 1990s (cabinet submissions are documents that outline ministry policy and program proposals; they form the basis of discussions and decisions at the cabinet level). The procedures not only focused on the information that ministers required to make good decisions, but also placed a premium on interministerial consultation. Internal consultation was further buttressed by the growth of interministerial committees. With the end of the Tory dynasty in 1985, the emphasis on consultation in policy development expanded to embrace external stakeholders – persons and organizations affected by government policies – under both the Liberals and the NDP.

During the period of institutionalization the balance of power between the civil service and ministerial political staff changed several times. Political staff are not part of the merit-based civil service; they are partisan appointees who engage in explicitly political work in ministers' offices. Under Premier Davis the civil service were the government's trusted advisers; political staff were few in number and kept a low profile. This changed significantly when David Peterson assumed power in 1985. His ministers directed large staff groups that were involved in cabinet and legislative committees and served as a parallel source of advice for cabinet decision makers. Cabinet committee meetings were largely the preserve of ministers and political staff; the deputy ministers met separately (in 'mirror committees'). However, the Liberals maintained the 'separate but equal' status of political staff and the civil service, particularly in the divide between the Premier's Office and the Cabinet Office and in the appointments to the deputy-minister class. Both the power and size of political staff reached new heights under Premier Rae. One prominent minister had thirty-three staff members (about 5 per cent of the ministry's complement). Anecdotal evidence suggested that in several cases political staff members were the 'gatekeepers' of ministerial access and, despite their inexperience with governing, had the minister's attention to a greater degree than the civil service. There was also a perception that the ranks of the senior civil service were politicized under the NDP, a development best symbolized by the appointment of David Agnew, Bob Rae's campaign manager in

1990, as the secretary of the cabinet – the top civil-service position – in September 1992.

In short, the institutionalized system reflected the expansion of the state's role and the notion that every set of interests, both inside and outside government, needed voice in the policy-development process. Political sensitivity competed with political neutrality as the key criterion for senior administrative appointments. It was a system that was complex and, at times, cumbersome. It was also a system that often placed structural and procedural sophistication ahead of clarity of purpose and the execution of political will.

CABINET GOVERNMENT UNDER THE NDP

The first NDP cabinet featured twenty-seven ministers, eleven of whom held more than one portfolio. The most notable aspect of the cabinet's membership was the presence of twelve women and the deliberate attempt by Premier Rae to create a cabinet system that reflected the principle of 'gender equity.' Eight cabinet committees were established and each minister had two committee assignments on average (approximately 40 per cent of the assignments were held by women). Female representation on the Policy and Priorities Board and Management Board, two key coordinating committees, was 50 per cent. Another unique characteristic of the cabinet was that eight of the thirty-two parliamentary assistants appointed by the premier sat on four of the committees.

Centralization characterized the processes associated with the NDP's cabinet committees. Two hierarchies existed, one for policy and legislation and another for the budget and resources management. The recommendations of the four policy committees (Social, Environment, Economic and Labour, and Justice) and the Legislation/Regulations committee reached the cabinet table only after they had been approved by the powerful Policy and Priorities Board, a committee that some viewed as an 'inner cabinet.' Neither Davis nor Peterson required that the Policy and Priorities Board approve all policy-committee items. Cabinet Office continued to provide support to the committees involved in the policy-approval process, but it moved beyond its traditional process orientation to a substantive policy-analysis role. In addition, the 'mirror' committees of deputy ministers created during the Liberal regime were eliminated and the deputies were reintegrated into the policy committee discussions, an approach also employed during the Davis years. However, time was set aside on the cabinet committee agenda for 'ministers only.' The only unique aspect of this procedure was that it was a scheduled item – ministers have long used the prerogative of 'throwing staff out' and talking privately.

During the latter part of his mandate Premier Rae expanded the number of policy committees, although not nearly to the extent of his predecessors. A Cabinet Committee on Jobs and two subcommittees (Aboriginal Issues under the Cabinet Committee on Justice and Industrial Assistance under the Cabinet Committee on Economic Development) were created.

The second hierarchy revolved around the creation of a Treasury Board in 1991. The concept of a Treasury Board was not a new one in Ontario. Schindeler observes that the first such body was created in 1886. It took almost seventy years, however, for the original Treasury Board to assume a formidable role in the formulation of corporate (govenment-wide) policy.

The original Treasury Board was replaced by the Management Board of Cabinet in the early 1970s on the recommendation of the COGP. The rationale for the reform was that the Management Board would provide a cabinet-level focus on resource utilization in government. The new board not only assumed the functions of the old Treasury Board in the areas of the expenditure budget, financial management, and administrative policy but also those of the Civil Service Commission in the sphere of personnel management. Although the Management Board provided integration at the political level, fragmentation still characterized the bureaucratic level in that the board received support from two entities, the Management Board Secretariat and the reorganized Civil Service Commission. In addition, the board and its staff were closely intertwined with the Treasury portfolio in the formulation of the expenditure budget.

Under the NDP's first round of cabinet reforms, the Management Board retained responsibility for budgetary and financial-management decisions and hived off responsibility for administrative and human-resources management policy to a new Operations Committee. However, the Operations Committee was essentially moribund and the Management Board functioned as both the 'chief economist' and 'general manager' of the corporate system. The initial arrangements foreshadowed the ultimate aim of creating a new Treasury Board and a reorganized Management Board. Although the creation of a Treasury Board was alluded to in the Treasurer's December 1990 economic statement, the notion of restructuring central-agency roles predated the assumption of power by the NDP. In the summer of 1990 a Central Agency Review, part of the so-called Tomorrow Project, was initiated by a group of senior civil servants. The review was timed to be implemented after the election of 1990, which was widely expected to return the Liberals to power. It contained a number of themes and findings, several of which were directly related to the establishment of a new Treasury Board and a revised budgetary process:

- weak linkage between the policy-development and resource-alloca-tion processes;
- neglect of the government's role as an employer and manager;
- absence of effective program review; and
- duplication between the Management Board and Treasury ministry in the development of the expenditure budget.

A bill to establish the Treasury Board was tabled immediately after the presentation of the new government's first budget in April 1991. The bill was passed by the legislature at the end of June and proclaimed by cabinet in August. The Treasurer (chair), Chair of Management Board (vice-chair), and four other ministers were the board's members. The Management Board's membership continued to adhere to the stipula-tions of its enabling statute, that is, the Chair of Management Board, a vice-chair (usually the Treasurer), and four other ministers.

The centralization that characterized the cabinet system increased dur-ing the middle of the NDP government's term. In February 1993, just a few months before the government's annual budget speech, Premier Rae took the first steps of what was to culminate in the Expenditure Control Plan and the Social Contract process. The former slashed ministry spend-ing by $4 billion in 1993–4; the latter involved the negotiation of $2 billion of compensation costs (for employee salaries and benefits) in the broader public sector that includes school boards, municipalities, universities, and social and health delivery agencies. In addition to giving the appear-ance of a smaller cabinet created by the appointment of ministers with-out portfolio, the premier sent shock waves through the OPS by consolidating several government ministries:

- The ministries of Treasury and Economics, Revenue, and Financial Institutions were combined into a Ministry of Finance.
- The ministries of Education, Colleges and Universities, and Skills De-velopment were formed into a Ministry of Education and Training.

- The Management Board Secretariat absorbed the Ministry of Government Services.
- The ministries of Environment and Energy were amalgamated into a Ministry of Environment and Energy.
- The Ministry of Culture and Communications lost its Communications Division to the new Ministry of Economic Development and Trade, but it assumed responsibilities in the areas of tourism and recreation.

Not since the implementation of the recommendations of the COGP in the early 1970s had the OPS experienced the degree of environmental turbulence that accompanied these changes in the structure of government. Several veteran deputy ministers were dispatched from their posts. Branches responsible for staff functions such as audit or human-resource management were also consolidated, a development that reduced expenditures and resulted in staff becoming surplus. Intra-ministry consolidation also furthered the process of 'delayering' – flattening the organization by eliminating entire levels ('layers') of managers.

The centralization thrust implicit in the ministry consolidation scheme was augmented by two new realities around the cabinet table. The first new reality was that the reforms pruned ministerial 'deadwood' and left strategic portfolios in the hands of those perceived as the most able ministers (for example, David Cooke at Education and Training and Frances Lankin at Economic Development and Trade). The second new reality involved the suspension of a practice that Premier Rae had initially put in place regarding the position of policy-committee chair. At first the premier decided against the practice of having members of the powerful Policy and Priorities Board chair the policy committees (the precedent for this approach can be found in the position of Provincial Secretary recommended by the COGP and implemented by Premier Davis). However, this change was, at best, a symbolic gesture of empowerment in a centralized system that revolved around the decisions of the premier and his key ministers sitting on the Policy and Priorities Board. As the NDP government faced the prospect of dealing with its fiscal problems in the run up to the next election, the ministers on the Policy and Priorities Board were assigned the additional responsibility of chairing the policy committees and moving key agenda items along in step with the government's new fiscal regime.

In sum, the reform of the cabinet system carried out by the NDP established three institutions of corporate decision making:

- Policy and Priorities Board / Cabinet Office, responsible for priority setting and policy management;
- Treasury Board / Ministry of Finance, responsible for fiscal planning and expenditure management; and
- Management Board / Management Board Secretariat, responsible for operational and public-service management.

The cabinet system under the NDP was complex in terms of structure and process and, as a result, the decision-making process moved slowly. The requirements of internal consultation were substantial and even included a role for the government caucus, either before or after an item was approved by the Policy and Priorities Board. In addition, anecdotal evidence suggests that, notwithstanding the power of the premier and certain ministers, cabinet consensus was often arrived at with much debate and great difficulty.

THE HARRIS CABINET SYSTEM

Premier Harris moved quickly to create a new cabinet system, one that bears a close resemblance to the pre-COGP model of the 1960s in terms of structural and procedural simplicity. It is a system that can implement quickly the clear agenda that the Progressive Conservative party promised voters during the June 1995 provincial election.

The Harris government intends to reduce the role of the state and create the maximum possible scope for the private sector. In addition, it wants the public sector to function in a more 'business-like' manner. These beliefs are set out in the *Common Sense Revolution* (*CSR*), the document that outlines unambiguously the policy agenda of the Harris government. This intent is also evident in the legislation that the government has passed since coming to office, as well as in its 1996 budget and prior economic and fiscal statements.

Given this focus, the premier has established a cabinet system that is 'built for speed.' The policy committees that proliferated under his predecessors and served as the point of entry for policy proposals into the labyrinth of cabinet decision making have been disbanded. The ranks of ministerial and central-agency staff that grew substantially under the two previous governing parties are much reduced. Several cabinet positions, including the ministers without portfolio, have been eliminated.

What remains is a cabinet consisting of nineteen portfolios including the premiership. The system is supported by three coordinating committees – the Policy and Priorities Board, Management Board, and Legislation and Regulations – and a streamlined Cabinet Office and Premier's Office. The Treasury Board has been disbanded and its staff reallocated to the Ministry of Finance and the Management Board Secretariat. The number of political staff has been well below the norm established under the Liberals and the NDP.

Each cabinet committee has six members, a number designed for arriving at consensus quickly. Only four ministers sit on more than one committee and four ministers do not sit on any committees. Policy and Priorities continues to be chaired by the premier and its membership encompasses the most powerful ministers in the new government, including the Minister of Finance and Chair of the Management Board (both of whom also sit on the Management Board). Both the Policy and Priorities Board and Management Board are key venues for the government's major decisions, including the budget. The Cabinet Submission guidelines employed by the former government are in place, but some consideration is being given to their revision.

This initial template for the cabinet system was redesigned before the end of the Harris government's first year in power. Between February and May 1996 three subcommittees of the Policy and Priorities Board were established, a development in line with the premier's stated intent to use ad hoc committees when necessary. The three subcommittees are:

– Jobs and the Economy, chaired by the premier and including five other ministers and two parliamentary assistants;
– Federal-Provincial Relations, chaired by the Minister of Intergovernmental Affairs and including the premier, five other cabinet ministers, and two parliamentary assistants; and
– Restructuring and Local Services, chaired by the Minister of Municipal Affairs and Housing and including seven other ministers and two parliamentary assistants.

The subcommittees range in size from eight to ten members and are larger than the three coordinating committees. Parliamentary assistants are included, and two have also been added to the Cabinet Committee on Legislation and Regulations (an approach adopted by previous governments).

Another change to the system was signalled by the announcement in the government's first budget speech that a Cabinet Committee on Privatization would be established. This committee is chaired by the Minister of Finance and includes three other members – the Chair of Management Board, the Minister of Labour, and a minister without portfolio.

The model employed by Premier Harris moves the focus of cabinet deliberations from policy formulation to policy implementation. It is a centralized system driven by the premier and his key ministers (one Tory backbencher has coined the phrase 'the imperial premiership'). The many decisions made by the government during its first year in office refute the notion that the government cannot act until substantial consultation has taken place both externally and internally, a key precept of the institutionalized system. The consultation process for the Harris government culminated with the June 1995 election when voters endorsed the CSR. For the new government, the choices are clear; the political will is strong and the new cabinet system is designed to get on with the job.

However, the emergence of subcommittees as part of the Policy and Priorities Board may be an indication that the system was too slim and too fast for the complexities of public-policy development. There is anecdotal evidence to suggest that cabinet set a new record for endurance by considering hundreds of items at a sitting in the run up to the Minister of Finance's November 1995 'Economic Statement' that resulted in unprecedented cuts in government expenditure affecting all segments of Ontario society. Also, ministry staff have observed that there is sometimes little time to analyse and comment on policy submissions or even frame their own proposals in accordance with the cabinet-submissions guidelines. The Harris cabinet system may be testing the limits to human rationality as well as the limits of the political culture that has evolved in Ontario since the 1970s, particularly the public desire for meaningful consultation in all stages of the policy-development process.

The Expenditure Budget Process

THE CONSULTATIVE APPROACH OF THE NDP

Shortly after coming to power the government led by Bob Rae was made aware of the fiscal crisis facing the provincial government. The small budgetary surplus bequeathed by the Liberals evaporated quickly in the harsh environment of the worst economic downturn since the 1930s. The first inclination of a social-democratic government was to prime the economy in a traditional manner by increasing public spending on job creation. However, the Keynesian bromide had little effect on the global economic forces of the 1990s and soon the combined impact of falling revenues as a result of the recession and the continued growth of expenditures left the government staring at the politically and economically unpalatable prospect of a $17 billion deficit by the middle of its term. At this point the emphasis shifted from implementing the government's extensive policy agenda as promised in the 1990 election manifesto, 'An Agenda for People,' to managing the deficit in a manner that would assuage the concerns of the public, business leaders, and the bond-rating houses in Canada and the United States. By the spring of 1993 the main instruments of budgetary policy were the Expenditure Control Plan (ECP) and the Social Contract. In particular, the Social Contract concept recognized a central fiscal reality for the Ontario government, that about 75 per cent of its expenditures are in the form of transfer payments to individuals and public organizations and about 50 per cent of its transfers finance employee compensation costs.

Under the NDP the approach to the expenditure budget process was designed to integrate strategic policy and resource decisions, enhance the government's role as employer/manager, redirect funds to higher priorities, and ensure public-service accountability. The process involved multiyear planning, a procedure employed during Premier Davis's first term but abandoned with the onset of minority government in 1975, and a more consultative process of decision making involving stakeholders inside and outside government.

The NDP's budgetary process encompassed four sequential planning phases: the determination of strategic policy directions and priorities by cabinet at its annual fall retreat; the development of a fiscal and management strategy; finalization of the fiscal plan and government priorities; and implementation of policy and budgetary decisions. Within the constraints imposed by the government's strategic policy directions and priorities as well as economic and fiscal realities, cabinet ministers focused on three streams of decision making: the base budget, new initiatives, and program reviews.

The Treasury Board reviewed the ministries' base budgets during the fall. A key element in this phase was the submission of workforce impact plans. These plans addressed a number of analytical elements within a framework of eight specific priorities: employment equity; positive union-management relationships; safe, healthy, and accessible workplaces; opportunities for youth; training, re-skilling, and development of people; balancing work and family responsibilities; employee participation in decision making; and flexible organizational structures.

By the 1993–4 fiscal year the government's need to reduce expenditures was evident in two new features of the base budget review. First, the Multi-Year Expenditure Reduction Plan (MYERP) set targets for expenditure reduction that had to be met through program elimination, rationalization, or consolidation; controlling cost escalation; improved efficiency; and the overall streamlining of government. Second, emphasis was placed on the generation of non-tax revenue. Non-tax revenue comes from sources such as fees, licences, royalties, sales and rentals, and fines and penalties; just under $240 million was raised in this manner in the 1993–4 fiscal year.

Within the new-initiatives stream, ministry spending proposals were first reviewed by the policy committees of cabinet. Each policy committee had a new-initiatives funding envelope established by cabinet that ranked ministry proposals in order of priority. New initiatives were subsequently reviewed by both the Treasury Board and Policy and Priorities Board.

The reallocation of government expenditures to fund the priorities of government was the third stream. In the fiscal environment of the 1990s, freeing up funds through a process of program review was perceived as the only way to implement the government's extensive policy agenda. The review process was both strategically focused and premised on full consultation with and involvement by internal and external stakeholders. Proposed policy and program changes were assessed in relation to targeted savings, economic renewal, labour-force and client impact, equity, and intergovernmental relations. Areas to be reviewed and basic policy objectives were established by cabinet. The review teams were led by line-ministry staff but also included central-agency staff, employees, clients, and delivery organizations. The time frame for reviews extended from six to twenty-four months.

The three streams of decision making were ultimately brought together to produce the government's throne speech, budget, and expenditure estimates. The most influential players within cabinet were the ministers on the Treasury Board and Policy and Priorities Board. Management Board reviewed the workforce-impact plans. The Cabinet Office played an important role in providing support and direction for ministries with respect to the new-initiatives and reallocation streams.

One strength of the expenditure-budget process that distinguished Premier Rae's approach from that of his predecessors was the emphasis on human-resources management through the development of workforce-impact plans as well as the involvement of stakeholders within and outside government. However, the reforms also created certain problems.

One of the rationales for the creation of a Treasury Board was to provide a dedicated focus on expenditures and financial-management matters. A corollary was that the Management Board would provide a dedicated focus on other elements of corporate policy, particularly human-resources management. The architects of the new system contended, not without foundation, that under earlier Progressive Conservative and Liberal governments the Management Board had subordinated its role as employer to the fiscal imperatives emanating from the Treasury ministry.

However, the solution chosen by the NDP begged the question of whether this neglect of the human element was a consequence of particular institutional arrangements or of ideological and partisan factors. The NDP government attempted to orchestrate a significant cultural shift in the public service with its support of policies such as employment equity and improved union-management relations. It can be argued that substantial structural change was not needed to accomplish these policy goals. The consequence, at least in the short term, was that the creation of a dedicated focus on separate areas of corporate decision making was accompanied by greater internal confusion and the absence of co-ordination. In this regard the reforms ignored the fact that while it is analytically possible to dissect resource requests into administrative, financial, and human dimensions, in reality these dimensions are interrelated. Is an administrative reorganization, for example, an administrative issue for the Management Board or a financial issue for the Treasury Board?

The consultative component, although laudable in democratic terms, was time-consuming and inherently driven towards program expansion and hence increased expenditure. Both the ECP and Social Contract processes eventually demonstrated that cutting expenditures required swift, decisive action by cabinet.

THE BUSINESS-PLANNING APPROACH OF THE HARRIS GOVERNMENT

Consistent with its political ideology and policy agenda of reducing the role of the state in the lives of the province's residents, the Harris government has adopted a business-planning approach as the centrepiece of its expenditure-budget process. This approach was one of the key recommendations of the Ontario Financial Review Commission (OFRC). The OFRC was appointed by the government in July 1995 to examine 'how the Province recorded its financial transactions, kept its accounts, managed its finances and organized its work' and to 'restore credibility and confidence in the reporting of the financial position of the Province.'[2] Its final report was issued in November 1995.

Ministry business plans are the component that links the traditional components of fiscal strategy and estimates. In its first year the government established the fiscal context early on through the release of two documents by the Minister of Finance: 'Ontario Fiscal Overview and Spending Cuts' (July 1995) and 'Fiscal and Economic Statement' (November 1995). Both documents outlined the government's intention to make substantial cuts in its expenditures, including transfer payments and staff complement.

Business plans are reviewed by the Policy and Priorities Board and Management Board and signed by the minister and deputy minister. Coordination of the process is provided by the Cabinet Office. The purpose of the planning process is to

- link the government's policy and fiscal agendas;
- develop a long-term strategy for fiscal sustainability;
- establish a ministry blueprint for fundamental changes; and
- improve accountability.

Each plan has four elements:

- ministry vision and core businesses;
- strategies for change;
- performance measures and reporting; and
- a marketing and communications strategy.

A condensed version of the plan used for internal purposes is available to the public after the delivery of the budget speech.

The ministry-vision and core-businesses element is intended to provide a clear sense of the ministry proposals for meeting government savings targets, defining its current and future (three to five years) core businesses, and identifying short- and long-term restructured delivery mechanisms. The strategies-for-change element explains how the ministry will manage the transition to fewer resources and changed core businesses over a three-to-five-year time frame. It must address a number of considerations: major changes in program delivery and cost-containment strategies; proposed significant policy shifts; legislative and regulatory requirements; major stakeholder and transfer-partner impacts; non-tax-revenue strategy; proposed staffing impacts; and impacts on other jurisdictions and ministries. The performance-measures and reporting element require measures for each core business area. Both output efficiency and specific program/policy outcomes must be measured and the indicators should allow for objective verification. The marketing and communications strategy deals with issues arising from both the ministry's business plan and estimates submission. The purpose of the strategy is to support the review of business plans by the Policy and Priorities Board and to develop an overall communications strategy. It must address several considerations including target audiences, key messages, tactics, inter-ministry coordination, and timing.

Ministry estimates submissions to Management Board are also signed by the minister and deputy minister. The process encompassed expenditure allocations and savings targets for 1996–7 and 1997–8. In line with the November 1995 statement by the Minister of Finance and a ministry's business plan, the strategic areas targeted for savings were reducing internal administration, restructuring government operations, reducing funding to agencies, boards, and commissions, and cutting government grants. As in the past, the scope of the submission included operating and capital expenditures and the ministry's non-tax-revenue strategy.

Ontario government ministries have engaged in numerous strategic and operational planning processes since the 1970s. Moreover, there have been prior attempts to measure the performance of government programs or shore up accountability mechanisms. The experiment with 'managing by results' during the Davis years is an instance of the former, and the 'shared accountability framework' during the Rae years is an instance of the latter. What is unique about the Harris government's planning exercise is its comprehensive and directive nature (although Alberta's business-planning process under Premier Klein occurred before Ontario's and did serve as a model). The first edition was a 240-page tome containing 21 ministry plans all scripted according to a common format and all consistent with the government's clear fiscal direction.

Not everybody agrees with the appropriateness of the ideological current underlying the process, that is, that government is a 'business' that is accountable to its 'shareholders.' Thomas Walkom, Queen's Park correspondent for the *Toronto Star*, has pointed out that this notion has nothing to say about democracy since a business can be controlled by a single, autocratic shareholder. In Walkom's view, the Ontario 'shareholder' who counts the most is the empowered, tax-paying members of the upper middle class, whose fiscal frugality is evident in the various measures of program performance (for example, measuring the performance of social-housing policy by the 'reduction in the per unit costs of existing subsidized social housing' not by the reduction in the number of homeless persons).[3]

Issues in the 1990s and Beyond

POLITICS AND THE OPS

Since 1918 the constitutional convention of political neutrality, as embodied in the Public Service Act (PSA), has defined both the fundamental relationship between the members of the OPS and the political executive and the wider political process. Among other things, the act has required that public servants be appointed on the basis of merit, that they refrain from participating in certain partisan political activities (for example, holding a party office) or criticizing government policy in public, and that they loyally implement the policies of the government of the day. Although employees in the private sector have also been subject to the principles of appointment by merit and loyalty to the employer, the restrictions on partisan activity meant that government employees enjoyed fewer political rights than other provincial residents.

During the 1990s the notion that public servants should be politically neutral has been challenged on two fronts. The first challenge concerns the extent to which public servants should participate in partisan politics. The second challenge relates to whether the main criterion for appointing senior public servants such as deputy ministers should continue to be political neutrality or their support of the governing party's policies.

The issue of participation in partisan politics was resolved during the NDP years in power. Consistent with its social-democratic ideology, the NDP government amended the PSA in 1993 to grant wider 'political activity rights' to the majority of OPS members, most of whom are represented by the Ontario Public Service Employees Union (OPSEU), a long-time NDP political ally. However, the widening of political rights was not entirely a partisan tactic, since the Supreme Court of Canada had struck down comparable statutory restrictions on federal public servants in 1991 and the Ontario Court of Appeal struck down the PSA provisions in July 1993. Therefore, the PSA amendment recognized the legal reality imposed by evolving judicial opinion in the context of the Charter of Rights and Freedoms and the democratic reality that the restrictions had made public servants, most of whom are involved in operational matters, 'second-class citizens.'

The amended provisions of the PSA apply to 'Crown employees,' that is, persons 'employed in the service of the Crown or any agency of the Crown,' but not the employees of Crown agencies that are employers in their own right (for example, Ontario Hydro). A Crown employee engages in 'political activity' when he or she

(a) does anything in support of or in opposition to a federal or provincial political party;
(b) does anything in support of or opposition to a candidate in a federal, provincial or municipal election;
(c) comments publicly and outside the scope of the duties of his or her position on matters that are directly related to those duties and that are dealt with in the positions or policies of a federal or provincial party or in the positions publicly expressed by a candidate in a federal or provincial election.
(Public Service Act, s. 28.1)

A Crown employee cannot engage in political activity in the workplace, associate his or her position with political activity, or participate in activity that could place him or her 'in a position of conflict with the interests of the Crown' (PSA, ibid.).

The PSA establishes two categories of employees for purposes of defining permissible political activities: restricted and unrestricted. The restricted category encompasses deputy ministers and persons with the rank or status of deputy ministers; members of the Senior Management Group (the top civil-service executives); full-time heads, vice-chairs, and members of agencies, boards, and commissions; and commissioned officers and detachment commanders of the Ontario Provincial Police. Members of these employee groups are still constrained by the traditional restrictions on partisan activity that affected all Crown employees before the amendment of the act. Restricted employees can vote in elections at the three levels of government, contribute money to federal and provincial political parties, contribute money to candidates in elections at all levels, be a member of a federal or provincial political party, attend all-candidates' meetings, and participate in municipal politics (including holding office) with the permission of their deputy ministers. Greater participation is sanctioned in municipal politics under the rationale that it is non-partisan, at least in formal terms. The employee's deputy minister can only grant a leave of absence to contest or hold municipal office if he or she 'is of the opinion that the activity or office would not interfere with the performance of the employee's duties and would not conflict with the interests of the Crown' (PSA, s. 28.4).

Unrestricted employees (all those not defined as restricted) can be politically active subject to a few exceptions. No leave of absence is required for participation in municipal politics unless the activity or office interferes with the employee's duties or conflicts with Crown interests. Running as a candidate in federal and provincial elections and commenting publicly on job-related issues requires a leave of absence. Crown employees who have supervisory duties or who deal with or exercise discretionary authority over members of the public must be on leave to solicit funds for political parties. The granting of leave by a deputy minister is automatic for unrestricted employees.

In a related amendment to the PSA in December 1993 the NDP government granted its employees 'whistleblowers' protection.' The purpose of this part of the act is to 'protect employees of the Ontario Government from retaliation for disclosing allegations of serious government wrong-doing and to provide a means for making those allegations public' (PSA, s. 28.11). Government wrongdoing is defined as an act or omission of an institution or employee that contravenes a statute or regulation, represents gross mismanagement, causes a gross waste of money, represents an abuse of authority, or poses a grave health or safety hazard to individuals or a grave environmental hazard.

Whistleblowers' protection is the responsibility of a counsel appointed by the cabinet from among the members of the Law Society of Upper Canada. The counsel is an officer of the Legislative Assembly who is appointed for a renewable five-year term and can only be removed by cabinet for cause by the legislature.

To date the most contentious aspect of the whistleblowers' protection is that the amendment has not been proclaimed (the final stage of a bill's passing into law, which requires cabinet authorization). This issue was raised publicly in December 1994 by Fred Upshaw, then president of OPSEU, in a letter to Premier Rae. Upshaw expressed 'deep disappointment' that the cabinet had not appointed a counsel, thereby depriving OPS employees of the right to expose government wrongdoing without revealing their identity or risking their jobs.[4] In the first year of their mandate, the Progressive Conservative government did not act to implement the whistleblowers' protection.

The second challenge concerns the issue of appointing supporters of the governing party to senior positions within the OPS. During the

NDP's tenure a perception persisted that the OPS was significantly more politicized than under previous governments. This perception was magnified by Premier Rae's appointment of David Agnew to the post of Secretary of Cabinet in 1992. Agnew had been the director of the NDP's successful 1990 election campaign and was later Principal Secretary in the Premier's Office. His appointment to the post traditionally reserved for apolitical, career civil servants sent shock waves through the OPS.

Graham White has observed that the degree to which the senior ranks of the OPS were politicized under the NDP 'is not at all clear.' On the one hand, the attitude of the NDP government towards the senior (and middle-management) levels varied between 'wary tolerance and outright hostility.' For some partisans, the occupants of these positions represented the 'establishment they had long fought.' On the other hand, not all deputy-ministers were certified partisans. Many of the appointments to the deputy minister class were career public servants who had served NDP governments in western Canada, especially in Manitoba, and who were recruited into the OPS during the Peterson years. Their strategic contribution was an understanding of the social-democratic policy agenda and the ability to move it along.[5]

The perception of politicization in the senior public service has not yet taken root with the return to power of the Progressive Conservative party. Shortly after assuming office, Premier Harris signalled that the role of the OPS would be shifting back to familiar ground. The first signal was the appointment of Rita Burak as the Secretary of Cabinet and Michael Gourley as Deputy Minister of Finance, both of whom were career civil servants within the OPS. The second signal was the firing of the deputy ministers who were closely identified with the NDP government. Premier Harris also sent other signals in a speech to deputy ministers in June 1995. He affirmed the traditional role of the civil service to provide policy advice and facilitate policy implementation, assured deputy ministers that they would have direct access to their ministers, and refocused the activities of ministerial political staff on day-to-day political tasks and communications. However, the deputies also heard the bottom-line message of the new government: the management agenda must follow the unforgiving thrust of the fiscal agenda.

The immutable character of the Harris government's policy agenda (as defined in the *CSR*) and its dominant ideological perspective that government should play a smaller role in Ontario society and operate 'like a business' has several implications for senior public servants. As White has observed, these developments diminish their role as policy advisers and place emphasis on their role as managers of business operations, a juxtaposition of past tendencies. Moreover, given the downsizing of the OPS through privatization, contracting out, and program rationalization, the scale of business operations will be much reduced in comparison to the expansion that has characterized the past forty years or so. In this new environment, a career in the OPS and the preparation and skills required for success therein will be substantially different.

LABOUR RELATIONS

The first collective-bargaining regime for the OPS was ushered in by the passage of the Crown Employees Collective Bargaining Act (CECBA) in 1972. This regime involved, among other features, compulsory arbitration (not the right to strike) as the primary means of dispute resolution and the exclusion of persons occupying confidential, managerial, and professional jobs from bargaining units. Therefore, approximately 23 per cent of Ontario's civil service did not come under the provisions of the act.

Since the passage of the CECBA, labour relations within the OPS have been characterized by many of the same issues that are evident in other jurisdictions. Among these are the conflict generated by government policies of financial restraint and privatization; the demand for greater political rights for public servants; the desire on the union side for an expansion of the scope of collective bargaining to include a number of non-monetary matters (for example, position classification); and the continual push by unions for improvements in the compensation and working conditions of provincial employees. These issues, and many others, have been on the agenda for negotiation between the Management Board (the employer) and certified employee bargaining agents, the largest of which is OPSEU.

In December 1993 the legislature passed Bill 117, a piece of legislation that completely revamped the CECBA and fundamentally altered the dynamics of labour relations in the OPS. The law was promptly proclaimed by the NDP government in February 1994. With a few exceptions (for example, the loss of compulsory arbitration as an alternative dispute-resolution option), OPSEU supported the CECBA reforms.

The legislation puts labour relations in the OPS under the broader framework employed in the private sector (that is, the CECBA is deemed to form part of the Labour Relations Act [LRA]). The key changes are the granting of the right to strike (with the parallel requirement to determine the number of workers who are considered essential and not allowed to strike) and the expansion of the matters subject to collective bargaining. The legislation provides for separate bargaining by six OPSEU bargaining units over issues such as wages, hours of work, shift scheduling, and shift premiums. All units bargain at a central table over grievance procedures, non-discrimination clauses, the posting and filling of vacancies, seniority, surplus employees (employees who have lost their jobs but have not been laid off or released), layoffs, bumping[6] and redeployment (the right of a laid-off employee to displace another with less seniority), pensions, long-term disability, and other benefits that apply across the public service. By mutual agreement between the union and the government, bargaining-unit issues can be moved to the central table.

Under the act, 'essential services' are those that are

necessary to enable the employer [the government] to prevent,
(a) danger to life, health or safety,
(b) the destruction or serious deterioration of machinery, equipment or premises,
(c) serious environmental damage, or
(d) disruption of the administration of the courts or of legislative drafting ...
(CECBA, s. 30)

Both the government and the union must 'bargain in good faith and make every reasonable effort to make an essential services agreement' (CECBA, s. 31.2). Negotiation of the essential-services agreement must commence at least 180 days before the expiration of the existing collective agreement, and disputes as to what constitute essential services are resolved by the Ontario Labour Relations Board (OLRB).

The CECBA reforms not only expanded the labour rights of OPSEU's members but also gave thousands of employees in managerial and professional jobs the right to join a union (managers who have the authority to hire, fire, and discipline employees still do not have this right). Although OPSEU attempted to obtain certification as the bargaining agent of these employees, ultimately managers and professionals opted to join the Association of Management, Administrative and Professional Crown Employees of Ontario (AMAPCEO), an organization formed in 1992. The main stumbling block in OPSEU's organizing drive was its insistence that the seniority rights of its existing members would override those of any managers or professionals who became members. AMAPCEO was certified by the OLRB in January 1995 as the bargaining agent for 4600 OPS employees.

Labour relations during the NDP years were also marked by the acri-

mony of the Social Contract process. The NDP's Social Contract legislation was passed in July 1993. It specified a 1 August 1993 deadline for
public-sector groups to reach agreements designed to achieve expenditure savings targets (set by the provincial government) that covered a
three-year period. Social Contract measures were not applied to employees earning less than $30,000 annually. Although it was hoped to attain
the savings without massive job losses, the 'fail-safe' provisions of the
legislation (deployed in the event that an agreement was not reached)
required public-sector workers to take up to twelve unpaid days off
during each of the three years and public-sector employers to lay off
staff, if necessary.

OPSEU's share of the sectoral savings target was $132.8 million in each
of the three years, to be met through voluntary unpaid days off, a freeze
on automatic salary increases linked to length of service, a moratorium
on classification grievances, overtime taken in compensating time instead of cash, and savings through reductions of waste and inefficiency.
Although this approach allowed OPSEU members to avoid lay-offs, the
imposition of the Social Contract created a substantial rift between the
NDP government and many of its traditional labour allies, including
OPSEU.

The election of the Progressive Conservative Party in June 1995 held
out the prospect of increased labour strife within the OPS (and in the
private sector). Two key policy planks in the *CSR* were the repeal of the
NDP's reforms to the LRA (largely affecting private-sector labour relations) and the downsizing of government operations to reduce both costs
and the role of the state. Downsizing included the cutting of some 13,000
provincial-government jobs.

The first battle occurred in the fall of 1995 with the passage of Bill 7,
legislation that repealed the changes to the LRA made by the former
NDP government. One of the provisions of Bill 7 stipulated that the
'successor rights' provisions of the LRA did not apply to the privatization
of provincial-government operations. Successor rights require a new
employer to honour a union contract and allow employees to retain
union representation.

The next skirmish involved the controversial Bill 26, the Savings and
Restructuring Act, 1995 (more popularly known as the 'omnibus bill').
Under Bill 26 the government acquired the authority to prevent the
partial wind-up of employee pension plans, an approach sometimes
used to assist laid-off workers. A prior attempt by the government to
achieve this objective through regulation had been contested in the courts

by OPSEU, and in December 1995 a Divisional Court struck down a cabinet order restricting the access of laid-off OPSEU members to their pension funds.

The battles over successor rights and pensions were dress rehearsals for the larger confrontation that would culminate in the first lawful strike in the history of the OPS. In the collective-bargaining negotiations leading up to the strike, the government put forward a position that advanced its program of cost reduction and the downsizing of operations. Job security, not increased compensation, quickly became the key issue for OPSEU members. Initial government proposals affecting this issue would have stripped employee job protection when government operations were privatized, contracted out, or divested (these employees would lose their seniority, wage scale, and contract and union representation); restricted the right of surplus employees to move to another position; reduced the provision for notice of lay-off to two weeks in some cases; lessened the impact of the criterion of seniority in determining lay-offs; and eliminated employee access to retraining. In addition, the government attempted to reclaim the determination of employee pensions, job classification, and wage scales as management rights, thereby depriving OPSEU of the right to negotiate and grieve these matters.

About 55,000 of OPSEU's 67,000 members went on strike in late February 1996. They faced formidable odds. Not only were they inexperienced in the use of the strike weapon, but they also were challenging a government that was pursuing a popular agenda. The strike lasted five weeks, much longer than most observers thought would be the case. When OPSEU's locals ratified the new collective agreement at the end of March by a vote of 95 per cent, the union's solidarity was high and it could claim victory on several matters relating to the issue of job security. These included

- pension-bridging protection for members laid off before they are eligible for early retirement;
- job protection for members affected by privatization;
- the rejection of a government proposal to institute short-term lay-offs with two weeks' notice;
- expanded bumping rights (for example, a laid-off employee can execute three bumps across the province within her or his own ministry);
- the matching of surplus employees with those who want to exit volun-

tarily (when the match is made the volunteer receives enhanced severance); and
– allowing surplus workers, who previously chose not to retire on a Factor 80 basis, to now do so (Factor 80 is a program whereby an employee can retire without penalty when her or his age and years of service total 80).

However, in the end, OPSEU could only blunt, not stop, the cost-reduction program of the Harris government. The strike also exacted a financial toll. During the five-week strike, OPSEU accumulated a $13 million debt, an amount largely owed to other unions. Subsequently, it was necessary to approve a temporary dues increase to pay off the debt over a two-year period. OPSEU was also forced to lay off some of its own staff and endure the embarrassment of a bitter strike.

The new collective agreement has not restored calm to labour relations within the OPS. As the government proceeds with its privatization strategy, the job-protection provisions in the collective agreement are being tested. The provisions represent a compromise between the revocation of successor rights under Bill 7 and the union's demands for complete job protection for members affected by privatization. The agreement requires the government to take 'reasonable efforts ... to ensure that employees in the bargaining unit are offered positions with the new employer.'[7] If the new wage scale is not at least 85 per cent of the public-service rate, or seniority or service credits are not recognized by the new employer, the employee can opt for enhanced severance and full bumping rights.

Indeed, the first test of this provision has resulted in the union filing a grievance against the government. The test case is the privatization of the Ministry of Transportation's highway-maintenance operations in the area between London and Windsor, a development that affects the jobs of 195 union members. From OPSEU's perspective, the 'tender packages give new employers almost no incentive to take on [Ministry of Transportation] employees.'[8]

The job cuts promised by the Harris government are also now taking hold. In April 1996 the Chair of Management Board announced that the government would cut over 10,600 jobs (including 1400 vacant positions) during the next two years. In May 1996 the first round of job cuts hit OPSEU's members. The largest cuts were in the Ministry of Natural Resources (915 jobs), Ministry of Labour (301), Ministry of Environment and Energy (245), and Ministry of Agriculture, Food and Rural Affairs (157).

ORGANIZATIONAL CHANGE

'Change' has been the watchword for the OPS during the 1980s and the first half of the 1990s. White and Lindquist have analysed the waves of change impacting on the OPS.[9] The major developments include the following:

- three changes in the governing party between 1985 and 1995
- the creation of a Treasury Board by the NDP and its dismantling by the Progressive Conservatives as part of the continuing reform of central agencies
- a substantial initiative by the Management Board in the early 1990s to improve service quality
- extensive re-engineering of government operations, including de-layering and greater use of information technology (organizational re-engineering has been defined as 'the fundamental rethinking and redesign of business processes to achieve dramatic improvements in critical, contemporary measures of performance, such as cost, quality, service, and speed'[10])
- employment-equity programs initiated by the Liberals, accelerated by the NDP, and terminated by the Progressive Conservatives
- a 'Shared Accountability Framework' developed under the NDP to improve ministerial and administrative accountability for the implementation of management reforms
- a 'business plan' approach developed by the Progressive Conservatives that emphasizes public accountability, the definition of core businesses for each ministry, and performance measures for public services
- the expansion of government relocation programs under the Liberals and the scaling down and termination of relocation plans under the NDP and Progressive Conservatives
- the exodus of experienced managers and professionals from the OPS, especially at the senior levels, through successive early-retirement or voluntary-exit programs
- the downsizing of government through privatization, contracting out, program reduction, and program divestiture, a trend that is reaching unparalled dimensions under the current Progressive Conservative government

In the final part of the chapter these developments will be examined from the perspective of demographic trends in Canada (demographic trends in Ontario mirror the national situation). The analysis presented below looks at the OPS as a segment of the public-sector labour force. The emphasis is not on the short-term consequences of organizational change but on the long-term results of continuing current approaches, particularly downsizing.

Canada's population is aging because of a prolonged period of low fertility and increasing life expectancy, trends that are likely to continue. Given Canada's population distribution, the age composition of the population will have a substantial impact on the provision of goods and services by both the public and private sectors.

The template of the 'baby boom, bust, and echo' generations provides the key analytical framework for understanding Canadian demographic trends during the past fifty years and the next twenty-five.[11] The baby boom between 1947 and 1966 accounts for almost one-third of Canada's 1996 population of 30 million people. An important sub-cohort within the boom generation is represented by those individuals born between 1960 (the peak of the boom) and 1966, the so-called Generation X, who number approximately 2.6 million. The baby-bust cohort, born during a period of declining fertility between 1967 and 1979, encompasses 5.4 million Canadians (about 55 per cent the size of the boom cohort). The echo generation, born during the 1980s and first part of the 1990s, is the offspring of the boomers. They are more numerous (6.9 million, or about 70 per cent of the boom) than the preceding bust generation, not because of an upswing in fertility but as a result of the sheer size of the baby-boom cohort.

In relating demographics and public-sector labour-force trends, three types of generic career paths should be identified: linear, spiral, and transitory (a fourth, the steady-state path, is not applicable to the public sector). One of the implications of current demographic trends in Canada is the transition from linear to spiral and transitory career paths. However, the current emphasis on downsizing – the stripping of jobs to enhance short-term profitability or reduce the deficit – is creating a situation of demographic imbalance within public and private corporate structures that will reduce long-term productivity and profitability.

The linear career path emphasizes upward movement through the numerous levels of a hierarchical ('triangular') organization. Individuals pursuing this career path may ultimately have two occupations, one on the service-delivery side of the organization and the other in senior management. The reward system is based on the progressive accumulation of both authority and compensation through promotion. A career within the police service or the military illustrates the linear conception well, but so do the careers of the thousands of workers who are employed in government agencies or large private corporations. During much of the postwar period, successive waves of workers have expected to pursue linear careers within triangular structures.

The spiral career path is characterized by both upward and lateral organizational movement. Individuals who pursue this career path can expect to have several occupations during their working years. One may start out as an accountant and then be promoted eventually to the position of director of financial services, that is, reach the first rung of the senior-management level. At this point one's next occupation may involve a lateral move to become the director of program evaluation. In sum, over time one progresses within the organization through a series of vertical and lateral moves.

A spiral path requires a substantially different organizational structure and reward system than that of the linear path. The organization is still a triangle but it is much flatter, with fewer management levels. Individuals are not motivated by the continual prospect of promotions but by the challenges of different occupations and the opportunities associated with re-education and retraining. The innovative restructuring of the Office of the Registrar General in Ontario's Ministry of Consumer and Commercial Relations during the past several years has applied many of the notions inherent in the concept of a spiral career path.

The transitory career path emphasizes lateral movement among different projects either within one organization or among several. Individuals pursuing this path will have many occupations during their careers. The concept of the temporary team is the organizational structure that fits best with the transitory career path. Independence, variety, and a flexible work schedule are the rewards; the absence of security and a fixed level of compensation are the constraints. Own-account workers within the ranks of the self-employed in Canada illustrate this career path.

The baby boom represents a twenty-year 'rectangle' of workers moving through a triangular corporate world. The central issue is that the boom generation challenges the leaders of traditionally structured organizations, where linear careers are the norm, to 'push a rectangle up a triangle.' The problem is 'plateauing' or career blockage for large groups of workers conditioned to regard upward mobility as the signpost of success. The response is de-layering and re-engineering to strip out unnecessary levels of management and work processes and create a flat and responsive organization. However, in too many cases another step has been taken – the downsizing of staff to contain financial costs. From the perspective of demographics plateauing, re-engineering, and de-layering, but not downsizing, are 'inevitable surprises.'

The impact of demographics on organizational structure and career paths is not simply an issue of the 1990s. This issue will become increasingly problematic over the next ten years. In 1981, as the last of the baby-boom generation began to enter the labour force (defined as workers between 15 and 64), the labour force still exhibited its traditional triangular shape, that is, a mass of younger workers at the base and increasingly fewer older workers as one moves towards the apex. By 2006 the baby-boom group will range in age from 40 to 59 with the peak at 46. Projections show this cohort as the broad top end of a barrel-shaped labour force. The bottom levels of the old triangular labour force (i.e., workers under 35) will be less occupied than in the past. Downsizing, as currently practised, accelerates this natural trend.

Federal-government employment data for 1995–6 lend further support to the thesis that the baby-boom cohort dominates organizational ranks (Ontario-government data are not readily available, but White cites statistics showing that the proportion of OPS workers under 25 years fell from 5 per cent in 1989 to 2 per cent in 1995[12]). During 1995–6 the federal work force was reduced by just under 8 per cent. Notwithstanding absolute drops in all major age cohorts, the proportion of workers under age 35 fell by more than 2 per cent and the proportion of workers 35 and over increased by more than 2 per cent. The increased share for 'older' workers favoured the baby-boom generation. Boomers increased their share by about 2.5 per cent. Furthermore, the older front-end and peak boomers (age 35–49) fared the best, with an increase of well over 3 per cent. 'Generation X' (age 30–34) declined slightly.

The juxtaposition of the huge baby-boom generation with the management strategy of downsizing raises several important questions for Canada's public services, including the OPS. How should organizations adjust their structures, policies, and procedures to manage the transition of the boomers (and pre-boomers) from linear to spiral and transitory career paths? How important will workplace training become as a means of maintaining morale and productivity? What are the longer-term economic and social consequences of the blunt instrument of downsizing?

Downsizing, either in place of or in conjunction with re-engineering, represents the conventional wisdom on how governments (and businesses) can escape their financial woes. As ministers face citizens' wrath over excessive levels of deficit spending and public debt, the reflex response to this pressure is to implement a scheme that works, at best, in the short term.

Downsizing as the preferred 'short term solution' typically involves three elements:

1 cutting staff, usually across the board or on the basis of seniority;
2 organizational restructuring that emphasizes greater centralization of senior-management authority; and
3 substituting technology for people, nominally to improve service delivery.

Although there may be short-term financial benefits, the long-term problems created by downsizing outweigh the benefits. The first problem is that the survivors of the corporate bloodletting are often left in a demoralized and less-productive state. Low morale was cited as a problem by both Robert Giroux, Secretary of the Treasury Board, and Bill Krause, president of the Social Science Employees Association, when the federal government job cuts were initiated in 1995. According to Krause: 'It's not just the pure economics of the [exit] package, because some will be worse off if they take it, but morale is so low that it's inducing people to take the package – they want out.'[13] It might also be argued that 'corporate loyalty' evaporates in the aftermath of downsizing.

There are other consequences of the short-term solution. Where younger workers (under 35) are the prime victims of cuts, governments run the risk of having a less computer-literate work force. Longitudinal studies undertaken by Statistics Canada have consistently demonstrated the inverse relationship between computer literacy and age (that is, the younger the worker, the higher the literacy level). The emphasis of downsizing on replacing people with technology (although some critics contend that downsizing is more focused on the short-term cost reduction obtained through cutting jobs, not on strategic investment in technology) fails to recognize that technological solutions are potentially ineffective in an aging society, both for the client and service provider. At this point machines are not an appropriate replacement for front-line staff. Technology must become extremely 'user friendly' to have the desired impact on effectiveness. Moreover, technology does not replace everybody; therefore, substantial training expenditures will be required to develop the skills of the workers who must use the technology. Training costs will be higher for the older work force left in the wake of downsizing compared to one that is demographically balanced.

Downsizing also results in the organization losing some of its best employees. This observation reflects the hypothesis that two categories of workers tend to exit as a result of downsizing: the 'young' (under 35), who have limited seniority but high potential and high computer literacy, and the 'old' (over 50), who have the experience and knowledge. Furthermore, it is likely that, regardless of age, those who depart are the government's most entrepreneurial and creative people – the people who feel that they can make it on their own with or without the assistance of an attractive severance package.

The exodus of 'good people' creates several 'organizational deficits.' An organization without a significant youth cohort runs the risk of exhibiting low levels of 'energy,' client responsiveness, and computer literacy. In this regard governments will face not only a competitive future market for workers under the age of thirty-five, but also an even more competitive market for the best workers. At the older end of the employee spectrum, the exit of 'good people' means the loss of strategic expertise and 'institutional memory,' deficits that often lead to inefficiency and ineffectiveness. Recent press reports from Alberta indicate that the cumulative impact of years of wage decreases and reductions in operational resources is inducing senior civil servants to seek (and obtain) higher salaries in the private sector. There is now concern that the government is losing strategic expertise and its most innovative managers.

Unfortunately, for Canada's public services the 'good people' liberated by downsizing are probably not coming back. Those with professional and management backgrounds are swelling the ranks of the self-employed and will be available as consultants. They will not form part of the 'core' employee group that the deputy ministers of downsized departments suggest is sufficient to reach even higher levels of productivity. They will revel in the variety and flexibility of their transitory careers.

Indeed, many governments make it relatively easy for the 'good people' to leave. The case of the federal government is instructive. During the 1995–6 fiscal year, just under 77 per cent of those who left the public service did so under various incentive programs, particularly the Early Retirement Incentive (29 per cent), Civilian Reduction Program (20 per cent), and Early Departure Incentive (18 per cent). The Early Departure Incentive (EDI) is potentially lucrative – depending on years of service and age it could pay out up to ninety weeks of salary and $7000 for counselling and retraining. The federal government initially estimated that about 4000 of the 50,000 eligible employees would take up the EDI. In 1995–6, 3557 federal employees accepted the EDI.[14] The 'job swap' program is also both popular and an indicator of the desire of some civil servants to start new careers. In 1995 it was reported that twice as many members of the Professional Institute of the Public Service opted to leave government as swapped jobs.

In sum, by the 1980s the sheer size of the baby-boom generation began to put pressure on the vertical structure and linear career paths characteristic of large-scale public (and private) organizations, thereby making the transition to flatter corporate structures with spiral and transitory career paths inevitable. By the 1990s economic factors, some global in origin, increased the pressure on government leaders to improve the fiscal situation. Downsizing, with its emphasis on containing costs through job cuts and related measures, meets this goal in the short term, but it creates longer-term problems that will be exacerbated by demographic trends.

Conclusion

As the millennium approaches, the OPS faces a period of unprecedented change. The democratic paradigm in Ontario is shifting from a state-centred society to a market-centred society. The challenge to the OPS is to maintain its legitimacy and vigour in a turbulent and potentially hostile environment.

Notes

1 Richard Loreto, 'The Bureaucracy,' in Graham White, ed., *The Government and Politics of Ontario*, 4th ed. (Toronto: Nelson Canada, 1990), 103–24.
2 Ontario Financial Review Commission, *Beyond the Numbers: A New Financial Management and Accountability Framework for Ontario* (Toronto: 1995), appendix.
3 *Toronto Star*, 4 June 1996, A1.
4 OPSEU news release, 22 December 1994.
5 Graham White, 'Change in the Ontario Public Service,' in Evert Lindquist, ed., *The Career Public Service in Canada* (forthcoming).
6 'Bumping' is a process common in collective-bargaining arrangements that allows a laid-off worker to displace ('bump') a worker with less seniority from his or her job, provided the first employee is qualified for the job.

Under certain circumstances, workers who are bumped may in turn bump
other workers with less seniority.

7 OPSEU 'News Update,' 31 July 1996.
8 Ibid.
9 Evert A. Lindquist and Graham White, 'Streams, Springs and Stones:
   Ontario Public Service Reform in the 1980s and 1990s,' *Canadian Public
   Administration* 37 (Summer 1994): 267–301.
10 Michael Hammer and James Champy, *Reengineering the Corporation: A
   Manifesto for Business Revolution* (New York: Harper Business, 1993), 32.
11 David K. Foot, with Daniel Stoffman, *Boom, Bust and Echo: How to Profit from
   the Coming Demographic Shift* (Toronto: Macfarlane Walter and Ross, 1996).
12 White, 'Change,' 17.
13 Krause, *Hamilton Spectator*, 10 July 1995.
14 Data from Government of Canada, Treasury Board, 'Employment Statistics
   for the Federal Public Service: April 1, 1995 to March, 1996.'

Further Reading

Loreto, Richard. 'Changes in the Ontario Cabinet System.' *Public Sector Manage-
ment* 2, no. 1 (Spring 1991): 28–30.
– 'Back to the Future: Ontario's Treasury Board – Part I.' *Public Sector Manage-
ment* 2, no. 4 (Winter 1991): 17–19.
– 'Back to the Future: Ontario's Treasury Board – Part II.' *Public Sector Manage-
ment* 3, no. 1 (Spring 1992): 25–7.
– 'Common Sense or Revolution: The New Cabinet System in Ontario.' *Public
Sector Management* 6, no. 4 (1995): 6–8.
Loreto, Richard, and Graham White. 'The Premier and the Cabinet.' In G.
White, ed., *The Government and Politics of Ontario*, 4th ed., 79–102. Toronto:
Nelson Canada.
Ontario Financial Review Commission. *Beyond the Numbers: A New Financial
Management and Accountability Framework for Ontario*. Toronto: 1995.
Ontario Management Board of Cabinet. *Doing Better for Less: Introducing
Ontario's Business Plans – A Project to Protect Priority Services within a More
Affordable, Innovative Government*. Toronto: Queen's Printer for Ontario, 1996.
Ontario Ministry of Finance. *1995 Fiscal and Economic Statement*. Toronto:
Queen's Printer for Ontario, 1995.
– *1996 Ontario Budget Speech*. Toronto: Queen's Printer for Ontario, 1996.
– *1996 Ontario Budget Papers*. Toronto: Queen's Printer for Ontario, 1996.
Progressive Conservative Party of Ontario. *The Common Sense Revolution* (1995).

SIX

Local Government in Ontario

David Siegel

The focal point of this book is provincial government, but a significant amount of 'governing' in Ontario is done by local governments. A book on provincial government is not complete without a discussion of the local governments in that province which are in some ways extensions of the provincial government.

This chapter begins with a discussion of the general role of local government in Ontario, followed by a description of the provincial-municipal relationship. The next two sections then describe the structure of local government in Ontario and provide a quantitative overview of its activities. The following section reviews the problems facing local government. The final section takes a look at the future of local government generally and focuses more specifically on recent initiatives of the Harris government in the municipal field.

The Ambivalent Role of Local Government

The statement was made above that local government is in some ways an extension of provincial government. This seems demeaning to local government, but it is a correct interpretation of the constitutional-legal status of the relationship between provincial and local governments. Under section 92(8) of the Constitution Act, provincial governments have complete control over all aspects of local government. Provincial governments create local governments, determine their geographical boundaries, assign them responsibilities, prescribe how those responsibilities must be carried out, and can terminate the existence of any and all local governments in the province. In practice, most provincial governments choose to exercise restraint in actually wielding these draconian powers, but the Harris government has chosen to use these powers to a greater extent than they have been used in the past to effect major changes in the local-government system in Ontario. These changes will be discussed in more detail later.

However, these legalities obscure the reality of the role of local government in the 1990s. Local governments have two major roles – citizen access and service delivery.

The citizen-access role derives from the fact that local government is the level of government that is closest to the people. When federal and provincial representatives are chosen, they are sent off to Ottawa or Toronto, never to be seen in the local area again (or so it seems sometimes). However, the average citizen is likely to meet her or his local councillor at the shopping centre, arena, or workplace. The average citizen can normally appear personally in the local council chamber and state her or his case directly to councillors.

The size and scope of local government promotes citizen involvement. We hear the common expression 'You can't fight city hall.' In fact, however, it is much easier to make your views known at city hall than it is to organize and present your views to the federal and provincial governments. The legislative chambers in Ottawa and Toronto are reserved for elected members who make laws by discussing issues with one another. Thus, local government has an important role in promoting citizen access and citizen involvement in the governing process.

However, local governments are also service-delivery agencies. Because they are so close to the people, they are deemed the best level of government to provide certain services. When the provincial government delivers a service, it must do so in a roughly uniform manner to all residents throughout the province. Local governments can deliver different kinds of services at different levels. For example, one community can decide to have a high level of services even though it means paying high property taxes, while a neighbouring community might favour low taxes even though this results in a low level of services.

The problem is that these two aspects of local government can conflict with one another. One dimension of that conflict arises from the fact that pursuit of efficient service delivery could cause a push for larger units of local government in order to capture economies of scale;[1] but larger units are also less amenable to citizen access.

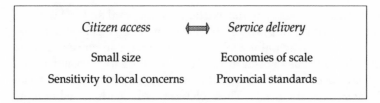

FIGURE 1 Local government's access-service conundrum

Another conflict arises when provincial governments are more interested in the service-delivery role of local governments than in the citizen-
access role. There are many examples of local and provincial governments
working together in the delivery of services. Most people only become
conscious of the seamless way in which the provincial and municipal
road systems normally fit together when there is some glitch. To the
extent that provincial governments use local governments as local service-delivery agents, this conflicts with meaningful citizen access. The
existence of provincial rules and standards means that local governments are not really making their own decisions. One of the thrusts of the
recent policy changes of the Harris government is to improve accountability by reducing instances of this sharing of responsibilities.

Figure 1 illustrates the conundrum that local government faces about
which of its roles it will emphasize. Of course, there are times when the
two streams fit together, but much of local government's time is devoted
to resolving the tension between these two roles.

This ambivalent role of local government is reflected in the rather
uneasy relationship between municipalities and the provincial government. Local governments see themselves as important governing bodies
deriving their legitimacy from their close links to the public. Provincial
governments sometimes see local governments as simply decentralized
service-delivery agencies. The turbulence of the provincial-municipal
relationship is caused by the fact that there is some truth in both of these
perceptions around a number of issues. While the immediate issue under
discussion varies quite a bit, the underlying issue being contested is
usually the appropriate level of municipal autonomy.

Provincial-Municipal Relations

The constitutional-legal status of local governments as creatures of provincial governments was discussed above. An important principle that

flows from this status is that local governments have no general mandate of authority to carry out their responsibilities. Before a local government can perform any actions, it must find specific authority for that action in some provincial statute.[2] This obviously imposes a significant restraint on the ability of local governments to be innovative.

The province of Ontario has tended to use its extensive powers in a restrained manner. It usually consults with local governments before it makes important decisions affecting them. This is not to suggest that this relationship is always calm and cozy. The Harris government is in the process of undertaking a major reorganization of local government that it contends is aimed at providing local governments with more autonomy. Paradoxically, many of these changes have been imposed on unwilling local governments because local officials have not always agreed with the precise nature of the changes.

Most provincial ministries have some dealings with local governments. The remainder of this section will discuss the nature of those relationships.

MINISTRY OF MUNICIPAL AFFAIRS

The Ministry of Municipal Affairs has the greatest frequency of contact with municipalities and is the ministry responsible for the overall operation of the municipal system. The ministry described its role this way in 1988, and it has not changed substantially since: 'The ministry is the key link in the province's relationship with the municipalities of Ontario and the services to the public provided by municipal governments. The ministry develops, co-ordinates and implements the province's policies and priorities relating to municipal government through the transfer of approximately $890 million to municipalities in 1987/88, the maintenance of close liaison with municipalities, the development and interpretation of policy, the provision of advice on administrative and management issues and the coordination of community and land use planning province-wide.'[3]

The ministry has a great deal of power over the municipal system under the Municipal Act and related legislation. In the extreme, the ministry can take over the administration of a municipality. This is done only in rare instances, when a municipality is in dire financial straits or when election irregularities leave a municipality without a council.

In practice, the ministry's main role is providing *funding* and *advice* to municipalities rather than exercising the heavy hand of supervision. The ministry also has a *legislative* function because it is responsible for proposing changes in legislation affecting municipalities. Finally, the ministry shares authority over *land-use planning* with the Ontario Municipal Board.

The Ministry of Municipal Affairs provides a significant amount of funding to municipalities, mostly on an unconditional basis. This funding is important to municipalities, partly because of the amount involved, but mostly because this is the only funding that municipalities receive from the province on a purely unconditional basis. Other ministries also provide significant funding, but it is always conditional on the municipality spending the money in a specified manner. The money from the Ministry of Municipal Affairs is the only provincial money that municipalities can use in any way they desire.

The ministry is also responsible for controlling municipal borrowing. Municipalities are free to make their own borrowing decisions as long as their annual interest charges do not exceed a fixed percentage of total expenditure. When a municipality wants to borrow beyond that amount, it must obtain the approval of the ministry. This is an important control, because it prevents any municipality from incurring excessive financial obligations and being unable to meet those obligations. This constitutes a vital protection for the entire municipal system, because if any municipality in Ontario went bankrupt it would impair the credit rating of all other Ontario municipalities.

As a part of its advisory function, the ministry has prepared many publications for municipalities dealing with such matters as financial management, election procedures, and selection of computer equipment. It also maintains a field-services branch with offices across the province. People from these offices visit municipalities, when requested, to provide advice to municipal officials. These advisory services are particularly helpful to smaller municipalities, which frequently do not have the complete range of in-house expertise that larger municipalities enjoy.

The ministry is also responsible for the overall organization of local government in the province. It has undertaken a number of studies dealing with both broad, general concerns such as the future of county government and specific matters such as the periodic reviews of regional governments. In some cases, studies of this kind result in advice to municipalities about administrative arrangements, but they can also lead to legislation implementing changes in municipal structures or electoral systems.

The Ministry of Municipal Affairs also represents the provincial interest in land-use planning matters. The province wants to ensure both that certain natural areas such as wetlands are used properly and that planning decisions taken in one jurisdiction do not unfairly affect neighbouring jurisdictions. To make sure these factors are considered by municipalities, the Ministry of Municipal Affairs works with other provincial ministries in the review of all land-use plans.

The operation of the Ministry of Municipal Affairs reflects the point made above about the constitutional-legal status of municipalities. The ministry *has* a great deal of power. In practice, it usually proceeds only in an advisory manner, unless serious problems develop.

ONTARIO MUNICIPAL BOARD

The Ontario Municipal Board (OMB) is a quasi-judicial agency reporting to the Ministry of Municipal Affairs. The Board shares responsibility for general management of municipalities with the ministry, but it operates in a much more judicial fashion, hearing the arguments presented by the various parties and issuing a binding decision. It has the authority to make a variety of decisions under more than one hundred different pieces of legislation, but its main impact on municipalities is in two areas:[4]

– Planning and zoning: The OMB functions as an appeal body for most planning and zoning matters. It reviews municipalities' official land-use plans and any proposed amendments. It hears appeals concerning zoning by-laws and other planning matters.
– Municipal boundaries: When two or more municipalities want to amalgamate or when a municipality wants to change its boundaries, usually by annexing lands from an adjoining municipality, the matter can end up before the OMB.

The Operation of the OMB
The board is a quasi-judicial body, but it tries to function in a less formal manner than an ordinary court. For example, the usual strict rules of evidence do not apply and board members will sometimes assist citizens in presenting their cases to ensure that all the facts are available. Board members travel throughout the province, so that hearings are usually held in the affected community.

Appeals of OMB Decisions
For all practical purposes, decisions of the OMB are final. There are some very limited grounds for appeal and judicial review, but these are seldom used.

OTHER PROVINCIAL MINISTRIES

Municipalities have frequent contacts with most provincial ministries concerning the delivery of municipal services in which ministries have some interest. Provincial ministries are usually concerned that services are delivered in a reasonably uniform manner across the province. For example, the Ministry of Environment and Energy has standards for water purification, sewage treatment, and operation of landfill sites that all municipalities must meet. In some cases, these standards are enforced by firm regulations or guidelines, while in other instances, ministries provide conditional grants that municipalities receive only if they provide services to a specified standard. Thus, one sees both the carrot and the stick employed.

The relationship between municipalities and these ministries can become tense, because municipalities sometimes feel that the ministries are either imposing unnecessarily high standards on them or are forcing them to pay for and provide services that ought to be provided by the province. This is another instance of the ambivalent role of local government as autonomous entity or provincial service-delivery agency. One of the main objectives of recent government policy has been to reduce the intrusive controls imposed by the ministries. This is a double-edged sword. Certainly, municipalities appreciate the additional automomy. The downside is that the lack of provincial standards could create a patchwork of policies across the province.

THE MUNICIPAL RESPONSE TO PROVINCIAL CONTROLS

Municipalities have an ambivalent attitude towards the various instruments of provincial control. On the one hand, most municipal officials recognize that some level of provincial control is necessary or even desirable. For example, the provincial control on municipal borrowing makes it unlikely that any Ontario municipality will ever default on a financial obligation. This guarantee of stability improves the position of *all* Ontario municipalities in the money market and reduces the interest rate that they must pay.

On the other hand, municipalities frequently complain vociferously when a provincial decision affects them negatively. The essence of their complaints can be captured fairly well in one sentence. The local politicians who put their jobs on the line every three years feel that they are more sensitive to the needs and concerns of the local population than public servants in Toronto or members of the OMB who spend a half-day in town before making a decision that will have profound implications for the future development of their community.

Achieving the proper balance of provincial control and local autonomy is very difficult. There are certain areas where provincial concerns must override those of the local municipality to ensure that the broader public interest is protected; for instance, in the preservation of unique natural areas. However, municipalities frequently claim that the province uses this apparently benevolent role to involve itself in purely local matters.

ASSOCIATION OF MUNICIPALITIES OF ONTARIO

The picture to this point seems to suggest that municipalities exist solely as the objects of provincial policy, with very little control over their own destinies. This is not really the case. Municipalities in Ontario are quite well organized to look after their own interests. The Association of Municipalities of Ontario (AMO) is a very strong organization, with approximately 700 members of the 839 municipalities in Ontario, representing 95 per cent of the total provincial population.[5]

The AMO has many of the characteristics of a trade association or interest group, and represents its members at Queen's Park and in Ottawa. It has regular meetings with the Minister of Municipal Affairs and other ministers who are developing legislation that will have an impact on municipalities, and prides itself on being consulted early in the policy-making process so that its members' concerns are taken into account in policy development.

The AMO operates on several levels. Its highest-profile activity is its large annual conference in Toronto, an important part of which is the passage of resolutions indicating to the provincial government what the major concerns of municipalities are. It also has a myriad of committees dealing with specific issues. These committees usually include municipal politicians and staff, and have frequent contact with provincial politicians and civil servants. The AMO also provides the usual kinds of services that trade associations provide to their members, collecting and disseminating information about such matters as labour relations, pay equity, and energy conservation.

The AMO is clearly a strong and viable association, but one of its continuing problems stems from the innate difficulty of representing over seven hundred municipalities of widely differing sizes, located in different areas of the province, and facing vastly different problems. This problem has been addressed by creating six sections within the AMO: counties, regions, small urban, large urban, northern Ontario, and rural. From time to time, one of these groups will argue that some restructuring of the association is required because its interests are not adequately represented. This has not proved to be a serious problem to this point, but if such splits become serious they could jeopardize the AMO's current strong position with the provincial government. A return to the pre-1982 situation of three associations speaking for municipalities would probably weaken the overall power of municipalities to make their case.

The Structure of Local Government in Ontario

THE COUNTY SYSTEM

The basis of local-government organization in Ontario is still the Baldwin Act, which was passed in 1849. This marked the beginning of real responsible local government in Ontario. Before this legislation, local administration was handled by provincially appointed judges. The basic unit of local government established by the Baldwin Act was the county. All of southern Ontario was divided into counties, which were in turn divided into towns, townships, and villages. In many urban areas, these counties have been replaced by regional governments, which will be discussed later, but most of southern Ontario is still organized on the basis of the county system of government.

One of the basic tenets of the Baldwin Act was that rural and urban interests must be kept separate – in part because the interests of the two were perceived to be so different that it was inappropriate to combine them. However, there was also a strong moralistic streak in old Ontario which held that urban dwellers were tainted in ways that people living in idyllic rural settings close to the soil were not. Therefore, it was beneficial to have this separation to prevent any contamination. This philosophy meant that the cities and larger towns located within counties were separate from them for administrative purposes. The idea was that the county and the city could each make its own decisions without regard to the other.

Counties have never featured particularly strong governments. The traditional image of a county sees it as having a farmer-dominated council whose main interest is in keeping taxes as low as possible rather than in providing services. Counties were initially established to provide only those few services that were beyond the scope of their constituent municipalities. The main services provided by counties have been senior citizens' homes, roads, social assistance, economic development, land-use planning, libraries, museums, and reforestation.[6]

County council is composed of one or two representatives from each of its constituent towns, townships, and villages. The number of representatives from each jurisdiction is determined by its population, although the huge variance in population of the constituent municipalities causes significant deviations from strict representation-by-population. The representatives are usually the heads of council of the constituent municipalities.[7] The head of county council, the warden, is selected from the members of council to serve a one-year term.

The county system of government worked well when Ontario was a predominantly rural province and still works reasonably well in rural areas of the province. However, as the province has become more urbanized, the Baldwin Act prescription of separating urban and rural areas has become increasingly meaningless. The advent of the motor car, in particular, led to development of extensive suburbs, which meant that people could live in one jurisdiction, work in another, and shop in several others. This required a greater integration of urban areas and their surrounding rural municipalities, which in truth were often areas in transition to suburban or urban development. Suburbanization highlighted the major weakness in county government in urban areas – the separation of rural and urban areas – and set the stage for the creation of regional governments.

REGIONAL GOVERNMENT

Even though there were clear problems with the county system, the introduction of regional government has been very contentious. This section will discuss how it operates and what its critics have had to say about it.

The first two-tier metropolitan government in Ontario was Metropolitan Toronto, which was established in 1954. It functioned like a federal government superimposed on the thirteen area municipalities in the southern portion of York County. There were two major innovations in the Metro system. The first was the combination in one government of the urban areas of the city of Toronto with the rural and suburbanizing outer jurisdictions such as Etobicoke, North York, and Scarborough. The second innovation was that Metro, unlike the counties, would have a much stronger role in governing. It was given responsibility for providing a full range of municipal services.

Metro was initially seen as a one-of-a-kind innovation, and the Ontario government did not seriously consider extending this structure to other areas of the province until the 1960s. Between 1969 and 1974, the Ontario government created ten regional governments, one district municipality, and one restructured county in response to the demonstrated need to update the local-government structure. No new regional governments were created after 1974 because of the political backlash that resulted from the creation of the first batch of regions. The system established in 1974 has been left largely undisturbed until the recent changes instituted by the Harris government which will be discussed later.

The two major differences between the regional governments created in the 1969–74 period and their predecessors paralleled the changes made when Metro Toronto was created. One was the end of the separation of cities and larger towns from the regional governments. The governing structure of the new regional municipalities consisted of representatives from both urban and rural areas.

The second difference was that the regions were a more active (and expensive) form of government than county governments had been. This change was brought about partly because the regions were providing more services than the counties had, but it was also a function of a rapidly changing environment. The increasing urbanization and suburbanization that were occurring at this time required major government expenditure on infrastructure such as roads, parks, water and sewer services, and schools. Regional expenditures were also affected by increased federal and provincial standards in such areas as sewage treatment. Previously, most municipalities disposed of their sewage by dumping it untreated into water courses. At roughly the time that regional governments were formed, federal and provincial governments considerably changed their pollution-control standards. Thus, the newly formed regional governments were forced to make large new expenditures that their predecessors had not faced. It is certainly true that regional government has been more expensive than its county predecessor, but it is unfair to forget that the two governments provide very different kinds and levels of service.

THE ELECTORAL STRUCTURE

Regional government is governed by a regional council. Seats on the council are allocated among the area municipalities on a rough representation-by-population basis, but the smaller municipalities are usually overrepresented. Councillors are selected in several different ways. *Indirect election* means that a person serves on regional council by virtue of her or his election to some office in an area municipality, for instance, the mayor or top vote-getter in a ward. *Direct election* means that a person is elected directly to serve on regional council and does not serve on the council of any area municipality.

The different modes of election create a very different dynamic on council. Indirectly elected councillors owe their first allegiance to the area municipalities to which they are directly elected. Most councillors work part-time at their position, which makes the job of regional councillor the secondary aspect of a part-time job. A person in that position is not likely to bring much energy or leadership to the regional council table. In more extreme cases, a local councillor gets elected on a 'region-bashing' platform and then find herself or himself serving on regional council.

Directly elected councillors do not have the same divided loyalties. Their reputation depends on making regional government work. When regional government was created, only Niagara had directly elected councillors, but over the years other regions have switched to having at least some positions directly elected.[8]

The head of regional council is the regional chairman.[9] In the past, all regional chairmen were selected in the same manner – a vote of council at its first meeting after a municipal election. By statute, council could select anyone for this position; the person did not have to be an elected councillor or even a resident of the region, although, in practice, councils usually either reappointed the previous chairman or selected a member of council as chairman. If the person selected holds a seat on council, he or she must resign and be replaced in that seat. In Hamilton-Wentworth and Ottawa-Carleton, the chairman is now elected by popular vote of all electors. This is a relatively recent innovation that has been discussed in other regions, but has not been adopted elsewhere.

DIVISION OF RESPONSIBILITIES

The division of responsibilities between the regions and the area municipalities varies widely between regions. It would probably be a mistake to think that all decisions about the division of responsibilities were well thought out and made on the basis of rational analysis. However, to the extent that conscious decisions were made, it seems likely that three general principles were employed in dividing responsibilities – economies of scale, responsiveness to local interests, and concern for protection of regional interests.

Services that generate economies of scale have usually been assigned to the regional level. Thus, responsibility for water purification and sewage treatment is generally found at the regional level, while responsibility for delivery of water and local sewage lines usually rests with the area municipality because there are fewer economies of scale to be generated.

Some functions have been lodged with the region because it is better able to take the long view and protect broader regional interests such as the preservation of unique natural areas. This is one reason why the region has a dominant role in land-use planning in all regions.

Services where responsiveness to local sentiments is most important have usually been allocated to the area municipalities. Some examples of these are the maintenance of local roads and recreation and cultural programs.

CRITICISMS OF REGIONAL GOVERNMENT

Regional government has been the subject of so much bitter criticism over the years that it is difficult to summarize all the negative comments that have been made. Attacking regional government has become such a significant part of the popular culture that many people have a knee-jerk reaction against regional government that they then have difficulty supporting with hard evidence.

Some criticism has flowed from the fact that the creation of regional government disturbed the traditional rural-urban split discussed above. Many people in rural areas did not want to be combined with the nearby urban areas, a process they viewed as subjecting them to the problems they saw developing in those areas. They also lamented the loss of local identity associated with the consolidation of smaller villages and hamlets into larger centres. At a more basic level, they resented having to pay property taxes to support urban levels of service when they were quite happy with the lower levels of service they had been receiving for years.

The cost of regional government has been another sore point. The previous county structures were very weak and provided only basic levels of service in most areas. When regional government was created, it was given a much broader mandate than the county had and the number of employees and size of operation increased accordingly. People perceived that property taxes were increasing rapidly as a result of this new layer of government.

A third criticism has been that regional government was imposed by the province without adequate consultation with local citizens. This viewpoint suggests that, while regional government worked well in Toronto, it was an unnecessarily complicated and expensive structure to impose on other areas of the province.

A fourth criticism is that two-tier government has resulted in duplication of services. In many cases, each tier of government has departments responsible for planning, roads and traffic, economic development, and other shared functions.

However, there is another side to these arguments. Some people like to wax poetic about protecting idyllic country settings from the ravages of urbanity, but the fact is that the increasing number of people being drawn to urban areas would have resulted in an encroachment on rural areas with or without regional government. The only question was whether that encroachment would occur in a haphazard manner or there would be a modicum of planning and improved service delivery to accompany this growth.

The cost of regional government has certainly been greater than the cost of the county system, although the level of increase might not be as great as some have argued when raw figures are adjusted to eliminate the effects of inflation and increasing population.[10] However, it is inappropriate to focus only on the increasing cost without also discussing the increasing level and quality of the service provided. Regional government was created at a time when both federal and provincial governments were interested in improving the quality of government services. As discussed earlier, this imposed a significant cost on regional government. Considering the tremendous pressure coming from both citizens and other governments to increase standards, it should not be surprising that the expenditures of regional governments exceeded those of their county predecessors.

Because of the size and scope of regional governments, it is likely that they have been able to do things that no area municipality could accomplish alone. The tremendous cost of new water and sewage-treatment facilities has already been cited, but other examples could be seen in the extensive Metro parks system in Toronto, the significant improvements in public transit in Ottawa-Carleton, and the rapid increase in infrastructure needed for development in the regions around Toronto.

The third criticism of regional government – that it was imposed on local citizens against their wills by aggressive and technocratic empire-builders at Queen's Park – is simply incorrect. By the early 1960s, it was becoming clear that the existing system of county government was outmoded for reasons discussed earlier. This was a feeling that was developing in many areas of the province, but was at first not accepted by provincial officials.[11] The groups advocating reform did not always agree on what form the changes should take, but they all recognized the need for reform. The only truth in the 'imposition' argument is that the province did have to decide on specific boundaries, electoral systems, and timing in the absence of local agreement on these details. However, the idea that the province imposed regional government on areas with no prior consultation with or input from local groups is simply incorrect.

The final criticism discussed above dealt with the duplication of services provided by the two tiers of government. This is an area where problems exist, but in some cases the problems are not as serious as they first appear. Two-tier land-use planning can cause difficulties for citizens because there can be confusion about which government has responsibility for which decisions. This is exacerbated when officials at one tier use the other tier as a scapegoat when problems arise. For other services, the apparent duplication is not really a problem. For example, there are two road systems, but the economies to be derived from combining them are not clear. In some areas, one tier already looks after some of the roads of the other tier on a contractual basis. A detailed study in Niagara determined that this system worked fairly well.[12]

On balance, the system of regional government has been beneficial, although there are clearly some problems. A later section will discuss the future of regional government.

LOCAL GOVERNMENT IN NORTHERN ONTARIO

Local government in the north has some similarities to that in the south.[13] The one regional government in the north – Sudbury – operates just like regional governments in the south. There are also cities, towns, townships, and villages that operate similar to those in the south, with the exception that they are one-tier governments. There is nothing similar to the counties in the north; all areas outside Sudbury are governed by one-tier governments. There are also large areas, sparsely populated tracts with effectively no local government as it is known in the south, or at best very limited forms of government providing limited services.

There are two structures that are unique to the north – improvement districts and unorganized territories. 'Improvement Districts are ... in essence, probationary forms of local government. They have the powers of a township but their board of trustees are [sic] appointed and are subjected to supervision by the province concerning by-laws and financial matters. They are usually set up in areas where new resource industries are being located and there is no established municipality.'[14]

As the name suggests, unorganized territories are not really local governments at all. Rather, they are small settlements in which services are provided either directly by the provincial government or by special-purpose bodies such as boards of education, local road boards, or recreation committees.

A Quantitative Overview of Local Government

Table 1 (p. 142) provides an overview of the number of local governments in Ontario.[15] The figures include all municipalities and some of the larger, higher-profile special-purpose bodies. This table illustrates the fact that traditional municipal governments are only one part of the total local-government scene.[16] If this table included all special-purpose bodies such as police services boards, cemetery boards, and boards of management of business improvement areas, the number of special-purpose bodies would easily exceed two thousand.

Figure 2 (p. 143) shows that the main sources of local government revenue in recent years have been property taxes and provincial transfer payments.[17] In the 1970s the importance of the property tax declined, but in the 1980s, as the importance of provincial transfers has declined, the property tax and user charges both became more important. The increase in the importance of user charges has been one of the major changes in municipal finance in recent times. Unfortunately, the most recent figures available are from 1991. More recent figures would certainly show a further decline in transfer payments and a continuing increase in user charges.

Some municipalities also receive a significant amount of funding in

TABLE 1
The scope of local government in Ontario, 1990

Municipal governments	
Regions, district municipalities, and restructured counties	13
Counties	26
Cities and borough	50
Towns	150
Villages	119
Townships	476
Improvement districts	5
Total municipal governments	839
Special-purpose bodies	
Boards of education	126
Public utilities commissions	363
Children's aid societies	56
Conservation authorities	38
Total special-purpose bodies	583
Total local governments	1422

Source: Ministry of Municipal Affairs, *Municipal Directory 1990*
(Queen's Printer for Ontario, 1990).

development charges. These are fees imposed on developers of new lots to cover the cost of the infrastructure that must be installed to service the new areas. This money is used mainly for the construction of roads, sewers, parks, and so forth. This is not a huge source of funding for the entire municipal system, but it is a very important funding source for growing municipalities. Without development charges, the cost of infrastructure would be a huge burden imposed on existing taxpayers. Development charges are effectively added to the cost of new development and so force the new residents to pay for the full cost of their lots. In most places, the charges amount to several thousand dollars and so substantially increase the cost of new development. These charges have been blamed for slowing down the growth of new development.

Figures 3 and 4 focus on the expenditure side of the budget. Figure 3 illustrates the impact of education on local expenditure. (Transportation is also shown to provide perspective.) Education must be shown on a separate graph because of problems of scale. It constitutes such a high percentage of local expenditure that it dwarfs the other categories. While expenditure on education has been declining slightly as a percentage of

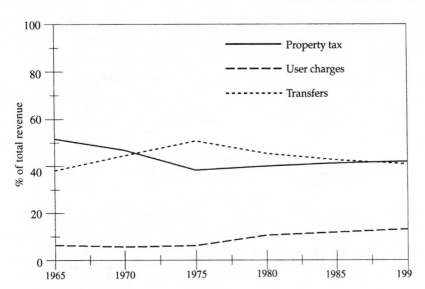

FIGURE 2 Municipal revenue, 1965–91

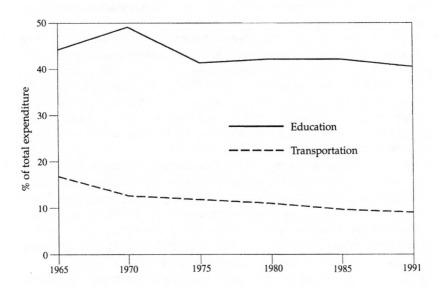

FIGURE 3 Municipal expenditure, 1965–91

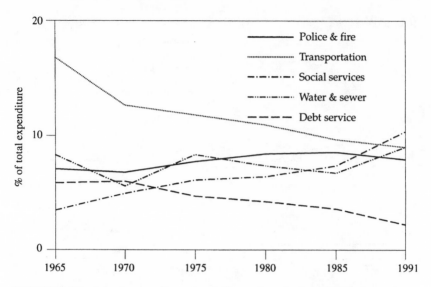

FIGURE 4 Municipal expenditure (excluding education), 1965–91

total expenditure in recent years, it is by far the largest single service on which local funds are spent.

Figure 4, which shows expenditure on the main expenditure categories other than education, illustrates some significant changes over the last twenty-five years. Expenditure on transportation (mostly roads, but an increasing amount on public transit) has declined significantly, while the major gainer has been social services. Another interesting trend is the significant decline in expenditure on debt service. This trend is at variance with the increasing expenditure on debt service at other levels of government.

One of the most interesting facts illustrated in figures 3 and 4 is the large amount of local-government expenditure that is beyond the control of municipal governments. The largest single object of local expenditure is education. This expenditure is controlled by boards of education, which are totally autonomous from municipal governments. Another major item of expenditure – policing – is under the control of police services boards, which are also not controlled by the municipal government. Thus, municipal governments control slightly more than half of total local-government expenditures, although they receive much more scrutiny than boards of education or police services boards. The actual level of municipal control is reduced even further when one considers the extent of provincially mandated programs and the effect of conditional transfer payments on municipal autonomy.

Municipal governments are likely to be in better financial condition than other levels of government. They are not allowed to go into debt except to fund major capital assets that will benefit future periods. However, there is no question that the reduction in provincial transfer payments and the downloading of certain provincial responsibilities onto to local governments have imposed significant financial problems on local governments. This and other problems on the horizon will be the topic of the next section.

Problems Facing Local Government

There are several problems facing local governments in Ontario. These problems will likely affect different communities differently, but few communities will escape some contact with most of the problems mentioned in this section.

THE PROPERTY TAX

The property-tax assessment system in Ontario is probably the worst and most antiquated in Canada.[18] In other provinces, property is assessed at its fair market value and the property tax is imposed on this value. In Ontario, the assessment system has been allowed to get very far out of date. In some communities, the last complete assessment was done in the 1940s, so properties in these municipalities still carry their 1940s values. This means that when an assessor assigns a value to a house built last year, he or she must engage in the fairy-tale activity of assuming that the house was built in the year of the last assessment for that municipality and assign a value accordingly. Assigning a 1947 value to a structure built in 1997 is an impossible task.

The lack of an objective standard creates numerous problems. In most communities, there is a feeling that new homes are assessed at a higher relative value than older homes and that apartments and commercial/industrial premises are assessed at a higher value than single-family homes. It is difficult to obtain firm evidence on this point, but to the extent that some properties are underassessed relative to others, the property-tax burden within a community is not shared equitably.

This problem also raises concerns about equity between municipalities. Area municipalities make contributions to the school boards and to the upper-tier counties and regions based on the municipality's share of the total property taxes within the larger unit. If different area municipalities have different assessment systems, then it is difficult to know if the total upper-tier or school-board levy has been allocated appropriately. The current patchwork arrangement requires the use of complex formulas to try to ensure some level of equity in these situations. However, there can be no assurance that equity is actually attained in the absence of some objective measure such as current market value.

This situation has been allowed to get into its current poor condition because succeeding provincial governments have not had the political will to introduce a more appropriate system. The political problem is that establishing fair market value will impose large changes in the status quo. Some taxpayers who have been paying an unreasonably low property tax (considering the real value of their property) will see their taxes increased significantly. This course has obvious political ramifications.

Currently the provincial government has sidestepped this issue by allowing individual municipalities to institute a system of market-value assessment if they choose. A growing number of municipalities have accepted this approach, but it is becoming obvious that this is only a piecemeal solution to a broad and serious problem. The only real solution is a provincial requirement that fair market-value assessment be used across the province. The longer the current inadequate situation remains, the worse the inequities become. The question is whether any government will have the political courage to correct this problem.

FINANCIAL PROBLEMS

By any measure, local governments have not been excessive spenders. Their share of gross domestic product has remained relatively constant over the last seventy years, while federal and provincial spending has been rising significantly.[19] Provincial legislation preventing them from borrowing to meet current operating expenditures has limited their debt. Surveys frequently indicate that the general public perceives that municipal governments provide services more efficiently than do other governments.[20]

However, there are pressures on both the revenue and expenditure sides of municipal budgets that do not bode well for the future. On the revenue side, there are the serious problems with the property-tax assessment system discussed above, but there are also concerns about the regressive nature of the property tax because it has a heavier impact on low-income than on high-income taxpayers. There has long been considerable controversy around this issue,[21] but the most recent evidence seems to be quite persuasive about the regressive nature of the tax.[22] For this reason, there is a great deal of reluctance to depend too heavily on the property tax.

An additional problem on the revenue side of the budget has been the decline in the level of provincial transfer payments. The first economic statement by the new Conservative government elected in 1995 stated that transfer payments to municipalities would be cut by over 40 per cent in two years.[23] Since provincial transfers account for approximately 40 per cent of municipal revenue, this amounts to a 16 per cent drop in municipal revenue – a tremendous loss for municipalities to digest in a very short time.

This cut is happening at the same time that the provincial government is downloading more responsibilities onto local governments. For example, the provincial government is in the process of transferring the care of a substantial number of provincial highways to municipalities with no increase in funding. The province is also considering transferring responsibility for property-tax assessment to municipalities. In addition to cuts in transfer payments to municipalities, the province is also reducing transfers to culture and recreation organizations, which will then likely request funding from municipalities to make up the shortfall.

The combination of reductions in provincial transfers while shifting more responsibilities to local governments will pose serious problems for local governments. The desire of the provincial treasurer to reduce the provincial deficit is laudable, but there needs to be an understanding that there are limits to how much this battle of deficit reduction can be fought on the backs of municipalities.

Relations with Special-Purpose Bodies

As discussed earlier, the complete system of local government in Ontario comprises more than just the municipalities that have been the major focus of this discussion so far. Many agencies, boards, and commissions have grown up around local governments. The formal and informal relationships between these bodies and municipalities vary quite widely. In some cases – for instance, school boards – the special-purpose bodies are wholly autonomous, sharing only the same tax base with municipalities, while in other cases (such as tourism advisory coun-

TABLE 2
Examples of special-purpose bodies

School board
Police services board
Conservation authority
Children's aid society
Hydroelectric commission
Committee of adjustment
Land division committee
Public health unit
Local architectural conservation advisory committee
Museum board
Trade and convention centre board
Economic development agency
Tourism advisory council

Note: These are meant as examples only. Not all
municipalities have all of these agencies, and there
are many that are not listed. Also the exact names
of the agencies vary in different municipalities.

cils) they are purely advisory bodies under the direct control of the
municipal council.

The existence of several bodies servicing the same clientele poses
problems. Both municipal social-service agencies and local children's aid
societies provide services to families. Because these two organizations
are separate and autonomous from one another, there is no way of
knowing that all the needs of families are being looked after in the most
effective manner.

The Future of Local Government in Ontario

THE COMMON SENSE REVOLUTION AND MUNICIPAL GOVERNMENT

In the 1995 election, the Progressive Conservatives led by Mike Harris
campaigned on a platform contained in the booklet *The Common Sense
Revolution*. Though it has sections devoted to several policy areas, *The
Common Sense Revolution* does not contain a section labelled 'local government.' If you want to know what the Harris government's views on
local government are, you must go to the subsection headed 'Less Government' in the section headed 'Doing Better for Less.' This section
makes it clear that this government's view of local governments is that

---

LESS GOVERNMENT

Canadians are probably the most over-governed people in the world. **We do not need every layer – federal, provincial, quasi-governmental bodies, regional, municipal and school board – that we have now.** We must rationalize the regional and municipal levels to avoid the overlap and duplication that now exist.

The example being set by a Harris Government, of a 24% reduction in the number of MPPs and a 20% cut in non-priority spending, will set the benchmark for municipal politicians and trustees. We will sit down with municipalities to discuss ways of reducing government entanglement and bureaucracy with an eye to eliminating waste and duplication as well as unfair downloading by the province.

Different solutions may well apply in different regions across this province. But by the end of our first term, taxpayers deserve a restructuring of these cumbersome bureaucracies.

Resolving the issue of efficient local government will take a great deal of hard work. It is rare that politicians and bureaucrats voluntarily surrender power. But it must happen. **It's time to stop government growth once and for all.**

> This will save Ontario taxpayers $250 million.

(*Common Sense Revolution*, 17; emphasis in original).

---

they are a 'cumbersome bureaucracy' that needs to be restructured to 'eliminat[e] waste and duplication.' Earlier in this chapter, it was mentioned that opinion polls indicate that the public generally feels that local governments are the best managed and most efficient levels of government. This is not a view shared by the Harris government.

As soon as the new government came to power in 1995, it began its assault on municipalities. In a peculiar one-two punch delivered in August 1995, the minister of municipal affairs warned delegates to the AMO annual conference that their transfer payments would be reduced by 20 per cent, while the premier said that the two levels of government should start acting like partners instead of schoolchildren fighting over who stole the candy.[24] If Mr Harris had been listening to his minister of municipal affairs, he would have known who stole the candy.

Under continual questioning in the legislature, the minister of municipal affairs stated that municipalities would be given more autonomy under this government so they would be happy to have a reduction in transfer payments.[25] This is a bit like saying that the poor and the rich have the same right to invest in the stock market. Granting more nominal autonomy with one hand, while using the other hand to withdraw the funding that allows municipalities to exercise that autonomy is a totally disingenuous gesture.

Actually a reduction in transfer payments can be beneficial in that the entire system of transfer payments – that is, spending someone else's money – muddles accountability, but this reduction must be balanced by a shift elsewhere to restore the municipality's financial status. It is true that the Harris government has been sympathetic to an increase in user charges, but municipalities have been using these for years anyway. What is more frightening to municipalities is that the minister is making noises about reducing the ability of municipalities to use development charges.[26]

So how does the Ontario government suggest that municipalities deal with this problem of reduced resources? When this issue was brought up in the legislature, the parliamentary assistant to the minister of municipal affairs argued that restructuring is the panacea that will allow municipalities to cope with any problem thrown at them.[27]

RESTRUCTURING AND AMALGAMATION AS PANACEA

The idea that restructuring and amalgamation would effect major savings is certainly in touch with the popular sentiment regarding improving the operation of governments. The 1990s could probably be characterized as the age of restructuring in government. Virtually all governments at all levels have come to feel that problems of efficiency and concerns about the size of government could be solved by the restructuring, and particularly amalgamation, of governmental units. The logic is that if there are fewer politicians and fewer government organizations, then less money will be spent. This is one of the arguments against two-tier regional governments – more politicians create more expenditure.

The empirical evidence that restructuring and amalgamation are the panaceas that some have thought is fairly weak at best, but this has not slowed the trend towards restructuring and amalgamation. The federal government undertook a major restructuring in June 1993 that reduced the number of cabinet portfolios but had little effect on its level of expenditure. When Mike Harris became premier, he boasted of having a small cabinet.

There had previously been several waves of amalgamation in local government in Ontario. Through the 1960s, the number of municipal-government units was reduced slightly from over 900 to about 840. At about the same time, the number of school boards was drastically reduced from 1300 to 125.[28] The conventional wisdom was that this was beneficial, although there is no empirical evidence that it reduced expenditure.

In the 1980s and early 1990s, there was some restructuring and amalgamation. Brant and Lambton[29] counties were restructured in ways that increased the size of their major cities, Brantford and Sarnia, respectively. A major restructuring occurred in Simcoe county (the Barrie-Orillia area), which resulted in a reduction in the number of area municipalities.[30] Again, the empirical evidence on the increase in efficiency was unclear. Many people liked to point to one particular municipality in Simcoe County where expenditure seemed to decline after amalgamation, but deeper examination raised questions about the validity of this claim.[31]

The Harris government seems intent on continuing this trend. To accomplish this goal it passed Bill 26, the ominously titled 'An Act to Achieve Fiscal Savings and to Promote Economic Prosperity through Public Sector Restructuring, Streamlining and Efficiency and to implement other aspects of the Government's Agenda.' The bill itself and the hype around its introduction created the impression that the provincial government was intent on reducing the number of municipalities by amalgamation. In spite of the minister of municipal affairs's protestations that amalgamations would generally be voluntary, municipalities felt that the atmosphere was such that if they did not institute voluntary amalgamations, they would be subject to amalgamations imposed by the province.

There are also questions about the future of county and regional government. The minister of municipal affairs has questioned whether two-tier governments are needed, but he has been careful not to suggest which tier should be eliminated.[32] At about the same time, the chairs of regional governments produced a document that raised the possibility of eliminating lower-tier municipalities at least in some areas.[33]

However, there is some question about whether restructuring and amalgamation are the panacea that some envision. In a recent edition of *Municipal World*, both C.R. Tindal,[34] a long-time academic commentator on local government, and Joseph Kushner,[35] an economist and veteran municipal councillor, raised serious questions about whether larger units of local government were necessarily more efficient. In separate articles, they both noted that one of the presumed advantages of consolidation of units is economies of scale, yet the empirical evidence is that economies of scale for most local services are attained at fairly low levels of population. Kushner, the economist, reminds us that there can also be diseconomies of scale – when organizations become too large, the unit cost of providing a service actually increases. Tindal argues that for the few services that attain maximum economies at higher levels, a better solution might be the extension of existing inter-municipal agreements to share services rather than the more radical change of amalgamation.

The strength of municipal government is that its small size and local nature mean that citizens feel close to it and know that they can have a real influence on its activities. Citizens' antipathy to regional government might well stem from its large size and separation from the local community. Obviously, the larger a government becomes, the further it appears to be removed from local control. Thoughtless amalgamation could provide the worst of both worlds – increased costs through diseconomies of scale and greater alienation of citizens from larger units of governments.

Who Does What and Who Pays for What?[36]

The Harris government has also been concerned with the division of responsibilities for the delivery of services between the provincial and municipal governments. The provincial government appointed David Crombie, former mayor of Toronto and a highly respected municipal expert, to head a group dubbed the 'Who Does What?' panel that had a mandate to review this division of responsibilities. The province did not accept all the recommendations of the panel, but there have been major changes in who does what that are summarized below.

Increased provincial transfer payments will greatly reduce dependence on the residential property tax for education funding. As indicated earlier in this chapter, education has taken up about half of the total property tax collected, so this was a huge windfall for municipalities, equal to half of the residential property tax collected. Alas, that is not the end of the story. At the same time, the province is shifting responsibility for funding public transit, public housing, and an increased portion of social assistance to the municipalities. While there is a certain fiscal balance here of increasing access to a revenue source and shifting responsibility for spending, there are some potential problems.

First, there might appear to be a balance for the entire municipal system, but that system is in fact composed of over eight hundred municipalities. It is likely that some municipalities will benefit from this change, but others could be severely damaged. A focus on the overall numbers obscures this very important consideration.

Second, increasing municipal responsibility for social assistance is problematic. Ontario is the only province in Canada in which municipalities have such a major role in social assistance. The problem is that social assistance is a redistributive program and it is highly problematic to redistribute wealth in a small geographic area. If a particular municipality is hit with the closing of a major industry, it will suffer double damage. Its ability to collect property tax will be reduced at the same time that large numbers of residents will be seeking social assistance and related government services. The concern in that this could produce a situation similar to what has happened in many American cities, where rich people have moved to exclusive enclaves to escape responsibility for social services, while poor people have remained clustered in poor cities that do not have the resources to provide adequate municipal services.

Governing the Greater Toronto Area

The structure of governance of Metropolitan Toronto has not changed significantly between 1954 and 1997. Over this time, the governing process has become much more complex and population pressures have caused the greater Toronto area (GTA) to expand into the suburbs to the east, north, and west of the city. This growth has caused considerable pressure to search for new ways of delivering services such as transportation and solid-waste disposal. The Golden Task Force was appointed by the NDP government to consider this issue. It recommended the creation of a GTA government that would be larger than the boundaries of Metro Toronto.

The Harris government did not accept this recommendation. Instead, it decided to restructure the Toronto area by eliminating the area municipalities and creating one large metropolitan government with the same boundaries as the previous Metropolitan Toronto. The intent is to reduce the number of municipal jurisdictions, reduce the number of politicians, and increase efficiency in government. The plan is that this new government would take effect with the municipal elections scheduled for November 1997.

The plan created a storm of opposition. Citizens who are attached to their existing area municipalities are upset at seeing those disappear. The efficiency benefits have not been demonstrated unequivocally. Varying studies indicate that the consolidated municipality can either save huge amounts or cost huge amounts depending on various assumptions. Despite an unprecedented grass-roots movement against the so-called Megacity bill, the province passed it into law in April 1997. This has created repercussions in regional governments, which assume that they are next in line for this treatment.

Conclusion

Local government is an important, but often overlooked, part of the governing process in Ontario. It struggles to reconcile two ambivalent roles – organ of local autonomy and instrument for local service delivery by the provincial government. It is now at an important juncture in its development. Radical reductions in provincial funding are forcing local governments to rethink their roles in the governing process. It will be very interesting to watch how this role changes in the next few years.

Notes

1 There is some question about whether there are major economies of scale to be captured in most services provided by local government. This will be discussed in more detail later, but the point here is that most people *believe* that economies of scale do exist.
2 Makuch, *Canadian Municipal and Planning Law*, chap. 4 and passim.
3 Ontario Ministry of Municipal Affairs, *Annual Report – 1987–1988*, opposite p. 1.
4 A partial listing of the legislation under which the Board obtains its powers is set out in OMB, *Annual Report '92–'94*, 12–13.
5 AMO *Annual Report*, 1994–5, inside back cover.
6 Ontario, Advisory Committee on County Government, *Patterns for the Future*, 48.
7 One of the criticisms of the existing arrangement is that the determination of which official goes to county council is complicated and not easy to understand. For the precise rules, see ibid., section III.

8 Mellon, 'Reforming the Electoral System of Metropolitan Toronto,' 38–56.

9 The sexist term 'chairman' is specified in the legislation. It has been suggested by several different bodies that this title be changed, but the province remains committed to the preservation of such language.

10 Niagara Region Review Commission, *Report and Recommendations*, chap. 5.

11 This situation is well documented with regard to Niagara in ibid., chap. 2.

12 Lionel D. Feldman Consulting Ltd, *Public Works in the Niagara Region* (Niagara Falls, Ont.: Niagara Region Review Commission, 1988).

13 There is very little written about the structure of local government in the north, but see Geoffrey R. Weller, 'The Evolution of Local Government in Northern Ontario.'

14 Ibid., 6.

15 The 1990 figures are the most recent available. These numbers change very little from year to year.

16 Warren Magnusson, 'The Local State in Canada: Theoretical Perspectives,' *Canadian Public Administration* 28, no. 4 (Winter 1985): 575–99.

17 The data in this and the following graphs is derived from the Statistics Canada CANSIM database. These are the most recent figures available. It is likely that there was little change between 1991 and 1995. As discussed later, large changes will likely be seen after 1995.

18 The full details of this problem have been set out in several places: see Niagara Region Review Commission, *Report and Recommendations*, chap. 6; Richard M. Bird and N. Enid Slack, *Urban Public Finance in Canada* (Toronto: Butterworths, 1983), 69–71; and Harry M. Kitchen, *Local Government Finance in Canada* (Toronto: Canadian Tax Foundation, 1984), 191–200.

19 Treff and Cook, *Finances of the Nation – 1995*, 18:6–7.

20 *Gallup Report*, 22 January 1983.

21 Richard Bird, 'The Incidence of the Property Tax: Old Wine in New Bottles?' *Canadian Public Policy* 2 (1976): 323–34. Cf. Ronald Meng and W. Irwin Gillespie, 'The Regressivity of Property Taxes in Canada: Another Look,' *Canadian Tax Journal* 34 (November–December 1986): 1417–30.

22 Ontario Fair Tax Commission, *Fair Taxation in a Changing World* (Toronto: University of Toronto Press, 1993), chap. 28.

23 Ontario, Legislature, *Debates*, 29 November 1995, 1113.

24 Martin Mittelstaedt, 'Harris tells municipalities it's time to be partners,' *Globe and Mail*, 23 August 1995.

25 Ontario, Legislature, *Debates*, 30 October 1995, 506; 1 November 1995, 606 and 609; 22 November 1995, 943 and 946.

26 Ibid., *Debates*, 31 October 1995, 542; 16 November 1995, 784.

27 Ibid., 2 November 1995, 691.

28 *Report of the Commission on the Financing of Elementary and Secondary Educa-tion in Ontario* (December 1985), 21.
29 David Foulds, 'A Local Solution to a Local Problem: Restructuring Comes to Sarnia-Lambton County,' *Municipal World*, November 1989, 296–7; Byron Montgomery, *Annexation and Restructuring in Sarnia-Lambton: A Model for Ontario County Government* (London: University of Western Ontario, 1990).
30 'South Simcoe Municipalities to Be Amalgamated,' *Municipal World*, February 1990, 33.
31 Editorial, 'Amalgamation or Misrepresentation?' *Municipal World*, March 1996, 2.
32 Allan Leach, 'The Future of Local Government: Efficient, Effective, Rel-evant,' *Cordillera Institute Journal*, December 1995, 7.
33 Regional Chairs of Ontario, *In Pursuit of Better Government* (October 1995).
34 C. Richard Tindal, 'Municipal Restructuring: The Myth and the Reality,' *Municipal World*, March 1996, 3–8.
35 Joseph Kushner, 'Municipal Reform: Is Consolidation the Answer?' *Munici-pal World*, March 1996, 10–11.
36 The material in this section was accurate at the time of writing in May 1997. However, this area is changing so rapidly that readers must seek more recent sources to ensure the accuracy of the details of changes described below.

Bibliography

Association of Municipalities of Ontario. *Annual Report* (various years).
Colton, Timothy J. *Big Daddy: Frederick G. Gardiner and the Building of Metropoli-tan Toronto*. Toronto: University of Toronto Press, 1980.
Higgins, Donald J.H. *Local and Urban Politics in Canada*. Toronto: Gage Educa-tional Publishing Company, 1986.
Leach, Allan, 'The Future of Local Government: Efficient, Effective, Relevant.' *Cordillera Institute Journal*, December 1995, 5–7.
Makuch, Stanley M. *Canadian Municipal and Planning Law*. Toronto: Carswell, 1983.
Mellon, Hugh, 'Reforming the Electoral System of Metropolitan Toronto: Doing Away with Dual Representation.' *Canadian Public Administration* 36, no. 1 (Spring 1993): 38–56.
Niagara Region Review Commission. *Report and Recommendations*. Toronto: Queen's Printer, 1989.

Ontario. Advisory Committee on County Government. *Patterns for the Future.*
  November 1987.
– Consultation Committee to the Minister of Municipal Affairs. *County
  Government in Ontario.* 1989.
– Royal Commission on Taxation. *Report.* Toronto: Queen's Printer, 1967.
Ontario Ministry of Municipal Affairs. *Annual Report – 1990–1991.* Queen's
  Printer for Ontario, 1991.
Ontario Ministry of Municipal Affairs and Housing. *Restructured Municipal
  Government in Ontario: Basic Information Booklet.* 1984.
Ontario Municipal Board. *Annual Report '92–'94.* Queen's Printer for Ontario,
  1995.
Plunkett, T.J., and George Betts. *The Management of Canadian Urban Government.*
  Kingston: Institute of Local Government, Queen's University, 1978.
Rose, Albert. *Governing Metropolitan Toronto: A Social and Political Analysis.*
  Berkeley: University of California Press, 1972.
Tindal, C.R. *You and Your Local Government.* Toronto: Ontario Municipal
  Management Development Board, 1982.
Tindal, C.R., and S. Nobes Tindal. *Local Government in Canada.* 4th ed. Toronto:
  McGraw-Hill Ryerson, 1995.
Treff, Karin, and Ted Cook. *Finances of the Nation – 1995.* Toronto: Canadian Tax
  Foundation, 1995.
Weller, Geoffrey R. 'The Evolution of Local Government in Northern Ontario.'
  Paper presented to the Annual Meeting of the Canadian Political Science
  Association, 2–5 June 1980.

SEVEN

Ontario in Confederation: The Not-So-Friendly Giant

David Cameron and Richard Simeon

Linchpin, prime beneficiary, milch cow, guardian of Confederation, smug defender of its own dominance. These are just some of the images that have been used to characterize Ontario's role in the Canadian federal system.

Geographically, economically, culturally, and politically, Ontario has always been at the centre of the federation, and has had the greatest stake in its maintenance. Until recently, most such images suggested a province and a people secure and comfortable in their perceptions of the federal system, and of their role within it. As by far the largest province in population, Ontario could be assured that whatever party was in power in Ottawa, a large proportion of that party's seats would come from the province, and its interests could not be ignored. As the largest and wealthiest economy, it could be assured that federal fiscal and economic policies would be crafted to satisfy Ontario's interests. Its industrial economy shaped by Sir John A. Macdonald's National Policy, Ontario was closely linked to the burgeoning agricultural and resource economies of the west. Sharing the great river valley of the St Lawrence and a long history, Ontario could have a close relationship with Quebec, and often act as an interlocutor between that province and other regions of the country.

In such circumstances, it was easy to believe that what was good for Ontario was good for the country, and vice versa. There was little tension between citizens' identities as Canadians and Ontarians: indeed, were they not the same thing? Other provinces and regions could develop strong regional identities and grievances – often directed at Ontario and its perceived dominance of the central government. Other provinces could press for change, as in the west's pressure for an end to the 'neocolonialism' of the National Policy, or Quebec's resistance to the federally led growth of the welfare state in the postwar period and its later calls to become *maîtres chez nous*. Ontario, by contrast, exemplified the status quo; it had no agenda for radical change. Instead, despite a few spectacular battles with Ottawa, discussed below, the provincial government saw itself as the mediator, the balance wheel in intergovernmental relations, concerned above all with harmonious and cooperative relations, and with political and economic stability.

In recent years, however, the imagery has begun to change. There is an emerging sense that Ontario is itself a region, in a highly regionalized country; that its position of dominance is threatened; that its interests no longer necessarily coincide with those of Ottawa; and that Ontario has its own grievances to pursue, and its own interests to defend. The first inkling of this change was during the 'energy wars' of the 1970s, when it appeared that a historic shift in the terms of trade between resource producers, largely in the west, and manufacturing centred in Ontario threatened the province's economic role. 'Petro-dollars, not constitutional lawyers' declared an Ontario position paper, 'are re-writing our constitutional system.'[1] In 1993, Premier Bob Rae asserted that Ontario had become 'the part of Canada that dare not speak its name.' It was time to abandon the 'premise that everyone else could speak ill of Ontario, and at the same time that this inherently wealthy place would continue to bankroll Canada.'[2] Premier Mike Harris, advocating the creation of a more functional federation by streamlining government and eliminating waste and duplication of services, declared: 'These changes, if done right, will lead to a country more decentralized in some respects and a national government that does less but does what it must well. Fiscal realities mean that no single government can dictate uniform behaviour across the country.'[3] The uncertainties and ambiguities in Ontario's role in Confederation today are nicely captured in the title of Thomas Courchene's article 'What Does Ontario Want?'[4]

This chapter seeks to explain these changes by examining the role that the province has played in Confederation since 1867. We pay particular attention to the recent seismic shifts in the Canadian and global economies, in Ontario's own social structure, and in the politics of national unity, all of which profoundly challenge the premises on which Ontario's historic role had been based, and which have provoked much soul-searching about the very nature of Ontario as a political community and about its position in the federal system. Do these shifts signal a profound change in Ontario's role in the federal system: in the goals it pursues, the political strategies it engages in, the alliances it forms? Are its relationships with Ottawa, Quebec, and other provinces changing? Is the assertiveness that recent Ontario governments have displayed a mere blip, brought on by specific events, or is something deeper going on? And if so, what are the implications for the future of Canadian federalism?

The Conventional Understanding of Ontario

In a 1968 article, A.R.M. Lower asked, 'Does Ontario Exist?' He concluded that a province with so little evident collective will could hardly be regarded as a political unit in any conventional sense.[5] In 1975, another historian, Peter Oliver, asked, 'Why should anyone attempt to write the history of a region which isn't' or 'try to define the regional characteristics of a society so elusive as to defy definition.'[6] Indeed, in most Canadian historiography, 'Ontario has not been seen as a region. Almost unconsciously, historians have equated the history of the province with that of the nation and have often depicted the interests of other regions as obstacles to the unity and welfare of Canada.'[7]

There are powerful reasons for this equation of Ontario and Canada, and for the historic lack of definition of Ontario as a distinct region. First is the enormous diversity and sprawling character of Ontario.[8] The differences between the wealthy, ethnically diverse, and industrial 'golden horseshoe,' the agricultural regions of the southwest, and the resource-producing north replicate many of the divisions in the country as a whole. It is therefore much more difficult for Ontario to speak with a single, united voice than it is for Saskatchewan, Alberta, or Newfoundland. Second, not surprisingly, given their numbers and geographic position, Ontario residents, of all provincial populations, tend to identify most strongly with the national government and the national community; there is little historic basis on which to mobilize a sense of Ontario as a region with strong grievances against a centre that they largely have controlled. With 103 of the 301 seats in the federal House of Commons, Ontarians can be assured of influence in Ottawa, whichever party is in power. They have therefore been less likely to turn to their provincial government as an instrument to redress a perceived lack of representation in Ottawa. Similarly, interest groups do not need to speak to Ottawa through the voice of Queen's Park. No 'province-building' economic elites tied to the provincial government have emerged in Ontario, as happened in Alberta or Quebec.[9]

All these factors have shaped Ontario's role in Confederation. They mean that there is no simple equation between the interests of 'Ontario' and those of the 'government of Ontario.' Federal politicians can equally claim to speak for the province. Indeed, the result may be that the concerns of the provincial government are less influential in Ottawa than those of other provincial governments, who can more credibly claim to be the most legitimate voice for provincial populations who feel unrepresented in Ottawa. Ontario's centrality also means that – with a few major exceptions – it has seldom been a 'demandeur' in federal-provincial or constitutional battles, and has never independently sought radical change. Indeed, Ontario has often resisted changes proposed by others that were seen to weaken the central government. As an institution, the Ontario government does, of course, share some interests with other provincial governments, such as concerns about fiscal arrangements and provincial autonomy, but these have been strongly tempered by its close relationship with Ottawa, and by the national orientations of its citizens. As a result, Ontario has often played the role of mediator between federal and provincial governments, has sought balance and compromise, and has customarily advocated a high level of cooperation and collaboration in federal-provincial relations.[10]

1. CONFEDERATION AND AFTER

Two powerful images dominate thinking about Ontario's role in the early years of Confederation: the 'Empire of the St Lawrence,' and the 'National Policy.' The idea of the commercial empire of the St Lawrence, the great waterway extending from the Atlantic ocean deep into the heart of North America, has permeated Canada's history from its earliest days. As historian Donald Creighton put it: 'Its owners, the Canadians, have held in it a unique possession; the realization of its potentialities has been one of the most persistent and compelling aims of their existence as a people. The river has inspired generations of Canadians to build a great territorial empire, both political and commercial, in the western interior of the continent.'[11] This was the backbone around which Quebec and Ontario were formed, shaping both their common interests in westward expansion and their competition for dominance in relations between the

Canadian heartland and the great western hinterland. It also profoundly shaped the relationships between Ontario and what were to become the western provinces.

The shared historical experience between Ontario and Quebec goes back to at least 1791, when the Constitutional Act divided the Province of Quebec into Upper and Lower Canada. Following Lord Durham's Report describing 'two nations warring in the bosom of a single state,' the two were reunited as a single province of Canada in 1840. Once the achievement of responsible government eroded the foundations of the Baldwin-Lafontaine reform alliance, the ensuing political deadlock pre-cipitated the Confederation settlement of 1867, recreating the provinces of Ontario and Quebec in a union embracing New Brunswick and Nova Scotia. But the larger ambition of Confederation was to project the em-pire of the St Lawrence westward to the Pacific and to create a single economy and polity on the northern half of the North American conti-nent. While provinces were given the responsibility of preserving their distinctive social and cultural lives, Ottawa was given the tools to realize this expansionary ambition, which was given policy form in the National Policy of Sir John A. Macdonald, in 1878. The National Policy provided the political and economic blueprint for Canada for almost a century. It embodied three main elements: completion of the railway to British Columbia (thus securing its entry to Confederation); a policy of high import tariffs, to increase federal revenues and to provide protection for an infant manufacturing sector, largely in Ontario; and aggressive poli-cies to settle western agricultural lands made accessible by the railway, thus increasing Canadian farm production and exports and providing a captive market for eastern manufacturing.[12] While achievement of its goals had to await the end of a world-wide recession towards the end of the nineteenth century, the National Policy profoundly shaped the poli-tics of Canadian federalism for almost one hundred years, and its echoes still faintly reverberate.

The policy was strongly shaped in the interests of manufacturing, transportation, and financial interests centred in Ontario and Quebec. Indeed, it was a clear example of Ontario using its control over the central government to achieve goals that it could not achieve on its own. Second, it succeeded in creating an east-west economy, but at the price of considerable regional tensions. To westerners, the National Policy looked less benign. Why should we be required to sell our products on volatile world markets, they asked, while we are required to buy our equipment from protected eastern manufacturers and transport our products on eastern-owned railways, all financed by the eastern banks? Wasn't the tariff just a barely disguised subsidy of eastern interests by westerners; and did not the National Policy condemn the west to being a permanent hinterland to the Central Canadian metropolis?[13] The resulting resentments fuelled a succession of western populist movements – the United Farmers, Progressives, Social Credit, and Cooperative Commonwealth Federation – all of which sought to redress the balance. While the policy underpinnings of the National Policy have long since eroded, these remain potent symbols in western attitudes towards central Canada, and especially Ontario.[14] They were revived strongly during the energy wars of the 1970s, when Ontario used its political leverage in Ottawa to push for lower oil and gas prices, and for greater sharing of western oil revenues with the rest of the country.

While the National Policy projected central power and the interests of Ontario and Quebec across the country, there were still some notable conflicts between Ottawa and Ontario in the early years of Confederation. Under Sir John A. Macdonald, early federal governments aggressively used the centralist policy levers found in the constitution, such as disallowance and the federal declaratory power, against the provinces.[15] Ontario Liberal Premier Oliver Mowat was an ardent defender of provincial rights, and strongly opposed this centralist vision, and indeed, it was he, not a Quebecer, who originated the 'compact theory,' defining Canada as an alliance of provinces in contrast to Macdonald's view of the provinces as creatures of Ottawa. In 1887 Mowat teamed with Quebec Premier Honoré Mercier to convene the first interprovincial conference, which produced a list of demands strikingly familiar to later Canadians: increased federal subsidies to the provinces, abolition of the disallowance power, limits on the declaratory power, and a provincial right to nominate members of the Senate.

There were economic conflicts too. Canadian politics in the nineteenth century were the politics of development – of railways, canals, roads, mines, and forests. The question was, Which of the competing economic interests would each level of government respond to, and around which would the major interests coalesce? Mowat's Liberal coalition consisted mainly of farmers and lumber interests, and like western farmers later, fought the high tariffs demanded by manufacturing interests allied to the federal Tories. By the turn of the century, however, the coalitions had shifted. Now the governing federal Liberals under Wilfrid Laurier were most sympathetic to agricultural interests, advocating free trade with the United States in the 'Reciprocity Election' of 1911 over the vigorous opposition of Ontario, where the manufacturing interests were now dominant. In addition, as the focus of economic development towards the end of the nineteenth century shifted to the 'new staples' of minerals, petroleum, and hydroelectric power, much of which lay under provincial control, the balance shifted. Ontario sought (with little success) to use its own economic powers to promote Ontario industry, notably with the 'manufacturing condition' – a sort of provincial national policy that included a ban on the export of raw timber and unrefined metal ore and restrictions on the export of hydro power.[16] This brought Ontario's actions squarely into conflict with federal powers over trade and commerce, navigable waters, and the like. Thus, the federal-provincial battles were in part proxies for the clash of interests within the province.

Ontario, as Canada's richest province, also sought to protect its financial base. As one writer puts it, 'To Ontario, the key aspect of federal-provincial relations is finance. It is not constitutional and jurisdictional matters.'[17] This was an important element in the long-running feud between fellow Liberals Mackenzie King in Ottawa and Mitchell Hepburn in Ontario. As Ottawa moved to assist poorer provinces almost bankrupted by the effects of the Great Depression of the 1930s, Hepburn attacked rising federal taxes and subsidies, arguing that they came disproportionately from Ontario and Quebec. He, along with Quebec and Alberta, refused to recognize the authority of a federally appointed royal commission – the Rowell-Sirois Commission established in 1937 – that was charged with reconsidering the financial basis of Confederation. He then bitterly attacked its recommendations aimed at greater redistribution and increased federal authority in social policy. Thus, through much of the early period – and indeed later – we see Ontario acting in a dual role: on one hand, as the main architect and beneficiary of federal economic activity embodied in the National Policy; on the other hand, as a provincial government, anxious to safeguard its jurisdiction and financial base against any federal encroachments and to protect its privileged position. In this role, it was frequently aligned with Quebec and, to a lesser extent, with the other richer provinces, Alberta and British Columbia.

2. THE POSTWAR 'NEW NATIONAL POLICY'[18]

Following the searing experience of the Depression and war, Canada, along with all other Western democracies, embraced a new policy blueprint, variously known as the Keynesian welfare state, the New Deal, or, in Canada, the 'New National Policy.' Its fundamental components were a turning away from protectionism towards freer trade and closer economic integration with the United States, management of the economy through the new tools of fiscal and economic policy, and the construction of the welfare state. Ontario emerged from the Second World War with a greatly strengthened manufacturing base and strong markets for its resource industries. It increasingly looked to the south, and U.S. ownership and investment in the province were rapidly increasing, as was north-south trade. Ontario was therefore an enthusiastic participant in the emerging new order.

However, the growth of the new welfare state had important implications for federalism. It pointed to a more expansive federal role: Ottawa took on responsibility for unemployment insurance, family allowances, and old-age pensions; other components of the welfare state, such as hospital insurance, Medicare, and the Canada Assistance Plan, were achieved through the use of the federal spending power to shape provincial policies. Finally, Ottawa embraced a greater commitment to interregional equalization. Federalism ensured that the new model would be achieved not through a wholesale centralization of power, but rather through initiatives undertaken cooperatively with provincial governments. Ontario helped ensure this would happen. On the one hand, the Ontario population clearly was strongly supportive of the new initiatives; on the other hand, these initiatives had major implications for the province's fiscal and policy autonomy. In addition, Ontario governments throughout this period were Conservative, while the new national initiatives were undertaken by the federal Liberals. Thus, Ontario joined with Quebec and others to block a sweeping set of centralizing federal proposals put forward at the end of the war.[19] With strong links to business and insurance interests, it resisted later developments such as Medicare (1968)[20] and the Canada Pension Plan (1966).[21] It consistently sided with Quebec in resisting increased fiscal centralization and seeking a larger share of the total taxation pool, as compared to that of the federal government. As well, it argued strongly that the new model should be developed with federal-provincial collaboration rather than through federal initiative alone. Nevertheless, while there were sharp disagreements over fiscal sharing, and alleged federal distortions of provincial priorities through conditional grant programs, the differences between Ottawa and the federal government, and Ontario and the other provinces, were not fundamental in this period. With the important exception of Quebec, all governments cooperated in building the welfare state. And in this case, unlike in later battles over energy, the central issues of the day did not divide the country along regional lines. Nevertheless, the tone did shift with changing leadership. Ontario's first postwar premier, George Drew, was a close ally of Quebec's Maurice Duplessis, and joined him in bitterly resisting Ottawa's expansionary aims, whereas his successor, Leslie Frost, agreed to the new tax-sharing arrangements and the principle of equalization. Frost's national instincts prevailed over his provincialism, setting a style followed by later premiers.

This was also a period in which Ontario attempted to mediate between Quebec and the rest of Canada. Perhaps the most dramatic Canadian political development of the 1960s was the Quiet Revolution in Quebec, leading Quebec to demand greater fiscal and policy autonomy in order to become 'maîtres chez nous.' Ontario sought to respond to these new aspirations, even as they challenged the economic and political arrangements that had served Ontario so well. Realizing the potential implications of these developments for the country's future – and in the face of a growing polarization between Quebec and the federal government on the future of Canada – Ontario Premier John Robarts convened the Confederation of Tomorrow Conference in 1967, to 'explore the measure of our consensus, and, perhaps, the range of our differences.' The key issues would be 'the place of French Canada in Canadian society' and 'the relationship between federal and provincial governments.'[22] This initiative may well be regarded as the first step in the search for a renewed constitution that has dominated federal-provincial politics ever since. The goal of the conference was not to articulate Ontario's own proposals for reform, but to ensure that Quebec's new concerns would be exposed to national debate. Robarts's dedication to a new accommodation with Quebec set a pattern that was followed by his successors, William Davis, David Peterson, and Bob Rae.

In the 1970s, federal-provincial conflict rose to levels unprecedented in this century. Two issues deeply divided the country – and on both Ontario displayed its fundamental affinity with a strong central government. The first was energy. In 1973, and again in 1979, oil and gas prices rose dramatically, and these externally generated shocks massively exacerbated interregional conflict within Canada.[23] The crisis pitted the interests of industry, consumers, and government in Ontario directly against the interests of western Canadian producers and governments. The former demanded that Canadians be cushioned against the rise in energy prices, and that a large share of the government revenues generated by the boom be captured by the federal government, to be shared across the whole country. The latter argued with equal passion that prices should be set at world levels, and that the lion's share of the resulting revenues should go to the western provinces who owned the resource. It was a pure zero-sum game, on regional lines; what one side won, the other lost. Ontario could do nothing on its own to affect prices or revenues. In order to achieve its interests, therefore, it had to rely on the exercise of federal powers over taxation and trade. It thus strongly supported Ottawa's moves to control prices and gain a larger share of revenues. These measures culminated in the Liberal government's 1981 National Energy Program, a draconian set of measures to centralize revenues, increase Canadian ownership of the oil and gas industry, and move energy development out of the provinces and onto federally controlled 'Canada lands,' especially in the North. The NEP immediately followed the 1980 federal election, in which the short-lived, and more western-oriented Conservative government led by Joe Clark was defeated, largely by Ontario votes. In that election, Premier Davis conspicuously snubbed his federal-party colleagues: regional interests trumped partisan loyalty. These positions, in turn, infuriated westerners, who once again saw Ontario using its muscle in Ottawa to make a barefaced raid on their resources.

The flow of wealth engendered by the shift in terms of trade between resources and manufacturing was accompanied by a strong desire on the part of the western provinces to use their economic resurgence to alter the balance of political power and put the final nails in the coffin of the National Policy. Alberta and Saskatchewan, in particular, embarked on ambitious efforts to diversify their economies, to ensure their control over resource development and revenues, and to increase their autonomy not only from Ottawa but also from central Canada. These developments placed Ontario on the defensive. There was much fear that the shift was permanent, so that Ontario industry would no longer be the engine of Canada's growth. Citizens and leaders alike felt their dominance in the Canadian system was eroding. As a result, Ontario increasingly took a defensive, 'province first,' position. While for the West the defence of provincial interests meant increased autonomy from federal power, however, for Ontario it meant an alliance with the federal government. As it turned out, however, the shift was not permanent: in the early 1980s energy prices collapsed, and it was Ontario that entered the long boom of the decade. The westward flow of people and investment was quickly reversed.[24]

The second major battle of this period was over the constitution.[25] Following the Quebec referendum on 'sovereignty-association' in 1980, a concerted effort at constitutional reform to build a 'renewed federalism' failed. In these discussions, Ontario lined up with other provinces on some issues, but on the key agenda items – the Charter of Rights, the nature of the Canadian political community, and the economic union – it was on the federal side. In the absence of provincial agreement, the federal government of Pierre Trudeau took a dramatic unilateral initiative, asserting that provincial consent for a request to Britain to amend the British North America Act was not constitutionally required. Ottawa, battling Quebec nationalists on one front and western energy producers on the other, rejected a province-centred model for the country and asserted the primacy of the federal government. Its amendments called for patriation of the constitution, a Charter of Rights and Freedoms, and an amending formula, but made no concessions to either Quebec or western calls for greater power. Quebec immediately joined seven other provinces in the 'Gang of Eight' to oppose the federal initiative. Trudeau's only provincial allies were the Conservative Premiers Davis of Ontario and Hatfield of New Brunswick. Again, when the chips were down, Ontario's interests were allied with those of Ottawa. When the smoke finally cleared, in November 1981, Ontario did return to the role of mediator, helping to hammer out the final agreement when negotiations resumed.[26] Significantly, however, the agreement was reached without Quebec. It was becoming harder and harder for Ontario to play the role of mediator between Quebec and the rest of the country. On the two key issues that poisoned federal-provincial relations in the 1970s and early 1980s, Ontario's government, and apparently most of its residents, strongly backed federal power.

These events suggest that deep cracks were beginning to appear in Ontario's traditional role in Confederation. As Tom Courchene suggests, the conventional view of Ontario in Confederation has been constructed out of a series of beliefs, namely:

– Ontario's size and dominant position have meant that national policy has typically been cast in a pro-Ontario light.
– Ontario has been and is in favour of strong central government.
– The political activities and loyalties of Ontarians have been directed more to the federal than the provincial government.
– Management of the big levers of economic stabilization have always been carried out with the Ontario economy in mind.
– Ontarians and their governments would much rather block federal or sister-province initiatives that are contrary to Ontario's interests than acquire greater provincial powers to pursue their interests autonomously.

– Ontario has traditionally supported the erection of barriers to external trade (the National Policy), while seeking to eliminate internal barriers to domestic trade.[27]

Despite the province's fundamental orientation to an Ottawa-centred Canada, there have been, as we have seen, numerous disagreements between Ontario and Ottawa since Confederation. Several factors seem to lie behind these episodes. First, as mentioned, despite its affinity with Ottawa on the big issues, the Ontario government does have its own institutional interests in mind, and hence has resisted perceived federal encroachments on its jurisdictional and financial autonomy. Second, conflicts have arisen when the coalition of interests reflected in the government at Queen's Park have differed from that prevailing in Ottawa: as when Mowat's government favoured agricultural and timber interests, while Macdonald's reflected manufacturing and commercial interests; or when Joe Clark's federal Conservative government was more sympathetic to western interests. Third, the aspirations, personalities, and ideologies of individual leaders have made a difference, as in the epic battles between Macdonald and Mowat, and Hepburn and Mackenzie King. Oddly, the partisan stripe of the governments at each level has not made a consistent difference. Energy and the constitution made allies of Conservative Davis and Liberal Trudeau, and opponents of Davis and fellow Tory Joe Clark.

A New Ontario?

Many elements of this conventional understanding remain in place. The legacy of the past casts a long shadow over the attitudes and aspirations of the present and future. Yet, by the 1980s some fundamental changes in Ontario's society and economy were at work, with the potential to reshape the province's understanding of itself, its interests, and its role in Confederation. Ontario began to march to its own drummer, and in several areas acted in uncharacteristically un-Ontario ways. There was a sense at Queen's Park that the postwar verities no longer held true. It is to these changes that we now turn.

1. IDEOLOGICAL DIVERGENCE

A powerful set of ideas, variously labelled neo-conservative and neo-liberal, swept North America and the world in the 1980s. The newly dominant ideology focused on the benefits of liberalized trade, on the need to restrain growing government debts and deficits, on the necessity of downsizing and rethinking the role of government generally, and on the pre-eminence of fiscal and monetary policies designed to restrain inflation. In Canada, these views were exemplified by the government of Brian Mulroney, which was elected in 1984, as well as by a growing number of provinces. Ontario, however, was ideologically 'off-side,' these ideas had little resonance for Ontario governments. In 1985, David Peterson's Liberal Party, with the help of a formal accord with the New Democratic Party, replaced the forty-two-year-old Conservative dynasty. Two years later, the Liberals were re-elected with a thumping majority.

The Liberals had little sympathy with Ottawa's restraint agenda. Through the 1980s, they rode an economic boom that produced increased revenues, while generating strong pressures for increased public spending to provide sewers, roads, schools, and hospitals for burgeoning new communities and to provide services for hundreds of thousands of new immigrants.[28] Thus, while federal finance ministers were preaching the need for restraint and deficit-reduction, the Ontario government was pursuing a quite contradictory policy, increasing both public spending and borrowing.

These policy and ideological differences were exacerbated when the NDP, led by Bob Rae, took power in 1990. The NDP had an expansive social-democratic agenda to implement and, more important, had to face the consequences of a severe economic downturn, leading to the deepest recession since the 1930s. Between 1989 and 1992, unemployment in Ontario went from 5.8 per cent to 11.3 per cent, plant closures and layoffs increased, and by 1993 10 per cent of Ontarians were on social assistance. Fears of 'de-industrialization' raised in the 1970s reappeared. The first NDP budget, in 1991, sought to address these problems with the traditional Keynesian counter-cyclical policy of increased spending, thereby sharply increasing the deficit and placing Ontario once more at odds with federal fiscal priorities, as well as with an increasingly dominant international fiscal orthodoxy.

2. ONTARIO'S POSITION IN NORTH AMERICA AND THE WORLD

Perhaps the central structural change Ontario is experiencing at present is the demise of the political economy of the National Policy, and of the predominantly east-west economy on which it is built. Put most bluntly, the Ontario economy and its primary linkages have shifted ninety degrees: from east-west, to north-south. This shift did not happen suddenly; indeed, in a sense it has been a continuous process since the Second World War. Perhaps the most significant step was negotiation of the Canada-U.S. Auto Pact in 1968, producing a virtually integrated North American market in automobile and parts manufacturing, Ontario's largest industrial sector. No longer would plants in Oshawa or Oakville produce small runs of many models for sale in the Canadian market; now the border would be erased. The Auto Pact was then followed by the Canada–United States Free Trade Agreement (FTA) in 1988 and its extension to Mexico in the North American Free Trade Agreement (NAFTA) in 1994.

These formal agreements both reflect and promote a fundamental realignment of the Ontario economy – becoming at the same time more integrated with, and reliant on, the U.S. market and less linked to domestic Canadian markets. Between 1981 and 1995, Ontario's exports abroad, predominantly to the United States, almost quadrupled from $38 billion to $140 billion; in the same period, exports to other provinces in Canada less than doubled from just under $37 billion to $62 billion. As a proportion of Gross Domestic Product (GDP) the contrast is even starker. International exports rose from just under 30 per cent of GDP to just under 45 per cent, while exports to other Canadians dropped, from 28 per cent of GDP to under 20 per cent. Similarly, Ontario's dependence on imports from other provinces as a proportion of all imports has been declining: from 11.1 per cent in 1984 to 8.8 per cent in 1989.[29]

These are fundamental shifts. What are their implications? First, Ontario has been deeply divided about them. On the one hand, it is clear that the province's prosperity depends on American and global markets, and that forces of global and North American restructuring and integration are immensely powerful; on the other hand, there are deep fears that the effects of globalization will lead to the loss of jobs to low-wage competitors, the loss of economic sovereignty, and the erosion of the social safety net that has become such a defining characteristic of Canadian identity. Ontario was the centre of widespread Canadian concerns in the 1970s about the implications of increasing foreign ownership. Ontario was also the centre of opposition to passage of the FTA and NAFTA.

While the debate on these issues engulfed the whole country, the greatest fears for the future were found among workers in manufacturing industries, worried about the impact of low-wage competition from abroad. Ontario and Prince Edward Island were the only provinces to oppose passage of the FTA. Later, the NDP government of Bob Rae also opposed NAFTA, seriously exploring the possibility of mounting a legal challenge to it on the grounds that it infringed provincial areas of juris-diction. In part, Ontario's opposition to the FTA and NAFTA reflected the social-democratic coalitions that sustained both the Liberal and NDP governments; in part it could be seen as a last-ditch defence by Ontario of the Canada created by the old National Policy[30] and of the privileged position in which it placed the province. Again, the reaction from else-where in Canada was that here was Ontario trying to maintain its old privileged position once again – along with the strongly expressed view by some that Ontario's opposition was foolish, and contrary even to its own interests.

In any case, opposition by the Ontario government to the FTA and NAFTA put it at odds both with the federal government and its provin-cial counterparts and with Ontario business interests, who now enthusi-astically embraced the free-trade ideal. Again, internal divisions in Ontario, this time closely related to class and, perhaps, gender, prevented it from speaking with a clear, united voice on the trade issue.

These events suggest that globalization and North American integra-tion are increasing both the volatility of the Canadian economy and its vulnerability to external forces. They also suggest that these forces are likely to affect different sectors, and therefore different regions, of the Canadian economy in different ways, making it more and more difficult to develop economic policies suitable for all regions and increasing the likelihood of federal and provincial, and interprovincial, disagreements about the appropriate response.

These forces of globalization have also had an impact on the politics of Canadian federalism. One persuasive line of argument suggests that the forces associated with globalization place more limits and constraints on national governments than do local or regional governments. Capital mobility and international agreements render the traditional tools of central government, such as fiscal and monetary policy, tariffs, and taxa-tion, less and less available. Conversely, policy instruments traditionally in the hands of regional governments, such as education, become more important. Such thinking has led to a growing conventional wisdom, especially among economists,[31] that the most appropriate response to these forces is to further decentralize responsibilities in the Canadian system. Such a strategy, it is argued, is both more appropriate to the new circumstances and more attuned to the provincialist aspirations of Que-bec and some other provinces.

This issue, too, has provoked much debate in Ontario. The long association of Ontario with a strong central government suggests that Ontarians would be reluctant to accept the decentralist model – and, indeed, much of the opposition to the decentralist elements in the Meech Lake and Charlottetown Accords (such as limitations on the federal spending power) was centred in Ontario. On the other hand, if the effectiveness of the federal government is now heavily constrained by international forces as well as by its fiscal deficits, and by the political necessity of responding to decentralist pressures from Quebec and elsewhere, then there is the strong possibility that Ontarians will increasingly find themselves looking to the provincial government to provide services of which the central government is no longer capable. Moreover, as residents of the largest and richest province, endowed with a substantial and experienced public service, Ontarians may perceive Queen's Park as the more effective political unit for achieving their goals.

Some straws in the wind indeed suggest that Ontario is less willing to link itself to federal interests. Recent Ontario governments strongly supported both Meech and Charlottetown, which did embody limited degrees of devolution, and more recently have supported intergovernmental agreements on the environment and social policy that also point in a decentralist direction. In the Charlottetown constitutional round, Premier Rae did respond to many in his coalition who were worried about the possible erosion of national standards – but he did so not by arguing for a strengthening of federal power to set and enforce such standards, but rather by advocating a constitutionally entrenched Social Charter, which would set standards for all governments.[32]

Similarly, Ontario has always been a strong proponent of the internal economic union, seeking to prevent provincial (or federal) policies that might undermine the free access of Ontario to the whole Canadian market. In recent years it played an important role in developing the intergovernmental Agreement on Internal Trade (AIT). Significantly, the agreement looks to intergovernmental cooperation and dispute resolution to strengthen the common market, rather than to strengthening constitutional guarantees or giving a stronger role to the federal government as the definer and enforcer of internal free trade. Thus, Ontario remains committed to what Bob Rae called the Canadian economic and social union,[33] but has declining confidence in Ottawa's ability to advance or protect it.

A broader but related issue is whether the economic trends that seem to be eroding the linkages among Canadian provinces and regions will also have the effect of eroding the social and affective or emotional ties linking Canadians to each other in a political union. If the cars that the auto worker in Oshawa makes are no longer sold in British Columbia or Nova Scotia,then what interest will he or she have in how well fellow citizens in the logging or fisheries industries are doing? Similarly, what about the commitment to equalization, or interregional redistribution, that is such a central part of the Confederation bargain? In an integrated east-west economy such transfers can be unifying: a dollar that goes from Ontario, via Ottawa, to, for example, New Brunswick, might be expected to find its way back to Ontario in the form of the purchase of Ontario goods and services. But in the new North American and global economy, that same dollar is more likely to be spent abroad. In such circumstances one might expect Ontarians' support for equalization to erode, and for Ontario to look increasingly to the well-being of the province, rather than that of the country as a whole.

There is little evidence of such a turning inwards so far. Across Canada, as Michael Adams and Mary Jane Lennon found,[33] there has been an erosion of support for national symbols such as the national anthem, the Governor General, and hockey. There was also a significant (13 per cent) drop between 1980 and 1990 in the proportion of respondents who said they identify more with Canada than with their province. As expected, Ontarians were more likely to identify with Canada than those in other provinces, but, significantly, the drop in national identification (a 17 per cent decline) was *greatest* in Ontario. There is no evidence of a declining commitment to support poorer regions of the country, but, while continuing to support the principle of equalization, Ontario politicians have increasingly argued that the redistribution built into other programs, such as Employment Insurance, is 'unfair' to Ontario.

3. DEBTS AND DEFICITS

Closely related to the geo-economic changes facing Ontario and Canada is the preoccupation of governments at all levels with managing their debts and deficits. By the 1990s, there was widespread agreement that prevailing levels of public-sector deficits and a combined federal and provincial debt approaching 100 per cent of GDP were unsustainable, consuming an ever-greater proportion of government revenues in debt-service payments, rendering Canada even more vulnerable to the vagaries of international financial markets, placing unconscionable burdens on future generations, and greatly limiting governments' ability to mitigate the effects of any future economic recession. Managing the fiscal crisis has become a central preoccupation of all governments. As we have noted, the Ontario government was slow to join the parade of deficit-cutters, placing it at odds with Ottawa and several other provinces. But by 1993, Premier Rae had become convinced that Ontario was about to hit a 'fiscal wall' – a combination of the squeeze between dramatically lower revenues and increased spending requirements – and that drastic action must be taken. His response was a stringent restraint program, capped by a three-year 'social contract' designed to restrain the public-sector wage bill while minimizing job losses. The Mike Harris government, elected 8 June 1995, dramatically escalated the attack on public spending, announcing on 21 July immediate spending cuts of $1.9 billion to bring the projected 1995–6 deficit down from $11.2 billion to $9.3 billion, and moving to reduce the size of the public service by about one-third. With the mantra of 'cut fast, cut deep,' Ontario had now enthusiastically joined the drive for balanced budgets across the country, with social and economic costs that remain to be counted.

One effect of budget restraint in a federal system with an extensive system of intergovernmental transfers is that each level of government will attempt to pass its fiscal problem on to others – from Ottawa to the provinces, and from provinces to municipalities and other transfer agencies, such as universities and school boards. In Ontario's case, a series of federal alterations to unemployment-insurance, training, housing, and refugee programs all increased the burden on the provincial treasury.

Most dramatic was the unilateral federal decision in 1990 to cap the growth of payments under the Canada Assistance Plan to those provinces (Ontario, Alberta, and British Columbia) not receiving equalization. The Canada Assistance Plan transfered federal funds to provinces to assist them in their support of provincial welfare programs. This meant that the 50:50 federal-provincial cost-sharing formula, which would continue to prevail in other provinces, would no longer apply to the three wealthiest provinces. The cap or growth ceiling would sharply reduce the federal share. This was a frontal assault on the treasuries of the affected provinces, especially Ontario, where the severity of the recession had resulted in the most rapid growth in spending on social assistance. CAP-eligible expenditures in Ontario rose from just over $3 billion in 1988–9 to close to $8 billion in 1992–3. By 1995, the federal decision was estimated to have cost Ontario $7 billion, and the federal share of welfare costs, once 50 per cent, had dwindled to 29 per cent.[34] The federal Liberals, elected in 1993, continued this policy and in the 1995 budget replaced existing transfer programs for welfare, health care, and post-secondary education with a new, combined Canada Health and Social Transfer (CHST), program that, while giving the provinces more flexibility in program design, would further reduce cash transfers by 15.2 per cent, or $7 billion, by 1996–7.[35]

These federal initiatives provoked the government of Ontario to reconsider the costs and benefits of federalism, and profoundly shaped the NDP's attitude and outlook to the federal system.[36] The NDP government developed what it called a 'fair shares' theory of federalism, suggesting that Ontario was receiving much less than it should in federal spending while bearing a disproportionate burden of the federal spending in other provinces. Not only was Ontario the major source of financing for the equalization system, but it also had to pay for extra redistribution built into other federal programs such as Unemployment Insurance. The NDP commissioned ten studies, by the Ottawa consulting firm Informetrica, to analyse in full detail the implications of federal-provincial fiscal arrangements for Ontario, thereby providing intellectual underpinnings to the fair-shares theory.[37] This argument – otherwise known as 'balance-sheet federalism' – has been continued in modified form by the Harris government, which, for example, sharply attacked a special federal subsidy to the Atlantic provinces to compensate them for harmonizing their sales taxes with the federal GST, and, in public advertisements, specifically blamed federal cuts for the need to introduce user fees for those receiving prescriptions under the Ontario Drug Benefit Plan.[38] Thus, the politics of fiscal restraint is a politics of shifting financial burdens (along with political blame). It is a politics that emphasizes a 'balance sheet' approach to federalism and a focus on the province's own immediate interests. It is likely to temper willingness to support redistributive policies. And to the extent that fiscal restraint reduces the federal government's presence in the daily lives of Ontarians, it is likely to reinforce a shift of linkages and loyalties from Ottawa to the province.

4. ONTARIO'S CONFEDERATION PARTNERS

Ontario's Confederation partners, the other provinces, are also changing, driven by the same forces of globalization and North American integration. They too are increasingly linked economically not to each other or to Ontario, but externally, whether to the United States or the Pacific Rim nations. Increasingly, even in provinces like New Brunswick, once heavily dependent on federal largesse, there is the sense that the federal government is a diminishing presence and that provincial residents must now look primarily to their own resources and talents to prepare for the future. Globalization in Canada – and indeed in other countries such as Belgium, Spain, Italy, and even Britain – seems to be associated with 'localization,' the flow of power away from the centralized nation-state to smaller, perhaps more homogeneous and manageable, units. The fundamental question for Canada is whether, as Thomas Courchene vividly put it, we can maintain an east-west social and political union on top of a north-south economy.[39]

Quebec presents a special case. As noted at the outset, Quebec and Ontario have been closely linked through the St Lawrence since Canada's earliest days. In negotiations on the constitution and other matters, Ontario governments have consistently sought to accommodate Quebec and to act as a bridge between it and other provinces. The traditional pattern has been followed in the recent period. Premier Peterson was an ardent supporter of the Meech Lake Accord. Believing that its success was essential to the maintenance of national unity, he expended enormous political resources in defending it, in the face of massive public opposition, much of it based in Ontario. In the last few months before the Meech Lake deadline expired in June 1990, he put aside virtually all other responsibilities to concentrate on the Meech Lake file; and in a last-ditch effort to save the accord, he even offered to give up several Ontario senate seats.

The same was true of his successor Bob Rae. He too defied many of his political advisers to play a central role in the Charlottetown negotiations, and, in the referendum debate that followed, like Peterson, Rae appears to have paid a large political price for having done so. Moreover, in the negotiations, which in their early stages were boycotted by Quebec Premier Robert Bourassa, Rae worked hard to ensure that the interests of Quebec were not ignored.

However, it is now an open question whether this traditional Ontario role will continue. The Quebec Referendum of 30 October 1995 brought the sovereignist Parti Québécois within a hair's breadth of success. It thus deeply altered the terrain of Canadian constitutional politics. In the rest of Canada, including Ontario, its aftermath appears to have been a hardening of opinion towards Quebec: a firmer rejection of constitutional special status for the province, an unwillingness to reopen the constitutional Pandora's box, an inclination to attempt to set tougher conditions for any future Quebec referendum, and a determination to bargain hard in any post-referendum negotiations. Such attitudes are perhaps especially strong among supporters of the Harris government, and among those who voted for the Reform Party (which came second in popular vote in the province in the 1993 federal election). Thus, at least in the short term, the Ontario government can be expected to play a less prominent role in national-unity debates than did its predecessors, and to be less accommodating to Quebec when it does.

5. A CHANGING ONTARIO SOCIETY

Ontario has itself been undergoing enormous change in its own society, which is also likely to affect its role in Confederation. Perhaps the most important change is its increasing ethnic diversity. Though it was always something of a caricature to describe Ontario society as 'British,' its elites and institutions certainly were. As we have suggested, it was the dynamic of British Ontario and French Quebec that did much to shape modern Canada. Ontario has become a polyethnic, multiracial, highly pluralistic society in which the 'British' now constitute just another minority. Immigration has transformed Canada's three largest metropolitan centres, the Lower Mainland of British Columbia, Montreal Island, and the Greater Toronto Area – nowhere more so than Toronto, which has emerged as an ethnically diverse, dynamic, vibrant city linked as much to the world as to its own provincial hinterland.

These changes are likely to have as yet uncharted impacts on Canadian political and social life. First, there is likely to be an increasing division within the province between Greater Toronto and the less diverse remainder of the province, a division replicated in lesser degree in parts of the rest of the country. This will create its own tensions, which provincial and local officials must manage. Indeed, managing and accommodating cultural diversity within the province is likely to become an increasing preoccupation for its leaders, at least to some extent pushing aside the historic preoccupations with Ottawa, the other provinces, and, especially, Quebec. The collective identities that motivate politics will be less those of province and language, and more those rooted in ethnicity, gender, and lifestyle. What will this diverse society have in common with Chicoutimi, 90 per cent of whose residents are of French origin, or with St John's, 93 per cent of whose population is British? The new Ontario is less and less likely to be sympathetic to a conception of Canada based on a partnership between 'two founding peoples,' one French and one English. These new social forces have already brought us a new set of political and constitutional concerns: multiculturalism, gender equity, and, above all, the universal rights embodied in the 1982 Charter of Rights and Freedoms. They have also challenged the elitist political style of the old Canada: it was mobilization from below, expressing many of these new concerns, that defeated both the Meech Lake and Charlottetown Accords. The challenge of diversity is likely to increase Ontario's focus on its internal concerns.

One indicator of Ontario's increasing diversity is the greater volatility of its politics. From 1943 to 1985, one party, the Progressive Conservatives, presided benignly over Ontario's extraordinary growth. In 1985, the mould was broken, and Ontario saw a bewildering succession of governments – Liberal, NDP, and back to Conservative in 1995. This suggests again more volatility in Ontario's policies as the vagaries of electoral politics bring rapid changes in ideological emphasis and in the personal predilections of leaders.[40] The contrast between Bob Rae's social democracy and Mike Harris's Common Sense Revolution is stark, playing out in a wide range of issues, from welfare, to employment equity, to Aboriginal affairs, to the very size, role, and purpose of government. Early indications are that there is likely to be much more continuity in Ontario's positions on intergovernmental affairs, but here too there are important shifts in emphasis, including, among others, far less willingness to take the lead in dealing with Quebec, the constitution, and national unity, and a new consensus with other provinces on the imperatives of deficit reduction.

All these factors – ideological shifts, the new political economy of Canada, the worries about debts and deficits and fair shares, changing relations with Quebec and other Confederation partners, and transformation of Ontario's society – were evident in Ontario participation in the Charlottetown round of constitutional negotiations in 1992. It is true that there was the traditional concern to accommodate Quebec. But no longer was there the sense that Ontario really had no constitutional agenda of its own except to ensure that all actors could come away from the table reasonably satisfied with arrangements, so that the system could function relatively smoothly. This time, Ontario had precise objectives both with respect to the process of constitutional discussion and with respect to substance. In terms of process, the province feared that Ottawa and Quebec would engineer a *fait accompli*, which would be imposed on the other provinces. So it took the lead in pressing successfully for a multilateral process. Moreover, the government, and especially the premier, argued, again successfully, for the inclusion of representatives of leading Aboriginal groups at the Charlottetown negotiating table. In terms of substance, the province had the most explicit, distinctive, and fully developed agenda ever presented by Ontario in constitutional negotiations. It included constitutional recognition of the Aboriginal right to self-government as a 'third order' of government in Canada,[41] a constitutionally entrenched Social Charter, stronger protection of the economic union, and resistance to western demands for a powerful elected Senate, with equal representation from all provinces.[42] Thus Ontario's position, vigorously promoted in the negotiations, was an artful crafting together of the province's traditional concerns for balance in the federation, strong intergovernmental cooperative processes, and accommodation with Quebec, along with contemporary concerns with 'fair shares,' the economic and social union, and Aboriginal rights.

With no large-scale constitutional negotiations on the horizon (short of a new referendum in Quebec), and with the Harris government preoccupied with implementing the Common Sense Revolution at home, the aggressive stance of the Rae government on the constitutional front will likely not soon be repeated. But we can expect an equally strong defence of Ontario's interests when they are seen to be threatened by the actions of either Ottawa or other provinces.

Conclusion

In what direction do the forces we have been discussing seem to point?

The geo-economic forces of globalization and North American integration have inexorably realigned vital parts of Ontario's economy away from the rest of Canada and towards the United States. Ontarians as citizens and patriots may still look to the east and west; as workers and managers, however – as economic actors – many now look south. Ontario relies less and less on other parts of Canada as a market for its products or a source of its imports. The logic of Canadian political economy embedded in the commercial empire of the St Lawrence and the National Policy is no more. The interdependencies among Canada's regions, which, as former Saskatchewan Premier Allan Blakeney once pointed out, made Canada a giant mutual insurance company, have been deeply eroded.

Debts and deficits tend to make all governments more concerned with their internal affairs. They lead to deficit-shifting and to the politics of blame avoidance and *sauve qui peut*. Economic forces tend to increase inequalities, both class and regional, while eroding the tolerance for sharing and redistribution.

Canada's Confederation partners are experiencing the same broad forces, with similar effects: increasingly linked by economics to the rest of the world, rather than to Canada and Ontario, increasingly preoccupied with their own affairs, and more likely to see Ottawa as irrelevant, if not oppressive. Most seek more autonomy to manage their own affairs, and thus support decentralizing trends. As Quebeckers have increasingly sought to march to their own drummer, the sense of deep common interests between the two dominant partners in Confederation has eroded.

And Ontario's own increasing social and ethnic diversity also has the effect of turning the province inward, as it seeks to manage its complex society. Moreover, the historic linkages both to Quebec and the west, which so defined Confederation and Ontario's role within it, are likely to play a much smaller role in the identities and self-images of Canadians who have made their home in Ontario since the Second World War. What we may be seeing here is not so much hostility to Quebec and its concerns as indifference.

All these tendencies, then, help explain the changes in Ontario's role in the federation we have described. They tend to confirm H.V. Nelles's comment about Ontario in the 1990s: 'Ontario will likely become much more assertive and determined to pursue its own agenda in national and international councils. In the process, Ontario's self-conscious identity as a distinct society, with imperatives separate from those of other provinces in the federation, will grow.'[43]

Our analysis has confirmed this view. However, we must be careful not to exaggerate these trends. For one thing, they may embody possibilities and potentials, rather than accomplished facts. True, the propensity of Ontarians to identify first with the national community may be declining – but national identification remains stronger in Ontario than in other provinces. True, Ontario may be more worried about the distribution of its resources to other parts of the country – but support for the basic principle of equalization remains strong. Indeed, the sensitivity to such changes may be greater among the province's political elites, attuned to such matters, than among most of its residents. In addition, while it is true that Ontario depends less on the rest of the country, and vice versa, than it once did, it also remains true that Ontario continues to have deep and intense economic linkages with the rest of country, and it cannot be indifferent to maintaining them.[44] While Ontarians, for example, may have embraced a less Quebec-centred view of the country than they held in the past, Ontario's economic, social, and political well-being remains deeply intertwined with Quebec. Quebec sovereignty would set in motion economic, social, and political disruptions with enormous consequences for the province. As we noted at the outset, Ontario's role in the federation has been deeply shaped by the basic fact that it is this province that has traditionally had the greatest stake in its survival. The stakes may now be a little smaller; but they remain large.

Finally, the forces of economic and demographic change that are at the heart of shifting orientations are indeed very powerful. They cannot be ignored. However, politics, culture, and society do not blindly follow economic or demographic determinants. If they did, Canada would not exist. There is no simple causal chain here; economics and politics are siblings and rivals. Human agency – the views and actions of governments and citizens – counts for much as well. In this sense, then, Ontario's future in Confederation remains a work in progress, to be constructed rather than deconstructed, by its people and its government.

Notes

1 Quoted in Richard Simeon and Ian Robinson, *State, Society and the Development of Canadian Federalism* (Toronto: University of Toronto Press, 1991), 237.
2 Bob Rae, 'Join Us to Make Canada Work Again,' speech to the Provincial Renewal Conference, Toronto, 8 November 1993.
3 Speech to the Canadian Club, Toronto, 12 October 1995.
4 In Thomas J. Courchene, *Rearrangements: The Courchene Papers* (Toronto: Mosaic Press, 1992), 1–42. The essay was first published in 1989.
5 *Ontario History* 60 (June 1968): 64.
6 *Public and Private Persons: The Ontario Political Culture 1914–1934* (Toronto: Clarke Irwin and Company, 1975), 7–8.
7 These words by the board of trustees of the Ontario Historical Studies Series occur in the preface to its volumes (see, for example, A. Margaret Evans, *Sir Oliver Mowat* [Toronto: University of Toronto Press, 1992]). These conflicting images multiply. Former Premier John Robarts liked to call Ontario the 'golden hinge' of Confederation; Northrop Frye called it 'surely one of the most inarticulate communities in human culture' (*The Bush Garden: Essays in the Canadian Imagination* [Toronto: Anansi, 1971], 7–8).
8 See Courchene, 'What Does Ontario Want?'
9 See Robert Young, Philippe Faucher, and André Blais, 'The Concept of Province-Building: A Critique,' *Canadian Journal of Political Science* 18 (1984):

783–818. For its application to Alberta and Saskatchewan in the 1970s, see John Richards and Larry Pratt, *Prairie Capitalism: Power and Influence in the New West* (Toronto: McClelland and Stewart, 1979).

10 For an excellent analysis of Ontario along these lines, see Don Stevenson, 'Ontario and Confederation: A Reassessment,' in Ronald L. Watts and Douglas Brown, eds, *Canada: The State of the Federation 1989* (Kingston: Institute of Intergovernmental Relations, 1989), 53–74.

11 *Towards the Discovery of Canada* (Toronto: Macmillan of Canada, 1972), 160–1.

12 See articles by Brown and Dales in R. Douglas Francis and Donald B. Smith, eds, *Readings in Canadian History, Post-Confederation* (Toronto: Holt Rinehart and Winston of Canada, 1982).

13 See, for example, David Bercuson, ed., *Canada and the Burden of Unity* (Toronto: Macmillan, 1977), 3.

14 See J.F. Conway, *The West: The History of a Region in Confederation* (Toronto: James Lorimer, 1983).

15 The former permitted the federal government to disallow provincial legislation, thereby annulling it; the latter permitted the federal government unilaterally to assume jurisdiction over a purely local work otherwise falling within the responsibility of the province. Both provisions may be considered dead.

16 See H.V. Nelles, *The Politics of Development: Forests, Mines and Hydro-Electric Power in Ontario, 1849–1941* (Toronto: Macmillan of Canada, 1974).

17 Joe Martin, *The Role and Place of Ontario in the Canadian Confederation* (Toronto: Economic Council of Ontario, 1974), 2.

18 The phrase was Donald V. Smiley's; see 'Canada and the Quest for a National Policy,' *Canadian Journal of Political Science* 8 (1975): 40–62.

19 See Simeon and Robinson, *State, Society*, 110–15.

20 'Medicare,' said Premier Robarts, was 'a deliberate attempt by the federal government top use federal fiscal power to intrude into areas that are the constitutional responsibility of the provinces.' But he went along.

21 For a discussion of federal-provincial relations in this period, see Richard Simeon, *Federal-Provincial Diplomacy: The Making of Recent Policy in Canada* (Toronto: University of Toronto Press, 1972).

22 Quoted in ibid., 92.

23 The best overview of the energy wars is G. Bruce Doern and Glen Toner, *The Politics of Energy: The Development and Implementation of the NEP* (Toronto: Methuen, 1985).

24 See Simeon and Robinson, *State, Society*, 304–6.

25 There is much written on this period. Perhaps the best overview is Roy Romanow, John Whyte, and Howard Leeson, *Canada Notwithstanding ...: The*

Making of the Constitution, 1976–1982 (Toronto: Carswell/Methuen, 1984).

26 Ontario Attorney General Roy McMurtry, Saskatchewan's Roy Romanow (now Premier) and Ottawa's Jean Chretien (now prime minister) worked out the final compromise in a back room of the National Conference Centre in Ottawa.

27 'What Does Ontario Want?' 21–4 (see note above).

28 See H.V. Nelles, '"Red Tied": Fin de Siècle Politics in Ontario,' in Michael Whittington and Glen Williams, eds, *Canadian Politics in the 1990s*, 3rd ed. (Scarborough: Nelson Canada, 1990), 76–97, and Rodney Haddow, 'Ontario Politics: "Plus ça Change ...?"' in James Bickerton and Alain-C. Gagnon, eds, *Canadian Politics*, 2nd ed. (Peterborough: Broadview Press, 1994).

29 All figures from Statistics Canada, reported in Greg Ip, 'The borderless world,' *Globe and Mail*, Focus section, 6 July 1996, D1, D5.

30 Despite the fact that, by the 1980s, Ontario had become 'the least reliant of all the provinces upon the national market ... [d]uring the 1970s, Ontario could be said to have become Canada's most economically independent province. Industrial restructuring in the 1980s furthered the process.' Nelles, '"Red Tied,"' 78–9.

31 See, for example, Thomas Courchene, 'Global Competitiveness and the Canadian Federation,' in *The Courchene Papers* (Oakville: Mosaic Press, 1991).

32 See, for example, the Rae government's discussion paper, *A Canadian Social Charter: Making Our Shared Values Stronger* (Toronto: MIA, September 1991).

33 'The Public's View of the Canadian Federation,' in R.L. Watts and D.M. Brown, eds, *Canada: The State of the Federation 1990* (Kingston: Institute of Intergovernmental Relations, 1990), 97–108.

34 Ken Battle and Sherri Torjman, *How Finance Re-Formed Social Policy* (Ottawa: Caledon Institute of Social Policy, 1995), 8. See also the Informetrica study, *Ontario and the Canada Assistance Plan*.

35 Battle and Torjman, *How Finance Re-formed Social Policy*, 7.

36 For example, it affected Ontario's position in the Charlottetown round of constitutional talks, as it allied with British Columbia and Alberta to push for a constitutional provision allowing for binding intergovernmental agreements to prevent Ottawa from changing transfer programs like CAP unilaterally.

37 The papers, while clearly commissioned to serve a political purpose, contain a wealth of data and information of use to students of Ontario government and politics. The ten papers, released in November 1993 and August 1994, are (1) The Distribution of Federal Spending and Revenue:

Implications for Ontario and the Other Provinces; (2) Review of the Established Programs Financing System; (3) Ontario and the Canada Assistance Plan; (4) The Consequences of Deficit Shifting for Ontario; (5) Labour Market Development and Training; (6) Recent Canadian Monetary Policy: National and Regional Implications; (7) Immigration Settlement in Canada and Ontario; (8) Social Housing; (9) Ontario and the Unemployment Insurance System; and (10) Regional and Industrial Development Assistance.

38 Advertisement appearing in Ontario newspapers, 11 July 1996.

39 See chapter 1 of *Social Canada in the Millennium* (Toronto: C.D. Howe Institute, 1994).

40 See Haddow, 'Ontario Politics,' 479–80.

41 The government had signed a 'Statement of Political Relationship' recognizing this right at a ceremony on Mount Mackay, on 6 August 1991.

42 The Charlottetown Accord did include an elected, equal Senate, but with 'effective' powers that were less than the proponents of a 'Triple E Senate' had sought.

43 '"Red Tied,"' 95.

44 Recent work by John McCallum and John Helliwell confirm the enduring importance of national borders in shaping trade among provinces. See John McCallum, 'National Borders Matter: Canada-U.S. Regional Trade Patterns,' *American Economic Review* 85, no. 3 (1995): 615–23; John Helliwell, 'Do National Borders Matter for Quebec's Trade?' *Canadian Journal of Economics*, forthcoming.

PART III

Politics

EIGHT

Elections and Campaigning:
'They Blew Our Doors Off on the Buy'

Robert J. Drummond and Robert MacDermid

At a minimum, in our system of government, elections represent an opportunity for the circulation of political elites. Electors are given a chance, at frequent though irregular intervals, to say whether they agree to retain the office-holders they selected on the last such occasion, or prefer to replace them with someone new. Where political parties are organized as more than mere electoral or patronage machines, and actually have some programmatic differences from one another, elections also allow for a change of direction in public policy. Of course, voters may vary in the extent to which they perceive the policy differences among parties, and they may change their support for a party without being fully cognizant of the policy effect of that decision. Nonetheless, political observers, whether in the academy or the mass media, commonly assess election results in terms of the 'mandate' that appears to have been given by the voters to one or another policy emphasis, philosophy, or political ideology.

Of course when more than two parties contend for office in a simple-plurality electoral system, the government chosen can rarely boast a majority of the popular vote, so that any assertion that its policies have secured the approval of the electorate is always open to challenge. The simple-plurality system does, however, ordinarily result in the winning party's getting a higher proportion of seats than votes.[1] This outcome is sometimes described as a virtue of our electoral system, since it makes majority governments more common; minority governments are assumed to be less stable. In a parliamentary system, of course, when the government party has secured majority control of the legislative assembly, it can (and often does) act as if it had the unambiguous backing of the popular will. On the other hand, minority governments are sometimes thought to be more responsive to voters and therefore more productive, perhaps because they must take account of some opposition views in order to pass legislation, and perhaps because they recognize their mandates are often short-lived – they will usually have to face the electorate again sooner than majority governments will.[2] The argument that a majority government with a minority of the vote does not represent the will of the people is not normally an impediment to the progress of its legislative agenda. After all, it has control of the legislature and usually no other party has secured more of the vote. But the argument can sometimes be used to good effect in the campaign that goes on between elections, especially as it centres on particular actions for which the government claims a popular mandate.

This chapter considers recent Ontario elections, and the campaigns mounted to contest them, by examining the rules under which they have been conducted, the campaign activities of the main participants, and the apparent meaning of the results. For citizens in a democracy, the means by which the members of the legislature are chosen is of critical importance, since the legislature effectively determines who will form the government. For political activists, explanations of voter choice are of similar importance, since politicians in a democracy can gain and keep office only if they are able to understand and respond to the message(s) voters are conveying when they go to the polls. Given the importance of understanding elections, from the perspective of citizen and activist alike, it is little wonder that academic students of politics have also attended closely to the matter of electoral choice.

In the last decade particularly, Ontario has posed a considerable challenge to those who would understand elections and electors. If the defeat of the Liberal government in 1943 signalled the beginning of a modern era of three-party politics in the province, it also began a period of remarkable stability in election results. From that point, the province was governed for a period of forty-two years by the Progressive Conservative Party. Admittedly, the PCs never held a majority of the popular vote in that period, and they were forced to govern with a minority of the seats following a third of the twelve elections they won. However, neither of the two opposition parties ever seemed strong enough to supplant the other and thereby pose a serious threat to the dominance of the Conservative party. Since 1985, however, both the Liberals (in 1985 and 1987)

TABLE 1
Popular vote vs. seats won among three parties (in percentage)

Year	% of votes			% of seats			Total seats	% of seats ÷ % of votes		
	PC	LIB	NDP	PC	LIB	NDP		PC	LIB	NDP
1943	36	31	32	42	18	38	90	1.17	.57	1.18
1945	44	30	22	73	16	9	90	1.66	.52	.40
1948	40	31	27	59	16	23	90	1.44	.52	.86
1951	48	32	19	88	9	2	90	1.83	.28	.12
1955	49	33	17	86	11	3	98	1.75	.34	.18
1959	46	37	17	72	22	5	98	1.57	.63	.30
1963	48	35	16	71	22	6	108	1.49	.63	.41
1967	42	32	26	59	24	17	117	1.40	.75	.66
1971	45	28	27	66	17	16	117	1.48	.61	.60
1975	36	34	29	43	26	30	125	1.19	.76	1.03
1977	40	32	28	46	27	26	125	1.15	.84	.93
1981	44	34	21	56	27	17	125	1.27	.79	.81
1985	37	38	24	42	38	20	125	1.14	1.00	.83
1987	25	48	26	12	73	15	130	.48	1.52	.58
1990	24	32	38	15	28	57	130	.63	.88	1.50
1995	45	31	21	63	23	13	130	1.40	.74	.62

and the NDP (in 1990) have formed governments, and in the face of such volatility, it is hard to say whether the Conservatives' regaining office in 1995 represents a return to the status quo or the continuation of a newly unstable era in electoral politics.

An important starting point for those who sought to understand election results at the beginning of this century, and one that continues to be of interest, is a review of the constituency results in an effort to categorize ridings as 'safe' or 'marginal' seats. In the absence of polling data, from which one could examine *individual* voter choice, the aggregated vote totals for constituencies (or for the polling subdivisions in which votes are cast and counted) at least provide some information about the past that may act as a guide to future results. Also the characterization of seats and polls in terms of their competitiveness has the advantage of identifying areas where campaign resources presumably can be deployed to optimum effect.

Of course, prediction of the future on the basis of the past relies on a degree of stability in voter choice that may not always be in evidence. As recently as the 1950s, voting was thought to be heavily influenced by the 'identification' of voters with parties, and elections with substantial shifts in constituency results were thus thought to signal either a 'deviation' of identifiers from their 'normal' support, or a 'realignment' of identification that would presumably be evident in future voting patterns. Regardless of the changes in an electorate as some voters died and others came of age, the observation that some seats were regularly dominated by one party or another was explained in terms of the long-term commitment of individual voters to their party. Similarly, the fact that some other seats consistently experienced closely fought contests between (or among) parties was not commonly attributed to voter volatility, but to the closeness of numerical balance between the committed supporters of one party and the equally committed supporters of the other(s). In recent years, however, there has been growing evidence that party identification is not as stable as was once believed, and that indeed, for some voters, identification with a party means little more than an intention to vote for that party at the next opportunity. That intention moreover may be highly volatile and open to influence from a number of directions.

Rules of the Game

Before any attempt is made to understand or predict the results of elections, it is probably wise to understand the rules governing the contests. Election law in Ontario has not changed much in the past decade (the last major alterations were in 1984 and 1986), and there is little indication that any party finds the system badly in need of reform. There are two main categories of election rules: (1) rules governing the enumeration of electors and the conduct of polling; and (2) those governing the registration and financing of political parties and candidates, as well as the conduct of election campaigns.

(1) Voters and polling: Electors in Ontario are enumerated (that is, entered on the list of those eligible to vote) before each election in a house-to-house canvass. The enumeration is conducted by persons nominated by the government party's probable candidate and by the probable candidate of the party with the greatest number of votes in that riding at the last election. The persons chosen are expected to conduct the enumeration in pairs – each is intended to assure the honest performance of the other – and if there is any bias in their instructions, it is towards inclusion, rather than exclusion, of names on the voters' list. Residents are normally taken at their word if they declare that they are eligible to vote, unless the enumerators have reason to suspect they are not. Enu-

merators are usually local people who know the community and who are paid a small amount to collect the names. For the governing party, enumeration is an opportunity for petty patronage. From time to time, there are allegations that enumerators have erred in including non-citizens, or in excluding eligible electors, but the system usually does not produce enough error to cause concern about an election result. There may well be systematic – even unintended – class, race, or gender bias in the enumeration. Homeless people are not enumerated because they do not have an address, recent immigrants who cannot speak English or who are unfamiliar with our democratic practices may not get onto the register, and it has been suggested that women escaping abusive relationships may not want their names publicly displayed on the register or may not wish to answer the door to strangers. There are well-publicized opportunities for prospective voters who have not been enumerated to get on the list before election day, and party canvassers regularly offer assistance with the procedure. In rural ridings, persons missed by the enumerators may vote if they swear that they are eligible and are vouched for by an eligible elector who is on the list. No such provision ordinarily applies in urban ridings, where enumeration is presumably less difficult to conduct and access to the process of 'revision' of the list is more convenient.

Voters in Ontario elections must be eighteen years of age. They must be Canadian citizens and must have resided in Ontario for six months before polling day. They must also ordinarily be resident in the constituency in which they propose to vote. No one may vote if prohibited by law from doing so. The vote is denied to inmates of reform or penal institutions.

The members of the Ontario Legislature are elected in 130 constituencies by simple-plurality vote (that is, the candidate with the most votes wins, regardless of how small a percentage of the vote is received; with more than two candidates usually in each seat, it is rare for a candidate to capture a majority of the vote, and not uncommon for candidates to win with less than 40 per cent). The present constituency boundaries were drawn by an independent Electoral Boundaries Commission (appointed in 1983) and approved by the legislature in time for the 1987 election. Despite the intention to create ridings with approximately equal numbers of voters, the provision of a guaranteed fifteen seats for Northern Ontario, the allowance of seats to vary up to 25 per cent from the average population, the agreement that even this 25 per cent limit could be exceeded if the commission considered it 'necessary or desirable,' and the fact that the boundaries are based on the 1981 census all mean that the ideal of 'one person, one vote' is now far from realized. At the present time there are large differences in the voting population of ridings. The largest riding, York Centre, had 129,108 names on the voting list for the 1995 election, while Rainy River had just 19,406 eligible voters. With the passage in late 1996 by the Harris government of the Fewer Politicians Act, which will reduce the legislature to 103 seats for the next election, some of these large differences will be eliminated. Since the provincial electoral boundaries will duplicate federal boundaries, the province will have effectively given control of its electoral map to the federal government.

The province continues to use paper ballots, which are counted by hand after the polls have closed. Since each election normally involves voting for only the one office, the system has not proved unwieldy and is likely to be maintained in the foreseeable future. The ballots bear only the names of the candidates in alphabetical order (unless two or more names are so similar that confusion is likely, in which case the Chief Election Officer – after consultation with all the candidates – will decide how the names are to be presented). In contrast to federal elections, the ballots make no mention of candidates' party affiliations. The consequence of this fact is that some proportion of any party candidate's campaign activity must be devoted to ensuring that voters (and especially party supporters) are aware of the link between the candidate and the party, and aware of the fact that the ballot will give them no clue as to that link when they have entered the polling booth.

Each candidate in a constituency may appoint scrutineers in each polling subdivision; 'outside' scrutineers are permitted to review the voters' list kept at the polling station from time to time while the polls are open, so long as they do not interfere with persons seeking to vote; 'inside' scrutineers (who may be the same persons) remain in the polling place after the polls have closed and observe the counting of the votes. Review of the list while voting is in progress is done in order to determine whether a particular elector has voted (names of voters are crossed off as they present themselves at the poll). The information is of use to candidates whose supporters have canvassed a poll and have identified possible supporters whom they wish to encourage or assist to attend the poll. The secrecy of the voter's choice is assured, since a ballot is deemed spoiled if any mark is placed on it that would identify the voter, and scrutineers and officials are expected to make no effort to determine how any elector has voted and are sworn to keep secret any such information if it should come to them by inadvertence. Ballot secrecy not only preserves the anonymity of each voter's choice, thus guarding them from possible retribution, but also ensures that buying a vote (besides being strictly illegal) is a risky proposition, given that the buyer cannot be absolutely sure that the seller has delivered the product.

(2) Registration and finance of parties and candidates: Candidates for election to the legislature must meet the same criteria of eligibility as electors, except that they need not be resident in the constituency for which they seek election. Since 1984, they have been required to post a $200 deposit (refundable if they secure at least 10 per cent of the vote) in order to be placed on the ballot.

Political parties are required, as a result of campaign finance legislation, to register with the province so that they may legally spend money on behalf of candidates for election, and so that their supporters may have the advantage of tax credits for political contributions. To qualify, they must have nominated fifty candidates in an election for the legislature or have garnered ten thousand signatures of eligible voters on a petition. At the present time, there are ten parties that have registered under the Election Finances Act.[3] The three principal parties (the Ontario Liberal Party, the Ontario New Democratic Party, and the Progressive Conservative Party of Ontario) qualified under the old legislation because at the time of its passage they had at least four members in the legislature. The Communist Party, the Libertarian Party, the Freedom Party (formerly the Unparty), and the Green Party all qualified by petition process under the old law, and the Family Coalition Party and Ontario Provincial Confederation of Regions qualified by petition under the new law. In 1995, the Natural Law Party qualified by the nomination process. As of 28 June 1995, only the three main parties had registered constituency associations in all 130 provincial ridings; among the others, only the Green Party came close to that number with 114 registered associations. The Family Coalition Party had 82 registered associations, and all the others only a handful each.

The Election Finance Commission also regulates the use of party names and abbreviations, and several individuals and organizations have registered names but have not developed parties to register under those names. Many requests for the registration of particular names have been rejected by the commission, in some cases because of potential confusion with existing parties. In the summer of 1994, the Reform Party of Canada was permitted to register the name 'Reform Party of Ontario,' despite the clear position of the national party that it would *not* run candidates in provincial elections. At the same time, the Reform Association of Ontario (a group who wanted to run provincial candidates under the Reform banner) was refused the right to use the name. The effect was to ensure that the national party, by registering the provincial name for its own use, prevented the running of provincial candidates under the Reform banner by the one organization that wanted to do so.

Party Competition

From 1905 to 1985, the Conservative (after 1942, Progressive Conservative) Party governed the province with only two brief interruptions – the Farmer-Labour government from 1919 to 1923 and the Liberal governments between 1934 and 1943. This record of apparent stability masks a transformation of the system of party competition in 1943, however, when what had been essentially a two-party system (with a short-lived deviation in 1919) became effectively a three-party system with the emergence of the CCF as a serious contender for power. The virtual collapse of the Liberals in 1943 made the CCF the Official Opposition, and although the Liberals regrouped in 1945, two-party competition was not restored. The CCF formed the Official Opposition again in 1948, and its successor, the New Democratic Party, became the Official Opposition in 1975. Following the election of 1985, the NDP entered into an agreement to sustain a Liberal minority government (in return for influence on the legislative agenda); they became the Official Opposition again in 1987, and formed the government of the province in 1990. In the period from 1943 to the present, no party has secured support from a majority of the electorate, and since 1967, none of the three main parties has fallen below 20 per cent of the popular vote.

Even as the province developed a three-party system, however, there were areas of the province where contests between only two parties were still the norm. Rural eastern Ontario remained a Conservative stronghold, with competition mainly from the Liberals. Conversely, rural southwestern Ontario was a Liberal bastion, threatened only by the Conservatives. As the cities and small industrial centres of southern Ontario grew in the 1960s and 1970s, the competitive presence of the NDP became more evident, and indeed in Windsor and Hamilton, and in parts of Toronto, the PCs often found themselves in third place. Metropolitan Toronto produced the most competitive struggles involving all three parties, but even within that region there were pockets where two-party competition was the norm. In the north, where the forestry and mining industries predominated, competition between 1971 and 1985 was often between the Conservatives and the NDP, with the Liberals a sometimes distant third. More recently, that pattern has been disrupted and there are seats in the north representing almost any pattern of competition one could imagine involving two or three parties.

Since 1987, however, it appears that the volatility of voter support for the three main parties has increased almost everywhere; there are few areas of the province in which any of the three can be said to be entirely secure, and few where any of the three have absolutely no prospect of success. There have been three general elections in the province (1987, 1990, and 1995) carried out using the current constituency boundaries. A review of results from those elections will demonstrate the changes that have taken place in party competitiveness.

In 1987, the Liberals won 95 seats and were second in 34; the PCs won only 16 seats, but were second in 54; the NDP won 19, and were second in 42. In 1990, the NDP won 74 seats (26 with less than 40 per cent of the vote, and 14 of those with under 35 per cent) and were second in 37; the Liberals won 36 and were second in 76; the PCs won 20, but were second in only 17. It would have been difficult to predict from these numbers alone that the Conservatives would win 81 seats in 1995 (28 with over 55 per cent of the vote and 20 of those with over 60 per cent) and come second in 30. The Liberals remained broadly competitive with 29 wins and 75 second-place finishes. The virtual collapse of the NDP vote allowed them to retain only 19 seats and to finish second in only 44. Clearly there has been enormous vote volatility in these three elections, though the Liberals were rather more consistent than the other two parties in first- and second-place finishes (129, 112, and 104 respectively, as compared with 61, 111, and 63 for the NDP and 70, 37, and 111 for the PCs).

There were 42 seats won by the same party in all three elections; one might be tempted to label these 'safe' seats, but not all were won by substantial margins, and some could very well change hands without a very substantial alteration in vote. Moreover, there are seats in the province that a party has lost after winning the seat in the previous election with over 50 per cent of the vote. Of the 42 seats that did not change hands after 1987, the Liberals won 19, the Conservatives 12, and the NDP 11. There were 53 seats won by two parties, but not by the third – 25 by either the Liberals or the PCs; 17 by either the Liberals or the NDP; and 11 by either the NDP or the PCs. Again, the seats vary in their margins of victory, and some can be said to be competitive among three parties, if the criterion is that each party regularly have at least 20 per cent of the vote. That leaves 34 seats that were won by a different party in each election – three elections, one each won by the Liberals, the Conservatives, and the NDP – and one seat (Elgin in southwestern Ontario) won by the Liberals, then the NDP, and then by the former NDP incumbent running as an independent. By the most conservative of criteria – that the seat have changed hands at least once in two elections (that is, in 1990 or 1995) – fully two-thirds of the province's seats can be said to be competitive. There remain, however, some variations across regions in the nature and extent of competition.

Let us look first at the 'safe' seats won in all three elections by the same party. Six of the NDP's wins were in northern Ontario seats, three were in Toronto (including the leader's seat), one was in the Niagara peninsula, and one was in Windsor. For the Conservatives, four of their consistent wins were in central Ontario, cottage-resort areas north of Toronto (including the leader's seat), three were in exurban areas on the fringe of Toronto, and five were in their traditional stronghold of eastern Ontario. The Liberals had six consistent wins in Toronto (mainly suburban), four in the north (including the leader's seat), seven in traditionally Conservative eastern Ontario (including three in Ottawa), one in the Niagara region, and one in Windsor. None of their consistent victories was in their traditional stronghold of rural southwestern Ontario.

Where are the seats that were won by a different party in each of the three contests? Only seven of the seats were in ostensibly competitive Metropolitan Toronto, though five were in the Toronto 'exurbs' and five were in the Niagara region of the 'Golden Horseshoe' around the western end of Lake Ontario. Three were in the central Ontario cottage-resort region north of Toronto and three were in eastern Ontario. By far the most volatile region by this criterion – number of seats held by different parties in three elections – was the southwest. Fully eleven of the changeable seats were in that area, as was the single seat that was won in 1995 by an independent candidate. In all thirty-four of the seats held by different parties in the three elections, the pattern was the same (and matched the pattern of the province as a whole): the seats were won by the Liberals in 1987, by the NDP in 1990, and by the Conservatives in 1995.

In the fourth edition of this book, one of this chapter's authors speculated that the 1985 election might represent an occasion of 'realignment' of party support, favouring the Liberals, and starting in the more diverse, urban, industrial areas of the province. The expectation was that the realignment (if such it was) would be evident in the more traditional, rural areas only in later elections, though even in 1987 the numbers cast doubt on that analysis. In the light of the three elections following 1985, the sense that a stable realignment of voter identification occurred in that year is completely overturned. Instead, the picture emerging from the riding-by-riding results in 1987, 1990, and 1995 is of a large 'floating' vote moving among the three parties in search of a government that can command longer-term allegiance. Whether this picture is accurate and, if so, whether the 'floaters' are likely to continue in motion cannot easily be determined without polling data that tracks individual changes in vote across the three elections, and vote intention at the next opportunity. One would have to remain cautious even about such poll results, however, since recollections of past voting are subject to considerable error and vote intention seems highly volatile. When the election of 1995 was called, for example, the Liberals had consistently held the support of a majority of respondents in a number of surveys over several months. Yet the Conservatives won a sizeable victory when the actual election was held.

Election Campaigns in Ontario

In seeking to explain this degree of volatility, political observers often turn to matters that are featured in election campaigning, such as changes in leadership, actions by government that divide voters in previously unexpected ways, or changes in party platforms that have the same polarizing effect. Leadership may indeed have been a factor in people's minds during the election campaign of 1995. Premier Bob Rae of course remained leader of the NDP, as he had been in 1987 and 1990, but the Liberals had selected a new leader after their 1990 loss of power and the Conservatives had selected their new leader just before the 1990 vote. Some press reports following the 1995 election blamed Liberal leader Lyn McLeod for turning an apparently insurmountable lead in the opinion polls into a defeat by election day. She was described as being indecisive and was accused of 'flip-flopping' on issues, but it is not the leader alone who should bear the responsibility for a campaign strategy that appeared uncertain whether to concentrate on the governing NDP (which was not expected to regain office) or the Conservatives (who started in third place in the legislature, if not in the polls). Premier Rae entered the contest running ahead of his party in approval – indeed, he was seen as one of his party's strongest assets – but his popularity was insufficient to improve the NDP's support. The NDP had little in the way of a campaign platform and tried to run on the integrity of not making promises and the leader's high ratings. Neither of these strategies translated into votes and appear to have been ill advised. Past Conservative campaigns had regularly centred on the leader, especially during the period when they formed the government of the province, and they did not change that emphasis much in opposition. However, Mike Harris was a little-known quantity in 1990, and the Conservative result in that election was so poor that a more experienced leader might have felt compelled to resign. By contrast, polls suggest that Mr Harris was a strong campaign asset in 1995; nevertheless, the Conservative platform, the 'Common Sense Revolution,' played an important part in the election. The Tories had been preparing their manifesto for the past four years, holding public meetings across the province and gathering input from those who favoured neo-conservative policy alternatives. Leadership may well be an important variable to help explain the last three general-election results in Ontario, but the explanation must be very complicated indeed. Bob Rae's leadership was insufficient to help his party retain its 'balance of power' role in 1987, was presumably more effective in 1990 when he became premier, and was again reduced in weight (or reversed in direction of effect) in 1995. Lyn McLeod led her party in only one election, but was party leader for most of the period when her party formed the Official Opposition to the NDP government. While she led her party in opposition, they were consistently on top of the opinion polls, but when the election campaign got under way, the Liberals turned potential victory into defeat. Finally, Mike Harris led his party to one of the worst drubbings in its history and one of its largest landslides as well. Clearly, something else besides leadership must have been at work.

We know that voters are not ordinarily all that well informed about candidates, leaders, and issues, even after a long election campaign. Yet somehow they appear to form impressions about those who seek their vote and to act on those impressions when the opportunity arises. Several factor may have come together to influence those impressions in the period from 1985 to 1995, leading to the volatile results reviewed above.

The Changing Technology of Election Campaigning

Campaigns have changed a great deal with the advent of new communications technology. Radio, telephone, television, multichannel television, satellites, cell phones, computers, and the Internet have all had effects on how campaigns are conducted. The radio gave parties their first opportunity to broadcast their message over a wider area than the crowd standing immediately in front of the speaker. Radio still has an important part to play in campaigns because it is relatively inexpensive, and because its audience is so fragmented, specific demographic groups can be effectively targeted. For example, the listeners to an all-sport radio channel will be mostly male, mostly urban, and mostly lower and middle class. If a party has a particular campaign message for this group, buying spots on sports radio will be an effective way of spending campaign dollars.

The telephone has had an equally important impact on campaigns in the last twenty years. Cell phones now allow instant communication and tighter control by central campaign planners over constituency campaigns and even the leader's tour. Strategists can literally be in the leader's ear, prompting with suitable answers to questions. But the telephone has had an even greater impact on polling and research. Twenty-five years ago, most polling was done by the slow and expensive door-to-door method or some less-reputable type of convenience sampling such as the person in the mall waylaying anyone who might take the time to answer. Not only were these methods expensive in staff costs and additional travel, but they were also, by today's standards, excruciatingly slow. Near universal access to telephones and the development of telephone sampling techniques and computer-assisted telephone interviewing has revolutionized polling, driving down costs, in many cases improving the quality of the data, and speeding up interviewing. Most campaigns will now be polling nightly, interviewing about two or three hundred people per day and adding these to the previous night's interviews to create a kind of rolling sample that gives strategists immediate answers to their questions about how the party's message is playing with the electorate. Polling can provide immediate feedback about new policy announcements, how a leader has done in a debate, how the television advertising campaign is being received, and how well future arguments might work if it is necessary to use them. Polling has become the scouting party of the election campaign. No credible campaign can hope to manage the party's message without polling information. Of course, campaigns never like to admit their extensive use of polling to affect all aspects of the campaign, and polling data is generally considered top-secret information, available to only a small number of campaign insiders, thus increasing their control over the entire campaign.

Television, with the multichannel universe the previous decade has brought us, has also become a crucial part of modern campaigns. Parties spend nearly half of their total campaign resources on television advertising, with the most spent on buying air time and producing commercials. Campaign ads are now crucial aspects of the campaign, and they are probably the only message that most people will receive directly from the party during the campaign, as very few take an active part in the campaign or attend campaign speeches. It is unfortunate, but true, that most voters' total involvement in and information about the campaign will be taken from a fifteen- or thirty-second ad, run during a television program and sandwiched between a beer ad and another for a new automobile. That means the impact of the ads is very important, and those who design ads and purchase air time become central planners of the campaign. They have a key role in determining the message in the advertising, how that message is realized in the sound and visuals of the ad, and what groups of people are targeted by the ad. The advertising industry keeps close track of who watches what programs as vital information to sell to prospective advertisers who have targeted certain demographic groups. This information is turned to the use of campaigners who may wish to vary their message according to the group that is most likely to hear or see it. The importance of television advertising to the modern campaign has centralized increasing amounts of power in a small group of strategists who design and create the ads and, further, has influenced political messages in the direction of commercial messages that the medium was designed to carry. We will return later to discuss these effects on campaigns.

Computers have gradually been affecting the way campaigns are run, and while it is just beginning to be important, the Internet via computers is also sure to have an effect on future campaigns. From its first use, the computer's value to campaigns has been in information storage and retrieval and the manipulation of large datasets that contain information about voters. Before campaigns were computerized, lists of supporters were laboriously typed and retyped, and probably never completely maintained. A tour through the filing cabinet of a riding association or even a central party would reveal piles of old, incomplete, surely partial, and badly identified records that are undated, half-written, half-typed, and often half-legible as well. The past twenty years have seen increased computer use in keeping the records of supporters and, more important, donors. The computer has been even more important in the development of fund-raising, particularly through direct mail. The Mulroney Conservatives developed this type of fund-raising to near gold-mine proportions. Computers generated personalized letters addressed to homeowners and addressing policy questions that were thought, on the basis of the analysis of census demographic data, to be of particular interest to the addressees. The campaign can not only direct tailored messages at those it feels are its most likely supporters, but it can keep track of and analyse the response in terms of donations and support.

Local campaigns, and national campaigns to a lesser extent, are all about lists – keeping track of known supporters and identifying potential supporters. Computerization has allowed campaigns to perfect this control and extend it by matching all manner of new databases with information on income, residence, family size, age, magazine reading habits, product buying, education, and so on. This information and the capacity to handle and manipulate it has permitted campaigns to target potential voters and craft policy messages and promises that it feels will be particularly attractive to certain sets of voters. This ability has once again concentrated power, and more specifically decision-making authority, in the hands of a small group of advisers whose job it is to deliver electoral victory, and whose tools are the fashioning of policy to convince some voters and be appealing to others. In this climate of persuasion and compliance, traditional party ideological and policy positions are usually the first casualties. Supposedly popular policies and promises that try to ingratiate the party with voters become the order of the day. It is small wonder that many of these promises and policy statements have little chance of becoming reality. Indeed, their reality was only that of a campaign effort to win support and power.

In the 1995 election, for the first time, all three parties had Internet websites. It is doubtful the sites had much influence on the campaign, since most of the information they contained was available elsewhere in print; and despite the hype that surrounds the Internet, users still represent a quite small percentage of the electorate and a select demographic group of well-educated high earners who are probably mostly male. At the present time, 'web sites' are just another targeting vehicle for parties, though the audience is rather small. Should the Internet become more widely available, its effect on campaigns may be most important outside of the main party campaign. American experience shows that a host of groups with an interest in the campaign have developed web sites to broadcast their messages and their analysis of the campaign as a way around the gatekeepers in the media who overlook what they imagine to be non-mainstream views.

Financing Elections

Courting the favour of voters is an expensive undertaking. Even with public subsidies for parties that are moderately successful, to get into the campaign business and have a chance of winning means that a party must have deep pockets. This fact all but rules out the possibility of new parties entering the electoral fray and stabilizes our politics around a number of conventional policy alternatives that all of the three parties in Ontario generally agree on. While editorial writers and op-ed commentators love to lash the parties for what appears to them to be profligate campaign spending, any other yardstick one can think of (for instance, U.S. elections) reveals that the money Ontario parties spend on elections is really quite modest. While advertising costs may seem exorbitant, put in perspective as a once-every-three-or-four-year expenditure (and in comparison to the advertising budgets of large companies, who spend these sums weekly or even daily), election spending is, if not trivial, at least modest. We may not agree with the manipulatory direction of campaigns, but as a cost of maintaining democratic elections, advertising seems very cheap indeed.

The regulation of campaign fund-raising and expenditure is performed by the Ontario Commission on Election Finances, which implements Ontario's Election Finances Act. The act is one of the most advanced pieces of legislation in democratic practice. It controls parties' fund-raising and expenditure through a number of easily stated, though not always easily realized, principles. First, the act requires that all central parties, constituency parties, candidates, and central and constituency campaigns be registered entities that must complete properly documented and audited annual or campaign-period returns. Second, it puts in place limits on the size, type, and source of donations to parties. A single donor could not give sufficient money to support even a modest local campaign. With these limitations, a single corporation, individual, or union cannot exercise undue influence over a party's campaign. The act also limits donors to those resident in the province and includes donations of services and free time that may advantage one party over another. Third, the act also limits the campaign expenditures of candidates, constituencies, and central parties with the application of a formula based on a cost per voter. In effect, this limits most local campaigns to under $50,000 and central campaigns to under $3,000,000. Fourth, the act mandates the public disclosure of all donations over $100 and all campaign expenditures over $1000. This allows the public to determine whether a candidate or party is open to undue influence by a single donor or group of donors. Fifth, the financing legislation provides for a direct public subsidy to support local and provincial campaigns, provided that the candidate garners at least 15 per cent of the vote. A public subsidy is also made available to parties that run a large number of candidates and attract a substantial percentage of voters. This provision diminishes the parties' reliance on private donors and, perhaps as a side effect, ensures that the parties' handling of money is above reproach. In the 1995 campaign, the winning Conservative party and the opposition Liberals both received public subsidies of just over $331,000 – about 11 per cent of the Conservatives' campaign-period income and 15 per cent of the Liberals' income. The parties also received public support through the generous 75 per cent tax rebate on donations to political parties. This amounts to a generous indirect public subsidy out of the provincial coffers, its purpose being to increase and stabilize the funding of political parties and to encourage smaller donors. It probably has had its greatest impact on the NDP, which is usually supported by middle- and lower-income earners who have apparently been susceptible to the argument that $75 of a $100 donation to the party is in effect a loan that will be repaid at tax time.

Campaign Spending

As table 2 (p. 206) shows, campaign spending in the past four elections between 1985 and 1995 has been gradually increasing. The one real exception to this trend was the mammoth $4.25 million losing campaign that the Conservatives ran in 1985. That campaign remains by far the most expensive of the period and probably of Ontario's history. The campaign-finance law has contributed to the equalizing of expenditure across the three main parties during the most recent election. A simple glance at the entire table and a little mental arithmetic easily confirms that expenditure is not related to success at the polls and winning parties are frequently outspent by losers. Fortunately, despite all the apparently effective tools of the campaign trade, expenditure is not a direct measure of success; there is still some room for the public mood and the art of reading it in determining election success.

What is perhaps more interesting about the table is the allocation of expenditures within the campaign and what these reveal about the differences between the parties. The most remarkable feature of the table is that for every party, at every election, advertising expenditures were by far the largest campaign expense and approached (and in some cases

TABLE 2
Central party campaign expenditures, Ontario 1985–95

	1995			1990			1987			1985		
	Lib %	NDP %	PC %	Lib. %	NDP %	PC %	Lib %	NDP %	PC %	Lib. %	NDP %	PC %
Advertising	45	41	68	49	53	41	50	48	54	43	59	49
Travel	13	17	13	9	17	13	9	14	9	7	12	14
Fund-raising	0	2	2	8	3	7	0	9	6	6	8	5
Research	9	7	2	19	7	4	16	4	9	8	3	11
Office	14	9	8	7	3	4	6	3	5	8	2	9
Salaries, consulting	0	10	3	0	6	0	4	12	3	8	13	6
Transfers	5	3	3	2	6	1	9	6	1	5	3	1
Other	14	11	2	6	6	30	5	4	12	14	0	6
Total $	2,789,323	2,528,343	2,585,625	2,987,138	1,624,810	2,402,159	2,597,785	1,475,423	1,974,702	1,596,235	1,353,198	4,262,845

exceeded) half of the total campaign expenses. Making television ads and buying airtime was by far the largest single component of advertising costs. For example, in 1995, the Conservatives paid Thomas Watt Advertising, a media buyer, $1.6 million for TV airtime, the Liberals paid Vickers and Benson $1.2 million, and the NDP gave $730,000 to Media Dimensions. The winning Conservative campaign was exceptional in dedicating close to 70 per cent of its budget to advertising, a far larger percentage than either of the other two parties.

The table also shows some important differences in how the parties are organized. The 'transfers' line in the table indicates sums given by the central party to the constituencies to assist in the running of local campaigns. The Liberal and NDP central parties are considerably more generous in assisting local campaigns than is the Conservative party. While this undoubtedly reflects the financial independence the Conservative party gives to its member constituencies – a mixed blessing to be sure – it probably also reflects the enormous debt that the party has carried throughout the ten-year period. While the Conservatives in office have preached deficit reduction, the party in practice has been engaged in deficit financing throughout the eighties and nineties, frequently carrying debt loads of as much as $5 million and failing to make significant inroads into the total, Mike Harris notwithstanding. Now that the party is in government, and fund-raising opportunities may therefore be more frequent, the debt will probably be significantly diminished.

The final noteworthy pattern in the table is in the salary and consulting line. The NDP, claiming to be a party of the working class, has always had significantly larger salary expenses than either of the other two parties, who apparently draw their expertise from people who can afford not to charge salaries. But that is not the complete story, for salaries, or commissions, or consulting fees are also buried in several other expense lines; one good example is polling and research, where charges undoubtedly hide some considerable fees. For example, the Liberal polling for the 1987 and 1990 elections was spectacularly expensive, and over the two elections Goldfarb Research charged the Liberal Party about $1 million for election polling.

Election Advertising

Despite the significance of advertising to overall campaign expenditures, few answers can be provided to some very simple questions about the parties' television-ad campaigns. For example, how often did the parties advertise?

There is little Canadian research that systematically shows how often parties advertised during a campaign. The widely held and incorrect assumption seems to be that campaign-advertising legislation dictates the airtime of the parties and keeps it roughly equal or at least reflective of the parties' share of seats in the legislature. In fact, there is no such legislation. In Ontario there are no requirements that paid television time be apportioned according to some formula for fairness. There are only two limits on the airtime a party can buy during an election: the inventory of advertising spots available and the global campaign-spending limits that the party must abide by. The current legislation leaves the parties free to determine their own mix of election spending. As will become clear below, there are good reasons to question this free-handed approach, for in reality it allows some parties to monopolize the airtime of particular stations, effectively shutting out the ads of other parties.

An analysis of logs kept for the Canadian Radio-television and Telecommunications Commission (CRTC) for a sample of eleven stations reveals some very large differences in the ad campaigns of the three main parties contesting the June 1995 Ontario election. Of the 2640 campaign commercials aired on eleven stations in the three-week advertising period between 17 May and 6 June, Progressive Conservative ads made up 53 per cent of the total, out-advertising the second-finishing Liberal Party by 2 to 1 and the incumbent government NDP by almost 3 to 1. When the numbers of ads are translated into air minutes, the NDP disadvantage is magnified: it trailed the Conservatives by 3.3 to 1 and the Liberals by 1.7 to 1, while the Liberals trailed the Conservatives by 2 to 1.

The large differences in the number of ads run by the parties is not the entire story, for it masks some considerable station-to-station variation across the eleven stations sampled. At the extreme, the Conservatives controlled the entire political advertising inventory on CKVR Barrie, a station that is carried on cable into Toronto and especially the outer areas of the GTA, the suburban and middle-class belt where the Conservatives gained seats from the Liberals and NDP. They also had large leads in the numbers of spots showing on CHCH Hamilton, CHEX Peterborough, CKCO Kitchener, and CKWS Kingston. The first three of these channels are also carried into the Toronto region by cable. The Conservatives trailed both the Liberals and NDP in spots showing on the two Toronto stations in the sample, CFTO and CITY. The relatively small Conservative buy on CITY may have been a targeting decision, for the youthful, urban viewers of CITY do not naturally appear to be part of the traditional Conservative electorate. CFTO is a slightly more complicated case, being the most expensive station on which to buy airtime and, through the Baton-CTV system, having a province-wide reach for some advertising spots.

It is obvious that the Conservative campaign had a well-considered media-buying strategy. The Conservatives were able to buy relatively inexpensive airtime on outlying stations and have the messages carried into Toronto and the suburban areas they had targeted as their potential electorate. In one case, constant viewers of a channel would have seen nothing but Conservative party ads. This apparent strategic success must have been the result of careful geographical targeting of the party's potential electorate and the organization and speed of the media buy. Since the NDP had the luxury of knowing the date of the election, they also had the advantage in placing their media buy. Interviews with campaign strategists suggest that this advantage was squandered, and the Conservatives (with the help of Jamie Watt, who in the words of one Liberal strategist 'blew our doors off on the buy')[4] began buying choice airtime as soon as the election writ was issued. In some cases, this resulted in the other parties being all but shut out, either wittingly or unwittingly, through the purchase of the entire advertising inventory. Leslie Noble, the Conservative campaign manager, indicated the importance of the buying strategy and the speed with which it was done: 'It was done the second the election was announced – we had our buy plan designed two months prior to the election so that it would be ready. Much of it is how much muscle and speed you can exert. Obviously there are election broadcast laws that legislate fairness, equal time as it were, that is not necessarily the best times. We designed our buy around the demographics we had to reach and where we thought we were going to get our biggest bang for our buck in terms of population, number of seats, and bought heavily in those areas.'[5] Alister Campbell, another key campaign adviser, underlined the importance of the Conservative strategy: 'We spent almost all of our money on the buy and we won the race on the buy. We ordered our ads hours before Rae called the election, the Liberals didn't get their buy in for another thirty-six hours so we won almost all of the avails, we had better positioning, better placing and also we disproportionately weighted our campaign to the back end. In the final week, when we operated on the assumption that the other two guys would be viciously negative against us that we would be able to match their combined throw weight.'[6]

The importance of media-buying strategies to campaigns deserves some comment. Media buyers are agents who act between the media (selling advertising time or space) and the customer who is selling a product. Buyers develop relationships with media sellers and often enter into contractual relationships to provide customers to media in return for reduced rates. Large and influential media buyers can offer customers reduced rates while guaranteeing sellers large blocks of sold time or space. Political parties may benefit in terms of expertise, and perhaps reduced rates, from a relationship with a media buyer. The Liberals have long had a close relationship with Vickers and Benson, and the media buy for the Liberals was done through Genesis, a company half owned by Vickers and Benson. The Conservatives used Thomas Watt, a London-based buyer.

Establishing the effectiveness of ad campaigns through observing their effects on voters is an impossibly complex problem to sort out. Voting decisions are a mixture of expressible and inchoate reactions to political ideas and personalities. But being too cautious has its limitations as well. There is sufficient evidence to venture some conclusions on the impor-tance of the ad campaigns to the outcome of the 1995 election.

Strategists of every party acknowledged the disciplined and focused Conservative campaign that managed not only to pick the issues that were most disturbing the electorate but also to sell these in a way that their solutions were credible and that they could be trusted to carry them out. The ad campaign reflected this long-term planning and discipline and laid the groundwork for the Conservative growth in support that carried them to office. As Leslie Noble put it: 'Our ads were extremely effective, they were simple and to the point, there weren't a whole bunch of them, the worst thing you can do in advertising is to mix your mes-sage, repetition is everything. Really, we only had four ads, the Liberals had ten or twelve ads, several of them running. When we look at the post-writ studies that we've done, people knew exactly what our mes-sage was, they had no idea what the Liberal messages were – they didn't know or they were specific – 70 percent of the people said they couldn't identify a Liberal policy or a Liberal message from that campaign. I think advertising played a very big role.'[7] Tom Long, the Conservative cam-paign chair, underlined Noble's comments in saying that 'the overall strategy was to keep it simple and to drive the points home and to dominate the media agenda and the issues agenda. The advertising simply fed into that. We wanted to be aggressively comparative with the Liberals so that people understood the difference between the two op-tions. We always believed that Bob Rae was irrelevant to the process.'[8] The Conservative ad campaign was further boosted by the spot advantage it held over the other two parties. Not only did they dominate the spot battle on several stations, but their buy was timed to provide plenty of response or attack possibilities at the end of the campaign. But it is still impossible to ascertain whether a good campaign brings victory or a victorious campaign always appears to be good. The Tories could have been dreadfully wrong. They certainly were in 1990, when their equally hard-hitting and focused ads gained them virtually no return. But that was in the context of some forceful NDP ads that seemed to catch the mood of frustration in the electorate in the same way the Tory ads did in 1995. It is probably more saying than truth that the winning party always has the best campaign advertising.

The Conservative advertising has to be seen in the context of the two ill-focused and badly managed advertising campaigns that ran in opposition to them. On the other hand, whether anything more successful could have been achieved by either the Liberal or NDP campaigns is open to question. They both lacked a clear message and were hobbled by decisions to have those messages conveyed by unpopular or unknown leaders. Their attempt to establish the credibility of their message through the leader were similarly doomed to failure. Inasmuch as the Conservative polling picked up these weaknesses, the NDP and Liberal strategists also should have seen them. The decision to place Bob Rae at the head of the campaign did nothing to win back alienated NDP supporters or gain new ones. And despite attempts to make Lyn McLeod seem like a leader, the Liberal ads only played into the hard-edged Conservative campaign that made her seem vacillating by comparison.

If there is a lesson, it may be the obvious one: that poorly managed ad campaigns usually reflect poorly managed campaigns in general – campaigns that usually end up losing. At least that much is true in the case of the 1995 Ontario election.

Conclusion

The Liberals came to power after the 1985 election, although they did not have the largest number of seats. The Conservatives had lost votes and seats, while the Liberals had made the largest gains. They were able to form a government principally because the NDP agreed not to vote against them on a matter of confidence for a period of two years, provided they received some influence over the legislative package the government would present. The 'accord' was a successful one for both parties in the sense that it produced quite a lot of government policy with which both could agree. It appeared to be of more value to the Liberals, however, in 1987, when the election of that year saw them achieve a majority government for the first time in fifty years.

If the 1987 result was an endorsement of the Liberals, born in part in the legislative achievements they had produced with the support (and prodding) of the NDP, the NDP victory of 1990 was in part a rejection of the Liberals because of a slowdown (absent such prodding) in the production of popular programs. In addition, however, the election result was probably affected by the haste with which the Liberals had sought a second mandate. While majority governments in the province's distant past had occasionally gone to the polls after only three years in office, only one government since 1951 had returned to the polls earlier than the fourth year of its mandate, and that had been the minority government elected in 1975. It was perhaps understandable that the Liberals sought to turn their popularity in opinion polls into a second term in 1990, but many journalists commented on the unnecessary rush, and some voters appear to have agreed.

Another not insignificant factor in 1990 was the appearance of substantial support (in some ridings) for independents and fourth-party candidates. The three main parties split almost 98 per cent of the vote in 1987, but they captured less than 94 per cent in 1990. To be sure, the 'other' vote did not draw uniquely from one party's supporters. However, there were twenty-one seats won by the NDP in 1990 where the margin of victory was less than the vote for independents and fourth-party candidates, and seventeen of those had been Liberal seats in 1987. In 1995, when the 'other' vote was not as high as in the previous contest, eighteen of the twenty-one seats went to the PCs. Fifteen of these seats were among the thirty-four that were held by the Liberals in 1987, the NDP in 1990, and the PCs in 1995.

If the Liberals were hasty in proceeding to the polls in 1990, the NDP delayed almost to the last possible moment in calling the 1995 election. Conventional wisdom in parliamentary politics holds that a government is in trouble if it waits until its fifth year in office to return to the voters, and that view was upheld by the result for the NDP in 1995. The party had come into office with the support of just over three voters in every eight; they had expected to find a budgetary surplus, only to see it turn into a deficit before they brought down their first budget; and they encountered a recession that lowered revenues while requiring increased spending on social-service supports. They approached the recession with conventional Keynesian remedies, increasing government spending (and hence the deficit) and seeking to create employment by stimulating aggregate demand. By the third year of their mandate, they concluded that they must rein in the deficit and embarked on a program of fiscal restraint, culminating in the summer of 1993 with the imposition of a 'social contract' that froze wages in the broader public sector and required that costs be cut, if other remedies did not suffice, by means of unpaid days off for public-sector workers. These 'Rae Days' (as they were colloquially known) combined an inconvenient interruption in public service with an affront to public-sector employees, whose existing labour contracts were in some cases simply broken. The government had failed to gain the support of the business community, who labelled them free-spenders because of increased welfare rates and other measures that had increased the deficit as the recession took hold. Restraint, when it came, was described as too little, too late. Small-business owners in particular also opposed the government's labour legislation that had outlawed strike-breakers and made it easier to organize unions. They also complained about the introduction of employment-equity programs that were caricatured as 'quotas' for minorities in employment. At the same time, the government had shelved its plans to introduce public auto insurance (despite the public's frustration with increased insurance rates) and, with the social contract, had angered important elements of the labour constituency on which it depended for campaign funds and workers. It then proceeded to an election campaign in which it did not articulate a clear plan of action for its second term. There was little surprise, given opinion polls showing the party below 20 per cent in support, when the government was defeated in the June vote. The Liberals, perhaps lulled into overconfidence by their lead in the polls, did not react quickly enough to the challenge of the rejuvenated Conservatives. And when they did recognize the threat from the right, they appeared as pale imitations of the very party they sought to criticize. The Conservatives planned a campaign that proposed simple, straightforward 'solutions' to the problems they thought were uppermost in the public's mind, and their Common Sense Revolution platform had a seductive clarity when compared to the vague promises of the Liberals and the absence of platform with the NDP.

The PC platform appealed with particularly good effect to a plurality of voters who could not devote much time and attention to detailed policy analysis. It promised tax reductions, spending reductions (in welfare, but not in health care; in educational bureaucracy, but not in the classroom), an end to 'quotas' in hiring (though quotas were not part of the employment-equity law), and the repeal of the NDP's labour legislation. The platform first implied that government was a simple matter and then undertook to make it simpler still by reducing the scope and size of the public sector. Voters responded favourably, although, like its predecessors, the Harris government took office with a majority of the legislature's seats but a minority of the popular vote.

Where will the province's electorate go next? The Conservatives appear to be counting on rapid progress in implementing their Common Sense Revolution to reduce the deficit and stimulate growth. The speed and clarity of their action is designed to find favour with voters who have found the other parties indecisive or disingenuous, and their offer to cut government and cut taxes seems grounded in the belief that voters would prefer a cheaper and narrower range of public services. The rhetoric employed by the government stresses the need to reduce the public debt, but the argument for less government goes beyond that issue. The danger the Conservatives face is that the particular public services they cut may have more support than they expected, and that voters who chose to vote PC in 1995 may turn away when their favourite government services are reduced or eliminated. Moreover, if the growth the Tories hope will result from a tax cut does not materialize, or if rising municipal taxes, other provincial levies, and user fees eat up taxpayers' gains, their reputation for good management of the provincial economy will be harmed. If it is true that governments get voted out, not in, then the fortunes of the Conservatives will largely depend on whether they impress more voters than they offend.

The hope of the opposition parties must lie in the expectation that a relatively small change in popular vote could result in a rather large shift in seats when the next election is called, probably some time in 1999. Both parties selected new leaders in 1996, and each will be hoping to capitalize on Conservative mistakes. Both will presumably be trying to craft election strategies that go beyond criticism of the government, however, since they will be competing with one another to be the place where voters go when they leave the Conservative fold. At the present time, the Liberals seem better placed to take advantage if the Conservatives falter, given the fact that they hold the second largest number of seats in the legislature, that they are not the party of the most recently ousted government, and that they have the most consistent pattern of support (in first- and second-place finishes) over the last three elections. However, one cannot ignore the collapse of the Liberals in the last campaign and the fact that the Conservatives went from sixteen seats in 1987 to eighty-one seats only eight years later. The NDP may console itself with the knowledge that the 1995 winner was in third place in 1990. In the face of the voter volatility represented by the results of the last three elections, only a braver scholar than the present authors would dare to predict the result of the next contest this far from its probable date.

Notes

1 The Liberals, for example, won the 1987 election with 73 per cent of the seats, but only 48 per cent of the vote; the NDP won in 1990 with 57 per cent of the seats, but less than 38 per cent of the vote; and the Conservatives won in 1995 with 62 per cent of the seats but less than 45 per cent of the vote.
2 The reason is not usually that the minority government is defeated in the legislature on a vote of confidence, but rather that it chooses at an early date to seek a more secure mandate, i.e., majority-government status. Examples include the Conservative government elected in 1975 and the Liberal government that took office in 1985; both went voluntarily to the polls two years afterwards. The Conservatives increased both their seats and votes, falling just short of a majority, while the Liberals acheived majority status.
3 An eleventh party, the Northern Ontario Heritage Party, was registered in 1977, but it was deregistered in 1985 for failing to file 1984 financial statements as required by the act.
4 Interview with Jim McLean, senior media adviser to Lyn McLeod, 23 August 1995.
5 Interview with Leslie Noble, Conservative campaign manager, 18 August 1995.
6 Interview conducted on 25 August 1995.
7 Interview with Leslie Noble, 18 August 1995.
8 Interview with Tom Long, 11 August 1995.

NINE

Ontario Party Politics in the 1990s: Comfort Meets Conviction

Robert J. Williams

Political parties are often considered the heart and soul of a larger process called 'politics'; the rise and fall of individual parties, inevitably linked to the personal fortunes of the party leader, usually demarcate the stages of evolution of a political system.

Post-Confederation Ontario was dominated by a single party, the Liberals, and a remarkable individual, Sir Oliver Mowat, who together laid the foundations of 'Empire Ontario' and its distinctive political tradition. The extraordinary success of the Conservative (later Progressive Conservative) Party over the first eighty-five years of the twentieth century, which consisted of winning the largest number of parliamentary seats in twenty of twenty-four general elections, left an indelible imprint on the actions of all Ontario political parties. Furthermore, scholarly interpretations of Ontario politics have emphasized qualities such as order, complacency, and balance that sprang from that environment.

In what will seem to posterity to be a sudden turnabout to this pattern (as it surely was those who lived through it!), the post-1985 period has revealed a different Ontario, one in which unpredictability became the norm, political upsets occurred with apparent regularity, and Canada's political 'Sleepy Hollow' was stirred by excitement and drama. The seemingly invincible Progressive Conservatives, guided by a new leader, Frank Miller, found themselves dislodged from government in 1985 through an extraordinary alliance between their long-time opponents. The Liberal Party, under David Peterson, transformed that opportunity into a sweeping majority in 1987, only to surrender its windfall through a combination of misjudgment and arrogance. The unintentional empowering of a New Democratic Party majority government by voters in 1990 was as big a shock to the party as it was to the electorate. However, in an increasingly repetitive script, the NDP was bundled out of office at the first opportunity by the regenerated Progressive Conservatives piloted by Mike Harris.

The roller-coaster fortunes of the provincial political parties are taken by some observers to be evidence that many of the earlier characterizations of Ontario's fundamental political values were either mistaken or obsolete, a conclusion that may have overlooked more prosaic electoral circumstances such as the strategic errors of judgment made by the parties themselves and the profound demographic, socio-economic, and technological changes that had been occurring throughout the province over the previous fifty years.

The challenge for observers in the late 1990s is to determine whether the return to office of the Progressive Conservative Party in Ontario represents (a) a return to the old familiar Ontario form, (b) a continuation of the decade of instability, (c) a new beginning, or (d) none of these. Unfortunately for prognosticators, there is evidence to support all four conclusions.

Unquestionably, the Progressive Conservative Party elected in June 1995 has pushed Ontario in new policy directions, but it remains to be seen whether the vagaries of the single-member plurality system and the partisan choices offered to voters in that election necessarily heralds a fundamental change in political values, any more than, say, the election of an NDP government did in 1990. These electoral outcomes are a product of the dynamics of a fifty-year-old three-party system and deliberate decisions about how political warfare is to be conducted in Ontario. The main difference between 1990 and 1995 seems to relate to a calculated shift from one type of political modus operandi to another. In turn, the suitability of this new strategy to the Ontario political milieu will be tested by all parties competing in subsequent elections.

Political Parties as Organizations

For all of their significance to voters (as well as journalists and political scientists), political parties in Ontario are actually fringe organizations. Few people belong to them in the sense of paying an annual membership fee. Political parties are also private associations in which most internal affairs and organizational arrangements are outside the purview of the public, the media, or even the state. An exception to this is the financial arrangements specifically related to the conduct of elections, but such provisions do not extend to the on-going operations of the parties. As a result, it is difficult – indeed impossible – to determine accurately the percentage of Ontario residents who could be said to be full-fledged members of the three major political parties – let alone the various smaller parties. A wildly generous estimate is that no more than 2 per cent of the population could be designated as party activists.[1] One repercussion of this situation is that few citizens seem to care what happens inside the parties or how they are run. Consequently, political parties may be seen as part of the 'problem with politics' today, rather than part of the solution. While it may be premature to declare the demise of the 'party' itself, it may be that the legitimacy of parties has been undermined in the last generation.

Ontario political parties have evolved in the latter part of the twentieth century, in part because of election financing arrangements and also because of new campaign circumstances such as the growing use of centralized media outlets. For example, rather than relying on personal contacts to fill their coffers, parties today raise money by direct-mail campaigns. They prefer expensive TV commercials to community events or door-knocking to sway voters at election time. Such changes mean that political parties have become more like other advocacy interests in society and less like their organizational antecedents.[2]

Political parties nevertheless perform many crucial functions within the political system: they select candidates and leaders and attempt to mobilize support for them at election time; they define electoral alternatives for uninformed, apathetic, or busy voters; and they ultimately influence the work of the legislature and the public-policy agenda through their elected members. The major parties differ only slightly from one another with respect to the performance of these roles.

For most of the fifty or so years since 1945, the major Ontario political parties have customarily been labelled pragmatic and opportunistic; the classic ideological self-descriptions – terms such as conservative, liberal, or social democratic – served mainly as 'flags of convenience' rather than being rigorous depictions of party objectives. The widely shared perspective seemed to be that ideology stifled the crucial flexibility needed to capitalize on the mood of capricious voters. Ideological debates, when they did occur, tended to be more intelligible to party activists than to the external community. In the early 1990s, as will be discussed below, Mike Harris set out to overturn these tenets of Ontario politics and in the process transformed not only the Progressive Conservative Party but possibly the entire political landscape.

Political parties are, ultimately, human organizations that can be directed with extraordinary skill or can be badly mismanaged. Parties are vehicles to carry a message of hope or a declaration of protest. They are groupings of the crassly ambitious and the wildly idealistic and all grades in between – conceivably all at the same time. In other words, political parties are enigmatic organizations with many different purposes and unique histories. Because of these limitations, one can go so far as to suggest that the way a political party is organized tells us very little about the impact that party may have on Ontario voters. More significant, possibly, are the relationships between and among the political parties.

Interdependence and Party Systems

Political scientists commonly refer to the 'party system,' but what is a 'system' of political parties? Peter McCormick suggests that the term 'system' carries the connotation of interdependence: it would be a 'distortion' to consider any one of the separate parts in isolation.[3] In the case of Ontario, it means considering the system's 'format' or 'shape,' which includes not just the number of parties, but their relative size, the intensity of the rivalry between parties, their philosophical principles, and the like. This contention suggests that the electoral prosperity of any one party is highly dependent upon, for example, the competitiveness of its opponents. First-past-the-post elections in Ontario also have a bearing on the shape of the party system: the manner in which votes are translated into seats almost consistently turns a plurality of votes into a majority of seats in the legislature. Conversely, the nature of the electoral system also means that a party with limited regional support can continue to play a role in the legislative arena because it will garner sufficient support to maintain a presence.

Although some aspects of the 1990 and 1995 elections will be examined later, the interdependence of the parties within the system can be illustrated through brief observations on the 1990 election. The PCs entered that contest with sixteen seats and a new leader. The NDP had nineteen seats and seemed to be losing direction. The Liberals had ninety-five seats and a substantial lead in the polls, but were burdened with a performance record tinged with scandal and a number of persistent and vociferous critics. The political arena was also marked by intensifying cleavages over religion, language, the environment and other concerns; several small parties (in particular Family Coalition, Confederation of Regions, Green, and Libertarian) were prepared to articulate them. Together, these four parties attracted over 240,000 votes (some 6 per cent of the aggregate vote) and also had an impact on the larger election outcome. Several questions follow: Did the fringe parties of the right attract enough votes, as some observers have suggested, to 'cost' the PCs as many as fourteen seats? If these parties had not been competing, would the PC party have finished third overall? Indeed, would the NDP have even won the 1990 election? Whatever the PC party's placing, would its performance have prompted the party's leadership to make the drastic change in electoral strategy embodied in the 'Common Sense Revolution' (CSR)? Without the CSR, in turn, would the PCs have won in 1995?

These questions cannot be answered satisfactorily, even by the most creative analyst, but they demonstrate that Ontario's party system is shaped by several factors, many of which are outside the control of the individual parties.

The Evolution of Ontario's Three-Party System

Ontario is unique among the Canadian provinces in that it has functioned with a three-party system, in one fundamental respect, since 1943. Up until that time, with two or three isolated exceptions, the Liberals and Conservatives dominated the popular vote and Ontario enjoyed a 'standard' party system as these two parties captured an overwhelming majority of the parliamentary seats. In the general election of 1943, however, three parties each captured more than 30 per cent of the popular vote. None of these parties has dropped below 15 per cent overall in the subsequent fifteen elections. Rather than being a transitional phenomenon[4] or a temporary aberration in the universe of the Canadian provinces, where two-party systems have tended to be the norm, the Ontario three-party system's fifty-year existence suggests that, if not permanent, it is at least venerable!

In the 1967 provincial election, the Ontario three-party system reached another stage of maturation. From 1951 to 1963, the CCF's (later the NDP's) credible popular vote (greater than 15 per cent overall in each election) did not translate into a viable legislative presence. Indeed, the party was only able to muster two, three, five, and seven seats in those four elections, hardly indicative of a healthy three-party system within the legislature. The 1967 breakthrough to twenty seats was a turning point in that all three parties have retained at least fifteen seats in every subsequent parliament, a number that allows an opposition party to perform a reasonable range of parliamentary duties in question period, debate, and committee work. In other words, Ontario has a three-party system not only at election time but in the on-going political life of the province as symbolized in the legislature.

In 1990, the Ontario three-party system reached another level of sophistication, since there were now three parties that customarily obtained a significant share of the popular vote and achieved a sizeable level of representation in the legislature, and had enjoyed the position of majority government. All this occurred without the displacement, disappearance, or dissolution of one or more the other parties. Ultimately, this development distinguishes Ontario's party system from all others in Canada.

'Hidden Dimensions' of the Ontario Party System

The frequent description in this chapter of Ontario as possessing a three-party system in this chapter is, actually, somewhat misleading in three respects.

1. From the mid-1940s to the mid-1980s, the provincial party system in Ontario featured a 'predominant party,' that is, a single party that was able to win parliamentary majorities in at least two consecutive elections. The Progressive Conservatives, of course, won twelve elections in a row, a remarkable accomplishment in almost any democratic society. Even its competitors seemed stuck in a monotonous groove, since the Liberals retained the status of Official Opposition on nine of those occasions and the CCF/NDP was repeatedly left with 'moral victories.' In this respect, the PCs rivalled the federal Liberal Party, which boasted a string of five victories from 1935 to 1953 and another five from 1963 to 1980.

Perhaps the most curious aspect of this phenomenon is the fact that the PC dominance persisted in a period of massive changes to Ontario's society and economy, changes that elsewhere in the world led to political instability, polarization, or mutations within the existing political parties and party systems.

The pre-1985 Ontario party system, therefore, was not a 'classic' democratic party system in which the control of government swung, pendulum-like, between rival parties on some more-or-less cyclical basis. The consistent success of one party and the consistent failure of the

others demonstrated a party system in which the parts were not comparable in popular support or in experience. One side enjoyed the aura of
political experience, even dignity; the other side was perceived as a band
of perennial losers. The post-1995 situation, one might suggest, is quite
unlike that earlier era, since all three parties have a core of parliamentar-
ians with cabinet experience. Moreover, all three parties have recently
enjoyed both the exhilaration of climbing to the top of the political perch
and the humiliation of falling from it with a resounding thud!

2. While sophisticated analysis can produce evidence that Ontario
political parties differ from one another in several important respects, the
most prosaic axiom is that the three major parties have each enjoyed
persistent success in certain regions and recurrent failure in others. In
other words, although it does not have 'regional parties' per se, Ontario
has a highly regionalized party system that reflects the diverse social,
economic, and geographic regions of the province.

The (Progressive) Conservative Party, for example, was always considered overpowering in rural and small-town eastern and central Ontario
during its years at the pinnacle, yet it has also been habitually successful
in winning urban (and more particularly suburban) seats around the
province in elections throughout this century.[5] At the same time, the
party has remained weak in Northern Ontario, where only Mike Harris
was elected in 1990 and 1995, and in the far southwest (Windsor and
Essex County), where in 1990 three PC candidates failed to garner even
5 per cent of the popular vote.

The mainstay of the provincial Liberal Party since the 1940s has traditionally been rural southwestern Ontario and several of the medium-
sized cities of that region, although Ottawa and the francophone
communities of eastern and Northern Ontario have been dutifully supporting the party for decades. Liberals have occasionally been elected in
suburban constituencies in what is now called the Greater Toronto Area
(GTA) – more consistently in those in which substantial numbers of
'ethnic' voters are concentrated. Over the last three general elections, the
Liberals are the least likely to be 'uncompetitive' (as defined below),
suggesting, possibly, that the party is the least 'regionalized' of the major
parties in its voter support base.

The NDP has historically been most successful in union-dominated
constituencies in Windsor, Hamilton, Toronto, Oshawa, and other urban
centres. Although the party made a breakthrough in numerous southwestern Ontario constituencies in 1990, this ascendancy proved to be
short-lived. In eastern Ontario and many of the more affluent suburbs of

TABLE 1
Geographic distribution of seats by party

	Liberal	NDP	PC	Total
	1. 34th Ontario General Election – 10 September 1987			
Southwest[a]	33	6	4	43
GTA[b]	37	7	4	48
East[c]	18	0	6	24
North	7	6	2	15
Total	95	19	16	130
	2. 35th Ontario General Election – 6 September 1990			
Southwest	4	32	7	43
GTA	17	24	7	48
East	11	8	5	24
North	4	10	1	15
Total	36	74	20	130
	3. 36th Ontario General Election – 8 June 1995			
Southwest	6	4	32	42[d]
GTA	9	5	34	48
East	9	0	15	24
North	6	8	1	15
Total	30	17	82	129[d]

Source: Based on Chief Election Officer of Ontario, *Election Returns with Statistics from the Records,* 1987, 1990, and 1995 general elections.
[a]Includes Simcoe County and the area west and south of Lake Simcoe not included in the GTA, as well as Hamilton and Niagara regions.
[b]The Greater Toronto Area (GTA) includes Metropolitan Toronto and the regions of Durham, York, Peel, and Halton.
[c]Includes the area north and east of Lake Simcoe, including the constituency of Parry Sound.
[d]Excludes one Independent elected in southwest.

the GTA (such as Markham, Oakville, and parts of Metropolitan Toronto), the party is inconsequential in the minds of most voters.

Unfortunately for the casual observer, the three successive landslide elections of 1987, 1990, and 1995 have all but obliterated these regional patterns in the parliamentary caucuses. Aggregate results do demonstrate, however, that a shift in party support in one region did not necessarily follow in other regions, as may be seen in table 1.

3. Returning to the statement made at the beginning of this section, the Ontario three-party system is actually a synthesis of a series of

(mostly) two-party contests that, in turn, occur as a result of the regional nature of the Ontario party system. Conversely, all three major parties are competitive in the same constituency only in a minority of cases.

These assertions can be supported through calculations based on official election returns for the 1987, 1990, and 1995 elections. If it can be assumed for these purposes – admittedly the figure is arbitrary – that a party that obtains a minimum of 20 per cent of the popular vote is 'competitive,' some interesting patterns can be discovered.

Beginning with the second point above, the three major parties crossed the 20 per cent threshold in 34 constituencies (about one-quarter of the cases) in 1987, with the Liberals winning 28 of those contests. The number of three-party struggles jumped to 67 (about 51 per cent of the cases) in 1990; the NDP won just under half of them (33). In 1995, three-party races occurred in only 49 constituencies (38 per cent), with the PCs winning 28 of those particular races. Just six constituencies are classified as 'competitive' in all three elections; Frontenac-Addington, Muskoka–Georgian Bay, St Catharines–Brock, Scarborough Centre, and York East mirrored the provincial trends in those contests by electing, in sequence, a Liberal, a New Democrat, and a Progressive Conservative candidate. Kingston and the Islands, the sixth case, bucked the pattern by electing a Liberal in both 1987 and 1995. In a further thirty constituencies (less than 25 per cent of all cases) the three-parties were 'competitive' in some combination of two of the three elections.

In reality, then, only a minority of the members of the parliamentary caucuses are elected in three-party competitions, as defined here. In most Ontario constituencies, one or more of the three main parties falls below 20 per cent of the popular vote (sometimes chronically); in other words, Ontario elections, especially in the years after 1967, consist of a disproportionately large number of two-party races that, when aggregated, produce the three-party system. Some data on these contests are found in table 2.

The three elections from 1987 to 1995 have, of course, been marked by wide fluctuations in the fortunes of the three main parties across the provincial system. It is worth noting that this pattern of volatility was also repeated within most constituencies: only six (as noted above) were three-party races in all three elections and only another fourteen consistently experienced two-party contests in all three elections (note that in some cases the competitive parties differed from election to election). Put in another way, in 1987 the NDP failed to capture 20 per cent of the votes in fifty constituencies, in 1990 it happened only five times, but in 1995 there were sixty-seven instances!

TABLE 2
Distribution of constituency elections by competitive type

Type	Winning party			
	Liberal	NDP	PC	Total
	1. 34th Ontario General Election – 10 September 1987			
Three-party[a]	28	2	4	34
Two-party:[b] L/PC	29	n/a	12	41
Two-party: L/NDP	29	17	n/a	46
Two-party: NDP/PC	n/a	0	0	0
One-party[c]	9	0	0	9
Total	95	19	16	130
	2. 35th Ontario General Election – 6 September 1990			
Three-party	20	33	14	67
Two-party: L/PC	0	n/a	4	4
Two-party: L/NDP	15	35	n/a	50
Two-party: NDP/PC	n/a	2	2	4
One-party	1	4	0	5
Total	36	74	20	130
	3. 36th Ontario General Election – 8 June 1995			
Three-party	8	13	28	49
Two-party: L/PC	18	n/a	41	59
Two-party: L/NDP	4	3	n/a	7
Two-party: NDP/PC	n/a	1	6	7
One-party	0	0	7	7
Total	30	17	82	129[d]

Source: Based on Chief Election Officer of Ontario, Election Returns with Statistics from the Records, 1987, 1990, and 1995 general elections.
[a]A three-party contest is considered to have occurred in a constituency in which the Liberal, New Democratic, and Progressive Conservative candidate each wins at least 20 per cent of the valid ballots cast.
[b]A two-party contest is considered to have occurred in a constituency in which candidates from only two of the Liberal, New Democratic, or Progressive Conservative parties wins at least 20 per cent of the valid ballots cast.
[c]A one-party contest is considered to have occurred in a constituency in which a candidate from only one of the Liberal, New Democratic, or Progressive Conservative parties wins at least 20 per cent of the valid ballots cast.
[d]Excludes one Independent elected in Elgin, where neither the Liberal nor NDP candidate received 20 per cent of the votes cast.

To complete the analysis, in a smaller number of constituencies one party's candidate captured an outright majority of the popular vote while neither of the other parties reached 20 per cent. In 1987 there were nine of these lopsided victories (all chalked up by Liberals), and five more in 1990 (four new Democrats and one Liberal). Not surprisingly, only PC candidates (seven) achieved this feat in 1995. These could be considered 'safe' seats using our extremely narrow definition, but only one constituency (Renfrew North, held by Liberal Sean Conway) actually appears more than once over the three elections. This is not to say that only one seat was a 'sure thing' for a particular party; there are many seats that have been held for several elections by the same party. Rather, in only one seat was all competition reduced to a token level for more than one contest.

Finally, as suggested earlier in the chapter, the impact of the so-called fringe parties on the party system in 1990 can be observed from these data, since there were fifty-five seats in that election where PC candidates failed to obtain 20 per cent of the votes cast (these are the contests where only the Liberals and/or the NDP were 'competitive'). The successful wooing of many of the people who voted for the minor parties in 1990 probably contributed to the size of the majority Mike Harris won in June 1995.

The purpose of this section, of course, is not to provide an analysis or explanation for why Ontario voters have supported the three major parties in this complex manner, but to explore some aspects of interdependence within the party system. The basic assumption is that, in a single-member plurality electoral system such as Ontario's, the larger picture is best understood as a series of smaller ones.

Formulas for Political Success in Ontario

Ontario's modern party system was built upon the foundations of the post–Second World War era. It was a time when affluence became widespread and when Ontario society grew more secular. These conditions nurtured an age when political ideology was declared redundant and even irrelevant.

The culture of affluence promoted parties of comfort. A political party that appreciated the worldly aspirations of the upwardly mobile would flourish, but to do so it had to avoid rigidity and espouse progress. The Progressive Conservatives succeeded by taking calculated safe steps forward and judicious steps backward – with the occasional lateral sashay when it was prudent! – always with the goal of seeking the safe middle ground. The Progressive Conservative Party – and its management style – took the politics out of governing in Ontario.

These were the years during which Ontario's political stability was directly related to the capacity of the PCs to maintain a political paradigm in which the parties were aligned in a classic left-centre-right spectrum, with the CCF-NDP isolated on the (discredited) left and the Liberals relegated to the cautious right, while the PCs successfully mastered the centre and prevailed to the right of centre. The party was effective at this strategy for about thirty years, in part because Ontario society continued to benefit from the party's pragmatic approaches to governing and in part because the party engaged in regular leadership renewal and developed a well-managed and patronage-fuelled party machine. The PC party, to be sure, gradually changed itself over time; this was, in fact, one of the secrets of its success (see note 2). Eventually it became known as the Big Blue Machine, a creation that 'repeatedly proved itself to be the most professional, innovative and successful organization in the election business.'[6]

A perhaps more compelling image, however, is the more unpretentious one used by the veteran journalist Eric Dowd, who once described the Progressive Conservatives of the early 1980s as 'the Harris tweed of political parties' (an ironic coincidence in light of its later revival as 'the Mike Harris party'). We can take this phrase to suggest that the party was as tough and enduring as the legendary sports jacket, that it was a mix of many colours that blended together into neutral shades and, perhaps most important (if it is not stretching the metaphor too much), that it was comfortable to those who 'wore' it.

The Progressive Conservatives' approach to governing, especially under William Davis (premier, 1971–85), has been variously described as non-doctrinaire, pragmatic, practical, or non-partisan. Its classic consensus style was meant to accommodate a broad spectrum of political beliefs both within the party and across the electorate. Its success seemed to demonstrate that Ontario preferred to elect governments of the centre; its longevity meant that the two opposition parties were forced to follow suit.

The Liberals were usually the runners-up, everyone's second choice. The party could never quite find an effective card to play, since it was frequently pushed and pulled between various intra-party interests (the federalist wing versus the provincial adherents, the rural backbone versus contemporary urbanites), none of which brought the long-delayed electoral success. By the early 1980s, the provincial party seemed to be chronically 'disorganized and demoralized.'[7] Like the outwardly invincible PCs, the Liberals seemed to want to be all things to all people. What many regarded as its 'ideological flexibility' was viewed by others as a lack of conviction or simply opportunism. In a political generation increasingly dependent on the opinion poll, Liberal supporters were nourished by months – if not years – of healthy survey numbers, only to find in both 1990 and 1995 that such voters had really only been 'Liberals by default.' When forced to make a mark on a ballot, many of them fled to other alternatives.

The CCF, the NDP's ancestor, had been almost obliterated by the anti-socialist propaganda of the cold-war years, but gradually gained credibility with the electorate and in the legislature. After it became the 'new party' in 1961, the NDP shambled along with dogged determination to pursue its social-democratic ideals into the 1970s, yet ultimately did not pose a serious threat to the government of the day. Under Bob Rae, however, after decades of trying 'to challenge what it thought of as the conventional politics of the old-line parties,'[8] the New Democratic Party took on a brokerage style of its own during the 1980s (despite resistance from many of its members who firmly believed that the party bore only a superficial resemblance to its forerunner). The NDP was ultimately successful in that pursuit of power but, as most observers agree, it soon lost its way trying to be 'everyone's government.' The siren call of the centre brought both victory and collapse.

As Joseph Wearing remarked in an earlier edition of this book, the three major Ontario parties were 'all attempting to crowd the centre of the political spectrum, because they know that is the road to political power.'[9] In more colourful language, Wayne Roberts and George Ehring submit that by the early 1990s, the NDP was '[d]efying the laws of both physics and politics,' since it was occupying 'the same space at the same time as not only the Liberals but often as the Conservatives as well.'[10] With politics driven towards consensus rather than polarization, the challenge for the parties – and their leaders – was to differentiate themselves sufficiently from one another to capture enough votes to form a government. In the mid-1990s, one party, the Progressive Conservatives, and one leader, Mike Harris, resolved that the old formula needed to be changed.

By the time Mike Harris was elected leader in 1990, the Big Blue Machine was but a faded memory. The party contested the 1990 election beset by new opponents and unsure of its own purpose. Rather than recreate the party in its old image as the route back to power, Harris and his closest associates traded in what was left of the Big Blue Machine on a new model, something decidedly different in the chronicle of modern Ontario political parties. The innovation that most clearly marks the Mike Harris Progressive Conservative Party from the Bill Davis party was the calculated shift from the comfortable moderate approach in Ontario politics to one in which conviction became the watchword. In place of traditional modus operandi, where flexibility eclipsed strongly held views, sharper positions and clear distances between the parties became the watchword. The 'Mike Harris party' developed new positions on a wide range of issues, blurred or discarded old ones, and challenged the status quo to win the support of voters across the conventional lines of party support.

These new convictions about what Ontario needed to do were embodied in a document known as the Common Sense Revolution; in the face of conventional wisdom, which increasingly held that voting decisions are largely determined by short-term images and issues forged in the heat of the campaign, the CSR was essentially 'road-tested' beginning in May 1994, a full year before the general election. Nearly all journalists, political commentators, and (most significantly) opposition politicians dismissed the CSR as inflexible, restrictive, premature, or unconventional and failed to take seriously the prediction of PC Party president Tom Long that the Common Sense Revolution would force 'a fundamental realignment' in Ontario politics.

Another element of the new PC formula for success involved maximizing electoral support by capitalizing on social tensions and attacking the state, in particular the welfare state. Instead of seeking a mellow consensus, the message of the CSR generated 'wedge' or 'hot button' issues that divided the Ontario community and polarized the electorate. Rather than re-endorsing the idea of a heavily interventionist government in Ontario (the kind of government, in other words, that the Progressive Conservatives had constructed from 1943 onwards), the CSR promoted a state that would play a far more restricted role and a society in which the logic of the market place would prevail. The net result was the articulation of a form of 'right-radicalism,' that is, an attempt to bring about rapid social change primarily for the benefit of 'the Ontario taxpayer.'

The Liberals in Ontario did not take the challenge of the CSR seriously until it was too late. As a government, the Liberals had basked in the glow of superficial change: they governed with a broad coalition of support that David Peterson had, in effect, merely inherited from the PCs, and the Liberal agenda appeared at times to be premised on making up for lost time rather than following a coherent strategy. In opposition, the party did not alter either its passive role as 'government in waiting' or its calculation that politics in Ontario would continue to operate in the 'comfort' zone. The Liberal Party launched its campaign in 1995 as it had governed from 1985 to 1990: its election promises were of the 'something for everyone' variety and its manifesto, officially known as the Liberal Action Plan, was a near clone of the federal Liberal Red Book that swept the 1993 federal election. However, what worked in that environment could not work in Ontario because the PCs had not only changed themselves but challenged the way party politics had operated in Ontario since mid-century. In contrast to the PC success in galvanizing its support through a definitive statement, the Liberal Action Plan merely appeared as 'a kinder, gentler' CSR or, less charitably, 'Common Sense Lite.'[11] As a formula for political success, equivocal messages did not work in 1995.

The NDP had already changed in the 1980s; in keeping with the age of electronic election campaigns, the party began to emphasize its leader and its style but played down (staunch adherents might say 'watered down') its ideology and core values. This formula was advantageous when the Liberals went into their tailspin in 1990, but proved distinctly unhelpful in guiding an inexperienced government through the economic and social upheavals of the early part of the decade. As a consequence, the NDP was abandoned by both its enemies and many of its traditional supporters even though it tried to satisfy 'all Ontarians.' Its wash-out as a government and its ridicule of the CSR when it was launched precluded the possibility of the NDP taking a uncompromising position when it returned to the hustings in 1995.

Both the Liberals and the New Democrats refused to believe that the old formula had been changed. As late as the spring of 1995, and indeed well into the election campaign, the PCs' opponents dismissed them as serious contenders and their remedy as disagreeable to the Ontario palate. In truth, however, enough Ontario voters were willing – indeed anxious – to swallow the bitter medicine that the CSR proffered that Mike Harris and his party easily won control of Ontario's thirty-sixth parliament.

The Progressive Conservatives and the Party System

Party systems tend to be durable but they are not necessarily eternal!

Social change and the emergence of new issues can lead to the periodic reshaping of a party system as new parties are created or the old ones adapt new positions or new strategies. The Ontario provincial party system, as has been shown, appeared to be in the midst of a genuine realignment in 1995 because one of the parties – the party that had played the predominant role in 'the politics of comfort' – successfully disconnected itself from the 'old political ways' to present itself in a new, uncompromising guise to voters.

To return to a point raised earlier, it is important to try to determine whether the return to office of the Progressive Conservative party in Ontario represents (1) a return to the old familiar Ontario form, (2) a continuation of the decade of instability, (3) a new beginning, or (4) none of these. As noted before, there is evidence to support all four conclusions.

1. *A return to the old form*: Ontario is once again being governed by the Progressive Conservative party, with a Liberal Official Opposition and the New Democrats as the third party in the legislature. After ten years of playing different roles, the players are back in their accustomed spots. It is almost as if nothing has happened. Even the influential CSR mimics the long-standing custom of downplaying philosophical postures in Ontario politics; voters were not asked to endorse a 'new conservatism' or any other ideology but 'common sense,' a phrase that almost defies definition.

2. *A continuation of the instability*: Ontario voters have been flexible partisans for most of the last twenty years, switching their votes in response to campaign tactics, media orchestrations, and bandwagon effects. Most do not see the existing political parties as reflecting significant social, economic, or demographic groupings as much as opportunistic organizations that need their votes not their commitment. The majority of voters are therefore detached from the parties and prefer to make up their minds afresh about who or what to support at each election. Voters behave, in other words, much like impulse shoppers who show little 'brand loyalty.' Finally, since the electorate has become increasingly cynical about the motives of elected officials, no party today can count on the fidelity of its supporters. In other words, it will take a notable record of achievement by the Harris government to break the cycle of instability that has gripped Ontario politics for a decade or more.

3. *A new beginning*: Ontario now has an agenda-driven government that has set high standards of performance for itself and has created high expectations among those who voted for it. There has been a metamorphosis of the Progressive Conservative Party of Leslie Frost, John Robarts,

and William Davis into a 'Mike Harris party' that seems to celebrate its hard edges and clear choices. Despite early tensions within the party between traditionalists and revisionists over this new orthodoxy, its leadership makes no apology for this change. The economic, social, and political conditions of the 1990s, they argue, demand new strategies, a new set of priorities, and, most important, a new 'world-view' if the people of Ontario are going to experience economic growth and personal security. To get to those ends, the Progressive Conservative Party changed the way it appealed to voters (actually, to taxpayers) and in the process reformulated the relationship among Ontario's political parties.

4. *None of these*: Many months before the election that brought him to power, Mike Harris asserted that his party would win because the political values of the people of Ontario had shifted. He predicted that his party's policies, which would fundamentally alter the role of government, would 'form the new centre of Ontario politics' and that 'what some thought was right wing is actually smack dab in the centre.'[12]

The values that particular political parties apply to the task of governing are not, however, equivalent to the community's political culture; normally they are one manifestation of it. That the political culture of Ontario itself may be gradually changing, because of technology and the media, in-migration, economic hardship, and other influences is certainly plausible but cannot easily be corroborated. Is a change in the 'political mood' the same as a change in values? Undoubtedly there is evidence of the former, but whether, for example, the recent period of political instability is a manifestation of changes to core values needs more investigation (and more thoughtful consideration than can be provided here).

Taken together, these four perspectives demonstrate that the potential exists for realignment in the contemporary Ontario party system.

The Future of the Ontario Party System

All things considered, party politics in Ontario has quickly changed from blasé to brusque. The three parties that have been active in Ontario's postwar party system were, for five decades, content to drive that system towards consensus rather than polarization. In 1995, a new mood of conviction entered the picture, bringing immediate electoral success but, as yet, no certainty that it will permanently transform Ontario party politics in the way its proponents would wish.

Scholars have consistently argued that – in contrast to the saga of provincial electoral politics in most other provinces – Ontario provincial party politics have been, with infrequent exceptions, remarkably predictable, bland, and unchanging. But in the late 1990s, the present is not what it used to be! The old political order may finally have changed.

Notes

1 Some empirical data on party memberships at the federal level are found in R.K. Carty, *Canadian Political Parties in the Constituencies: A Local Perspective* (Toronto and Oxford: Dundurn Press, 1991), volume 23 of the Research Studies for the Royal Commission on Electoral Reform and Party Financing. The estimates in the text are not drawn explicitly from Prof. Carty's work.

2 It should not be assumed that this is a brand-new phenomenon. See a discussion about changing party practices in the PC party in an earlier period in John Morris and Robert Williams, 'Leslie M. Frost, Patronage and "Grass-Roots Political Work,"' *Ontario History* 84, no. 2 (1992): 105–18.

3 Peter McCormick, 'Provincial Party Systems, 1945–1993,' in A. Brian Tanguay and Alain-G. Gagnon, *Canadian Parties in Transition*, 2nd ed. (Scarborough: Nelson, 1996), 349.

4 John Wilson and David Hoffman, 'Ontario: A Three Party System in Transition,' in Martin Robin, ed., *Canadian Provincial Politics* (Scarborough: Prentice-Hall, 1972), 198–239.

5 The best discussion of the emergence of the pattern of party support that prevailed for most of this century is found in Charles W. Humphries, 'Sources of Ontario "Progressive" Conservatism, 1900–1914,' Canadian Historical Association *Annual Report*, 1967, 118–29.

6 Rand Dyck, *Provincial Politics in Canada*, 2nd ed. (Scarborough: Prentice-Hall, 1991), 338

7 Rand Dyck, *Provincial Politics in Canada: Towards the Turn of the Century*, 3rd ed. (Scarborough: Prentice-Hall, 1996), 348.

8 Thomas Walkom, *Rae Days* (Toronto: Key Porter, 1994), 264.

9 Joseph Wearing, 'Ontario's Political Parties: The Ground Shifts,' in Graham White, ed., *The Government and Politics of Ontario*, 4th ed. (Toronto: Nelson, 1990), 234.

10 Ehring and Roberts, *Giving Away a Miracle: Lost Dreams, Broken Promises and the Ontario NDP* (Oakville: Mosaic Press, 1993), 356.

11 Patrick Basham and Michael McHugh, 'Son of Newt? The Marketing of

Ontario's *Common Sense Revolution*,' paper presented to the Canadian Political Science Association, June 1996, 20.
12 Martin Mittelstaedt, 'Ontario Tories get together to organize a revolution,' *Globe and Mail*, 19 November 1994, A5.

Further Reading

In addition to the titles listed in the notes, the following studies add to our understanding of contemporary party politics in Ontario. Pre-1985 interpretations are useful for a historical perspective.

Azoulay, Dan, '"A Desperate Holding Action": The Survival of the Ontario CCF/NDP, 1948–1964.' *Ontario History* 85, no. 1 (March 1993): 17–42.

Blizzard, Christina. *Right Turn: How the Tories Took Ontario*. Toronto and Oxford: Dundurn Press, 1995.

Brownsey, Keith, and Michael Howlett. 'Class Structure and Political Alliances in an Industrialized Society.' In K.B. Brownsey and M.H. Howlett, eds, *The Provincial State: Politics in Canada's Provinces and Territories*. Mississauga: Copp Clark Pitman, 1992.

Gagnon, Georgette, and Dan Rath. *Not without Cause: David Peterson's Fall from Grace*. Toronto: HarperCollins, 1991.

Haddow, Rodney. 'Ontario Politics: "Plus Ça Change ...?"' In James P. Bickerton and Alain-G. Gagnon, eds, *Canadian Politics*. 2nd ed. Peterborough: Broadview Press, 1994.

Johnson, David. 'The Ontario Party and Campaign Finance System: Initiative and Change.' In F. Leslie Seidle, ed., *Provincial Party and Election Finance in Canada*. Vol. 3 of Research Studies for the Royal Commission on Electoral Reform and Party Financing. Toronto and Oxford: Dundurn Press, 1991.

Manthorpe, Jonathan. *The Power and the Tories: Ontario Politics 1943 to the Present*. Toronto: Macmillan, 1974.

Speirs, Rosemary. *Out of the Blue: The Fall of the Tory Dynasty*. Toronto: Macmillan, 1986.

Wearing, Joseph. 'Ontario Political Parties: Fish or Fowl?' In Donald C. MacDonald, ed., *The Government and Politics of Ontario*. Toronto: Macmillan, 1975.

– 'Ontario Political Parties: Fish or Fowl?' In D.C. MacDonald, ed., *The Government and Politics of Ontario*. Revised ed. Toronto: Van Nostrand Reinhold, 1980.

- 'Ontario Political Parties: Fish or Fowl?' In D.C. MacDonald, ed., *The Government and Politics of Ontario*. 3rd ed. Toronto: Nelson, 1985.
Williams, Robert J. 'Ontario's Party Systems: Federal and Provincial.' In Hugh Thorburn, ed., *Party Politics in Canada*. 5th ed. Scarborough: Prentice-Hall, 1986.
- 'Ontario's Party Systems: Under New Management.' In H. Thorburn, ed., *Party Politics in Canada*. 6th ed. Scarborough: Prentice-Hall, 1991.
- 'Ontario's Provincial Party System after 1985: From Complacency to a Quandry.' In H. Thorburn, ed., *Party Politics in Canada*. 7th ed. Scarborough: Prentice-Hall, 1996.
Wilson, John, and David Hoffman. 'The Liberal Party in Contemporary Ontario Politics.' *Canadian Jouranl of Political Science* 3, no. 2 (June 1970).
Woolstencroft, Peter. '"Tories Kick Machine to Bits": Leadership Selection and the Ontario Progressive Conservative Party.' In R. Kenneth Carty, Lynda Erickson, and Donald E. Blake, eds, *Leaders and Parties in Canadian Politics: Experiences of the Parties*. Toronto: Harcourt Brace Jovanovich, 1992.

TEN

Spinning Tales: Politics and the News in Ontario

Frederick J. Fletcher and Rose Sottile

'This is not my last press conference. You may well have me to kick around.'
Bob Rae, announcing his resignation as NDP leader, 13 January 1996

In this chapter, we view the news media as a political institution, examining its role in Ontario politics and its relationship to other key political institutions, particularly the government and opposition political parties and interest groups. In addition to describing the key elements of politics and news in Ontario, we discuss important examples in text boxes throughout the chapter.

While there are many forms of political communication, from discussions among friends to party conferences, few are independent of the news media. For governments, the news media are important, not only to publicize their accomplishments, but also to inform the public about new policies and programs. The opposition parties must rely on the media, not only for information, but also to communicate to the voters their criticisms of government actions and their alternative programs. Without news coverage, much political activity would lose its significance. The daily political drama in the legislature, for example, would play only to the small minority of citizens who watch the legislature TV channel. Public hearings would not be very public and demonstrations would mobilize only the already committed. Modern election campaigns would be impossible without the media, with their ability to reach large audiences quickly, cheaply, and conveniently. For the foreseeable future, the conventional media – print, radio, and especially television – will continue to play a major role in the process of political communication. The structure of the media system, the standard practices of political journalism, and the way the news media are used by politicians and interest groups influence not only the operation of the political system but also the ways in which we understand politics. Increasingly aware of media influence, politicians and interest groups work hard to put their own spin on news coverage, so that they have as much influence as possible on the information and interpretations made available to citizens.

The Press Gallery

The most influential gatekeepers of information on provincial government and politics are the members of the legislative press gallery. The gallery, made up of reporters with special responsibility for covering Queen's Park, is on a day-to-day basis the single most important instrument of political communication in the province. Despite the development of new channels of information, such as the legislative television service available by satellite and cable throughout the province, government and opposition, as well as major interest groups, view the press gallery as crucial. Although they often try to bypass the gallery by using regional media, cable community channels, and open-line shows, as well as newsletters and the Internet, most politicians and political advisers recognize that it is the gallery that has the greatest influence on the public agenda.

The mass-media system that serves Ontario citizens is a highly developed one, made up of some forty-five daily newspapers and more than three hundred weeklies, thirty television stations (with five networks) and 154 radio stations, not to mention national specialty services, such as Newsworld and Vision, that carry some Ontario news. These news outlets are linked by a variety of news services, the most important of which is the Canadian Press (CP), a cooperative news-gathering and distribution agency owned collectively by the nation's daily newspapers. Broadcast News (BN), a division of CP, provides a basic news service for broadcasters. For all but the larger newspapers and broadcasting stations in urban areas, CP and BN are the major sources of non-local news. BN relies heavily on CP for the material in its hourly news summary, and CP, in turn, gets much of its copy from its larger member papers, supplemented by the work of its own small reporting staff (which covers the legislature quite thoroughly). The basic coverage of provincial politics provided by CP/BN is supplemented by the correspondents and special-ized services operating out of the Queen's Park press gallery.

In 1996, the gallery had fifty-two active members (reporters with of-fices at the legislature), representing twenty-eight news organizations, and fourteen associate members. In addition, several community and student newspapers, as well as less news-oriented broadcast outlets, send in reporters to cover major stories. Only nine of the forty-five Ontario dailies have staff writers among active gallery members. For many years, smaller centres in Ontario have relied on Thomson newspa-pers, a chain twenty-three dailies, which had a bureau of two or three reporters in the gallery. By 1990, Thomson had only one reporter at Queen's Park and, with the recent purchase of a number of these news-papers by Hollinger, a chain controlled by Conrad Black, it is unlikely that a separate bureau will be maintained at Queen's Park. Since Hollinger has also purchased a controlling interest in the Southam chain, it is probable that the smaller Hollinger papers will use Southam News Serv-ices, while the other small Thomson dailies will turn to CP. Except for some Toronto stations, few broadcast outlets have reporters in the gal-lery, relying on CP/BN and Toronto stations that provide taped reports to affiliates. Only three stations outside Toronto – CKCO (Kitchener), CHCH (Hamilton), and CFPL (London) – are represented in the gallery. Most bureaus are one-reporter operations, but a few have two (some-times with reporters having other duties as well); television outlets have technical staff as well. The major bureaus are Southam, which is a coop-erative operation, with reporters from four newspapers and a columnist (from the Ottawa *Citizen*), as well as a full-time researcher, and the *Toronto Star*, which has four reporters and a columnist. CP/BN has a staff of four, while other major news organizations, like the *Globe and Mail* and the CBC, have only two reporters at Queen's Park.

Rapid turnover in the gallery is a factor in the coverage. With the exception of half a dozen veterans, most reporters have been at Queen's Park for less than two years. Many organizations rotate their correspond-ents regularly, fearing that reporters might come to identify with a par-ticular party or get caught up in the insular world of politicians and lose touch with their audiences. Turnover also results from a tendency for reporters to drift into government or political jobs. These posts are attrac-tive, not only because they offer better pay and working conditions, but also because they offer new challenges, a chance to be involved in the decision-making process, and often better job security. The list of assist-ants to ministers, media-relations officers, and advisers to party leaders who were once gallery members is long. The notion that reporters might downplay criticism of government in the hope of getting a job does not stand up to scrutiny, since many of those hired have been among the most critical in the gallery. The real concern is the draining of experienced and able people from the gallery.

One problem with this high rate of turnover is that reporters need time at Queen's Park to master the arcane procedures of the legislature and the complicated structure of the civil service, as well as to acquire the contacts necessary to get background information. For example, when opposition MPPs use procedure to hold up government legislation, as in the case of the 'omnibus' bill in 1995 (see box 4), reporters are often unable to explain the rules or the traditions involved. Because policies often develop over long periods, new reporters lack the background to understand events. While acknowledging that novice reporters are often able and eager, one senior correspondent remarked that they often miss the point of developments or make embarrassing errors. Another commented: 'Reporters change here constantly; they don't know what happened here last year or the year before. With some papers, they're making a habit of changing reporters so often they don't know when something is announced whether it's only half of what the government originally promised, or whether it's a reversal of what the government promised, or if it's something the opposition parties have been demanding for years.' Lacking background, reporters are vulnerable to manipulation by their sources. As a former Queen's Park columnist remarked: 'Half of the press gallery doesn't know when it is being had.'

Gallery output is also influenced by the backgrounds of its members. For most of its history, the gallery has been a male preserve. More recently, women have been better represented, but few reporters come from the recent immigrant groups that make up such a high proportion of Ontario's population. Observers in the 1980s noted that the advent of a significant number of women in the gallery had led to a marked increase in attention paid to previously neglected issues, like day care and domestic violence. Despite their professionalism, it seems clear that the life experiences, education, and culture of gallery reporters influence both the items they select for coverage and their interpretation of these items.

In terms of democratic theory, the gallery's most important role is its coverage of the legislative process. The parliamentary ritual acquires its significance, in large part, from the public attention it gets. The incentive for opposition members to question ministers, criticize government policies, and develop alternative proposals lies more in the hope of accumulating public support for the next election than in shaming the government into changing its policies. The primary motive for delaying passage of a government bill is to attract public attention in the hope that public opinion will persuade the government to change course. The competition between a government anxious to look good and opposition parties striving to expose its weaknesses is central to parliamentary government, but it is an empty ritual without an audience. Though many Ontario citizens have access to legislative proceedings and committee hearings on the legislative channel, most still rely on reports from the press gallery for information as well as interpretation. Even in the information age, with voters able to watch televised legislative proceedings or scan the Internet, journalists remain crucial interpreters of political events, signalling what is important and placing events in context. The gallery remains, therefore, an essential part of the system that holds the government accountable for its actions.

The press gallery's status as an essential institution in the legislative system is recognized in many ways. Its members have the right to take notes in the legislature (in their own gallery), a right traditionally denied to visitors, though many reporters now follow question period and the debates on television monitors provided by the assembly. They are also allowed to examine copies of the budget and other major government policy statements a few hours before they are read in the House. Along with opposition MPPs and staff, and interest-group representatives, reporters are given access to the documents but are not permitted to leave the room – called a 'lockup' – or communicate with anyone outside until the documents have been publicly released. The gallery is provided free of charge with offices and a lounge in the legislature building, and with a variety of other costly services, including free copies of most government publications. Reporters also have access to areas closed to the public, such as the legislative library, and can call on the legislature's research service for assistance. These privileges are part of the gallery's 'traditional right of access to the legislative process to inform the public,' as it was expressed in the gallery's brief to the Ontario Commission on the Legislature (Camp Commission) in 1975.

HISTORY AND DEVELOPMENT

For many years, the gallery consisted of a handful of correspondents, often with close ties to political parties. The gallery of the 1950s was clearly part of the inner circle of the legislature. Reporters were often invited the office of Premier Leslie Frost for intimate briefings on cabinet decisions. It was common for correspondents to supplement their incomes by taking minutes for legislative committees and, in a few cases, writing speeches for MPPs. Long-standing gallery members were often friends and advisers to politicians and, according to one veteran reporter, had to develop a sense of just how much of the inside information they acquired should be published. During this period, the quality of information and analysis regarding provincial affairs reaching the public depended even more than it does now on the initiative, judgment, and integrity of a few reporters.

These cosy relationships between reporters and government – and, to a lesser extent, opposition – politicians did not survive the 1960s. The days of blatantly partisan newspapers, so much a part of the politics of earlier decades, were over and editors came to expect greater detachment on the part of their reporters. At the same time, the constitutional responsibilities of the provincial government were increasing in importance and the government itself was growing larger and more complex. These developments caused editors to take the gallery more seriously and led to some growth in the gallery. At the same time, cabinet ministers and MPPs were given more staff and services. The old intimacy was no longer possible and, with the addition of more associate members who come and go, is even less so today.

The attitudes of reporters also evolved in response to political developments. One turning point came in 1961, when John Robarts succeeded Frost as premier. In *The Power and the Tories* (1974), Jonathan Manthorpe, a former gallery member, traces the emergence of a more critical style of reporting to Robarts, whose evident distaste for journalists contrasted sharply with Frost's amiable relationship with the gallery and provoked a more detached and critical style. The more critical tone was taken up by the new group of reporters who entered the gallery in 1971. Developments at Queen's Park corresponded with the rise of adversarial journalism in the United States and Ottawa. Political scandals in the United States, especially Watergate, made adversarial journalism fashionable. At the same time, the growing tension between the news media and then prime minister Pierre Trudeau helped to break down any inhibitions Canadian political reporters might have had about tough-minded reporting. The large Conservative majority in the 1971 Ontario election led some news organizations – most notably the *Globe and Mail* – to take an adversarial approach in covering the provincial government, in a self-conscious attempt to supplement the weakened opposition parties.

Manthorpe notes that the new emphasis on investigative reporting was a response not only of concern for the public interest, but also, and more important, to the fear that a government with an entrenched majority would be boring, providing little of interest to report. While the personalities of reporters and editors – among other factors – come into play, it appears that the toughest investigative reporting has tended to take place in periods of majority government (1971–5, 1981–5, and since 1987). Each of the three new governments (Liberal, 1985–90; NDP, 1990–5; and Conservative, elected in 1995) has, after an initial 'honeymoon' period, faced tough scrutiny, particularly from news organizations sceptical of the governing party's priorities.

One effect of the increase in critical reporting was a growing awareness among reporters that they themselves had to avoid conflicts of interest, a major concern of investigative journalism. By the 1980s, there was a general attempt by correspondents to avoid the appearance of partisan ties and to limit their acceptance of free services offered by government and opposition parties; for example, all of the news organizations that assigned correspondents to travel with party leaders have since 1985 paid a fee to the parties to cover costs. However, there is still debate among reporters about the rent-free space and services provided to the gallery, with some concerned about its propriety and others defending it as a service to the public, since it enables free-lancers and reporters from smaller organizations to cover Queen's Park.

Aggressive investigative reporting is the exception rather than the norm; most reporters are content to follow up the revelations of others. In a number of cases, such as the Patti Starr Affair that plagued the Liberals in 1989–90, a scandal was exposed by reporters from outside the gallery. (See box 1.) In fact, not all gallery members see probing investigation as part of their jobs. Some argue that reporters should spend more time looking critically at new policies, exposing difficulties in government programs (and to a lesser extent in opposition proposals and activities), and seeking out injustice and inefficiency in government ministries. Others feel that these activities should be left to opposition caucuses and affected groups and that reporters should be neutral channels of information, simply reporting government statements and actions, opposition criticisms, public complaints, and government responses. Investigative reporting is done primarily by the larger newspapers, such as the *Globe* and the *Toronto Star*. It is 'too expensive and cumbersome for television,' according to one broadcast veteran. The scandal-mongering that sometimes passes for investigative journalism – such as exposing

Box 1

THE STARR AFFAIR

The Starr Affair, a party fund-raising scandal, is an instructive example of investigative journalism. The story broke in the *Globe* in February 1989, as a result of digging by Linda McQuaig, and was kept alive by McQuaig and columnist Michael Valpy, neither of whom was a member of the gallery. Gallery reporters did mainly reaction and follow-up reports. Central to the Starr case were the public records kept by the Commission on Election Finances, records that would not have been available before the reforms of the 1970s. As the story continued to develop, information came to light from a variety of sources (some volunteered), and eventually key aides to then Premier David Peterson were implicated, forcing resignations and a public inquiry to control disclosures and limit political damage. This process took several months, and the story would likely have died had the *Globe* not devoted resources to pursuing new angles. Journalistic persistence is often required to keep governments accountable and force change. In the end, criminal charges were laid and some modest reforms enacted. Although the premier was not implicated, the continuing scandal derailed the Liberal's communication agenda in the months leading up to the 1990 election, raised concerns about the honesty of the Liberals, and put Peterson on the defensive during the televised leaders' debate during the 1990 campaign. Reporters' access to public Commission on Election Finance records was a key part of the investigation.

minor conflicts of interest or checking on politicians' expense accounts – requires little effort and does not contribute much to democratic dialogue.

For the news media, Ontario politics has become much more interesting over the past decade since David Peterson's Liberals took power in 1985, ending more than forty years of Conservative rule. The advent of Ontario's first social-democratic government, with the NDP victory in 1990, brought widespread media attention. It was, noted one veteran reporter (repeating the words of Bob Rae), the 'return of politics.' There were clear ideological divisions in the legislature, with the attendant conflict and drama. All of this made Ontario politics more newsworthy and led major news organizations to pay more attention to Queen's Park. Interest was heightened with the election of the neo-conservative government of Mike Harris in 1995 and the profound social change promised by its election manifesto, the *Common Sense Revolution*.

WORK PATTERNS

On a day-to-day basis, the quality of Queen's Park coverage is largely determined by the customary work patterns of gallery members. Despite some differences among print, radio, and television reporters, there are some common patterns: reliance on government announcements and question period for the bulk of news, a concept of newsworthiness that stresses human interest and drama over issues, and a lack of resources and time.

The hour-long question period, which takes place early each sitting day, remains central to the work of most gallery reporters. This is especially true for broadcast journalists, one of whom defines his job as to 'try to bring the question period to the people through tape.' Some days, as many as 80 per cent of the stories filed from the gallery may be based on this single hour, in particular the first twenty or thirty minutes, which feature questions from the leaders of the opposition parties. Question period provides the essential elements of news as understood in Canadian journalism: immediacy, brevity, conflict between identifiable individuals, and of course potential significance, since important issues are often raised. It provides little, however, in the way of reasoned argument, longer-term perspective, or concern with underlying social and economic conditions or conflicts.

Nevertheless, preparation for question period is a major element in the media strategies of both government and opposition parties. Caucus research staffs spend a good deal of their time preparing questions and ministerial staffs work hard to anticipate questions and brief their ministers. For the opposition leaders, question period is not only their main media hit of the day, it is also their best opportunity to raise doubts about government priorities and undermine government support. Media attention is the foundation for accountability and drawing that attention requires drama. In addition, question period is a major testing ground for opposition critics and cabinet ministers. The media, and to a lesser extent the public, assess their competence on the basis of their performance in question period and in the scrums that follow. Debates and committee work are harder to cover and thus get much less attention.

After question period, reporters generally return to their offices to write and send in their stories. Most follow the debates on the legislature's television service in their offices or the gallery lounge. They also cover the regular Wednesday cabinet meetings, waiting outside the cabinet room for announcements and to catch ministers for statements on current issues. In addition, they attend news conferences called by government or opposition politicians or interest groups and sit in on committee meetings they think might be newsworthy, although these too are often covered by monitoring the legislature's internal television service. Reporters must also sift through the flood of news releases, speeches, and reports they receive every day from government agencies, opposition parties, and other groups, as well as follow up on issues raised in the House or in reports by talking with ministers, opposition critics, civil servants, or the occasional outside expert. Overall, studies show, government announcements and question-period interchanges tend to be the most important sources of news about provincial politics.

The advent of full-service television in the House has had only modest impact on actual coverage (see box 2, p. 246). The pictures still tend to be used as backdrops for reporters' summaries, and although coverage has broadened somewhat to include more from debates and committees, the focus remains on question period. The scramble for interviews – with twenty or more broadcast and print reporters crowding around political figures (scrums) – has continued much as before in the halls of the legislature. Broadcasters often seek to have announcements, questions, and comments repeated in briefer form (even the relatively brief exchanges of question period are often too long for broadcast news), while newspaper reporters often press for reactions, further details, or clarifications. Some reporters prefer to observe the scrums and to save their key questions for private interviews.

Deadlines are a central feature of gallery work patterns. Radio reporters must produce fresh forty- to sixty-second reports throughout the day and are expected to record items for use after they leave work. For many of these stories, clips from the House or scrum must be supplemented with interviews. Television and print reporters have more time but must still keep an eye on the clock. Tight deadlines often make it difficult to seek out background materials or examine announcements critically. Time pressures are exacerbated by the fact that most bureaus consist of a single reporter, without filing or research assistance. As one veteran reporter put it: 'There are a lot of good stories that should be looked at, a lot of press releases have a good story behind them, but how much time do you get? There is a lot better story there than you can dig up by making four or five quick phone calls.' Lack of time also makes reflection

Box 2

TELEVISING THE LEGISLATURE

A major change in the working environment of the gallery occurred in October 1986 with the inauguration of the Ontario Legislature Television Service. While television cameras and audio recorders had been allowed into the chamber in 1976 (in recognition of the growing importance of broadcast journalism), they had been used primarily to provide clips from question period for Toronto-based stations. The new service, a product of the Liberal-NDP accord following the 1985 election, has had much greater impact. When the House is in session, the service provides thirteen hours of daily coverage (in French and English) to all households with cable service, including repeats in prime time of question period and debates, as well as important committee hearings. The service also carries important news conferences. About 200,000 viewers tune in on any given day. The broadcasts appear to have increased the recognition level of Ontario MPPs, both through direct exposure and because television newscasts throughout the province can carry clips of the action in the House by recording them from the satellite feed that carries the signal to cable companies. Local stations can create the appearance of effective coverage of Queen's Park without the expense of a correspondent, using the satellite feed and reports from news services.

In addition to the broadcasts of house proceedings and committee hearings, a variety of channels are available only to those with offices at Queen's Park. At any time, a reporter may be able to follow the live action in the House, a committee on television and two more on audio, and events in the media studio, such as news conferences, as well as checking in on the information channel, which rebroadcasts public-affairs programs dealing with Ontario politics, provides a digest of television news, and lists scheduled events. Reporters can work more efficiently, keeping an eye on the action while working in their offices. These services have had their greatest impact on television reporters, providing them with a wider range of visuals and more time to formulate interpretations of events.

and analysis difficult. Breaking stories take precedence and the immediate often crowds out the important. Between sessions, the pace slackens and reporters get a chance to do feature stories, examine issues, and investigate policies. However, reporters – especially broadcasters –

are often given other assignments and come to Queen's Park only for cabinet meetings, news conferences, important committee hearings, or demonstrations.

Within the gallery, the CP bureau is expected to provide comprehensive basic coverage of the government and legislature, leaving other bureaus free to pursue stories of special interest to their news organizations. Smaller news outlets rely heavily on CP and its subsidiary, Broadcast News (BN). The bureau attempts full coverage of question period, important debates, all major government releases and reports, committee work, and public speeches by government and opposition leaders, also produces background reports and occasional commentaries. Because it serves broadcasters as well as newspapers, CP must work quickly. Major stories, which are usually filed on the run, are brief and, because CP serves many masters, rather general. The bureau lacks the staff to dig deeper, but it does respond to specific requests for stories of local interest.

RELATIONSHIPS AND INFLUENCE

In general, relationships between reporters and politicians at Queen's Park are much closer than those in Ottawa. Reporters, politicians, and staff are all part of a network of rumour and information exchange. Each node in this network is the product of carefully cultivated relationships and each exchange influences the tone and type of news that is generated. Relationships exist on three levels: those between members of the gallery; the institutional relationships between a party and a specific news organization; and the personal ties between government members (and the backbench) and reporters.

Although the gallery members are individuals working for different news organizations, they are in many ways in the same boat. In the hothouse setting of Queen's Park, it is not surprising that they influence one another's work. The pattern of influence depends in part on the medium and the messenger. Between elections, the major daily newspapers often set the coverage agenda, but television predominates during campaigns. Television's overall influence has increased in the last decade. The Toronto news organizations have disproportionate influence because they are available to gallery members and officials at Queen's Park.

For many years, there was an influential inner circle in the gallery. There was little doubt that confident old hands could set the tone for major stories. As one long-time observer put it in an interview: 'There are a few independent souls but by and large they all want to be singing the same tune. During an election, when many new reporters come in they depend on the gallery members to tell them what is going on. Many of them don't even know what riding they're in or who holds it. They pile on the bus, perk up their ears and listen to what the senior guys have to say. In the gallery, they come in for a coffee or a beer to find what the line on a story is. They's no doubt they're influenced by one another.'

However, the tutorials in the press-gallery lounge no longer have the influence they once had. Thomas Walkom, the respected Queen's Park columnist for the *Toronto Star* argues that, while reporters do read each other and discuss events, there is no attempt to decide what the news is and how it should be covered. The similarity of reporting out of Queen's Park is, in his view, more a result of unwritten rules about what news is and how it should be structured.

Traditionally, the *Globe* has had the greatest influence, based on its elite readership and emphasis on provincial affairs. In recent years, however, its emergence as a national daily has led to reduced coverage of Ontario politics. The *Toronto Star*, with its large circulation and close ties to the Liberal government, was a major influence from 1985 to 1990, and remains important because of the attention it devotes to provincial politics. With the advent of the Harris government in 1995, the *Toronto Sun*, which is generally sympathetic to the Common Sense Revolution, is likely to gain in influence. Other important players include CP, the CBC (radio and television), Global ('Focus Ontario'), TVO ('Studio Two,' 'Fourth Reading'), and various radio and television public-affairs and phone-in shows. The news decisions made by a few key journalists have a direct influence on the issues stressed by Queen's Park journalists and on the press gallery's interpretation of key events.

For some years, the opposition parties have catered to the *Star* and the *Globe* because both newspapers have the resources and the willingness to follow up on issues and keep the heat on the government. Shrewd media-relations people knew that the *Star* would run with social issues and the *Globe* with economic ones, while personal scandals and issues of welfare fraud would interest the *Sun*.

In all modern democracies, the relationship between politician and reporter is one of mutual dependency. Reporters need information and quotes from recognizable sources and politicians need publicity, preferably favourable. The correspondent who reports only public information is unlikely to be a great success. The politician who attracts little media attention often loses influence and weakens prospects for advancement and, in urban areas at least, re-election. Thus, ambitious politicians seek high-profile cabinet posts or, in opposition, assignments as critics of controversial portfolios.

The relationship between the news media and the opposition parties is symbiotic. Whereas the government has the advantage in routine coverage, the opposition is able to seize the initiative from time to time by raising issues or uncovering scandals that attract press and public attention. On a routine basis, the opposition parties rely heavily on the media for the daily assault on the government in question period (Liberal questions often come from the *Toronto Star*, for example). Wayne Roberts has written that the major news organizations usually set the agenda for question period: 'The opposition parties rarely generate their own issues, or dig up their own stories. They're not research driven, nor policy driven. They're publicity driven.'[1] In fact, opposition party researchers do generate issues and pick up leads from interest groups and citizen complaints. However, they also monitor the media closely and tend to follow the news, as well as supplementing press investigations and occasionally instigating them.

As we have seen, much of the activity at Queen's Park involves networking. Politicians and journalists strive to develop effective relations with one another. What is exchanged in these relationships is information (a two-way flow) and publicity. Journalists cultivate sources; politicians cultivate journalists who can influence their public standing. We have noted above the relationship between the Liberals and the *Toronto Star*; Conservatives tend to have closer ties to the *Toronto Sun* and CFTO-TV. Personal relationships are also important and often transcend ideological divisions. For example, a reporter from the *Star* might have a good relationship with a Conservative MPP, despite the *Star*'s editorial policies that are critical of the Harris government.

Although the gallery remains overwhelmingly male (of the 51 full-time and 14 associate members, only 13 are women), the old boy's network that characterized the gallery in the past is no longer a major factor. Nevertheless, some systemic barriers still exist. For example, the annual hockey game between the MPPs and the gallery inhibits the participation of women. There is no dressing room for women and reporters not playing are not permitted to attend, even as spectators. Women, unless they choose to ignore the unwritten rules, are consequently excluded from the socializing and important networking that follows. As *Toronto Sun* columnist Christina Blizzard points out:

'These opportunities are how you build contacts and ... women are excluded ... If you raise this as an issue, you're laughed at.'

In practice, the relationships between reporters and senior politicians are increasingly mediated by media-relations professionals on the staffs of the parties and cabinet ministers. Their work can be of major importance in establishing the public images of the premier, ministers, and opposition party leaders. Mostly former reporters, they must walk a tightrope between their bosses and the gallery, presenting the gallery viewpoint to the premier, for example, as well as promoting the premier with the gallery. An understanding of the gallery and credibility with its members are key requirements for an effective media-relations officer. Therefore, there are limits on how much 'spin' they can put on a story. Paul Rhodes, media point man for Premier Harris, is, like most of his predecessors, a former gallery member. The fact that over the past two decades many gallery members have 'crossed over' to work for party leaders and cabinet ministers is a cause for concern. Orland French, former Queen's Park columnist for the *Globe*, argues that the 'brain drain' from the gallery results in a potential imbalance, with political strategists knowing more about the media than journalists do about politics, that leaves reporters vulnerable to manipulation.

News Management

Given its central position in the political process, it is not surprising that the press gallery is faced with constant efforts to influence its work. Interest groups, as well as government and opposition parties, compete to shape the media agenda. While interest groups seek to block or promote policies, the parties are engaged in constant image management. The government has an advantage in that reporters cannot ignore statements by the premier or senior ministers if they have any substance at all. The volume of information has increased dramatically over the past decade, forcing reporters to be more selective in their coverage – a development that helps the government, with its enormous public-relations resources, to set the agenda and requires the opposition to work harder to attract media attention.

The relationship between cabinet ministers and the gallery revolves around announcements and leaks of inside information, with access to publicity being exchanged for newsworthy information and good quotes and visuals. Ministers frequently leak proposed policy changes as 'trial balloons' to obtain public reaction. The 'spin doctors' in government often leak parts of a new policy in an attempt to control the interpretation of a government initiative. At times, leaks are the result of conflicts within the government. A minister or civil servant may inform reporters of a plan in the hope of generating public support or opposition as a weapon in the internal debate within cabinet or the party caucus. Proposed cutbacks in program budgets, for example, are often leaked with the intention of raising an outcry against them. Such leaks have been quite common since the election of the cost-cutting Conservative government in June 1995. Leaks often reach the media indirectly, with sources providing information to an opposition MPP, who either passes it on to reporters or raises the issue in question period.

The best recent example of a deliberate leak that backfired is the case of John Piper, the communications director in the office of Premier Bob Rae. In an attempt to discredit a woman who had charged a cabinet minister with misconduct, Piper released information on her criminal record. He called in Anne Dawson, a *Toronto Sun* reporter with an interest in the case, and offered her the information. Although the criminal record was public knowledge, Dawson recognized that the major story here was the attempt of Piper, a senior official in the Premier's Office, to influence coverage of the scandal involving the minister. In the end, the scandal cost Piper his job and seriously damaged the NDP government's media relations.

While the House is in session, backbench MPPs can generate media coverage on Thursday mornings, during Private Members' Public Business, when they can introduce bills or resolutions. MPPs can raise issues important in their ridings or try to bring attention to larger concerns. Media-savvy members provide relevant information to local media, where they usually get good play, and to the gallery, which occasionally takes an interest. A good example was the introduction in 1996 by NDP justice critic Marion Boyd of a resolution calling on the government to introduce a Disabilities Act. She accompanied the resolution with a press conference featuring groups representing persons with disabilities. Her actions put the issue back on the public agenda.

In recent years, interest groups have become more media-oriented. Rather than simply lobbying behind the scenes, groups are increasingly more likely to seek to bring pressure on government through the media, particularly when they feel the government is not listening. Besides sending news releases and 'open letters' to reporters, interest groups can gain access to the gallery by holding MPP-sponsored press conferences in the legislature's media studio. Politicians encourage groups to tell their stories because they are likely to have more appeal to the media and the public than yet another statement by a politician. The symbiotic relationship between opposition politicians and groups is illustrated by the fact that they not only assist such groups to gain access to legislature facilities, but also have been known to hold seminars on media strategies for sympathetic interest groups (as the NDP community and social-services critic did in 1996). Although reporters approach interest groups with caution, as they do anyone with an 'agenda,' they find access to them useful because they represent citizens affected by government initiatives and their stories can add balance and realism to a news report.

Politicians have also become increasingly sophisticated in dealing with the media. Besides cultivating personal relationships with key reporters, politicians and their staffs try to present their concerns in ways that meet the needs of the reporters. Many provide items ready for printing or broadcasting, which smaller outlets often use without editing. Politicians representing larger centres, who must use the media to reach constituents, have learned to conform to media standards by making themselves available to comment on current issues and keeping their messages simple, brief, and catchy. It has become increasingly necessary to use gimmicks to get sustained coverage. Opposition MPPs have in recent years brought many 'props' into the House, from cans of tuna to radar guns, and have taken to holding up posters with quotes from the premier or other ministers, suggesting promises broken. More generally, the opposition seek media attention through committee hearings and various public consultations. Both government and opposition parties have organized travelling road shows – pre-budget consultations, task forces on health care, northern issues – that are designed not only to gather public input but also to gain media attention, to promote or oppose certain policies.

The opposition parties rely on media feedback to decide whether or not to pursue an issue. Their general policy is to keep raising issues – in the House or, with less effect, outside – until one catches the attention of key news organizations. Lacking resources, they try to compete with the government on a single major issue and gain control of the issue by making reporters dependent on their research. They try to keep a story going by coming up with a new revelation or angle every day, knowing that repetition is crucial to make a dent in voter perceptions. Some stories catch on, especially scandals, while others are one-day wonders. The goal of the opposition parties is, of course, to portray the government as incompetent, dictatorial, or out of touch with the public. The government, by contrast, tries to focus public attention on policies with broad public support and to portray the opposition as carping critics or the captives of 'special interests.' Each side tries to anticipate issues and get its story to the media first so that it can provide the framework for the issue. There is a certain circularity to the process, since many issues arise first in the media and are then fed back to the media through statements or questions in the House or in committees. In the end, the media – and public reaction – determine how far an issue will go.

An important element of news management is what some analysts call 'flak,' that is, criticism of the work of journalists who displease someone in power. Governments often try to bypass or intimidate reporters by complaining to their supervisors or media owners. Given that media owners tend to be sympathetic to pro-business governments (which many readily admit), this tactic may have special force when used by a Conservative government, although all governments complain about the coverage they receive. The hostility of both the Liberal and NDP governments to some members of the press gallery (or the gallery as a whole) has been noted by several observers. The independence of individual journalists from the interests of media owners is both important to democracy and at times very fragile.

Another tactic, which has been fairly common over the years, is for a government to respond to critical or embarrassing reports by trying to undermine the credibility of the news organization or reporter involved. Sometimes government spokespersons allege bias or conflict of interest on the part of the news organization. At others, governments encourage journalists sympathetic to them to 'smear' a journalist whose work concerns them. This was more common in the era of the partisan press, but it still happens today. (See box 3, p. 254.)

Media and Policy

While there are many forms of pressure placed on the government – from backbenchers, the opposition parties, interest groups, or the recommendations of civil servants – publicity in the media can have a major impact on the priority that government accords to an issue. Thomas Walkom argues that press coverage is sometimes a necessary condition, but never a sufficient condition to put an issue on the government's agenda. It seems clear, however, that media attention can move an item rapidly up the list of issues with which a government must deal, especially if press attention is widespread in the province and generates public reaction.

Box 3

ATTACKING THE MESSENGER

In May 1996, Martin Mittelstaedt, a highly regarded reporter for the *Globe and Mail*, became a target when he followed up on an investigative report by colleague Estanislao Oziewicz (a former gallery member) that detailed expenditures incurred by Premier Harris as Conservative party leader in the year leading up to the 1995 election that were covered by his riding association. The issue was that riding association funds come from tax-deductible donations. No legal issue was raised. Subsequently, someone faxed information to journalists sympathetic to the Harris government revealing that Mittelstaedt had donated $250 to an NDP riding association in 1990 (*before* he was assigned to Queen's Park). This information was used as the basis for an attack on the *Globe* stories by John Downing in the *Toronto Sun*. He did not name Mittelstaedt, but accused the *Globe* of 'hypocrisy.' Mike Duffy – who says he was faxed the information – treated it as a question of journalistic ethics. Paul Rhodes, senior media adviser in the Premier's Office, told reporters that he was aware of the donation, noting that such checking of donor lists is routine, but denied leaking the information. It seems likely that whoever leaked the information was seeking to discredit the stories and to deflect attention from the premier. Richard Brennan (*Windsor Star*, 3 May 1996) commented: 'The message was unmistakable: write stories that embarrass Premier Mike Harris and there will be repercussions.' He went on to predict that 'this political intimidation will backfire.' Unfortunately, however, the public often does not learn of stories that are not reported or pursued for fear of repercussions.

Opposition parties also respond to media attention, adjusting their strategies and tactics according to press-gallery interest. If an issue raised in the House receives favourable attention, it will be pursued. If not, it will be abandoned. The media serve as a barometer of the public's appetite for certain issues and for opposition tactics. Both government and opposition parties employ communication directors whose work is not so much routine media relations as issue management. The best strategists understand longer-term cycles in Ontario politics and try to anticipate issues and develop plans to deal with them before they come to public attention.

Media attention and public reaction are not usually sufficient to create a new policy or to veto one that is on the government agenda, but adjustments are often made in response to media coverage. Several instances in the past decade can be identified in which sustained media attention contributed to a change in government intentions. It seems clear, for example, that the NDP government reconsidered its plans in 1992 for public auto insurance in part because a clever lobbying campaign raised the spectre of large-scale job loss that was picked up by the media. The Conservative government's omnibus bill in 1996 was altered in several of its provisions as a result of the media attention generated by Alvin Curling's refusal to vote on the bill or leave the House and by the public hearings that the government agreed to as a result. (See box 4, pp. 256–7.)

The media probably have their greatest impact through reaction to embarrassing facts or conditions brought to light through investigative or exposure journalism. For example, in conflict-of-interest cases unearthed by the *Globe* in 1985, the government moved to tighten regulations only when it became clear that the revelations were generating significant public reaction. The key appears to be sustaining media attention long enough for public reaction to surface. There seems little doubt that the Conservatives adopted rent control as policy during the 1975 election campaign because the *Toronto Star*, followed by other news outlets, made a crusade of it, following up NDP revelations by featuring stories of evictions and inhumane living conditions day after day. It remains to be seen whether or not such coverage will take place – or make a difference – if the Harris government seeks to remove or severely weaken rent controls. It also seems likely that the public inquiry into violence on the picket line during the OPSEU strike – which featured a clash between the Ontario Provincial Police and strikers – might not have been called so quickly without the sustained media attention that the incident received. The power of the images broadcast by television news played an important role.

According to a senior strategist in the office of Premier Harris, the Conservative government is 'agenda-driven' and is not open to external influences. Each government announcement is derived from the *Common Sense Revolution* (the campaign document that outlined the party's agenda) and the role of the communications strategist is confined to timing and packaging. Government announcements are carefully planned in an attempt to control media coverage. Opposition strategists are simultaneously engaged in attempts to seize the agenda by raising issues the

Box 4

THE OMNIBUS BILL

The notorious 'omnibus bill,' Bill 26 – introduced in the House in November 1995 – was a complex act that amended forty-four statutes, created three laws, and repealed two others. The bill contained several controversial provisions and was unusually broad in its scope. The government viewed it as the foundation of its cost-cutting, pro-business strategy, while the opposition parties were concerned that it was bringing major social change to Ontario and expanding executive power without proper debate.

It seems clear that the government hoped to avoid controversy by introducing it when attention was focused elsewhere – on the government's first Economic Statement – and to get it passed quickly so that negative public reaction would not have sufficient time to develop. The House was scheduled to recess in just eight days for the holiday season. In addition, the government made several positive announcements at the same time, involving for example investments in cardiac surgery, hospitals, measles immunization, and dialysis. The gallery could be expected to cover all of these 'good news' items, as well as the Economic Statement, which would provide considerable fodder for analysis. In fact, the bill was introduced while MPPs and reporters were in a 'lock-up,' reviewing the Economic Statement before its introduction. The government seemed to be using most of the weapons in its news-management arsenal on this bill.

At the outset, it appeared that the opposition's substantive concerns about the bill – in particular, issues of the privacy of medical records, increased executive powers to alter programs without legislative authorization, and greater power at the municipal level to levy fees – would get very little media attention. Indeed, the media viewed it as a 'process story,' involving arcane issues of parliamentary procedure – about whether the bill should have been introduced as several separate bills, since it covered so many topics – and therefore of little interest to the public. However, the opposition parties were able to change the frame of reference when they orchestrated an overnight sit-in the House to protest the bill. The drama involved gave the story a human dimension – focused on Liberal Alvin Curling, the first MPP to refuse to vote or leave the House – that raised pointed questions about the new government's commitment to democratic procedures. By the end of the evening, every television station in the country was carrying pictures from Queen's Park. In the end, the House leaders of three parties were able to negotiate an end to the deadlock, with the government agreeing to delay the bill until public hearings could be held in January 1996.

The story sustained media and public attention throughout the hearings and important elements of the bill were exposed to public debate. In the end, the government made a number of amendments – which, some ministers conceded, improved the bill – without altering its fundamental elements. For example, stricter guidelines were implemented to ensure confidentiality of medical records and the taxation powers of municipalities were limited. The government, having learned the lessons of the NDP's first budget, used a full range of tactics to get its harsh medicine through the legislative process with minimal debate. However, the opposition was able to gain media attention through drastic tactics in the House – tactics that can only be used sparingly for fear of alienating voters and the media – and they succeeded in mobilizing enough public concern to bring about modest changes in the bill. This case is an excellent example of the relationships involved.

media cannot ignore. Government strategists, in particular, try to understand the nature of media attention and attempt to anticipate events. They are also concerned to control communication within government in order to reduce attention to internal divisions and be able to ensure that when the major changes they are implementing are completed they can be written as success stories. The omnibus bill (Bill 26) is a good example of media strategy and the relationship among the government, opposition, and media.

The insurance industry was able to derail the NDP government's plans for public auto insurance in 1991 through an extensive lobbying campaign that included not only well-researched representations to government, but also a media lobbying campaign that was capped by the appearance of the 'pink ladies.' The pink ladies, so named because of the pink slips they believed they would get when they lost their jobs in the auto-insurance industry, approached the gallery and also demonstrated at Queen's Park. The novelty of hundreds of female clerical workers demonstrating, and in particular the irony that it was the NDP that was said to be threatening their jobs, made them newsworthy. Their actions appeared to be spontaneous but, according to Thomas Walkom,[2] were in fact orchestrated by high-powered lobbyists. The Rae government, faced with the threat of job losses and adverse publicity, backed down.

The NDP government's first budget in 1991 was a public-relations disaster. The unexpectedly high deficit – the result largely of factors beyond the government's control – played into an established stereotype, that the NDP was a 'tax and spend' party that could not be expected to provide sound fiscal management. This stereotype had been reinforced by a campaign begun the day after the 1990 election by NDP opponents who raised fears about the party's performance in office. From a communications point of view, the NDP failed to give its supporters the necessary arguments to counter the negative reaction. For example, the government failed to explain the causes of the deficit effectively and did not prepare data to show that Ontario's deficit and debt situation were actually better than those of most other provinces on a per capita basis. It is not surprising, therefore, that the budget received a negative press, even in newspapers that might have been supportive of its policies, like the *Toronto Star*. As Walkom[3] describes it: 'The ferocity of the reaction against the budget took the government by surprise. By 1991, it had become accepted wisdom in both business circles and the media that government debt was bad. However, the Rae government did not understand how deeply this neo-conservative orthodoxy had seeped into society. It did not understand that nerve – and lots of it – was required to run an economic policy directly counter to the perceived wisdom of radio and television talk shows.'

The government learned important lessons from this experience and had a much better communications strategy in place for its second budget, which was also more fiscally conservative, and did receive more favourable media reaction. By that time, however, it was too late. The slide in the polls had already begun and the NDP's image as a threat to economic stability was established in the minds of many potential swing voters. (See box 5.)

The case of the NDP's labour-law reforms, which included a ban on replacement workers, triggered a major media blitz from elements of the business community and raised questions of conflict of interest for newspapers. The campaign, which began in late 1991, was, according to Walkom,[4] 'one of the fiercest anti-government campaigns ever witnessed in Ontario.' The campaign involved lobbying, advertising, and 'media management.' The public nature of the campaign was unusual, since business had previously lobbied governments privately for the most part, but the sense of lack of access to the NDP cabinet and the success of

Box 5

HITTING THE WALL

The NDP's budget difficulties created the context for an extraordinary reaction to a public-affairs program. In February 1993, CTV broadcast an episode of its public-affairs show, *W5*, that presented New Zealand as a country that had hit the debt wall predicted for Ontario, taken drastic measures to reduce government services, and gotten back on the road to prosperity. The program's interpretation of events and their applicability to Ontario were disputed by many, but the program was used by Premier Rae and Treasurer Floyd Laughren to try to persuade reluctant members of the cabinet, NDP caucus, and others that drastic action was necessary to tackle the provincial deficit. Tapes of the program circulated throughout the government. It was an unusual case of a single program influencing media perceptions and becoming part of the policy process.

the pro–free trade coalition in 1988 persuaded business to go public. From a media point of view, the key element of the campaign was a series of strident advertisements placed by the Canadian Daily Newspaper Association warning of massive economic disruption if the proposed amendments went forward. The newspapers were concerned that labour disruptions would hit them hard if they could not use replacement workers, since, like other service industries, they cannot stockpile their products. In many cases, the ads were accompanied by editorials and commentaries opposing the amendments. The NDP government, already convinced of the hostility of the *Toronto Sun* and other conservative dailies, now perceived a general media hostility, extending even to the *Toronto Star*. They felt – with some reason – that newspapers had a clear conflict of interest with respect to the issue and did not accept the argument that the business and editorial sides of the newspaper industry were separate. The controversy played a major role, along with media attention to several trivial scandals, in souring NDP relations with the gallery. Although the press was by no means uniformly negative, and there was considerable support for the social-contract initiative, the NDP, like the Liberals before them, felt that they were unfairly treated by many media outlets. Both avoided interaction with the gallery as their mandate approached its end, a response that may have damaged their re-election efforts.

The Flow of News

In a large province like Ontario, the flow of news is important. For many years, the limited flow of Queen's Park news to voters outside the Greater Toronto Area has meant that the activities of the opposition parties in the legislature have had little impact outside the Metro area. Except in ridings held by the opposition parties, where incumbent MPPs can get their messages out by supplying smaller news outlets with news releases (including sound and video tapes), the government has a clear communications advantage. It can use announcements, awards, ceremonial openings of public facilities, and tours by ministers to attract local media attention. The Liberals were just as adept as the Conservatives in making use of this advantage. The NDP government made extensive use of these tactics in the last two years of its mandate, but ran into a somewhat more hostile media than did the other two parties. Polls over the past twenty-five years show that voters in the GTA are more aware of events at Queen's Park and of opposition-party activities than voters in other areas.

Opposition parties, if their penetrating questions, constructive criticisms, and alternative policy proposals in the chamber are not getting through to the public, must turn to other tactics. One long-standing technique is to have party leaders visit media centres outside Toronto for open-line shows and television and newspaper interviews. Politicians of all stripes like to bypass the gallery, which is often critical, and use communication channels that give them more control over the message. These include phone-in and interview shows, community radio and television shows, as well as meetings outside of Toronto that attract local media. In addition, MPPs send out constituency newsletters (at taxpayers' expense) and send information to local media. In recent years, parties – and even the government – have used direct mail, advertisements, or even 800 numbers to promote or oppose policies. For example, the Harris government invited the public to ask for a copy of its first Throne Speech by calling in. In 1992, Bob Rae made an unprecedented television address to discuss the province's fiscal problems. As required by Canadian broadcasting regulations, the opposition parties were given an opportunity to respond. Most recently, some MPPs have established web sites and invited the public to respond. Conservative MPP Tony Clement has raised issues in question period at the request of constituents who post questions to his site.

While it is true that Ontario citizens outside the Greater Toronto Area do not have as ready access to news from Queen's Park as Metro residents, information about political concerns outside Toronto gets even less attention in the major media. Because gallery members rarely travel beyond the 'precinct,' that is, Queen's Park, northern concerns, for example, are not usually part of the provincial public agenda. The case of access to air travel in Northern Ontario surfaced in 1996, when government-owned NorOntair cancelled its service to five northern communities. The cancellation raised the general issue of access to services in rural communities and connections among Ontario regions, but it received limited news coverage outside the north until the reeve of one of the affected communities held a news conference at Queen's Park (under NDP auspices). In the end, the government was able to negotiate an agreement with a private carrier to serve the areas, but the issue could easily have been forgotten. Similarly, the issues surrounding the expected revenues from a casino on a reserve in the north got little media attention until a native leader brought it to the gallery at Queen's Park.

The major consequences of a pattern of communication that does not focus on Ontario affairs are that the common images that create a sense of community are not equally distributed throughout the province and important information is not available in some areas. This raises important democratic issues, since public participation requires an understanding of provincial issues and the viewpoints of citizens across the province. Overall, the expanding circulation area of the *Toronto Star* and the availability of Ontario-oriented public- affairs programming on the CBC, Global, and TVOntario have brought a marked improvement in the flow of Ontario political news, but the gaps identified above remain a problem.

Election Coverage

During election campaigns, the media step up their coverage of provincial politics. In the process, they make the campaign visible and through their selection and presentation of news help to shape the images of candidates, define campaign issues, and influence the tone of the election. In liberal democracies, the media are expected to provide sufficient impartial information to permit citizens to make a reasoned voting choice. In 1990, for example, two-thirds of a sample of Ontario voters said they found media coverage of the campaign important in making their voting decisions.[5] In recent years, newspapers have joined radio and television in avoiding overt partisan bias in their news coverage, but some news organizations make little effort to hide their ideological preferences. The fact that the NDP rarely receives editorial endorsements, for example, reflects the pro-business bias of the media in general. Many commentators, in newspapers and on radio and television, made clear their desire to see a government other than the NDP.

In a pioneering study of campaign coverage in the Toronto media during the 1971 provincial election, University of Toronto political scientist Stephen Clarkson noted that the media place greater emphasis on the governing party than on opposition parties (and on party leaders at the expense of other candidates) and tend to limit the capacity of parties to communicate their platforms to the electorate by stressing only a few major issues. The dominance of party leaders has been evident in all media since 1971, but especially in broadcast news. The coverage generally gives the impression that elections involve a choice among leaders rather than among platforms, philosophies, or party 'teams.' Apparently responding to media practices, the parties have increasingly been planning their campaigns around the leaders and the bulk of the election coverage focuses on the leaders' campaign tours. In general, the news media make it virtually impossible for the parties to deal with more than a few issues in a campaign or to focus widespread attention on candidates other than the leader. As a consequence, most campaigns focus on a few key issues and on the personal appeal and competence of the party leaders. In 1995, according to an analysis by York student Carmen Pignataro, only three substantive issues received significant coverage in a sample of daily newspapers: taxes, welfare, and the deficit. These were the Conservative campaign issues and indicate the success of their campaign in influencing news priorities. However, leadership received most coverage. Pignataro also found that Liberal leader Lyn McLeod was far more likely to be referred to negatively in newspaper coverage (a ratio of four negative for each positive reference) than Rae (2:1) or Harris, who had a slight positive balance.

Leaders debates have become an important feature of Ontario elections. Except for 1981 and 1985, when the governing Conservatives refused to take part, there has been at least one televised debate in every campaign since 1975. Post-election polls in 1985 indicated that Conservative Premier Frank Miller lost media support and votes as a result of his refusal to debate. In the past, incumbent premiers have refused to debate when they had a clear lead in the polls, reasoning that they had nothing to gain by giving their opponents a platform to attack them. By 1990, however, it appeared that televised leaders debates had become such an accepted part of provincial election campaigns that refusal to debate would risk public and media disapproval for any leader. The debates in 1990 and 1995 both seemed to have some influence on the outcome of the election, although neither was decisive. In 1995, for example, the media refused to declare a winner, but poll results suggested that the slide in support for Lyn McLeod and the Liberals, which had been evident in the previous week, was accelerated by the debate.[6]

As far as election results are concerned, it is not unreasonable to argue that the nature of news coverage has had some influence on the outcome of recent Ontario elections. In 1985, the media were critical of the new Conservative premier, Frank Miller, for his uncharacteristic unwillingness to talk to reporters or take part in the proposed leaders debate and for the widespread perception that he was too far right for many Ontario voters. Poll results made it clear that Miller's support dropped during the campaign, probably in part because he failed to project a positive media image. In 1987, the media portrayed Peterson as a winner and the Liberal majority was portrayed as inevitable. The electorate was prepared to go along. By 1990, however, having governed for five years, Peterson had more negatives to contend with. The Starr Affair and the failure to achieve a solution to constitutional issues were important factors. Equally important, however, may have been the tension between the premier and the press gallery that had emerged in 1989 and 1990 and, in particular, the 'protester phenomenon' that captured media attention during the campaign. The campaign got off to a bad start for the Liberals when the premier's press conference to announce that he was calling an early election was disrupted by a Greenpeace protester. That protester, and others, plagued Peterson throughout the campaign and the Liberals were unable to develop an effective response. The 'winner' who breezed through the campaign in 1987 did not look like a winner in 1990, despite starting the campaign with more than 50 per cent of voter support. The media, already cynical about the early election call (which they thought was a ploy to avoid facing some difficult issues and scandals), made a conscious decision to cover the protests. Liberal strategists felt it was this factor that cost them the election. However, the stunningly effective NDP advertising campaign, which reminded voters of Liberal scandals, was arguably just as important.[7]

The Liberals also began the 1995 campaign with a substantial lead in the polls. The Conservatives, however, appear to have been much better prepared. They handled the news media much more adroitly than the other two parties, ran the most effective advertising campaign, and used innovative techniques, such as circulating their platform months in advance of the election call and making extensive use of direct mail and videos delivered to swing voters in their target ridings.[8] John Doyle points out that 'Harris sold his ideas through TV news – he provided the perfect backdrop and props for illustrating his policies and the TV reporters lapped it up.' Believing that 'most people sum up an election in TV images,' Conservative strategists mapped out an 'illustrative image' for each day of the campaign well in advance. Doyle identifies three defining moments: (1) a flatbed truck with thirty-one chairs driving away from Queen's Park to illustrate how many seats a Conservative government would eliminate from the legislature; (2) the leader at a Consumers Distributing store to show what voters could buy with the promised tax cut; (3) a sign announcing a town called Welfare, Ontario, population 1,300,000.[9] The Conservatives were able to focus coverage on their issues, which no doubt helped them win the election.

Explaining the Patterns

In general, as we have seen, the news media constitute an arena of struggle for control of the Ontario political agenda. In this struggle, the media are not neutral, since they have their own interests at stake, but they are subject to continual attempts at manipulation by government and opposition parties, as well as by interest groups of all stripes. The coverage that results is shaped by the interaction of these news sources with media practices. Many of the strengths and weaknesses of the coverage stem from the backgrounds, values, professional norms, and work patterns of journalists. The Queen's Park reporters are the primary gatekeepers in the system, but they work within guidelines established by their news organizations. These guidelines are influenced by a wide variety of factors, the most important of which are the general cultural norms of Ontario and the commercial interests of media corporations.

The traditional low level of attention to Ontario politics, for example, may be explained in part by the lower salience of provincial politics in Ontario relative to other provinces. However, a major factor is the profit orientation of most news outlets. Since they are primarily in the business of selling audiences to advertisers, many see little reason to spend money on improved coverage of provincial politics. This is particularly true of the broadcast media, whose main product is entertainment. One could argue, therefore, that the increased interest in provincial politics in the past decade is a result not only of the fact that Ontario politics has become more important, as the federal government withdraws from many policy areas, but also – and perhaps more importantly – from the fact that Ontario politics has become more interesting. The higher level of conflict and drama that has emerged as a result of voter volatility and the resulting changes of government as well as difficult economic times in the province are a major factor in the increased coverage, since they have made Ontario politics more newsworthy.

The relative lack of hard-hitting investigative reporting noted by many media critics can be traced to several related factors. First, for the most part, only larger news organizations are willing to make the long-term commitment of reporters to projects that may produce nothing publishable. The services of experts and the threat of libel suits make such reporting too expensive for most editorial budgets. Second, many news organizations shy away from being too controversial. In their quest for large audiences, many outlets are reluctant to offend any major segment of their communities that is attractive to advertisers.

More generally, Ericson, Baranek, and Chan note that reporters appear to be influenced in their news selection and presentation by such factors as (1) the 'political affinities' of their news outlets, (2) editorial budgets that force reporters to depend on official sources, and (3) fear in some circles of loss of advertising (including government advertising) if reporting is too critical. While little evidence is offered for these assertions, there is no denying that the major media organizations are themselves well-established parts of our present economic and social system and have no desire to undermine it. This was reflected, for example, in the less than generous attitude of many news organizations to the NDP government. Like others, media owners and managers tend to identify their interests with the public interest.

Reporters and editors are frequently more venturesome than their employers, but they are often inhibited by a subtle set of newsroom norms that discourage some kinds of reporting and encourage others. There is, in fact, little direct suppression of news or opinion, but reporting that upsets community norms or threatens local economic interests is often discouraged. It is safer, as well as easier, to avoid sceptical reporting and analysis in favour of summarizing what others have said and done. Only a few news organizations have the resources and commitment to seek the rewards of public service as well as profit. These exceptions, however, do often influence the coverage provided by others.

When provincial politics is not adequately covered, the democratic process suffers. Governments have less reason to be responsive to public needs and preferences. The governing party benefits greatly from media neglect, since few Ontarians would know about government blunders without the media. Thus, the current higher level of attention is to be welcomed. Much of value can be learned from the best work of press gallery correspondents; the challenge is to encourage more high-quality journalism. Citizens can, by using a variety of news sources, look beyond the tales spun by politicians and the stories told by journalists and create their own public agenda.

Notes

This is the fifth version of this chapter, which was first published in 1975 and has been substantially revised for this edition. The senior author has been assisted by several legislative interns, as well as graduate students and research assistants at York University. The chapter also draws on the research of several York University undergraduates including, for this version, that of Carmen Pignataro. Many of these contributions are acknowledged in earlier editions. Most important, over the years, a large number of gallery members and media-relations people have agreed to be interviewed. We discussed the gallery and its work with many members of the gallery and other Queen's Park observers in 1996. We are grateful to all of those who have helped us to understand better the complex relationships between media and politics at Queen's Park. We, however, remain responsible for errors of fact or interpretation.

1 *Now*, 23 February – 1 March 1989.
2 T. Walkom, *Rae Days: The Rise and Follies of the NDP*. (Toronto: Key Porter Books, 1994), 75–6. Patrick Monahan naively attributes the initiation of this campaign to the spontaneous action of individuals. See P. Monahan, *Storming the Pink Palace – The NDP in Power: A Cautionary Tale* (Toronto: Lester Publishing, 1995), 82–3.
3 Ibid., 103.
4 *Ibid.*, 127.
5 Georgette Gagnon and Dan Rath, *Not without Cause: David Peterson's Fall from Grace* (Toronto: Harper Collins, 1991), 248.
6 Christina Blizzard, *Right Turn: How the Tories Took Ontario* (Toronto: Dundurn Press, 1995), 109.
7 Gagnon and Rath, *Not without Cause*, 252–5.
8 Blizzard, *Right Turn*, chap. 9.
9 *Broadcast Week*, 24–30 June 1995.

Further Reading

Ericson, Richard V., Patricia M. Baranek, and Janet L. Chan. *Negotiating Control: A Study of News Sources*, esp. chap. 4. Toronto: University of Toronto Press, 1989. Presents a detailed study of reporter-source relationships at Queen's Park, carried out in 1982–3.

Fletcher, Frederick J., and Robert Everett. 'Mass Media and Elections in Canada.' In F.J. Fletcher, ed., *Media, Elections and Democracy*, 179–222. Toronto: Dundurn Press for the Royal Commission on Electoral Reform and Party Financing, 1991. Discusses the role of the media in Canadian elections, with comparisons to other democracies.

– 'The Mass Media and Political Communication in Canada.' In Benjamin D. Singer, ed., *Communications in Canadian Society* (4th ed.), 237–59. Toronto: Nelson, 1995. Provides an overview of political communication in Canada.

Fletcher, Frederick J., and Daphne Gottlieb Taras. 'The Mass Media and Canadian Politics: Private Ownership, Public Responsibilities.' In Michael Whittington and Glen Williams, eds., *Canadian Politics in the 1990s* (4th ed.), 292–319. Toronto: Nelson, 1995. Surveys the major issues regarding news coverage of politics.

Gagnon, Georgette, and Dan Rath. *Not without Cause: David Peterson's Fall from Grace*. Toronto: HarperCollins, 1991. An interesting discussion of the Liberal government and the election of 1990, with attention to media relations.

Manthorpe, Jonathan. *The Power and the Tories: Ontario Politics – 1943 to Present*. Toronto: Macmillan of Canada, 1974. A reporter's-eye view of Ontario politics and the press gallery (see esp. pp. 228–41).

Speirs, Rosemary. *Out of the Blue: The Fall of the Tory Dynasty in Ontario*. Toronto: Macmillan of Canada, 1986. Describes in detail the events that shaped the 1985 election campaign and its aftermath.

Walkom, Thomas. *Rae Days: The Rise and Follies of the NDP*. Toronto: Key Porter Books, 1994. A review of the NDP in power, including discussion of its relations with the press gallery, by a long-time gallery member.

White, Graham, ed. *Inside the Pink Palace: Ontario Legislature Internship Essays*. Toronto: OLIP/CPSA, 1993. Contains several revealing essays on media relations at Queen's Park. See esp. pp. 1–20, 57–128, 186–228, and 294–309.

ELEVEN

Judging Women's Political Success in the 1990s

Cheryl N. Collier

The 1990s have been a roller-coaster ride for women in politics in Ontario. At the beginning of the decade, women saw unprecedented gains in their political representation in the legislature, cabinet, and elite levels of the bureaucracy. As well, women were able to acheive substantive policy gains in areas of particular interest to them[1] as a result of this increased political participation. However, this decade has also seen the first drop in women's representation in electoral politics after twenty-five years of successive increases. And perhaps, as a direct result, many of women's policy gains have subsequently been stripped away.

While gender parity has yet to be reached in Ontario politics, the recent unevenness in women's political success raises questions as to whether women will be able to sustain political gains over time in the province overall. What seems to be increasingly clear, however, is that the party ideology of the government in power has played a significant role in determining how sussessful women have been in both numeric and substantive representation in the 1990s. The social-democratic New Democratic and the neo-conservative Progressive Conservative parties that formed governments during this decade had very different approaches to women-centred or feminist policy issues. As well, each party in Ontario has a different approach to promoting women to contest party nominations and run in elections, also with distinct results. In the end, the evidence indicates strongly that, even in times of fiscal restraint and decreasing federal transfer payments to the province, women are much more successful in politics under a left-wing than a right-wing government.

This chapter will evaluate women's numeric and substantive representation in Ontario politics with a particular focus on the 1990s in order to illustrate the trends summarized above. The first section of the chapter will describe women's numeric representation in the legislature, the cabinet, and appointed elite bureaucratic positions, paying particular attention to the different promotion tactics of all three political parties. In this section, the paper will argue that women are still largely underrepresented in the Ontario legislature but that different affirmative-action practices of the parties have resulted in different levels of success for women, depending on which party is in power. Of note are the high numbers of women appointed to the cabinet under the NDP and the substantial numbers of women to reach the elite bureaucracy under the NDP and PC regimes.

The second section of the chapter will evaluate women's substantive representation – their ability to achieve policy gains and to exert influence over general public policy. This section will first evaluate the government machinery put in place to deal with women's issues and then will review substantive policy gains and losses for women during the 1990s. It will argue that although some strides have been made in sustaining substantive policy gains in areas of particular interest to women, those gains have been threatened or completely dismantled under the new era of neo-conservatism that has swept the province under the PCs. As well, government machinery put in place to deal with women's issues has become less and less effective in influencing the policy process and that machinery's very existence is currently in jeopardy. In the end, the evidence indicates that policy results that favour women will more often occur when a large minority of women, especially feminist women, hold elected and appointed office under a social-democratic government. When those women are absent, so are women's policy gains, especially when a neo-conservative government is in power.

Women's Electoral Representation

Ontario has historically been an important setting for English Canadian women's movement activity. This began with the 1877 founding of the Toronto Women's Literary Society, which is the first suffrage-movement activity recorded in Canada, and continues on past the more recent founding of the Toronto-based Committee for '94, which focused on achieving gender parity in the federal legislature by 1994.[2] The campaign of the Canadian women's movement to increase the numbers of women elected to federal and provincial legislatures specifically can be traced to

TABLE 1
Women elected by each party since 1945

Year	Progressive Conservatives	New Democrats (CCF)	Liberals	Total No. (%)
1945	0*	0	0	0 (0)
1948	0*	1	0	1 (1)
1951	0*	0	0	0 (0)
1955	0*	0	0	0 (0)
1959	0*	0	0	0 (0)
1963	1*	0	0	1 (1)
1967	1*	1	0	2 (2)
1971	1*	0	0	1 (1)
1975	3*	2	1	6 (5)
1977	3*	2	1	6 (5)
1981	4*	1	1	6 (5)
1985	3	3	3*	9 (7)
1987	1	3	16*	20 (15)
1990	3	19*	6	28 (21)
1995	11*	4	4	19 (15)

Source: Canadian Parliamentary Guides (1945–94); Canadian Press, 1995.
*Indicates government party.

the early stages of the second wave of the movement[3] and the 1970 federal *Report of the Royal Commission on the Status of Women*. The report identified women's electoral projects as important goals for women, and during the 1970s women started to see a steady growth in their numeric representation at the federal level and in many provinces across the country.

Ontario was no exception to this trend. When we look at table 1,[4] we can see that from 1945 until the mid-1970s women were virtually non-existent in the Ontario legislature: only once during this period did as many as two women sit as MPPs, and in three successive elections no women were elected. Finally, in the mid-1970s half a dozen women were elected. From that decade through the 1980s, and peaking in 1990, women in the Ontario legislature saw a steady increase in their numbers from about 5 per cent in 1975 to 21 per cent in 1990. Unfortunately, in 1995 those incremental increases were halted by the first drop in numeric representation in the province in twenty-five years to 15 per cent of the legislature. This drop in numbers is quite substantial and surprising when compared to the fact that women's numeric representation in parliament and in provincial legislatures across the country has been consistently on the rise since the 1970s.

Much research has been done to explain women's absence from legislative office. Early work in this area identified cultural and role constraints that worked against women's involvement, concluding that women did not see themselves as fitting into the traditional public, male arena of politics and that their isolation in the private sphere of the home as wives and mothers created time constraints that curbed their ability to participate in politics. Subsequent electoral and candidate selection studies identified women's relative inability to earn money and to raise campaign funds when compared to men; the tendency of parties to try to discourage women from running by playing dirty tricks on them during nomination campaigns; and the unwillingness of parties to run women in 'winnable' ridings as being major barriers to women's ability to get elected.[5]

While most of these barriers still exist to a certain extent, more recent literature focuses specifically on the crucial role of parties as gatekeepers to elected office. Since fringe parties and independent candidates lack legitimacy in the Canadian political system, in order to have any hope of winning a potential candidate must be identified with a major party. This fact gives parties substantial power in deciding who makes it to the legislature. Researchers have found that candidate selection is locally controlled, but that women have the best chance of being elected in parties that actively aid, promote, and convince women to run for a constituency nomination.

In Ontario, the three major provincial parties have different approaches to the promotion of women as candidates for public office. The Ontario New Democratic Party takes the most proactive approach by actually setting and encouraging specific target figures for the number of women nominated as candidates. However, these targets are not enforced as quotas, as compliance by riding associations is voluntary. The party almost enacted a quota system to promote women as candidates for election, but this strategy ran into some resistance within the party ranks, where there was some worry about 'negative press.' In the end, the party settled on a system in which process is mandatory but outcomes are not. In 1982, the NDP became the first provincial party organization to adopt an affirmative-action resolution, drafted by the NDP Women's Committee. This resolution had four major objectives: emphasizing policies of interest to women; providing leadership training programs for women; recruiting female candidates in strong ridings and helping with child care and household expenses; and encouraging at least 50 per cent representation in riding executives, provincial-council delegations, the provincial executive, and party committees. In 1989, the NDP extended this affirmative-action resolution to cover nomination and candidacy for not only women but also visible minorities, people with disabilities, and Aboriginal peoples. Also, in order to help women raise enough money to run for public office once nominated (a key to their chances of being elected) the federal NDP in 1983 established the Agnes Macphail Fund, which has a provincial counterpart in Ontario. This fund helps support female candidates for election at the federal and provincial levels. For example, in 1988, the federal NDP disbursed $1000 to each of its eighty-five female candidates to help them run for office.

The Ontario Progressive Conservatives have a similar fund to aid women in need of money to run for office once they have been nominated, as do the Ontario Liberals. The federal PC Ellen Fairclough Fund, established in 1986, is available at the provincial level as is the federal Liberal Judy LaMarsh Fund, established in 1984. None of these funds, however, can be used by a woman seeking a nomination because of fears the money would be used against incumbents. To help women at the point of seeking nomination, the Ontario PCs set up the Women in Nomination (WIN) program in 1987. WIN, which is still an active program in the party, also runs training programs and consulting services for women to help them pick ridings in which to run, set up campaign teams, and organize fund raising. Unlike the NDP, the PC provincial association's constitution does not encourage ridings to adopt a 50 per cent target for women candidates. Similarly, the Ontario Liberal Women's Perspective Advisory Committee was formed in 1982 to encourage an increase in women's participation within that party and in electoral office, but tended to promote voluntary or informal efforts to accomplish this goal.

Looking back at table 1, it is clear that most women were elected to the party that captured power during each election. Given the massive shifts in the parties' electoral fortunes in Ontario since the mid-1980s, this suggests that women are swept into office when an unexpected shift in voter support for a party brings in candidates nominated in what would otherwise be considered unwinnable ridings.[6] Parties are often charged with running women in unwinnable ridings, so women in particular would benefit from this kind of electoral sea-change. In the 1990 Ontario election, for example, NDP candidate Marion Boyd ran against Liberal leader David Peterson in the riding of London Centre and defeated him in an unexpected electoral 'sweep.' In 1995, however, fewer women were swept into office with the PC winning tide, even though that election saw the most PC women ever being brought into the legislature

TABLE 2
Women run by the parties, 1987–90, by percentage (number)

Year	PCs	NDP	Liberals	Total
1987	18 (23)	35 (45)	21 (27)	95
1990	15 (19)	30 (39)	21 (26)	84
1995	15 (19)	29 (37)	24 (31)	87

Source: Provincial Chief Electoral Results, 1987, 1988, 1990, 1995

at any one time. This latter difference in the numbers of women swept into office – nineteen women by the NDP in 1990 (the most ever by any one party in Ontario's history) and eleven women by the PCs in 1995 – can best be explained by the affirmative-action policies of both parties and the fact that the NDP has tended to run more women candidates than the PCs.

Indeed table 2 clearly shows that the NDP has consistently run more women than either the Liberals or the PCs since 1987, hovering between 30 and 35 per cent. However, the overall number of women candidates fielded by the major parties in Ontario has fallen in each election year from a high of ninety-five candidates in 1987 to eighty-seven candidates in 1995. This disturbing trend may indicate that more needs to be done in the area of promoting women in all parties to run for office if gender parity is ever to become a reality in the Ontario legislature.

Appointments to Cabinet and Elite Levels of the Bureaucracy

The provincial policy process is generally dominated by three important actors: the government, or more specifically the cabinet and premier; the bureaucracy; and, to varying extents, interest groups. Increasingly, feminist political scientists are judging women's political success not only on the basis of increasing women's electoral representation but also through achieving policy gains that benefit women. In that light, it is important to evaluate women's influence and representation within the cabinet and elite decision-making levels of the bureaucracy, as these are crucial locations in the provincial policy process and can be a deciding factor as to the presence or absence of feminist policy.

Table 3 indicates that the differences among the parties do not stop at affirmative-action programs to promote nominees and candidates. There is also a clear distinction between the parties' willingness to promote women, once elected, to powerful cabinet positions, with the NDP again proving to be more willing to promote women. In 1990, NDP leader Bob

TABLE 3
Women cabinet ministers

Year	Government party	Percentage (no.) of women ministers
1987	Liberals	15 (4/26)
1990	New Democrats	44 (11/25)
1995	Progressive Conservatives	20 (4/20)

Source: Campbell 1987, 1993; Leroux and Artuso 1995.

Rae appointed the highest percentage of women to any cabinet in the history of Canadian politics. In that twenty-five-member cabinet, eleven, or 44 per cent, were women, a situation approaching gender parity. It is possible that these eleven women ministers constituted a 'critical mass' or a significant minority large enough to effect major shifts in policy.[7] Indeed, the 44 per cent tally surpasses a 30–35 per cent target area used by Scandinavian political scientists to identify the presence of a critical mass.

It is also important to note that the majority, if not all, of these eleven NDP women ministers had publicly identified themselves as feminists and were predisposed to promote and implement policies and programs presumed to benefit women. Feminist ministers such as Frances Lankin, Marion Boyd, and Evelyn Gigantes were particularly 'adamant [that] their fight for sexual equality [wouldn't] be compromised by power.'[8] Current political-science research has raised questions about the assumption that women, once elected, will consciously represent and promote feminist or women-centred policies. Much research does indicate that for the most part women will represent women's interests even if they do not see themselves as being elected to represent women per se. However, the increasing presence of anti-feminist and neo-conservative women in legislatures indicates that a blanket assumption that all women legislators will represent women is probably a false one. One might suggest, then, that the election of *feminist* women is a precondition to sustain women-centred policy outcomes. Along with the public identification of certain cabinet ministers as feminists, informal women's caucuses existed within the NDP cabinet as well as in the larger party caucus. These informal caucuses would specifically discuss ways to get women's policy items on the government agenda.

The Ontario PC government elected in 1995, however, promoted women to only 20 per cent of the cabinet positions available after Premier Mike Harris chopped the cabinet to twenty members, its lowest level in three

TABLE 4
Women in party caucuses, by percentage (number)

Election Year	PCs	NDP	Liberals
1987	6 (1/16)	16 (3/19)	17 (16/95)
1990	15 (3/20)	26 (19/74)	17 (6/36)
1995	13 (11/82)	24 (4/17)	13 (4/31)

Sources: Canadian Parliamentary Guides (1987–95); Chief Election Officer (Ontario) 1987, 1990, 1995.

TABLE 5
Women's appointment to elite bureaucratic positions, 1995–96,
by percentage (number)

Year	Deputy ministers	Assistant deputy ministers	Agencies, boards, and commissions
1995	40 (8/20)	42 (38/90)	34 (42/122)
1996	40 (8/20)	43 (39/90)	43 (52/122)

Sources: Corpus Administrative Index (1995); Government of Ontario telephone directory, fall/winter 1995–96.

decades. The percentage of Tory women in the overall 1995 caucus was also smaller, at 13 per cent, than the NDP's 1990 percentage of women in the caucus, which stood at 26 per cent (see table 4). None of the PC women cabinet ministers have publicly identified themselves as feminist nor does a women's caucus appear to exist within this cabinet or the wider caucus. Whereas NDP women cabinet ministers were given higher-profile portfolios, including Attorney General, Health, and Economic Development and Trade, the PC women cabinet ministers were for the most part marginalized in traditionally feminine cabinet posts, including former PC leadership contender Dianne Cunningham, who was relegated to the lesser posts of Intergovernmental Affairs Minister and Minister Responsible for Women's Issues.

Table 5 shows that both the NDP and the PCs have appointed significant numbers of women to elite levels of the bureaucracy. About 40 per cent of all deputy ministers (the most senior level of the bureaucracy) under both governments were women, based on a tally of eight out of twenty-one DM positions under the NDP and nine out of twenty-one DM positions under the PCs.[9] This 40 per cent is quite a significant increase from two decades earlier, when only one or two of the deputy ministers were women. These DM appointments were both in traditionally feminine departments, such as Citizenship, Culture and Recreation and Community and Social Services, as well as in less-traditional departments, including Solicitor General, Health, and Management Board. Many of the specific DMs changed from one administration to the next, but the overall number of women DMs did not change. This same trend is apparent with women assistant deputy ministers (the second most senior level of the bureaucracy), whose numbers hovered just over 40 per cent under both governments.

The high levels of women in the elite bureaucracy under both recent provincial regimes may be linked to the existence of employment-equity legislation in the public service since 1987, when it was first introduced by the Ontario Liberals (and subsequently improved under the NDP). This has resulted in a larger pool of experienced women bureaucrats from which to draw for merit-based appointments to ADM and DM positions. In 1992, for example, women made up 47 per cent of the provincial public service. Indeed this merit-based trend in hiring explains why Rita Burak, a highly respected, non-partisan career bureaucrat, was appointed by the Tories in 1995 as the first-ever woman Cabinet Secretary, the highest civil-service position in Ontario. This could also help explain the increase in the appointment of women to chairs of agencies, boards, and commissions in the province, which went from 34 per cent under the NDP to 43 per cent under the PCs.[10]

Women's Substantive Representation

As was mentioned above, feminist political scientists do not measure women's success via their numerical representation in elected and appointed office alone. It is often assumed that the more women elected to the legislature, the greater the chances that those women will articulate women's interests/needs[11] and push for policy gains to address those interests/needs. To that end, this section will attempt to evaluate how well the bureaucratic machinery put in place specifically to articulate women's interests is working. As well, the section will also evaluate the women-centred policies enacted or scrapped by each government in the 1990s to try to suggest the existence of a link between women's numeric and substantive representation.

In the 1990s two main bureaucratic bodies have been responsible for articulating women's interests within the provincial government. These are the Ontario Women's Directorate (OWD) and the Ontario Advisory Council on Women's Issues (OACWI). The OACWI was the successor to the Ontario Advisory Council on the Status of Women, which was created in 1973 in partial response to the 1970 federal *Report of the Royal Commission on the Status of Women*. The RCSW Report recommended that a national advisory council be developed to represent women's needs within government and that once that national body was in place, provincial councils should also be established that mirrored the federal example. The Ontario Status of Women Council underwent a sunset review in 1983 that resulted in then-Premier Bill Davis and the provincial Progressive Conservative government creating the OWD and the OACWI, after much lobbying by provincial women's groups and the Ontario Advisory Council on the Status of Women to enhance the offices' capacity for more effective policy input. After 1983, both government agencies were to report to the newly created minister responsible for women's issues to, in the words of Bill Davis, 'provide a needed focus and a coordinating role in the delivery and communication of programs and policies designed to assist and encourage women in all aspects of life.'[12]

In 1995, the OWD had a staff of about eighty-five and a budget of about $18 million. Its original mandate was to make recommendations to cabinet through the minister responsible, brief the minister, and maintain a policy staff to work with policy advisers to develop programs and policies for the betterment of women. Subsequently, however, this role shifted to a more passive one as adviser to government. The more active policy role appears to have been taken over by specific policy offices such as the Women's Health Bureau, the Pay Equity Commission, and the Human Resources Secretariat, which divided the focus of women's issues within the provincial government. Under the NDP, the Office Responsible for Women's Issues budget, which includes that of the OWD, was frozen between 1991 and 1994 at approximately $24 million. Under the PCs, funding for the OWD has been slashed dramatically, the Office Responsible for Women's Issues has had twenty-seven jobs cut, and its overall budget has been trimmed by $2.9 million, mostly affecting programs put in place for the prevention of violence against women.

In 1993, the OACWI had fifteen members and a budget of approximately $384,000. Established in 1983, its original mandate was to monitor and evaluate existing legislation and programs related to the status of women, to illuminate areas where the government needs to focus specific attention, to make recommendations to government in these areas, to consult with public women's groups province-wide, and to respond to specific requests by the minister responsible for women's issues for advice and consultation. The NDP initiated a new mandate for the OACWI in 1991 that stressed the need to improve communications between the OACWI and provincial women's groups. In 1992 a second new mandate was established following a full-scale review of the OACWI stressing a need for more continuity in appointments to the Council and a move away from a research focus to a greater community-outreach role. The OACWI, however, was constrained in this outreach role as a link between grass-roots women's groups and the provincial government owing to both the size of the women's movement and the budgetary limitations of the Council itself.[13] Under the NDP, the OACWI budget decreased from $500,000 in 1989 to $374,200 in 1993, but at least the OACWI was kept alive. The Tories, by contrast, decided to fold the OACWI altogether in the spring of 1996 just before the announcement of their first provincial budget.

Women-Centred Policy Results

Several factors constrained both the NDP and PC governments from enacting policy in areas of particular interest to women. These included a country-wide recession and a subsequent decline in federal transfers via the Canada Assistance Plan and the Established Programs Financing plan, which shrunk the revenues available to the province during the 1990s. Both governments were forced to practise their own brand of fiscal restraint. For the NDP this meant cautious spending, but an overall increase in spending by 13 per cent nonetheless (which also helped to substantially increase the province's deficit). For the PCs restraint has meant deep spending cuts, especially in policy areas of particular interest to women, and no spending increases, with the goal of a balanced budget by the year 2000 and a 30 per cent cut in provincial tax rates, the phase-in of which began the summer of 1996. These drastically different ideologies – and arguably the existence of a critical mass of women in one cabinet versus a small number of women in another – would lead to very different results for women in the policy arena.

During its term, the NDP did implement a significant number of women-centred policies, many of which were started by the previous Liberal government, including making the employment-equity law for provincial public-sector workers mandatory; changes to child-support regulations that allowed the government to deduct money from the income of defaulting spouses; an increase of over 10,000 new child-care spaces; improved parental leave; new funding for sexual-assault centres and women's centres; increased access to abortion services; legislation that eliminates the time limits on filing sexual-assault cases; and legalized midwifery via a provincial degree program that legitimized its practice.

The Ontario PCs, when elected, did their best to dismantle many of these policy gains that women were able to achieve under the NDP. Their goal was to reduce the provincial deficit and to conform to neo-conservative ideology, which saw women as 'special interests' and did not favour state quotas or aid programs to help bolster women's equality. Cuts to women-centred policy included a loss of nearly 4000 subsidized child-care spaces when the JobsOntario program was stopped; a cap on pay-equity wage increases for underpaid women; the scrapping of the NDP's Employment Equity program on the grounds that it imposed strict 'quotas' to the detriment of merit-based hiring; the elimination of second-stage women's shelter counselling funding and a 7.5 per cent cut to shelters' budgets; a freeze on wage grants put in place to top up the meagre salaries of child-care workers; and, most seriously for women, a 21.6 per cent reduction in benefits to welfare recipients (the elderly and disabled were spared this cut). During the spring 1996 budget, however, the PCs did manage a promise to increase child-care funding by $200 million between 1996 and 2001, including a three-year $7.7 million investment in child-care-centre building renovations across the province.

Researchers have noted that women are more likely to be poorer than men and to be the primary caregivers of young children and the elderly. As a result, they are disproportionately affected by cuts to social programs and have more of a stake in ensuring that many of these 'welfare-state' programs stay intact. In addition, a disproportionate number of women work in the health, education, and social-services sectors, which all received substantial cuts under the Tories, resulting in a large number of women losing their jobs. Therefore, the reality of life under the neo-conservative PCs in Ontario is a bit crueler for women. It seems clear that this neo-conservative ideology, combined with the lack of women within the government caucus and specifically the cabinet, precipitated these negative policy results for women, whereas the presence of feminist women under the social-democratic NDP seemed to be enough to protect existing programs and even promote new social programs to benefit women, even during an era of fiscal restraint and recession.

Conclusions

An Environics poll published in the *Toronto Star* in April 1996 showed an unprecedented gender gap in support for the provincial Tories that was not seen in the previous NDP or Liberal terms in office. Overall, 62 per cent of women polled said they disapproved of the Harris government and its 'Common Sense Revolution,' while 55 per cent of men said they approved of the Tories. This gap can perhaps best be explained by the remarkable contrast between what the Tories have *not* done for women in the province and what the NDP administration before them *had* done for women. For the first time in its history, the province has seen a decrease in the number of female legislators; at the same time, women-centred programs and even bureaucratic departments set up to deal with women's issues (ironically, by a more centrist version of the Tories under Bill Davis) have been cut or eliminated. In stark contrast, at the beginning of the decade, women were close to achieving gender parity in the Ontario cabinet, were experiencing the highest numbers of women legislators in the province's history, and had seen substantial policy gains in areas that matter to women. Clearly, what this shows is that party ideology matters quite a lot to women in Ontario and to their success in provincial politics.

However, it is too soon to lay too much praise at the doorstep of the NDP. While the gains in women's numeric and substantive representation under this government were impressive compared to the past and present, they still signified women's underrepresentation and failure to reach gender parity. It is also important to recall that the overall number of women candidates for the provincial legislature dropped from 1987 to 1995. This indeed is a disturbing trend that seems to indicate that more needs to be done by all the parties to help women seek and gain nomination for office. As well, the recent scrapping of employment-equity programs in the province can only hurt the gains women have achieved in the public service and elite bureaucracy. This too is an area that needs to be addressed if gender parity is to become a reality. And only when women can achieve equal levels of representation in the legislature, and can ensure their interests are being expressed and dealt with via substantive policies and programs, will they truly be successful in politics in Ontario.

Notes

The author wishes to thank Lisa Young, who graciously read and commented on an earlier version of this chapter.

1 Recently feminist political scientists have cautioned against dealing with so-called women's issues to the detriment of discounting other policy areas that are of distinct interest to women. See Sandra Burt, 'The Several Worlds of Policy Analysis: Traditional Approaches to Feminist Critiques,' in S. Burt and L. Code, eds, *Changing Methods: Feminists Transforming Practice* (Toronto: Broadview, 1995) and Janine Brodie, ed., *Women and Canadian Public Policy* (Toronto: Harcourt Brace, 1996). However, most research still tends to identify policy areas of *particular* interest to women as including areas such as child care, employment, and pay equity. This chapter will focus on these policy areas of particular interest to women, but will also discuss general public policy (i.e., welfare policy) that affects women differently than men.

2 The Committee for '94 was also very involved in Ontario politics and arguably has had a stronger impact on the province's parties than on federal ones.

3 The women's movement in Canada has gone through two specific waves. The first wave occurred around the turn of the century and mainly focused on women's goal to gain the vote in federal and provincial elections. After the federal franchise was won, the women's movement then went through a hiatus period until it was revitalized in the 1960s (as it was in the United States and other Western democracies) with a focus on equal rights and equal treatment for women.

4 It is important to note that all numbers and percentages mentioned in this chapter are only snapshots of particular moments in time, as all of these numbers are constantly changing owing to resignations, promotions, by-elections, and so on.

5 On barriers that hinder women's electoral success, see Janine Brodie and Jill Vickers, *Canadian Women in Politics: An Overview* (Ottawa: CRIAW, 1982); Janine Brodie, *Women and Politics in Canada* (Toronto: McGraw-Hill Ryerson, 1985); and Sylvia Bashevkin, *Toeing the Lines: Women and Party Politics in English Canada*, 2nd ed. (Toronto: University of Toronto Press, 1993).

6 Recent research suggests that the trend of parties running women in unwinnable ridings is subsiding somewhat and notes that women's steady electoral gains in federal and provincial legislatures can be explained by the increased number of women who participate in the paid workforce and by women's higher levels of education and subsequent political interest. See Donley Studlar and Richard Matland, 'The Growth of Women's Representation in the Canadian House of Commons and the Election of 1984,' *Canadian Journal of Political Science* 27, no. 1 (1994).

7 The concept of a critical mass comes from nuclear physics, where it refers to

the quantity needed to start a chain reaction. In the feminist study of politics, 'critical mass theory' argues that a large minority can still make a difference even if it is still a minority. For more discussion on feminist critical-mass theory, see Helge Maria Hernes, *Welfare State and Woman Power: Essays in State Feminism* (Oslo: Norwegian University Press, 1987); Drude Dahlerup, 'From a Small to a Large Minority: Women in Scandinavian Politics,' *Scandinavian Political Studies* 11, no. 4 (1988).

8 This quotation was taken from a 4 September 1990 *Ottawa Citizen* article: 'Women in politics: Paying a heavy price for power,' B1.

9 This is based on a tally of the current twenty-one DM positions listed in the Government of Ontario Telephone Directory, but not including other DM-equivalent status positions.

10 These percentages are based on a tally of the 122 principal agency, board, and commission appointments made, as listed in the *Corpus Administrative Index*.

11 It is important to note here that women in Ontario are not one monolithic group, but are in fact diverse and distinct according to their region, race, colour, sexual orientation, class, age, and ability. As a result it is extremely difficult to speak of all women's interests/needs as being the same. Women-centred or feminist policy should take this fact into account to some extent.

12 This quotation was obtained from an OWD anniversary edition of its internal publication *Currents* (1993).

13 Information on the OACWI's mandates was obtained from Pauline Rankin in a personal interview in April 1995.

Further Reading

Arscott, Jane, and Linda Trimble, eds. *In the Presence of Women: Representation in Canadian Governments*. Toronto: Harcourt Brace Canada, 1997.

Bashevkin, Sylvia. *Toeing the Lines: Women and Party Politics in English Canada*. 2nd ed. Toronto: University of Toronto Press, 1993.

Brodie, Janine, ed. *Women and Canadian Public Policy*. Toronto: Harcourt Brace Canada, 1996.

Burt, Sandra. 'The Several Worlds of Policy Analysis: Traditional Approaches to Feminist Critiques.' In Sandra Burt and Lorraine Code, eds, *Changing Methods: Feminists Transforming Practice*, 357–78. Toronto: Broadview, 1995.

Campbell, Elaine (Ontario Legislative Research Services). *Female Representation in the Senate, House of Commons and Provincial and Territorial Legislative*

Assemblies. 1st and 2nd eds. Toronto: Ministry of Government Services, 1987, 1993.

Gingras, François-Pierre, ed. *Gender and Politics in Contemporary Canada.* Toronto: Oxford University Press, 1995.

Gotell, Lise, and Janine Brodie. 'Women and Parties in the 1990s: Less than Ever an Issue of Numbers.' In H.G. Thorburn, ed., *Party Politics in Canada* (7th ed.), 54–71. Scarborough: Prentice-Hall, 1996.

Leroux, Jacki, and Antonella Artuso. 'Harris' number comes up.' Ottawa *Sun,* 27 June 1995, 4–5.

TWELVE

Politics and Policy in the North

Geoffrey R. Weller

The political patterns that are observable in northern Ontario are described here as the politics of disaffection. This is characterized by a tendency to vote for the party in power at both the federal and the provincial level in the hope of getting some return that will correct or at least mitigate the worst effects of hinterland status. At the same time, there is a strong undercurrent of radical politics. In addition, there are occasional calls, usually very weak, for separate status. The party in power usually undertakes initiatives that are intended to retain or obtain the allegiance of the voters in the region but not to eradicate the root causes of disaffection and, thereby, the nature of politics in the region. These characteristics of the politics of disaffection are complicated by the fact that there is a significant indigenous population in the region whose politics is somewhat separate in that it is played out in largely different arenas and according to some different rules, although it is also motivated by a profound sense of disaffection.

The politics of disaffection are largely a reflection of a deep sense of grievance and alienation among many of the residents of northern Ontario. This sense of grievance is partly a reflection of a perceived ignorance of the north on the part of those in Queen's Park or the south in general. It is also partly because there are marked differences between the north and the south in terms of economic well-being, health status and services, education and educational services, and most other indicators. In addition, this sense of grievance is partly the result of an awareness that the region is unable to do much about its own situation given its

relatively small percentage of the total provincial population and conse-
quent lack of political influence.

It should be noted that the political patterns and grievances observable
in northern Ontario have many unique features but are not unusual.
They are very similar to the situation found in most of the northern parts
of the provinces.[1] Moreover, there are a number of similarities with the
political patterns and the social and economic characteristics of the regions that constitute what is now known as the circumpolar north.[2] Some
of the strongest similarities are with northern Finland, northern Norway,
and northern Sweden. Some parallels can also be drawn between northern Ontario, the northern parts of Russia, and parts of Alaska. Unfortunately, the policies of the governments responsible for these regions have
often been more extensive, imaginative, and successful than those of
successive governments of Ontario. Despite this, little notice seems to be
taken and few lessons appear to have been learned.

This chapter will begin with a description of the setting of politics in
northern Ontario. The conditions that result in the strong sense of grievance that is at the root of much of the region's politics will then be
detailed. The manifestations of the politics of disaffection that are characteristic of politics in northern Ontario will then be analysed. This will be
followed by an analysis of the actions and statements of governments
and political parties relating to the north up until the election of the
present government in 1995. These actions and statements involved considerable government intervention to help develop the north, whatever
the political party. The final section of the chapter attempts to assess the
likely effect on the north of the Conservatives' 'Common Sense Revolution,' a revolution that largely abhors governmental activism. The chapter concludes by arquing that the politics of disaffection are likely to
continue into the foreseeable future and to be exacerbated by the beliefs
and actions of the current government.

The Setting

Northern Ontario consists of three distinct subregions. The northeast and
the northwest between them comprise the mid-north of the province.
This consists of a scattering of small cities and towns, most of them
heavily dependent upon the extraction of a single natural resource. The
northeast is primarily dependent upon mineral extraction, whereas the
northwest is primarily dependent upon forest resources. Another clear
distinction between the two is the much higher percentage of franco-

phone Ontarians in the northeast. The third subregion is that of the far north, beyond 50 degrees latitude, where the population is very sparse and consists largely of a few widely scattered Indian communities heavily dependent upon welfare and the traditional economy of hunting, fishing, and trapping.

Northern Ontario is huge. It constitutes 88.4 per cent of the total land area of the province, or 810,411 square kilometres of the total of 916,734.[3] To put this in perspective, northwestern Ontario at 287,159 square kilometres is about the same size as Italy (294,000), and northeastern Ontario at 523,000 square kilometres is much the same size as France (547,000), western Europe's largest nation. More than 90 per cent of this huge land mass is publicly owned in the form of Crown land, and its use is regulated by the provincial government. Moreover, the system of local government (the Baldwin system) found in southern Ontario does not apply in the north.[4] Both of these factors help create an impression that the region is virtually a colonial, resource-rich appendage to southern Ontario.

To call the region 'northern' Ontario is misleading, although it is indeed north of the golden horseshoe, but then so is 99 per cent of Canada, including all of the Maritimes. It is misleading because it would be much more accurate to talk of it being western Ontario, since the vast majority of the region lies well to the west of the golden horseshoe. Only a very tiny portion of Ontario lies to the east of 80 degrees longitude (Hamilton), and the western boundary of the province is at 95 degrees longitude, which is far to the west of Lake Superior, bordering on Minnesota. The word 'northern' is also misleading because the region is not very northerly in comparative terms. Much of the region is to the south of the southern boundaries of the western provinces with the United States. Thunder Bay, for example, is well to the south of Winnipeg, yet is only 64 kilometres north of the U.S. border and at roughly the same latitude as Quebec City or Paris. Even the most northerly point of northern Ontario at the Manitoba border on Hudson Bay is only at 57 degrees latitude, the same latitude as Copenhagen or Edinburgh.

The geology and climate of northern Ontario are what produce its northern ambience rather than its actual physical location. Most of the region is located on the Canadian Shield, which dips down at the midpoint of the continent. This geological formation is rich in mineral resources, but it makes agriculture difficult. The climate of the region is typically mid-continental, with cool summers and cold winters, which also mitigates against agricultural settlement. The southern part of the region is covered with forests, but the northern one-third, some of which is above the tree line, consists of swampy lowlands along Ontario's lengthy sea coastline from Moose Factory to the Manitoba border. Thus, geologically and climatically northern Ontario is very similar to regions such as northern Scandinavia and parts of Alaska, which are at far more northerly latitudes. The geology and the climate have a marked effect on settlement patterns, which consist largely of scattered pockets of population around resource extraction sites or transportation hubs.

Although northern Ontario's land area is enormous, its population is small relative to that of southern Ontario. In 1991 the population of northern Ontario was 814,000, or only 8.07 per cent of the 10,084,000 total population of the province. Of this total, 574,000 (5.69%) lived in north-eastern Ontario and 240,000 (2.38%) lived in northwestern Ontario. Approximately 75 per cent of the regional population lives in five major centres and over one-third in the two largest cities, Thunder Bay (124,427) and Sudbury (157,613). While the northeast has several larger cities and towns such as Sudbury, Sault Ste Marie, Timmins, and North Bay, the northwest has only one major city, Thunder Bay, which has approximately half of the total population of northwestern Ontario. Outside northern Ontario's major centres, the population lives in 162 municipalities. Fifty of these are single-resource communities, with over 60 per cent of them having fewer than 2500 inhabitants.[5] The population of northern Ontario has remained virtually static for many years, while the total provincial population has been increasing rapidly. Thus, northern Ontario's proportion of the province's total population declined from 10.4 per cent in 1971 to 8.07 per cent in 1991.

Northern Ontario's population is physically remote from the centre of economic and political power in the province, namely Toronto. This fact has an economic cost and it no doubt also contributes to the sense of political alienation and disaffection. Sudbury, on the southern and eastern edge of the north, is relatively close to Toronto as it is only about 320 kilometres away by road. Kenora, however, on the southern but western edge of the region on the Ontario-Manitoba border, is 1930 road kilometres to the west of Toronto. People in Kenora can get to Denver as easily by road as they can get to Toronto; in fact, it is easier, as the roads to Denver are nearly all four-lane and divided, as opposed to the low-quality, two-lane ones to Toronto. For those in Toronto it is a shorter flight east to Halifax than it is west to Kenora. These huge distances and this remoteness are magnified by the fact that the quality of northern roads and communications in general tends to be poorer than for the rest of

Ontario and by the fact that transportation and communications within the region are more difficult than between the region and the rest of the province. For example, when flying commercially from Thunder Bay to Sudbury, or anywhere else in the northeast, it is necessary to go through Toronto. With the area to the north of the Great Lakes encompassed by just one province, Ontario, while the area to the south of the Lakes is encompassed by eight American states, it is not surprising that there is a feeling of remoteness among many of the residents of Northern Ontario. No doubt there would also be among the residents of Duluth, Minnesota, if their state capital were as distant as Buffalo, New York.

The population of northern Ontario is very mixed racially, ethnically, and in terms of religious conviction. This is the result of both the type of economic development that has occurred and the particular time at which immigration took place. There is a significant Native population that amounts to half of the total Native population of Ontario; about half of these are registered Indians living on reserves, with the rest being non-status Indians and Métis. The high birth rate among the Native population and the outmigration of young non-Natives means that the proportion of the population that is Native is rapidly increasing. The non-Native population is very mixed, with the most notable element being a large concentration of Franco-Ontarians in northeastern Ontario that constitutes roughly one-third of all of Ontario's francophones.

The economy of northern Ontario is resource-based. The major industries are mining, forestry, power generation, transportation, tourism, and the traditional economy of hunting, fishing, and trapping. There is very little agriculture and little manufacturing. Mining predominates in the northeast, forestry in the northwest, and the traditional economy in the far north. The economy has been largely structured on the needs of southern Ontario and this is clearly reflected in the transportation network, which has been designed largely to facilitate the movement of bulk commodities to the south rather than for intraregional communications. In short, northern Ontario does not have an integrated, reasonably self-reliant regional economy. This is also partly the consequence of the major enterprises in the region being owned or controlled by groups headquartered outside the region.

Northern Ontario is nearly always compared to southern Ontario; however, it is instructive to make other comparisons. Northern Ontario has an area that is larger than that of Saskatchewan and much larger than all of the Atlantic provinces. Northern Ontario's population is slightly less than Saskatchewan's and that of Nova Scotia. Moreover, the gross provincial product of northern Ontario is not much less than Saskatch-ewan's and more than Nova Scotia's. In fact, given the very different nature of the northern Ontario economy from that of southern Ontario, one can almost think of northern Ontario as being a province within a province.[6]

The Causes of Political Disaffection

Much of the politics in the north is motivated by a sense of grievance or alienation. This is partly the result of a perceived ignorance on the part of those in Queen's Park and the south in general. It is also partly the result of some major economic differentials between the north and the south. This is compounded by clear differences in areas such as health care and education in terms of both services and status. Added factors are some serious grievances on the part of francophones and Natives and some major environmental grievances relating to specific problems and the general matter of resource-use conflicts. Finally, political disaffection may also stem from the region's lack of political clout and a generalized feeling that the region has not been allowed to fulfil its historical prom-ise, but rather has been forced to play the role of southern Ontario's resource reserve hinterland.

One of the biggest problems faced by northern Ontario is simply an ignorance of its nature and its problems on the part of those in a position to do something about the problems. Nearly every resident of the region is able to present an amusing story revealing the often-profound igno-rance of provincial civil servants or southern residents in general about northern Ontario. Whether this ignorance is willful or not, it produces a sense of grievance in the northern population. The problem is of long standing, for some time ago both the Procedural Affairs committee of the Ontario Legislature[7] and the Report of the Advisory Committee on Re-source Dependent Communities in Northern Ontario[8] remarked upon it. The Procedural Affairs committee criticized ministers and senior bureau-crats for failing to travel to the north to acquaint themselves with the problems facing the region, and stated that 'it appeared to the Committee that in some cases there appeared to be a deliberate effort to avoid such trips – this situation is inexcusable.'[9]

There is a continuing marked difference in economic well-being be-tween northern and southern Ontario. The northern population is not only less well off than the southern population, it is also exposed to the uncertainties that come from working in industries that suffer from boom-and-bust cycles and that are always heavily dependent upon world prices for their health. In addition, the natural-resource sector has become steadily more capital-intensive, which means that jobs are steadily being lost in northern Ontario in mining, forestry, and related industries.[10] In addition, the range of jobs available is not as great as in southern Ontario; thus, there are few alternatives to turn to should there be a downturn in the regional economy. Most of the new employment opportunities have been created in the service sector, but many of these, such as the ones in tourism, are low-wage and seasonal. In addition, northern residents are faced with higher costs for most goods and services than is the case in southern Ontario. This is especially true in the remote communities of the far north. The nature of the regional economy generally results in far higher rates of unemployment in northern than in southern Ontario. This, in turn, has resulted in youth outmigration which affects not only the rate of population growth but the demographic structure of the regional population.

The northern sense of grievance also stems from the region's relatively poor health-care statistics and a relative lack of health-care services. Mortality and morbidity rates are considerably higher for northern Ontario than Ontario generally.[11] For the Native population the situation remains tragic despite significant improvements in recent years. The mortality and morbidity rates for this segment of the population are worse than for a number of Third World nations.[12] However, the causes in northern Ontario are rather different – suicide, poisoning, violence, and alcoholism, a combination indicative of profound social breakdown rather than health-care problems as such. Northern Ontario also suffers from a relative lack of health-care facilities and personnel. Generally there is a much less favourable doctor-to-patient ratio than in southern Ontario. In fact, while some say that the south has too many doctors, the north clearly has too few. There are some extremely severe shortages in northern Ontario, including psychiatrists, psychologists, hematologists, geriatricians, physiotherapists, occupational therapists, and audiologists. The combination of measures undertaken to deal with these shortages, while they have clearly prevented a bad situation from becoming worse, have not overcome the problem, as several recent (and uncoordinated) studies into health manpower problems by different ministries indicate. Some northerners are not pleased that the Scandinavian model that has been successfully used to tackle the same problems has not been employed in northern Ontario, or even recognized as a possibility. Put simply, the Scandinavian approach to the same set of problems was to train people in the disciplines in short supply in the underserviced region.[13]

The northern sense of grievance is also rooted in part in the region's lack of educational services and poor educational indicators relative to Ontario generally. At the secondary-school level there is not the same range of programming or the same rate of graduation as for Ontario in general. At the post-secondary level there is a lower rate of participation than for the province as a whole. In addition, a full range of programs is not offered by the three universities (Lakehead in Thunder Bay, Laurentian in Sudbury, and Nipissing in North Bay) despite the region's population being nearly that of Saskatchewan's and bigger than Nova Scotia's. The most glaring example here is that, apart from nursing, there is no health-profession training in the north. In addition, no institution offers law or is able to give many degrees at the doctoral level.[14] A former deputy minister of northern affairs, Mr George Tough, is reported to have commented that 'their mistake was that they created northern clones of southern universities.'[15] As with health-care services, many northern residents are not pleased that the different and successful approach to university education in northern Norway, Sweden, and Finland was not used in Ontario and never seems likely to be. Put briefly, the Scandinavian nations were not driven simply by access concerns when they established universities in their northern regions at much the same time as Lakehead and Laurentian were established in the mid-sixties.[16] The Scandinavians used their new northern universities and colleges as instruments of economic, social, and cultural development and began their institutions with schools of medicine, dentistry, social work, engineering, teacher education, and the like. It seems most unlikely that Ontario's northern universities will ever be accorded the same role or ever get medical, dental, and other regionally relevant training programs.[17]

The northern Ontario sense of grievance also stems from a feeling that its environment is threatened, a feeling that often takes two contrasting forms. First, there are those who regard the region's major industries, notably forestry and mining, as big polluters of the regional environment and who see these industries as being controlled by southerners with little respect or direct concern for the northern environment. Second, there are those who resent the southern environmentalists who want to preserve vast tracts of northern Ontario as pristine wilderness for vacation and other purposes and want to deny northerners the ability to take a multi-use approach to the land. This was the theme of the incoming president of the Ontario Professional Foresters Association in a speech in 1988, when he spoke of an 'understanding gap between northern and southern Ontario.'[18]

To the general list of grievances can be added the specific complaints of those groups that are strongly represented in the region, namely the francophones and the Native peoples. Francophone Ontarians, who are heavily concentrated in northeastern Ontario, feel that there are insufficient services provided for them in French and that they are an especially disadvantaged group. Over half of Ontario's Native peoples live in the north in extremely disadvantaged circumstances. Moreover, their situation is complicated by the fact that those on the reserves largely relate to the federal government, while those not living on reserves relate mainly to the provincial government. Given their economic and social circumstances and the bifurcated governmental responsibility for Native affairs, it is not surprising that Northern Ontario's Native peoples are embracing the concept of Native self-government even if it has not been very clearly defined to date.

The sense of grievance in the north also has something to do with the fact that northern Ontario is a region that many regard as not having been allowed to achieve its original promise and that now, because of a lack of political influence, will never be able to do so. The early residents of northern Ontario did not expect that they would long reside in a resource hinterland area. Cheap hydro power in Sault Ste Marie and in other areas led to early industrial developments. In addition, there was an expectation that manufacturing and service sectors would develop in the wake of the development of the mines and the building of the pulp and paper plants. Many thought the population growth would be rapid and that many cities would become sizeable. Some, for example, believed Thunder Bay would become Canada's Chicago because of its similar geographic position as the 'gateway to the west.' Instead, it became Canada's Duluth.[19] These expectations have long ago been put to one side as the city and the whole region have been largely bypassed, with industry and the associated population being located elsewhere. For many this bypassing of the region is symbolized by the oil pipelines from the west that dip below the U.S. border just east of Winnipeg to reach Ontario soil again at the nearest point in southern Ontario, namely Sarnia. The bypassing of the region has meant that it has little political influence; in fact, its political influence is decreasing. At present the entire region returns only 15 members of the legislature out of a total of

130 – just enough to be of significance only in a tightly contested election. After the next election only 10 of 103 MPPs will represent northern Ontario.

The Politics of Disaffection in Northern Ontario

The politics of disaffection manifests itself in a variety of forms. There has been a pattern of voting for the party in power at both the federal and provincial levels, although that tendency is not as strong as it once was. There has also been a strong undercurrent of voting for the left. In addition, there have been small, but significant, attempts to either create a separate province out of northern Ontario or lead parts of it into union with Manitoba. Each of these manifestations represents a way in which it is thought the problems of the region can be overcome. Another manifestation of the politics of disaffection is a tendency to opt out of the struggle altogether and concentrate on local politics. Each of these manifestations will be analysed in turn.

The voting pattern in northern Ontario shows that, in very general terms, its residents have predominantly voted for the party in power at both the provincial and federal levels. This pattern stands in marked contrast to the conventional wisdom about the reaction of voters in many provincial and supra-provincial hinterland regions, who are normally regarded as being likely to vote for opposition or third parties as a means of changing their situation. Provincially, northern Ontario supported the Progressive Conservatives throughout their long period in office from 1943 to 1985.[20] In 1987, when the Liberals formed the government, the region switched and elected seven Liberals, six New Democrats, and only two Progressive Conservatives.[21] In 1990, when the NDP became the government, the north switched to very strong support for that party, electing ten members of the governing party from among the fifteen ridings in the region. However, in 1995, when the Progressive Conservatives again formed the government, the pattern was truly broken, with the north increasing its support for the NDP by electing eleven members of that party, three Liberals, and only one Progressive Conservative. However, the Progressive Conservative in question was Michael Harris, the premier of the province.

This general tendency to vote for the party in power has most likely been an attempt by voters to make the region useful politically to the party in power, in this way hoping at least to obtain a few handouts. Certainly, it would not be possible for the region to threaten a ruling party to any significant degree. Northern Ontario simply does not have much political clout, with only 15 of 130 seats in the legislature. Given the long periods of one-party rule in the province until recently, there was a certain degree of logic to this pattern of voting. Clearly, it was likely to produce goodwill of some kind on the part of the governing party. On the other hand, it might lead to the governing party assuming support in the region. Certainly, many in the region are aware that it is reliant on nothing more substantial than goodwill.

Another manifestation of the politics of disaffection in northern Ontario is the fairly strong vote for the New Democratic Party or other parties further to the left and the support of fairly radical union organizations. The NDP, until the 1990 provincial election, has traditionally been the second party in the region – whichever of the other two parties held the majority of seats. In this respect, northern Ontario is like many other provinces: the further north one goes, the greater the support for the NDP. Another element of this reaction has been the relatively strong support accorded political parties to the left of the NDP. The Communist party, for example, has had a significant amount of support over the years in northern Ontario and has had an influence on the strongly unionized workforce in the region. In the past, undercurrents of political radicalism and protest actions have been manifested in strong support for the International Workers of the World (IWW) and the One Big Union (OBU). However, the left in the region has always been factionalized, often along ethnic lines, and has never succeeded in being a major political force in northern Ontario.[22] The relatively strong support for the NDP, and parties further to the left, indicates that there is an element of protest voting in the north but that it has not been and is not as strong as it has been in the supra-provincial regions such as western Canada. That is, protest voting has not been and is not the dominant pattern.

Yet a further manifestation of the politics of disaffection in northern Ontario are the periodic protest movements and even calls for separate status. The most recent protest movement was the 'Save Our North' campaign launched by a coalition of communities, organizations, and individuals located mainly in the northeast who are concerned about the future of the natural-resource industries in the north.[23] There have been several calls for a separate province of northern Ontario. The first such call was in the 1870s, when Simon James Dawson, the member of the Ontario Legislature for Algoma, argued that his district should become a separate province. There were periodic but very minor calls for separation from the 1870s until the First World War; then there was a gap until the 1950s, when they were renewed. The nineteenth- and early-twentieth-century calls were based upon a spirit of optimism and a feeling that a separate province would be a powerful entity. The later ones were founded on a spirit of rebellion against a subservient hinterland status that had developed over the decades. Principal among the later calls for separate status were those of Hubert Limbrick and Ed Diebel. In 1950 Limbrick declared that northern Ontario was isolated and neglected by the provincial government and that the only way to rectify this situation was to create a new province to be called Aurora. Despite hundreds of people attending public meetings the movement fizzled quickly. In 1973 Ed Diebel of North Bay, believing that the only way that northern Ontario would be listened to would be if there was a party that represented the interests of the whole region, formed the Northern Ontario Heritage Party. One of the party's planks was a call for a new province in the north. While the party obtained the 100,000 signatures necessary for it to become an officially recognized party in Ontario for funding purposes, it never was able to establish a viable organization.[24] In the early 1990s Donald D. McKinnon, a Cochrane prospector, concluded that secession might be necessary.[25] He started the Ontario North Territory movement, but it received little attention and few adherents.

In northwestern Ontario the politics of disaffection has also been revealed in the occasional call for union with Manitoba. The Ontario-Manitoba border, as originally proposed in the late nineteenth century, shifted several times, on occasion well to the east of Thunder Bay, before it was finalized in its present location. A number of individuals have argued over the years that it would have been far more logical to make what is now northwestern Ontario part of Manitoba. One of these was Hubert Limbrick, who turned to this alternative when his suggestion of a new province went nowhere. The arguments seem to amount to saying that northwestern Ontario, being closer to Manitoba, would benefit by being regarded as an integral, rather than a peripheral region. It was argued that the result of such a provincial realignment could well have been better communications, such as a four-lane divided highway from Winnipeg to Thunder Bay (which would have been Manitoba's second city), greater use of the port of Thunder Bay and the elimination of the need to develop the port of Churchill, and generally a more vibrant economic environment in the northwest. Whether or not this would indeed have been the result we shall never know.

The nature of Native politics in northern Ontario could also be regarded as another component of the politics of disaffection. The northern

Native population is truly on the periphery of the periphery in terms not only of location but also of their language, their economic base, and the social and economic services delivered to them. They exist largely separately from the non-Native population of the north in threatened and unstable circumstances. It is not surprising that disaffection exists in this society, and it is encouraging to see that the push to Native self-government is progressing, however ill-defined it may be. At least it holds out the promise of change and improvement along with a chance to regain self-respect.

The nature of francophone politics in northern Ontario could be regarded as yet another component of the politics of disaffection. The proportion of francophones is higher in northeastern Ontario than in other parts of the province and the problems faced there have a greater visibility. In recent years a kind of Franco-Ontarian societal movement has arisen that, while not markedly asserting itself at the electoral level, has produced powerful political undercurrents that are difficult for any government to completely ignore.

It has been argued that another manifestation of the politics of disaffection has been the avoidance of politics at the provincial level altogether and a concentration on local politics. Don Scott has contended this tendency may be partly the result of the parochial nature of the media in northern Ontario.[26] This emphasis on local politics is said to be manifested in high turnout rates in local elections and a concentration on local issues or, as in the case of Thunder Bay, local rivalry between the two former cities of Port Arthur and Fort William.[27]

Northern Development and Government Intervention

Until the present Harris government was elected, governmental intervention or activism to try to overcome or mitigate political disaffection in Northern Ontario has been extensive and of various types. It consisted of handouts of various kinds, studies and conferences to analyse the problems, the creation of a special ministry for northern affairs, and a wide variety of piecemeal economic and social-development initiatives. However, the current government espouses a philosophy that supports a significant reduction of the role of government in the economy and society. While this is having a great effect on the entire province, it is likely to have a particularly large effect on a region more heavily dependent upon governmental activism than most others. The era of governmental activism will be reviewed in this section and the impending new era in the next.

The traditional response of successive provincial governments to try to reduce political disaffection in the north has been what I have previously called the politics of handouts.[28] These handouts have taken many forms, but perhaps the most dramatic and effective was the moving of many government jobs to the north in the late 1980s. The Rosehart Report, otherwise known as the Advisory Committee on Resource Dependent Communities in Northern Ontario, had recommended that 5000 jobs out of a then provincial total of 80,000 be transferred to the north by 1991. In 1986 the Liberal government announced a more modest 1200 would be transferred. The headquarters of the Ministry of Northern Development and Mines was moved to Sudbury, the Ontario Lottery Corporation and the forestry branch of the Ministry of Natural Resources to Sault Ste Marie, the headquarters staff of the Ministry of Correctional Services to North Bay, and the Registrar General's Branch of the Ministry of Consumer and Commercial Relations and the Student Awards Branch of the Ministry of Colleges and Universities to Thunder Bay. The transfers meant not only job diversification in these cities but also the construction of new buildings. In the event, they also meant job creation locally, for most of the incumbents did not wish to be transferred. Other handouts have been piecemeal and have affected many areas over the years. In health care, for example, these have included a Northern Health Travel Grant, which was instituted in 1986, a program of incentive grants to specialists to locate in the north, and enhanced cancer treatment in the region.

Another traditional form of response has been to undertake studies and conferences that are ostensibly intended to point the way to mitigating or removing the causes of disaffection in northern Ontario. This device has been used so frequently and with such little apparant effect that northern residents often treat them with a well-justified scepticism. In recent times, the most well-known of the studies have been the Design for Development Studies for the northeast and the northwest[29] and the Hartt Commission, which later became known as the Fahlgren inquiry.[30] The Design for Development studies contained few suggestions for fundamental change and became largely irrelevant when the province-wide planning process of which they were a part was halted. The Hartt/ Fahlgren commission, properly known as the Royal Commission on the Northern Environment, ended up as the longest-running and very nearly the most expensive provincial inquiry ever, with possibly the least useful output of any before or since. None the less, some of the studies have had a significant effect. For example, many of the recommendations of the Rosehart Report were acted upon in the late 1980s by a Liberal minority government in need of electoral support in the north. No doubt the current government will be able to continue to use this approach as it costs little but has the appearance of activism.

A response that has been very useful for the north was the creation in 1976 of a Ministry of Northern Affairs, now called the Ministry of Northern Development and Mines. This ministry was part of a general trend on the part of several provincial governments at that time to establish agencies to deal with their northern regions in a manner intended to reduce political disaffection and either ensure the retention of political support in the region or to gain that support. The type of agency established in Ontario which I have elsewhere called a coordinating ministry contrasted with the all-powerful type of ministry established in Saskatchewan, the Department of Northern Saskatchewan (DNS), and the limited ministries found in Manitoba or Quebec, where the role was limited to local-government or indigenous-peoples affairs.[31] Initially, under the leadership of its first minister, Leo Bernier, sometimes referred to as the 'Emperor of the North,' the Ontario ministry seemed to be a sophisticated mechanism for taking the politics of handouts to greater heights.[32] However, as the ministry has steadily become more established and employed by the Progressive Conservatives, the Liberals, and the NDP, it has become not only increasingly useful to the region but more inclined to undertake long-range projects and more economic planning. Particularly notable are the ministry's efforts over the years in terms of enhancing much of the infrastructure in the north, especially that related to the creation of airfields and telecommunications. The creation of a related network of Northern Development Councils and the sponsoring of resource centres and databases at Lakehead and Laurentian universities indicate a desire to enhance the ministry's capacity for long-range development planning.

A wide variety of economic-development initiatives have been undertaken in relation to northern Ontario in recent decades by both the federal and provincial governments. These initiatives have been largely of three varieties. The first is what could be considered a 'more of the same' approach. That is, a great deal of money has been expended on what are essentially subsidies to enhance industries already located in the region, namely forestry and mining. The second type of initiative has tended to enhance outmigration: for instance, the construction of universities and colleges that train people for jobs that largely exist outside northern Ontario. The third sort of initiative has centred on infrastructural developments, such as roads, airports, and telecommunications systems. These have largely been of assistance to the primary industries already located in the region. Until recently, none of these economic-development initiatives was undertaken with a view to trying to expand the range of employment opportunities in Northern Ontario, although some infrastructural developments are, of course, helpful in this regard. In the 1980s, the emphasis changed and a much greater effort was directed to job creation and economic diversification. Within this goal, however, a great deal of emphasis was placed upon developing the tourist industry in the region, even though this is a low-wage, seasonal industry. The shift in emphasis is the result largely of the realization that the region's primary industries, mining and forestry, are rapidly becoming more capital-intensive.[33]

Despite the change in emphasis, the economic-development initiatives undertaken did not remove the root causes of disaffection or change the nature of politics in the region. This is because, first, the actions were not taken as part of any long-range plan. In fact, there was an inadequate knowledge base for long-range economic planning. (The creation of the resource centres and databases at Lakehead and Laurentian universities have, however, helped to solve this problem.) Second, there was no integration of planning efforts between the federal government, the provincial government, and local agencies. Third, an integrated view of what constitutes economic development seems not to have been adopted. For example, the two northern universities have been accorded no, or minimal, roles in helping in economic development – in marked contrast to the role of universities in similar northern regions in Sweden, Finland, and Norway.

Northern Development and the Common Sense Revolution

On 8 June 1995 a Conservative government that believes in greater reliance on the private sector, a significant reduction in government activism, and a downsizing of government itself was elected. This is likely to have a significant effect upon the way in which the north is dealt with and, indeed, upon the north itself. The reduced reliance on the public sector should logically result in a reduction in the use of the politics of handouts. It is certainly already being revealed in a reduction of public subsidies to government corporations with extensive operations in the north. Moreover, the downsizing of government may adversely affect a region more heavily reliant on the public sector than others, both economically and in terms of its limited political representation.

The likelihood of governmental intervention or activism continuing on the same scale as before is slim given the tenor of the economic times and the non-interventionist, downsizing approach of the present government. The tenor of the economic times is reflected in a belief, held by some in the north, that the region will prosper best in a more competitive, privatized environment. This is the view of the editor of *Northern Ontario Business*[34] as well as of two Lakehead University economists who have argued that, rather than prop up the regional economy with business subsidies and job creation in the public sector, government should concentrate on infrastructure development, especially in the area of telecommunications.[35]

However, it is unlikely that the region would prosper best in a more competitive and privatized economy because, in addition to possessing a relatively poor infrastructure, the region suffers from many competitive disadvantages. These include, among many others, small-sized regional markets, great distance from other markets, increasing competition from cheap and abundant sources of natural wealth both within Canada (such as Voisey Bay, Newfoundland) and outside (in low-wage developing economies). Moreover, it seems often to be forgotten just how dependent the region is upon governmental activism. Such activism has been behind much of the job creation, and certainly the job diversification, in the north, and many of the new jobs are themselves government ones. The experience of Sudbury is only the most glaring of the examples. That city has received support from both levels of government, but primarily the provincial, in the form of the headquarters of the Ministry of Northern Development and Mines, the headquarters of the Ontario Geological Survey, Science North (an innovative science and technology centre), a neutrino research laboratory, a major cancer treatment centre, a federal taxation data centre, a new civic square complex, and much else besides. It has even been remarked that 'the cynical began to refer to Sudbury as the pork barrel capital of Canada.'[36] However, maybe the premier will be sympathetic to governmental activism in the north as he comes from there and because, as one reporter put it, 'Harris and his father had not been above applying for government money to underwrite a planned $400,000 expansion of Nipissing Ridge Ski Hill.'[37]

The effect of reduced provincial-government subsidies is already highly visible in the north. The provincially owned Ontario Northland Transportation Commission (ONTC) had its budget cut by $6 million in November 1995. That led to the closing down of NorOntair on 29 March 1996 and the sale of the airline's assets. NorOntair served seventeen locations throughout the north and had been in operation for twenty-three years. Some in the private sector, such as Cliff Friesen of Bearskin Airlines in Thunder Bay, think the public will benefit; still, he didn't think it would mean reduced air fares.[38] While private airlines have picked up many of the routes, some communities are wondering if they will lose their air service.

The promised downsizing of government and reduction of federal transfer payments will affect operations throughout the north over the years ahead, although only time will tell if the north will suffer disproportionately compared to the rest of the province. The north is more vulnerable, however, in that it is more reliant than other regions of the province on public employment for its well-being. There seem to be conflicting definitions of what constitutes 'public employment,' but it is fair to say that northern Ontario has double the proportion of public-service jobs of other regions of the province. One report stated that there are 26,000 public-administration jobs in the north and that these outnumber the 25,000 primary-industry and 10,000 non-resource manufacturing jobs.[39] The premier's own home town of North Bay is itself heavily dependent upon the public sector, and some of its residents fears were summed up in placards waved outside his constituency office after the September 1995 Throne Speech that read 'No jobs. No pay. No North Bay.'[40]

The present government's intent of diminishing the size of government will also affect the political representation of the north. The reduction in the size of the legislature means that northern Ontario will lose five of its current 15 seats. Traditionally, it was generally accepted that the vast distances, the sparse population, and the limited transportation facilities justified ridings in northern Ontario having smaller populations than those in the south, but this principle will no longer operate. In fact, northern Ontario lost proportionately far more of its legislative representation in the Harris redistribution than any other region. As a result, 'It will be more difficult to convince "Toronto" to adopt policies, laws and budgets that benefit the north.'[41]

Conclusions

Governmental activism in relation to northern Ontario taken in the period up until the election of the Harris government in 1995 succeeded in stopping the development of any political movements that were likely to lead to any serious consequences for the political forces in the south. It also prevented anything more serious than an undercurrent of protest voting and the New Democratic Party being strong in the north. However, no fundamental change was made in the nature of centre-periphery relations as a consequence of the initiatives undertaken. The attempts to diversify the economy of the region were piecemeal and were not nearly extensive enough to have more than a marginal effect.

There appeared to be then, and there appears to be now, a lack of vision concerning how to deal with the north and a lack of political will to do anything more than whatever is sufficient to prevent serious political dissent. This lack of vision and will applies not only to those in the south but also to those who live in the north and who are responsible for its development. This is reflected in two tendencies. The first is a tendency to reject automatically anything that even hints of planning on a reasonably comprehensive basis, be it in the economic or the social sphere, a tendency enhanced by the recent election of a government enamoured of a less-intrusive public sector. Thus, there is little evidence that much thought has ever been given to how federal and provincial actions can be synchronized or how universities might be able to contribute directly to development, as has been the case in many other nations. The second tendency is a resistance to looking at what other nations have done in their similar northern regions, even though they have had levels of success tackling similar problems that are far greater in many fields than is the case in northern Ontario. No official comparative studies have been undertaken and there have been few visits abroad.

The short-run future for northern Ontario is not particularly bright. Only very limited sectors of the economy of the region are likely to thrive in the more competitive business environment that the current government wishes to promote. This is largely because the north has few areas of natural competitive advantage. Moreover, the region is more heavily dependent upon the public sector than most, so it is unlikely to thrive in an era of government downsizing. Consequently, the politics of disaffection is likely not only to continue into the foreseeable future but to intensify.

Notes

1 Geoffrey R. Weller, 'Political Disaffection in the Canadian Provincial North,' *Bulletin of Canadian Studies* (U.K.) 9, no. 1 (Spring 1985): 58–86.
2 Geoffrey R. Weller, 'Comparing Northern Hinterlands: The Case of North America and the Nordic Countries,' a paper presented at the Maple Leaf

and Eagle Conference on North America, University of Helsinki, Finland, 11–13 May 1988.

3 Ontario, *Business Facts Ontario Canada* (Toronto: Queen's Printer for Ontario, 1993), 72, 74.

4 Geoffrey R. Weller, 'Local Government in the Canadian Provincial North,' *Canadian Public Administration* 24, no. 1 (Spring 1981): 44–72.

5 Ontario, *Northern Ontario: Economic Overview and Outlook* (Toronto: Ministry of Northern Development and Mines, 1988).

6 Ontario, 'Comparisons with Other Provinces' (Toronto: Ministry of Northern Development and Mines, 1984): a slide show accompanying the deputy minister's general speech on the ministry.

7 Ontario, Standing Committee on Procedural Affairs and Agencies, Boards and Commissions, *Report on Agencies, Boards and Commissions* (no. 11) (Toronto: Legislative Assembly, 1st Session, 33rd Parliament, 34 Elizabeth II), 3–6.

8 Ontario, Advisory Committee on Resource Dependent Communities in Northern Ontario, *Final Report and Recommendations* (Toronto: Ministry of Northern Development and Mines, 1986).

9 Ontario, Standing Committee on Procedural Affairs, *Report*, 5.

10 The Ontario Ministry of Northern Development and Mines estimates that between 1970 and 1985 some 25,000 jobs were lost in mining, forestry, and related industries in Northern Ontario. See Ontario, Ministry of Northern Development and Mines, *Strategic Priorities for Northern Ontario and Ontario's Mining Industry 1986–1996* (Toronto: Ministry of Northern Development and Mines, 1986), iv.

11 Geoffrey R. Weller and Pranlal Manga, 'The Feasibility of Developing an Integrated Health Care Delivery System in the North: The Case of Northern Ontario,' in David Young, ed., *Health Care Issues in the Canadian North* (Edmonton: Boreal Institute for Northern Studies, 1988), 140–50.

12 T. Kue Young, *Health Care and Cultural Change: The Indian Experience in the Central Subarctic* (Toronto: University of Toronto Press, 1988). See also James B. Waldram, D. Henning, and T. Kue Young, *Aboriginal Health in Canada: Historical, Cultural, and Epidemiological Perspectives* (Toronto: University of Toronto Press, 1995).

13 See Geoffrey R. Weller, 'Universities, Change and Development in the Scandinavian North,' a paper presented at the joint meeting of the International Studies Association and the British International Studies Association, University of London, U.K., 28 March–1 April 1989.

14 See Geoffrey R. Weller and Robert G. Rosehart, 'The Politics of Government Intervention in Higher Education: A Case for the North,' in Cecily Watson,

ed., *Readings in Canadian Higher Education* (Toronto: Ontario Institute for Studies in Education, 1988), 48–76.

15 See *Financial Post*, 2 March 1987, 'The Other Ontario.'

16 See Geoffrey R. Weller and Robert G. Rosehart, 'Universities, Politics and Development in Northern Ontario and Northern Sweden: A Comparative Analysis,' *Canadian Journal of Higher Education* 15, no. 3 (1985): 51–72, and Geoffrey R. Weller, 'Universities in the Circumpolar North: A Comparative Analysis,' in P. Adams and D. Parker, eds, *Canada's Subarctic Universities* (Ottawa: Association of Canadian Universities for Northern Studies, 1987), 3–17.

17 See Geoffrey R. Weller, 'Universities, Politics and Development: The Case of Northern Ontario,' in Fred Lazin, Samuel Aroni, and Yehuda Gradus, eds, *The Policy Impact of Universities in Developing Regions* (New York: Macmillan, 1988), 210–22.

18 See *Northern Ontario Business*, April 1988.

19 See Daniel J. Elazar, 'Constitutional Change in a Long Depressed Community: A Case Study of Duluth, Minnesota,' *Journal of the Minnesota Academy of Science* 33 (1965): 49–66.

20 See Geoffrey R. Weller, 'Hinterland Politics: The Case of Northwestern Ontario,' *Canadian Journal of Political Science* 10, no. 4 (Winter 1977): 444–70.

21 See Geoffrey R. Weller, 'The North in the Provincial Election of 1987,' a paper presented at the annual meetings of the Western Social Science Association, Denver, 27–30 April 1988.

22 See, for example, A.W. Rasporich, 'Factionalism and Class in Modern Lakehead Politics,' *Lakehead University Review* 7 (1974): 31–65.

23 Save Our North, *Save Our North* (Timmins: Save Our North, no date).

24 See Gordon Brock, *The Province of Northern Ontario* (Cobalt: Highway Bookshop, 1978) for an account of these separatist tendencies. See also Geoffrey R. Weller, 'Algoma and Superior: Prospects for Separation in Northern Ontario and Northern Michigan,' a paper presented at the annual meetings of the Western Political Science Association, San Diego, March 1982.

25 Donald D. McKinnon, *A Future in the North for Our Children* (Cochrane: McKinnon Prospecting, 1991).

26 Don Scott, 'Northern Alienation,' in Donald C. Macdonald, ed., *Government and Politics in Ontario* (Toronto: MacMillan, 1975), 235–248.

27 See M.E. Arthur, 'The Landing and the Plot,' *Lakehead University Review* 1 (1968): 1–17, and 'Interurban Rivalry in Port Arthur and Fort William, 1870–1907,' a paper presented at the Western Canadian Studies Conference, Calgary, 1974.

28 Weller, 'Hinterland Politics,' 743–46.

29 Ontario, Department of Treasury and Economics, *Design for Development: Northwestern Ontario Region* (Toronto: Queen's Printer, 1970) and Ontario, Ministry of Treasury, Economics and Intergovernmental Affairs, *Design for Development, Northeastern Ontario: A Proposed Planning and Development Strategy* (Toronto: Queen's Printer, 1976).

30 Ontario, Royal Commission on the Northern Environment (Ed Fahlgren, Commissioner), *Final Report and Recommendations* (Toronto: Ontario Ministry of the Attorney General, 1985).

31 Geoffrey R. Weller, 'Provincial Ministries of Northern Affairs: A Comparative Analysis,' in R.W. Wein, R.R. Riew, and I. Methven, eds, *Resources and Dynamics of the Boreal Zone* (Ottawa: Association of Canadian Universities for Northern Studies [ACUNS], 1983), 480–97, and Douglas C. Nord, 'Establishing Political Institutions for the Periphery: A Comparative Analysis,' a paper presented at the 14th World Congress of the International Political Science Association, Washington, 28 August–1 September 1988.

32 See Toronto *Globe and Mail*, 5 May 1987, 'Tory "Emperor of the North" to abdicate after 21 years.'

33 See Weller, 'Provincial Ministries of Northern Affairs.'

34 See editorial by Michael Atkins, 'Making Austerity Work Will Help Us All,' *Northern Ontario Business*, January 1996.

35 See *Northern Ontario Business*, November 1993, 'Governments Must Rethink Their Role in the North's Economy: Lakehead Professors.'

36 C.M. Wallace, 'The 1980's,' in C.M. Wallace and Ashley Thomson, *Sudbury: Rail Town and Regional Capital* (Toronto: Dundurn Press, 1993), 279.

37 See John Lownsbrough, 'Mike the Knife,' Toronto *Globe and Mail, Report on Business Magazine*, February 1996, 59.

38 See *Northern Ontario Business*, January 1986, 'Private Carriers Show Interest in NorOntair Flights.'

39 Statistics Canada data cited in 'In Pursuit of a Unified Strategy,' *Northern Ontario Business*, May 1995.

40 Lownsbrough, 'Mike the Knife,' 55.

41 See Iain Angus, 'Let's Keep Communication Alive,' *Northern Ontario Business*, April 1996.

Further Reading

In addition to the works cited in this chapter, there are several books that would be useful to those interested in finding out more about Northern

Ontario. An excellent bibliography of recent works on northern Ontario is Ashley Thomson, Gwenda Hallsworth, and Lionel Bonin, *The Bibliography of Northern Ontario 1966–1991* (Toronto: Dundurn Press, 1994). For earlier works, consult Ontario, *A Selected Bibliography of Documents Relating to Northern Ontario, 1869–1977* (Toronto: Economic Development Branch, Ministry of Treasury, Economics and Intergovernmental Affairs, 1978). Although dated, a general reference work that would help individuals orient themselves to the geography of the region is Royal Commission on the Northern Environment, *North of 50: An Atlas of Far Northern Ontario* (Toronto: University of Toronto Press, 1985).

The history of the development of northern Ontario is discussed in Morris Zaslow, *The Opening of the Canadian North, 1870–1914* (Toronto: McClelland and Stewart, 1971) and *The Northward Expansion of Canada, 1914–1967* (Toronto: McClelland and Stewart, 1988). These volumes place the development of northern Ontario in the general context of the development of the Canadian north. For an interesting and lavishly illustrated history of northern Ontario, see Matt Bray and Ernie Epp, eds, *A Vast and Magnificent Land: An Illustrated History of Northern Ontario* (Sudbury and Thunder Bay: Ministry of Northern Development and Mines, 1984). This volume contains chapters on most of the region's major industries as well as on culture and sports. A now classic study of the history of the state's involvement in the development and regulation of the natural-resource industries in Ontario is H.V. Nelles, *The Politics of Development: Forests, Mines and Hydro-electric Power in Ontario, 1849–1941* (Toronto: Macmillan, 1975). For a wide-ranging history of the logging industry in Northern Ontario see Ian Radforth, *Bush Workers and Bosses: Logging in Northern Ontario* (Toronto: University of Toronto Press, 1987).

THIRTEEN

The New World of Interest-Group Politics in Ontario

Henry J. Jacek

The election of Mike Harris and his majority Conservative government in June of 1995 not only marked the most dramatic shift in public policy in over fifty years, it also heralded a completely new era in Ontario interest-group politics. This new regime, however, appears to be more complex than simple ideological explanations indicate. Some interest groups are in a sense being deinstitutionalized and forced into what some may see as primarily political movements. Others, such as comprehensive business interest associations (BIAs), are being given even more privileged access than before. Finally, some, in a surprising way, are likely to be given large amounts of public power (as private-interest governments) as public bureaucratic functions are handed over to private associations through a form of privatization.

In an important sense this is not new. The same type of complex interest-group/government relations began with the election of Margaret Thatcher as British prime minister in 1979. Thus, although some of the substantive policy ideas of Ontario's Conservatives can be traced most immediately to the radical American Republicans elected in 1994, the form of interest-group/government relations are influenced by the election of a neo-conservative government within a parliamentary regime.

The Changing Roles of Ontario Interest Groups

The complexity of roles of interest groups in any partisan political regime tend to be underestimated. Political commentators emphasize the more visible roles of lobbyist organizations and social movements, but pay less attention to interest groups as quasi-business firms or private-interest governments. These roles and their relative importance in any interest group depends on the strength of its member-orientation versus a concern for policy influence and the emphasis on either policy formation or policy implementation (see figure 1).

Traditionally, Ontario interest groups have been most concerned with having influence at the policy-formation stage. The association leaders normally define the members' long-term strategic interests, obtain support from their members periodically for these definitions, and then try to convince the government decision makers of the wisdom of their views. The policies pursued are public policies in that the benefits of the policies are open to all Ontario residents. This strategy is sometimes called the 'conservative strategy.'

Unfortunately for most interest groups, the Conservative government of Mike Harris is not interested in engaging in a policy-formulation process with interest associations. This government party believes that its policies have been defined by its campaign statements. Traditional interest groups, except for the privileged business interest associations, such as the Ontario Chamber of Commerce, are viewed as special pleaders by the Conservative cabinet. Thus, most interest groups are now frozen out of the policy process.

While most interest groups are now formally excluded from the policy process (or at least were in the early days of the Harris administration), some groups are treated with outright hostility. In general, these are the employee groups such as the Power Workers Union and the Ontario Liquor Boards Employees Union. One of the basic goals of Conservative public policy is to reduce the autonomy of employees and increase the power of employers. We can see this in the repeal of some labour legislation developed over the past fifty years, in the repeal of the employment-equity legislation and in many provisions of the omnibus Savings and Restructuring Act, such as the repeal of the many provisions of the Pay Equity Act. The view of the Conservative government is that employees should be more docile and have fewer rights and resources in relation to their employer.

This approach has led a number of associations to change from being mainly lobbying-type organizations to being more like a social movement. We can see this change in the days of protest against the provincial government in 1995 and 1996. The largest demonstrations of the first year of the Harris administration occurred on 23 and 24 February 1996 in Hamilton. On the second day, approximately 100,000 people protested

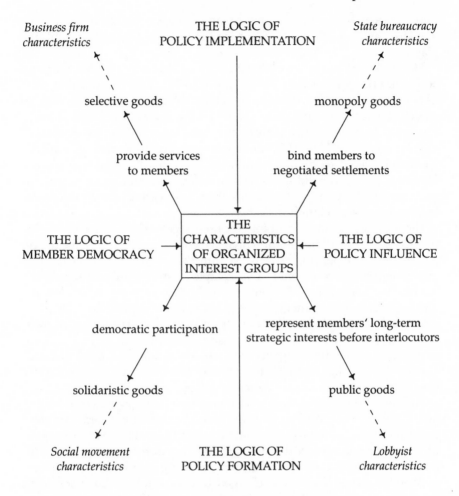

FIGURE 1 The Possible Roles of Organized Interest Groups

Note: An adaptation of figure 10.1, 'The diverse (and sometimes competing) logics of associability,' chap. 10, Philippe C. Schmitter and Luca Lanzalaco, 'Regions and the Organization of Business Interests,' in William D. Coleman and Henry J. Jacek, eds, *Regionalism, Business Interests and Public Policy* (London: Sage Publications, 1989), 214.

the policies of the provincial government. Gone was the solely 'conservative strategy.' A new 'militant but legitimate or legal' strategy took its place.

The backbone of the protest parade of 24 February was the Ontario Secondary School Teachers Federation (OSSTF). This organization was now responding primarily to its members' needs. The tactic was democratic grass-roots participation – being on the streets in political protest. The immediate benefit available to members was a feeling of widespread member solidarity. The OSSTF, among others, partially deinstitutionalized itself and tended to become somewhat more like a social movement. However, the OSSTF did not rely only on a single-track strategy, since it maintained a hospitality suite inside the Conservative policy conference held in downtown Hamilton that weekend.

The most complex aspect of interest-group/government relations of the new Conservative administration involved conflicting signals on the use of interest groups to perform government functions – what have been termed 'private-interest governments.'[1] One complex case that will be discussed in the next section involves the Ontario Medical Association, which lost its 'private-interest government' status given to it by the previous NDP government (1990–95). On the other hand, the Conservatives have handed over the government's Ontario Travel Industry Compensation Fund to a committee representing travel agents and tour and motor-coach operators and have agreed that the Ontario Trucking Association will administer compulsory training for truck tire and wheel installers.

The one type of interest-group tendency seemingly not affected by the new Conservative government is the market-oriented business firm tendency. Local automobile clubs affiliated with the Ontario Motor League fit this description the best. The main function of these local clubs is to provide services to their members, for the most part at no additional fees or at lower prices than those charged to non-members. Such services, thus, are selectively offered to members, but within the context of a commercial market. Political activities are clearly secondary.

The Traditional Functions of Interest Groups in the Public Policy Process

It is now useful to step back and look at the traditional function of interest groups in Ontario politics. We can thereby put into context the dramatic changes brought about by the NDP and Conservative governments of the 1990s. Interest groups in society tend to be underestimated because their total role is unknown to most non-members. Political scientists generally concentrate on the public-policy role of interest groups (and only part at that), despite the fact that most well-established interest groups develop commercial functions for their members as individual consumers. The two central functions within the broad public-policy role – formulation and implementation – tend to operate independently within the interest group.

Interest groups are usually linked to the making or formulation of public policy. Here we think of a chaotic struggle among groups trying to claim a dominant role in the making of public policy that is of special interest to their members, while leaving the actual implementation of policy to public officials. Thus, the interest groups seek to exercise power, but not the responsible authority that promotes the public interest. Such a form of interest politics we describe as pluralist.

However, many business, professional, and labour associations actually partake in the authority of the Ontario government. While the implementation of public policy is often shared with government officials and/or other associations, sometimes de facto monopolistic authority devolves upon an interest association, thus creating a private-interest government. The Law Society of Upper Canada (Canada's oldest continuing interest group) and the College of Physicians and Surgeons of Ontario are examples. Both have disciplinary authority (police powers and judicial-like capacities) that have the force of provincial law. The same is true of some other professions such as architects. The authority granted the Ontario Association of Architects goes back to the Architects Act 1935. When interest groups start to take some responsibility for the execution of public policy, we can speak of a corporatist tendency in public policy.

While most scholars use pluralist theory to explain policy making in Ontario (and Canada in general), corporatism explains some important aspects of public policy. Briefly, corporatism involves the formal – if not the legal – incorporation of organized interest groups in the implementation of public policy. When this happens, the usual distinction between the public and private sectors breaks down. Instead of conveying their members' views to government officials, interest groups now enforce public policy by encouraging their membership to conform to government policies. Such a process turns a system of interest representation into one of government by formerly private interest groups. The following section illustrates the analytic utility of the pluralist and corporatist conceptions of interest-group politics. It also demonstrates the dramatic shift in the relationship between the Ontario Government and key interest groups under the Harris government.

An Illustrative Case: The Ontario Medical Association under Different Party Administrations

Over the past twenty-five years, health-care costs have grown dramatically, to the point of consuming over one-third of the provincial budget. By 1990 that portion of the budget consistently outstripped the rate of inflation. This health-care ticking time bomb led first the NDP government and then the Conservative government to experiment with dramatic policies to cap one of the most expensive aspects of Ontario health care, the salaries of physicians. These new policies involved changing the relations between physician interest groups and the Ontario government.

Among all health-care interests, physicians and surgeons are the most powerful. While this group is represented by many different types of organizations, the most common variation is by specialization, such as family physicians, dermatologists, or plastic surgeons. Organizations may be differentiated by their relationship to other organizations – such as hospitals or governments, as in the case of interns and residents, medical teachers, or coroners and medical examiners – but the most important associations are general ones, such as the College of Physicians and Surgeons of Ontario and the Ontario Medical Association (OMA). While these two associations represent the same medical practitioners, their functions – deeply rooted in Ontario history – are fundamentally different and give rise to frequent conflict and tension during public debates about health policy.

The making of Ontario's health policy cannot be understood without understanding the traditional dual associability of Ontario's physicians and surgeons. The College is a compulsory body concerned with questions of quality medical care, while the OMA is a voluntary organization that represents the financial interests and individual freedoms of the medical profession. The OMA had a density rate (the ratio of actual members to potential members) of approximately 80 per cent around 1990. In addition, the OMA had monopoly rights granted by the Ontario government to negotiate for physician fees. How this situation came about requires a brief overview of the development of the profession as a whole.

Since the beginning of medical practice in Ontario, there have been controversies over who should be allowed to practise and what standards should be followed, or, indeed, whether regulation should take place at all. The basic conflict resulted from the clash of two value systems. The regulatory tradition, which is compatible with corporatist policy making, supports the notion that any group possessing corporate property rights should be subject to rigorous self-regulation.[2] Thus, physicians who 'own' the skills, techniques, and traditions of medicine must, as a group, regulate the standards and the methods for the use of their 'property.' The opposing tradition held that the skills and techniques of medicine belonged to the individual and that the standards and methods for their use were, therefore, to be determined by the market. Presumably, only the best doctors would survive the rigours of the market place.

The regulatory tradition began as an idea imported from Britain and manifested itself early on in attempts to establish a system for examining and licensing medical practitioners. These attempts at regulation were frustrated over the years by a massive influx of immigrant practitioners who had been certified in various places under varying conditions. Further, a large portion of these immigrants arrived from the United States, where standards were loose and where the second market tradition of medical practice held sway. Over time, however, the British conception of regulatory medicine strengthened. The College of Physicians and Surgeons of Ontario, founded formally in 1866, moved to impose a compulsory annual fee on all doctors in the late 1800s, in order to finance the building of a headquarters and general organizational maintenance. Despite strong resistance, the College prevailed, winning the authority to license and set standards for the profession as a whole. Today, the College is defined by its corporatist properties: membership is compulsory; members must pay the annual fee set by the College in order to practise medicine in Ontario; the College enjoys a representational monopoly and, perhaps most important, it has the authority to regulate and discipline its individual members.

In June 1881, not long after the College's founding, the Ontario Medical Association held its first annual meeting. Dual associability was established, that is, physicians were permitted to belong to both the OMA and the College. The OMA complemented the College by promoting the financial interests of its voluntary members. The relationship between the two associations started to change in the 1960s as health policy evolved from a private service to one that was publicly funded. The two major aspects of this policy change were (1) a widespread acceptance that all citizens should have equal access to medical treatment and (2) the transference of responsibility for medical-care costs from individual householders to the provincial treasurer.

In the years to come, these two characteristics of Ontario health policy

would affect physician income and increasingly became the most contentious part of Ontario health politics and, more specifically, of the functions of the two main medical associations. Initially, physicians prospered
under the Ontario Health Insurance Plan (OHIP). As usage increased,
their incomes rose; more important, they could count on receiving payment for every patient. In addition, payment from the government was
rapid and office administrative costs declined relative to the monies
collected. Physicians easily maintained their position as the best-paid
occupational group as their average income ballooned to five times that
of the average taxpayer. However, by the end of the 1970s, their relative
position declined under double-digit inflation and sluggish increases in
their fee schedules.

Some disgruntled physicians began to extra-bill their patients – that is,
charge more for services than the provincial government would reim-
burse them for – in order to increase their incomes and at the same time
keep pressure on the Ontario government to more aggressively push up
the fee schedules. The negative public response to this tactic – it was seen
as an assault on the principle of equal access – led to the 1984 passage,
under the federal Liberal government, of the Canada Health Act, which
contained a financial penalty for the Ontario government if it allowed
extra billing to continue. The decision of the newly elected federal Conservative government of Brian Mulroney to enforce the Canada Health
Act provoked, in the summer of 1986, a bitter physicians' strike, which
ended with a devastating defeat of the OMA. How a formerly astute
interest group could allow itself to be so badly outmanoeuvred by the
Ontario government has been the subject of a great deal of analysis,
much of it centring on physicians' fears for the future.[3]

The conflict also marked a major change in the public-policy roles of
the two associations. Historically, the College concerned itself with the
quality of patient care, not finances, going out of its way, in fact, to
distance itself from the monetary aspirations of the medical profession.
Indeed, it focused more on its legal mandate than on the interests of its
members. Yet, over time, the issue of the quality of medical care started
to become partially intertwined with the issue of physicians' incomes.
The College came to view abnormally high earnings by a physician as
indicative of an overly high patient load, which decreased the quality of
service. It was hoped that a cap on individual physicians' earnings
would prevent superficial medical treatment, but its indirect effect was
to reduce the size of payments to practitioners.

Nor was the pluralist body, the OMA, immune to developing corporatist

properties. Before the passage of the Canada Health Act and its implementation in Ontario, there were concerns that in some areas certain
specialists, such as obstetricians and anaesthetists, would all demand
extra payments from patients. The OMA, anticipating public outrage
over such an action, guaranteed that patients – especially low-income
patients – would be able to obtain help without personally having to
make payments to a physician.

However, when the minority Liberal government moved to end extra
billing in 1986, the OMA reverted to its pure pluralist activity of lobbying
– only now, instead of relying on its traditional conservative style, the
association turned to the militant mode. The nightly news from Queen's
Park featured angry doctors behaving in ways totally at variance with
the public's image of doctors as self-controlled and reasoning authority
figures. Such behaviour provoked negative reactions from the government, the opposition parties, and the public. But it was the College that
ultimately restored order. It did so not by confronting the extra-billing
issue directly, but rather by stressing the obligation of the corporate
profession to provide medical care to the people of Ontario – a direct
attack on the militant pluralist style chosen by the OMA. Forced to
choose between the contrasting political tactics of the OMA and the
College, physicians bent to the dictates of the conservative (yet forceful)
College. The more corporatist mode had won out over the pluralist
mode.

But more change was to follow. The new NDP government faced
financial problems even worse than for the Liberal government that
preceded it. A long, deep recession in the first half of the 1990s eroded
government revenues; first the federal Conservative government and
then the Chrétien Liberal government kept reducing transfer payments
at the same time as government expenditures were rising to deal with the
failing economy.

In order to decrease once again the rate of increasing physician costs,
the Rae government attempted to work through the OMA and set up a
full-blown corporatist medical-policy process along with an appropriate
corporatist medical structure. Not only would this reinforce the OMA's
monopoly over salary negotiations, but also it would offer binding arbitration and, most important, compulsory membership of all physicians
in the OMA. Each of the approximately 20,000 physicians became obliged
to pay about $1100 a year in membership fees. If a physician refused to
pay his/her fee, then the OMA would tell the government in late winter
and the membership fees would be deducted from the doctor's health-

insurance payments. As well, the OMA was given control over some programs such as recruiting and subsidizing young doctors to spell those in isolated communities when the latter needed a rest.[4]

Despite grumbling by some physicians, the Ontario government–OMA relationship prevented a repeat of the turbulence seen in the Liberal years. Then came the new Harris government and its omnibus Savings and Restructuring Act (Bill 26). This bill allowed the government to revoke the representational rights of the OMA and all of the 1991 Framework Agreement. Under Bill 26's Schedule I, the Physician Services Delivery Management Act, all contractual rights of the OMA and all previous agreements between the Ontario government and the OMA were abolished. For the first time in Ontario history, the power to set doctors' fees rested not with individual physicians or with their interest group, but with the provincial minister of health. The OMA was reduced to being a purely pluralist association with no public functions whatsoever.

Recognizing its changed status, the OMA gave up its right to compel all Ontario physicians to pay membership fees. The expected loss in revenue resulted in a cutback of social functions and staff. Before the Tory legislation, the OMA had an annual operating budget of $15 million and two hundred staff members. The result of the February 1996 OMA decisions to become, once again, a purely voluntary interest group will have an uncertain impact on the OMA. Since 95 per cent of the OMA's budget comes from membership dues, any significant drop in membership will have an important effect on its overall budget.[5] One could also expect a significant drop in the number of full-time OMA employees paid out of the operating budget. Thus, over the course of ten years (1985–95), the Ontario Medical Association has gone from being a voluntary association, with negotiating rights generally binding on all physicians, to a pure corporatist 'private interest government,' to a now purely pluralist organization with no real public-administrative function and with only lobbyist characteristics. However, faced with increasing militancy by individual physicians and spontaneous proposals for an embargo on accepting new patients, the Harris government informally and quietly accepted the OMA once again as the negotiating partner representing Ontario physicians by the beginning of 1997.

The Specific Activities of Interest Associations

As in other liberal democracies, interest groups in Ontario perform four

distinct functions: public-policy formulation, public-policy implementation, advancing members' economic interests, and selectively providing
benefits to members. Table 1 (p. 318) summarizes the activities of interest
groups that are characteristic of the four functions, in terms of specific
tactics, the targets of interest-group activities, the frequency of interest-
group activity, and the personnel involved in activity. Public-policy formulation is usually done in one of three levels of intensity. First, business
interest associations, such as the Ontario Division of the Canadian Manufacturers Association, use a *conservative style* that involves meeting quietly behind closed doors with the premier, cabinet ministers, and senior
bureaucrats. Such a style is adopted because the group, confident in the
interest it represents, expects a favourable reception. Business interests,
especially in manufacturing, enjoy a special relationship with the Ontario government, whether Conservative or Liberal. A healthy and prosperous business community means a strong provincial tax base and an
affluent population with well-funded public services, all of which serve
to boost public support for the government of the day.

Interest groups that are less confident of a sympathetic reception from
government often adopt a *moderate style*. Such groups engage in the same
type of activities that one finds in the conservative style, but they exert
more vigorous pressure. This pressure usually assumes two forms. First,
elected non-cabinet members are contacted. These include not only
backbench government party MPPs and opposition members, but also
politicians at the regional and municipal level. Second, the public-
relations strength of these associations is cranked up to influence public
opinion, increasingly through the use of paid political advertising in the
mass media. This type of promotion is called 'advocacy advertising' to
distinguish it from commercial advertising. It is driven by the assumption that an aroused public opinion will pressure the cabinet to be more
sympathetic to the interests of the group involved.

The third and most intense type of pressure activity is the *militant style*.
This occurs when the group leaders believe that they are confronting
hostile government authorities, or when they feel that their opponents
are more dangerous to the government's stability. The extra political
muscle needed in this style may take the form of mass action, such as
letter-writing campaigns or, at the legal extreme, protest rallies. The
latter occur physically close to the government, either in front of the
legislative building at Queen's Park or wherever the premier happens to
be. Often politically unsophisticated groups unthinkingly adopt a militant style. Some do so out of the belief that the government will respond

TABLE 1
The functions, activities, targets, frequency, and personnel of interest groups

	Functions	Activities	Targets	Frequency	Personnel
1	Public-policy formulation (pluralist emphasis)	Lobbying, advocacy advertising, demonstrations	Politicians, senior bureaucrats, public opinion	Intermittent depending on issues	Chief Executive Officer (CEO)
2	Public-policy implementation (corporatist emphasis)	Working partnership	Middle-level bureaucrats	Regular and frequent	Technical manager
3	Economic policy (commercial emphasis)	Contractual negotiations, commercial advertising	Business associations, labour unions, marketing boards, large corporations, potential consumers	Regular and infrequent; intermittent depending on threats from other economic actors	Economic specialists
4	Selective benefits (consumer emphasis)	Service: Agency-client, business-consumer	Members, some sales to outsiders	Varies depending on demands of members and revenue needs of the association	Service director

only to aggressive forms of pressure, not reasoned argument. Others take the naive view that normal pressure-group tactics in the United States can be transferred to the Canadian setting with equal success.

In general, the militant style is more likely to be associated with small, transitory, single-issue groups or those with limited involvement in politics. These groups have relatively little impact on public policy (although they capture a disproportionate amount of newspaper space and television time). As we pointed out earlier, employee groups have adopted this style since the Harris government came to power in 1995.

When interest groups are involved in the implementation of public policy, their style of political activities changes dramatically. They are now insiders in the policy process and, most important, are partly responsible for the success of public policy. Confrontation between state officials and interest-group leaders gives way to cooperation, pressure lobbying to a working partnership.

It is a mistake to discuss only the overt political activities of interest groups. The political power of these groups is, in fact, enhanced when they meet the non-political needs of their members. One of these needs is the ability to deal with, on a collective basis, other powerful interests in Ontario. Thus, contracts may be negotiated between two interest groups. This happens most visibly in the area of labour relations, where an association of employers negotiates a labour contract with a trade union and the workers it represents. Broad collective negotiating of this type is fairly common in the Ontario construction industry. Still another form of interest group economic activity is commercial advertising, whereby consumers are urged to use the generic products of an Ontario industry, be they dairy products, such as milk or butter, or specific building materials such as clay bricks.

Finally, interest groups also provide their members with individual benefits on a selective basis. These benefits may be given upon request to all members in good standing, or they may be sold to members at a special low price. Benefits may be social (for example, the right to attend certain entertainment events) and so designed to build the solidarity of the group and provide the association with a valuable resource for its political activities. Thus, understanding the non-political activities of an interest group gives us insight into why some groups seem more powerful in the political process than others.

The Targets of Interest Groups

The functions of interest groups in Ontario can be differentiated not only by the activities of these associations, but also by the intended targets of these specific activities. The target of group activity under pressure pluralism is the top policy elite of the province, namely the cabinet and senior civil servants. If direct efforts seem to lack the expected persuasive impact, then groups may choose to affect decision-makers indirectly by mobilizing public opinion. In general, it is the cabinet that is most open to this pressure, since its members depend on periodic electoral support to maintain their positions. Public opinion may reach the cabinet via backbench government MPPs who use the secret governmental caucus to urge the cabinet to make policy adjustments. Cabinet response is affected by at least two major political conditions. First, the government status – that is, majority or minority – of the party in power is taken into consideration. Minority governments are extremely sensitive to public opinion on major issues since they may be defeated at any time the legislature is in session and forced to fight an election on the current policy under dispute. Second, in a majority-government situation, the longer the period of time that has elapsed since the last election, the more important becomes the issue of public opinion.

When an Ontario interest group is involved in the implementation of public policy, not only does the nature of the activity change dramatically, but the target of attention shifts downward in the governmental structure. In this situation, lower-ranking government officials and interest-group personnel share similar policy performance goals and are ready to help one another in seeing that public policy meets its objectives.

With the shift to economic-policy functions, the targets or interlocutors shift again. Negotiations and agreements may be made with other economic interest groups, such as business associations, labour unions, or professional bodies. Some of these groups may have a quasi-public character, as is evident in various agricultural marketing boards. In some settings, negotiations may be held with provincial crown corporations such as Ontario Hydro, or with large private firms. Finally, the interest group may focus its attention on the consumers of the goods or services its membership produces.

In the case of selective benefits, the members of the association may be treated as preferential customers. Typical among this group are the members of the various local automobile clubs that make up the Ontario section of the Canadian Automobile Association or the 650 local credit unions that are members of the Credit Union Central of Ontario. Interest groups can generate extra revenue when they sell goods and services to non-members at prices that are normally higher than the cost to members.

Frequency of Activities

The frequency of interaction between an interest group and its targets or interlocutors varies depending on the classification of the association's activities. In the area of public-policy formulation, the level of frequency is highly variable depending on the political agenda. As long as issues related to the group's core interest or domain are off the political agenda, the group is likely to engage in minimal, routine, low-intensity communications with political authorities. However, should a relevant issue arise in the political environment (especially one that threatens to impose new costs on the interest group's members), then we can expect intense political activity. In general, interest groups mobilize more to prevent changes they view as hostile to their current position than to gain from opportunities. This well-known principle, which dates back to the writings of Machiavelli, helps explain why policy change is difficult to achieve.

In contrast, the working partnership between interest groups and provincial authorities in the implementation of public policy requires almost daily contacts, certainly by phone and often face-to-face. Since the work involved in implementation is usually highly technical and complex in some of its details, frequent clarification between the partners is necessary, very often in such areas as the development and revision of regulations, as well as their enforcement by association officials on their own members.

The commercial functions of interest groups vary constantly in their timing. Commercial negotiations on behalf of an interest are often held annually, or in the case of labour negotiations every two or three years. The normally predictable cycle of commercial functions can, however, be severely disrupted by the sudden intrusion of hostile economic forces into the interest group's environment. Often this threat is the result of an unintended or unexpected consequence of a change in public policy involving trade or technological innovations that propel the restructuring of economic sectors. Individual members who find it difficult to respond on their own will look to their association to defend their interest. The textile industry, for example, in the face of the necessity for cost-cutting brought about by changes in trade policy would more effectively defend its interest on an association-to-union basis than on a firm-by-firm basis.

Finally, the voluntary interest group needs to maintain a high membership density, that is, a high rate of actual members to potential members. In order to do this, most groups offer membership services to encourage loyalty to the organization. However, the successful interest association must respond to members whose needs for association services may vary greatly from year to year. At the same time, however, the need for membership fees and sales of goods and services to members and non-members is constant; the interest group, like other organizations, requires a stable and predictable cash flow.

Interest-Group Personnel

Like most organizations, interest groups attempt to make themselves more efficient by creating specialized roles for different individuals within their ranks. This division of labour is also seen in the four different interest-group functions. Since public-policy formulation is such a highly visible and symbolic activity, one should not be surprised to see in interest groups the active presence of a chief executive officer (CEO), the most senior full-time staff member of the organization, who normally assumes the title of 'president.' At times when symbolic political support is especially crucial, the CEO is helped out by the highest-ranking member, who chairs the board of directors – normally for a period of one year – and generally goes under the title 'chairman of the board.' If a delegation to the cabinet or to an individual minister is called for, other board officers may become involved. On more routine political lobbying, a director of government relations or public affairs may be the leading figure.

When public-policy implementation is at centre stage, the personnel changes. This function is usually described as 'merely technical' in order to insulate its activities from the high-pressure, overtly political arena. The work to be done takes place under the purview of expert techno-crats, whether middle-level bureaucrats in the government or their coun-terparts, the technical managers in the interest group. The educational and work-experience backgrounds of both group and provincial officials are usually the same. Among this group, substantive knowledge and technical skills take precedence over political skills. However, this should not obscure the fact that the assumptions driving public-policy imple-mentation activity are highly political; at the same time, the portrayal of a policy as 'technical' discourages the politically aware public from tak-ing an active interest, thereby allowing the policy makers and interest groups greater leeway.

The interest-group personnel involved in economic policy also has distinctive specialized knowledge and skills, particularly in such areas as taxation, labour relations, and contract law. This is the world of account-ants, lawyers, and industrial-relations specialists.

Finally, the provision of selective benefits calls for people with very good interpersonal skills who can promote the organization as they sign up new memberships, renew existing members, and market the goods and services offered by the organization. The motto of this group is 'Don't give away for free what you can sell.'

Ontario and Federal Comparisons

Ontario and federal interest groups can be compared on the basis of two major variables – first, the degree and strength of their internal organization and, second, the division of policy responsibilities between Ottawa and the Ontario government.

Canada's relatively decentralized federal governmental system puts pressure on interest groups – many of which operated in a local or provincial context before coalescing into national associations – to be similarly decentralized. Some interest groups resist decentralization – others embrace it. Business interest associations that are nationally integrated by a small or medium number of large firms are among the most resistant (particularly so if the industry they represent is highly exposed to international competition, as seems to be increasingly the case). In Ontario, by contrast, labour, professional, and farmer interests are more organizationally developed at the provincial level. Labour unions, for example, discover their locus of power in individual unions, which are geographically concentrated. Indeed, union power is often devolved down to the level of powerful local units.[6] With respect to agriculture, the cultivation of crops and the raising of livestock are subject to local climate and physical geography, which not unexpectedly creates strong regional bonds among farmers.

The second factor affecting the integration of interest groups is the division of policy responsibilities between Ottawa and the Ontario government. When Ottawa has overriding authority (and actually exercises it), the national interest group is likely to be strong and autonomous from regional subunits. However, when the Ontario government either has constitutional jurisdiction or controls policy through, for example, the expenditure of funds, the Ontario group is more powerful than is commonly believed.

Federal and Ontario interest groups can vary in terms of their impact. The 'Ontario' association is generally much more important within the provincial context than is the national 'Canada' association within the federal context. Association members usually perceive a greater impact on their day-to-day lives from provincial-government policies. As a result, these members are usually willing to devote more money and work to build up their provincial association compared to their federal interest group. Thus, the Ontario Federation of Agriculture is a stronger presence on the provincial scene than is the Canadian Federation of Agriculture on the federal scene. The same holds true for other provincial associations such as the Ontario Medical Association, the Ontario Federation of Labour, the Council of Ontario Construction Associations, the Ontario Forest Industries Associations, and the Credit Union Central of Ontario.

In discussing the relative roles of federal and provincial interest groups, it is useful to examine the interests in a specific sector such as the Ontario food industry. This industry, broadly defined, is a key component of Ontario's economic prosperity, despite the popular image of Ontario as an industrial province. It includes at its source farmers and those businesses that service them: seed growers; fertilizer, pesticide, and herbicide manufacturers and dealers; farm-machinery manufacturers and dealers; and the financial-services industry – both private and public – that supports farming. Wholesalers, retailers, and employees in the food-processing industry all benefit from these supports. Co-production work by consumers, which occurs in 'pick your own' operations, is another important feature of the Ontario food industry.

Interest groups are indispensable in coordinating the relationships among the various economic actors along the food chain, as well as public policy for the food industry, which is negotiated between Ottawa and Ontario. Especially important are farmers' organizations at the provincial level. Since single-commodity farmers tend to be geographically concentrated, organization is easier to develop at the provincial than at the federal level. The provincial organizations promote and defend local farming interests against the federal government (which is often more preoccupied with the problems of farmers in Quebec or western Canada) and against the major corporate purchasers of farmers' produce.

The major form of commodity farm organization in Ontario is the marketing board. The Ontario government has been a major stimulus to the creation and growth of this association of farmers. The marketing board has been granted a wide array of legal, compulsory powers (although each board has its own unique mix of powers and limitations). In the commodities of greatest strength – milk, cream, chickens, eggs, turkeys, and tobacco – the individual boards that make up the marketing board are corporatist organizations that control entry into whatever type of farming is under review, license the amount of the commodity each farmer can produce, and determine who can buy these farm products and for what purposes. Clearly, the locus of power in the policy systems lies in these provincial farmer groups.

Conclusion

The purpose of this chapter was to give the reader an understanding of the public-policy role of interest groups in Ontario. As a first step, we showed that there have been dramatic changes in the relations between the Ontario government and Ontario interest groups in the 1990s. In order to understand these complex shifts, four roles of interest groups were outlined. In a sense, the Harris government has revitalized a large number of institutionalized employee groups by pushing them into a much more member-oriented, democratic-social-movement role. Purely lobbying organizations have been limited by the strong political-party orientation of the Conservatives, except for broad-based business interest associations.[7] Some heavily institutionalized groups, like the Ontario Medical Association, have lost their public-policy implementation functions, while others have taken on this type of function because of the privatizing of government activity.

Associated with various interest-group roles and functions are a set of characteristics based on visible group activities and their specific targets, the frequency with which these activities are undertaken, and the personnel within the interest group that performs the activity. In analysing the roles of Ontario interest groups in the policy process, we tried to show how different patterns fit the concepts of pluralism and corporatism. When public-policy formulation is characterized by intermittent interaction among competing interest groups lobbying politicians, senior civil servants, and public opinion, interest groups can be said to exhibit a pluralist policy role. In contrast, when public-policy implementation is characterized by antagonistic interest groups that develop a working partnership and regularly brainstorm with middle-level civil servants (who share their technical competence and commitment to problem-solving), a corporatist approach is indicated.

While it is fair to say that the usual form of interest-group activity in Ontario is pluralist, one should not ignore the apparent growth of strong long-term corporatist tendencies in some areas. This is true especially in narrow economic sectors in the Harris government, in contrast to the New Democrats' attempts to institute a more broadly based macro-corporatism in the health, agricultural, labour, and business arenas. The most visible, of course, was 'the Social Contract,' a concept derived from European corporatist practices.

What we know for sure now is that the mould for stable relations between Ontario interest groups and the Ontario government is now broken. In the course of ten years, from 1987 to 1996, Ontario went through three major changes in these relations. Each premier seemed to have a different conception of the proper form of the relationship. With these abrupt changes, the old truths about the stability of Ontario state-society relations are now part of Ontario's history, and are not at all accurate for describing Ontario's present.

Notes

1 For an elaboration and explanation of this concept with Ontario examples, see Wyn Grant, ed., *Business Interests, Organizational Development and Private Interest Government* (New York: Walter de Gruyter, 1987).

2 The understanding of health policy in Ontario owes a great deal to the years of research by Carolyn Tuohy. See her 'Pluralism and Corporatism in Ontario Medical Politics,' in K.J. Rea and J.T. McLeod, eds, *Business and Government in Canada: Selected Readings*, 2nd ed. (Toronto: Methuen, 1976), 395–413; 'Private Government, Property and Professionalism,' *Canadian Journal of Political Science* 9, no. 4 (December 1976): 668–81; and 'Medicine and the State in Canada: The Extra-Billing Issue in Perspective,' *Canadian Journal of Political Science* 21, no. 2 (June 1988): 267–96.

3 See Robert G. Evans et al., 'Controlling Health Expenditures – The Canadian Reality,' *New England Journal of Medicine* 320, no. 9 (2 March 1989): 575.

4 Robert Sheppard, 'A union busted,' *Globe and Mail*, 29 February 1996, A19.

5 Interview with Ann Todd, Chief Financial Officer, Ontario Medical Association, 24 May 1996.

6 For a sense of the flavour of local union power in Ontario, see Bill Freeman, *1005: Political Life in a Union Local* (Toronto: James Lorimer, 1982).

7 The resistance of the Harris government to most forms of traditional lobbying has had a very depressing impact on the commercial activities of professional lobbyists in Ontario.

Further Reading

Atkinson, Michael M., and Robert A. Nigol. 'Selecting Policy Instruments: Neo-Institutional and Rational Choice Interpretations of Automobile Insurance in Ontario,' *Canadian Journal of Political Science* 22, no. 1 (March 1989): 107–35. This excellent article explores the utility of two currently favoured approaches to political-science interpretations of the relationships of interest groups and government in Ontario politics. A close reading is necessary, but the reader will be well rewarded.

Coleman, William D., and Henry J. Jacek. 'The Role and Activities of Business Interest Associations in Canada.' *Canadian Journal of Political Science* 16, no. 2 (June 1983): 257–80. The original version of table 1 was first presented in this article, which contains discussions of Ontario interest groups in the food-processing industry and the role of farmers/marketing boards in the public-policy process.

Jacek, Henry J. 'Pluralist and Corporatist Intermediation, Activities of Business Interest Associations, and Corporate Profits: Some Evidence from Canada.' *Comparative Politics* 18, no. 4 (July 1986): 419–37. This article elaborates upon the classic definitions of pluralism and corporatism enunciated by Philippe Schmitter, and attempts to apply them systematically to the Canadian public-policy process. Some material on Ontario interest groups is included.

Pross, A. Paul. *Group Politics and Public Policy*. 2nd edition, Toronto: Oxford University Press, 1992. This is the basic Canadian study of interest groups in the public-policy process. A few Ontario examples are included.

Schwartz, Mildred A. 'North American Social Democracy in the 1990s: The NDP in Ontario,' *Canadian-American Public Policy*, no. 17 (April 1994): 1–46. This article discusses the problems the NDP government had with its natural employee constituency over the Social Contract Act, enacted 7 July 1993.

Skogstad, Grace. 'The Farm Policy Community and Public Policy in Ontario and Québec.' In William D. Coleman and Grace Skogstad, eds, *Policy Communities and Public Policy in Canada: A Structural Approach*, 59–90. Mississauga, Ont.: Copp Clark Pittman Ltd, 1990. This chapter shows how the strong capabilities of the federal and Ontario governments combined with fragmented interest groups impede policy formulation.

Thorburn, Hugh G. *Interest Groups in the Canadian Federal System*. Toronto: University of Toronto Press, 1985. Volume 69 in the series of research reports of the Royal Commission on the Economic Union and Development Prospects for Canada (MacDonald Commission). Part of this report deals with the evolution of interests in Ontario.

PART IV

Change and Continuity in the Ontario Political System

An Insiders' View of the NDP Government of Ontario: The Politics of Permanent Opposition Meets the Economics of Permanent Recession

Chuck Rachlis and David Wolfe

On 6 September 1990, with 37 per cent of the popular vote and 74 of 130 seats, the New Democrats were elected as the thirty-fifth government of Ontario; on 1 October Bob Rae became premier. Almost five years later, on 8 June 1995, the NDP was defeated as Mike Harris's Conservatives elected 82 MPPs.

After forty-two years of Conservative party government in the province, voters have chosen three different political parties in the three general elections since 1985. Some see this as evidence of major inconsistency on the part of the Ontario electorate. Others interpret the differing outcomes in 1987, 1990, and 1995 as a consistent search on the part of electors for solutions to the persistent economic problems they experienced in the 1980s and 1990s. We side with the second interpretation – that Ontario voters have been more consistent than they are frequently given credit for.

An important factor in voter motivation over the past decade has been the declining standard of living experienced by the majority of Ontario families. A succession of statistics indicates that families are working more hours collectively, earning lower real incomes, and losing a higher proportion of their declining real incomes to taxes. They feel a pervasive anxiety about their (and their children's) economic prospects; at the same time, they are angered that the growing bite that taxes take out of their income has not resulted in better or more services. Instead, they see a growing proportion of public-sector revenues being absorbed by debt interest charges, rather than funding programs or delivering services.

The election of the NDP in 1990 reflected voters' anxiety and their belief that the Liberal government elected in 1987 had failed to deliver solutions to these problems. Among other factors, the drift evident in the Liberal government despite its buoyant finances, anger at Premier Peterson's having called an election only three years after winning a massive majority in 1987, unhappiness over his government's inability – despite brave talk to the contrary – to do anything about the Canada-U.S. Free Trade Agreement, and concerns about political integrity raised by the government's political scandals contributed to the resonance in public opinion of the basic NDP election message: that the Liberals and Tories were on the side of an unacceptable status quo; change was spelled N-D-P.

The support for the NDP government of many Ontarians who had voted NDP for these reasons would continue on the condition that they felt the government was moving to change things – fundamentally, that it was delivering services in a more efficient and cost-effective manner and that it would improve their prospects for good jobs and rising incomes. Whether the NDP government could have successfully held their support can only be a matter for speculation. What is clear is that during the course of its mandate, the NDP government was subjected to conflicting pressures that made winning a second mandate more difficult. The discipline of government – the ability to resist the pressure to respond to short-term political demands for the sake of building a longer-term base of support – did not exist at the outset of the government's mandate, or even many months into it. By the time this discipline was achieved, several critical decisions with lasting political costs had already been taken.

These pressures were both external and internal. They were the result partly of the NDP's pre-1990 years as an opposition party and partly of the dire economic circumstances the new government faced as the economy plunged into the depths of recession in the winter of 1991. Constrained by its past, and deluged by the demands of trying to navigate a new course, even as it learned to manage the controls of an ill-equipped and slow-to-respond ship of state, the NDP did not transform itself quickly enough to avert the loss of much of its public support. Once lost, that support proved impossible to recover.

Our story about the NDP government of Ontario is a story of politics and economics, and of their intersection in a particular parliamentary practice and a set of (mostly) economic policy areas. Our account is focused on these areas, and ignores important initiatives in the areas of child care, pay equity, education, social assistance, training, employment equity, and long-term care. It also ignores the constitutional follies of 1992. It is necessarily a subjective account, reflecting our direct participation in the events described. These factors do not, we believe, affect our story; they do make it less than the history of the NDP government.

More Work for Less Pay: Anxiety and Anger

Recent studies have established that the long postwar economic boom referred to as the 'Golden Age' came to an end in the mid-1970s.[1] The old truism of a rising tide that lifts all boats has given way to a more sombre reality of stagnant and declining incomes. Between 1980 and 1994, average family income in Canada increased by only half of 1 per cent. Since 1989, it has declined by 5 per cent.[2]

More and more young workers (including, and in addition to, disproportionate numbers of women, people with disabilities, and members of visible minorities) are stuck, perhaps permanently, in part-time or temporary jobs – 'non-standard employment,' the Economic Council of Canada calls it.[3] The traditional prescription that better skills and more education are the appropriate government policy responses seems inadequate, as evidence mounts that 'young workers entering the labour market face a "demand deficit" rather than a "skills deficit."' Education and training cannot address the full dimensions of the problem: in isolation, they simply produce 'better educated unemployed people.'[4]

These conditions contribute to a powerful voter appetite for change, based on anxiety and mounting distrust of the 'same old thing.' In 1990 in Ontario, the desire for change coincided with real differences in the political choices on offer. To a considerable extent (thanks to Reaganomics in the United States and its Canadian emulators), voters saw government itself as a major part of the problem. This image would prove problematic for an NDP government committed both to an activist approach to governing and to a fundamental even-handedness: as Premier-elect Rae said on election night, 'We have to work with all the sections of the community to build confidence in the future of our economy and confidence in the future of our society.'

From Opposition to Government

The NDP's election in 1990 was the culmination of a long process of defining the party's electoral platform in terms of the demands of significant constituent communities of interest. There was little in the way of an overarching or 'big picture' analytic framework. Significant tensions were either ignored or assumed away. One significant attempt to fashion a broader policy framework was the economic policy review conducted in 1988–90 by the then Treasury critic, Floyd Laughren, which enlisted the services of more than a dozen academics, policy activists, and trade-union staff to explore new approaches to NDP economic thinking.

The review was a stimulating and provocative experience for those who participated in it and it produced some important ideas that contributed to initiatives of the future government.[5] However, most of the work was carried out in isolation from the party membership, and the limited attempts to present the results of the policy review to party activists met with a less than overwhelming response. Most significantly, the review had little direct impact on the party's supposed platform in the 1990 election – the *Agenda for People*. This gap between the policy thinking of some activists and others connected to the caucus at Queen's Park and the broader party membership evidenced long-standing tensions that would resurface in a more serious form during the mandate of the government.

The NDP's success in opposition was the ability of the caucus to mobilize opposition around demands for government action that were precise in terms of output, but that never had to address questions of priority, sequencing, or means. In the absence of overt contradiction at the level of policy, almost any opponent of the government was a friend of the NDP. This inclusiveness did not, however, extend to the rank and file of the party. The NDP's parliamentary arm – first the opposition caucus and then the cabinet and backbench – was quite removed from the movement for social change that the party harnessed and attempted to steer. Indeed, the party apparatus played a distinctly subordinate organizational and fund-raising role.

For the NDP, the practical politics of legislature-focused opposition resulted in a view that denied the importance of issues that did not resonate with identifiable oppositional allies. In particular, key issues of government finance and operations were seen as distractions that concealed or misrepresented the real issues. Through the 1980s, major elements of the NDP's support – including many trade-union activists, environmentalists, and members of 'equity seeking groups' – adopted similar views. The result was that they ignored many critical areas of policy and management that the government of the day must deal with, whatever else its ambitions. To the extent that the NDP did express its views on issues of public finance and fiscal policy, it adopted a reflexive Keynesianism that took no account of managing the public sector.

This self-conception was reinforced by the peculiar dynamics of legislative politics, and the fact that there is virtually no media coverage of Ontario politics apart from that provided by the Queen's Park press gallery, a very uncritical body to say the least. The focus of media attention is the daily question period, supplemented by scrums with ministers, including the premier. Just as in an election campaign, where there are contradictory messages flying in all directions, the key to attracting coverage and voter attention is product differentiation. Hyperbole, simplification, and the 10-second sound bite are effective in attracting attention, especially when contrast and confrontation are reporters' criteria of what is newsworthy. Nuance and moderation usually fail the test.

There is little market for complexity or reflection in such an environment. And even those politicians and reporters who tire of the daily diet of filler find little appetite for substance among their caucus colleagues or back at the newsroom. Over the term of a government's mandate (for this is the natural rhythm of provincial political life), the result is increasingly partisan packaging of ideas that have been simplified – or 'dumbed down' – for easy media and public consumption.

The political economy of NDP support was tension-ridden, anchored in the we/they dynamic of its opposition practice, and dependent on an expanding economy. In the mid- and late 1980s, pre–Free Trade economic expansion and steadily rising taxes generated rapid growth in government revenues and new programs. The period of the NDP/Liberal Accord from 1985 to 1987 legitimized many NDP policy concerns, even though the initial beneficiaries of the accord were the Peterson Liberals.[6] At the same time, growing unhappiness with the federal Conservatives depressed the voter appeal of the rudderless provincial Tories.

The ambitious and progressive reform agenda defined by the Accord in 1985 and its uneven implementation created an expectation among many NDP supporters that the NDP government would rapidly implement the undiluted version of the Accord agenda – including those items proposed by the NDP that the Liberals had not agreed to implement. This excessive level of expectations collided directly with the dramatically changed economic circumstances of the new government in the aftermath of the Free Trade Agreement and the Bank of Canada–induced recession of 1990.

The Fiscal Challenge Begins

The worst recession since the 'dirty thirties' hit Ontario in 1990. At the same time as provincial Treasurer Bob Nixon was rehearsing his proud claim in the 1990 Budget that 'last year we achieved a balanced budget for the first time in 20 years,' the destruction of hundreds of thousands of jobs in the industrial heartland was beginning. By election day, in September 1990, there were 107,000 fewer Ontarians employed than at the beginning of the year. By the spring of 1992, a total of more than 330,000 jobs would disappear. However, general awareness of how bad things were was delayed by the lag in statistical reporting and a two-month election campaign during which the previous government never missed an opportunity to trumpet that it had eliminated the deficit and that the provincial balance sheet was in surplus. It was certainly not apparent in 1990 that this was the worst recession since the 1930s. Still, it was understood early on that the government's task would be difficult. 'I wanted to be premier in the worst way,' joked Bob Rae. 'I had no idea my wish would be granted so literally.'

One of the early events in the life of the new government was a briefing from senior Treasury officials on Monday, 10 September, four days after the election. Going into the briefing, little more was known than what had been tabled in the 1990 Liberal budget, which predicted revenues of $44.5 billion and a $30 million surplus. In fact, as the premier and his senior advisers learned, the much-touted surplus was in reality a sizeable deficit that would likely exceed $2 billion during the current fiscal year. The projections for future years were even more alarming.

For years, the deficit had played an iconic role in discussions of fiscal policy in the legislature and the provincial media. The much-prized AAA rating bestowed on Ontario debt by the bond-rating agencies symbolized for many the fiscal rectitude of Canada's wealthiest province. It frequently was invoked by Premier Bill Davis and his supporters to justify both the slow pace of change under Conservative governments and their concern about deficit finance. (Although the deficit was a standard fixture in provincial budgeting, it was modest in size; even the 1981–2 recession had pushed it only as high as $2.5 billion, against revenue of $20.5 billion.)

Only four days after becoming premier-elect, Bob Rae was told that if nothing changed, the revenue shortfalls now evident would produce a deficit of more than $6 billion in year two of his government (without considering any of the spending items promised by the NDP before the election).

The Dilemmas of Governing

Taking power was a huge job. Of the 74 New Democrat MPPs, only 17 had been MPPs before 1990. None had ever been part of a provincial government. One-third of the cabinet members were newly elected to the legislature, and had to learn two jobs – MPP and cabinet minister – simultaneously.[7] Hundreds of political staff positions had to be filled, ranging from drivers and scheduling assistants to policy advisers and executive assistants. Senior positions in the Premier's Office were vacant for weeks. The time pressures were immense. The government was sworn in on 1 October, and the legislature began its thirty-fifth session with a Speech from the Throne on 20 November, only seven weeks later. Initial tasks included getting key staff placed in ministers' offices, getting ministers and staff briefed by ministry staff, dealing with a barrage of 'can't wait' issues, and preparing for the fall session of the legislature.

The NDP was not well prepared to govern. It had given little thought to the mechanics and structure of government and no effort had been made to tie together the various strands of the party's policy prescriptions into a program for government.[8] Few within the leadership of the party or the caucus thought the NDP would ever win an election. Indeed, the party's strategists shared that view even as the 1990 campaign headed for the finish.

Election campaigns are incredibly intense, in part because of the multitude of situations requiring decisions, many of which must be taken within hours, or even minutes. The 1990 NDP campaign was typical. Despite meetings held throughout each day, in person and by phone, Saturday nights were an opportunity to assess and plan on a slightly longer scale. The Saturday evening meetings were also a chance for campaign strategists to review the results of recent polling data and try to understand overall dynamics.

At the 25 August meeting, just twelve days before the election, party pollster Dave Gotthilf delivered a bombshell: not only was the NDP campaign doing extremely well, he advised that the strategists should start thinking about an NDP minority, or possibly even a majority, government. The reaction was telling. After a moment's stunned silence, the group broke into guffaws. 'What's the matter, haven't you been paid yet?' asked the caucus research director. The meeting moved on.

The attitudinal shift required of the new government was made more difficult by the high degree of suspicion and uncertainty that existed in the early days between new ministers (and their political staff) and public servants. Blame for this falls on both sides. The public service was even less prepared than the NDP for a change of government. Before the election, much of the senior echelon of the public service had been absorbed in an internal administrative reorganization and streamlining exercise, safely assuming the Peterson Liberals would be returned to office.[9] The election result caught them completely off guard and much of the transition period was taken up by ministry staff scrambling to acquaint themselves with the *Agenda for People* and translate their own priorities into its language. The internal policy-making capacity was poorly attuned to the kind of strategic consideration of issues that the new ministers wanted.

For his part, the premier resisted advice to create a central planning secretariat, like the ones created by NDP governments in Manitoba and Saskatchewan, to act as the brain trust for the new government. Instead, he turned to several bureaucrats with prior experience working in NDP governments to create a new policy-planning and expenditure-management system. While the new system was staffed overwhelmingly by career civil servants, both the rapid promotion of several key individuals to deputy minister status and the more activist policy role assigned to staff in the central agencies aroused the suspicions of the older line bureaucrats and laid the basis for the false but often-repeated assertion that the NDP was politicizing the public service.[10]

The early weeks of the new government were largely taken up with sifting through a huge array of policy issues to prepare for its first throne speech and the treasurer's economic statement. The task facing the new cabinet was both exhilarating and exhausting. By the time the legislature resumed in November, it had hammered out an initial agenda that touched many of the bases of traditional party concern, but lacked both strategic focus and internal consistency. Furthermore, it was created without much consideration of the fiscal constraints the government would shortly have to face. The government's first economic-recovery initiative – the Anti-Recession Program – reflected its uncertainty about its future fiscal direction. Some advisers argued that the amount of stimulus (with some municipal participation, just under $1 billion) was insufficient to have much impact on the recession and that a larger package in the order of $2 billion was required to have any effect on the level of demand and employment. However, senior ministers, still in shock from their initial Treasury briefings, were reluctant to take on that degree of additional debt.

Thus, the government's initial fiscal stance set the direction it was to follow for the next two years: 'tax and spend' Keynesianism in the eyes of most business and Bay Street critics, but not sufficiently stimulative to have a real impact on unemployment in the eyes of many of the government's own supporters.

The Fateful Spring of 1991: The Suits Fight Back

The initial policy and fiscal planning decisions in the fall of 1990 set the stage for the most critical period in the NDP government's life: the fateful spring of 1991. Two fundamental policy initiatives – rent control and labour-relations reform – and the government's first budget set it on a collision course with the province's business community and began its downward slide in the opinion polls – a loss of support that proved impossible to recover from.

Legislation to enact rent control was introduced by then Minister of Housing Dave Cooke in late November 1990. Rent review initially had been introduced by the Conservatives, as a result of pressure from the NDP under Stephen Lewis before and during the 1975 election campaign. Under the law that existed in 1990, rent increases were limited to a maximum percentage amount. However, landlords could apply for increases above this amount, to pay for renovations and for new costs associated with refinancing arrangements. The issue that prompted the NDP's legislation was that landlords were obtaining approval for rent increases far in excess of the basic figure. Attacks on these rent increases and eliminating increases for capital or financing costs (strict rent controls) were prominent elements of the NDP's 1990 campaign.

However, when Bill 4 was introduced, the landlord community was outraged. First, the bill virtually eliminated their ability to go above the control figure. Second, and worse, Bill 4 denied direct cost recovery to many landlords who had already completed renovations and filed applications for rent increases based on these already incurred expenses, as well as to some of those seeking increases based on refinancing expenses. As the landlords saw it, these aspects of the legislation were punitive and unreasonable.

The landlord community quickly mobilized itself into various organizations, the biggest and most active of which was the Fair Rental Policy Organization (FRPO). The landlords represented a small proportion of the business community, but the rapidity with which they organized, the intensity with which they lobbied, and their ability to portray the government as unreasonable and their own well-heeled industry as oppressed, impressed many others. FRPO lobbied vigorously across the province throughout the spring, and while it had little impact on the legislative result, its activities set important precedents for future confrontations between the government and the business community.

While the conflict over rent control was still raging, a second point of confrontation emerged to supersede it – the issue of labour-relations reform. The question of labour-relations reform had been on the government's agenda from the outset, but initially took a back seat to a wide range of other issues. Throughout the fall of 1990 the Ministry of Labour responded enthusiastically to the election of the new government and rushed to cabinet with proposals to implement a wide range of new initiatives. These included the extension of pay equity to women excluded from existing coverage by the Pay Equity Act; improvements to the Employment Standards Act to deal more effectively with the problems of plant closures and labour adjustment; measures for improved parental leave; implementation of the NDP's commitment to raise the minimum wage to 60 per cent of the average industrial wage; and initial steps to implement the proposal of the former Premier's Council to create an Ontario Training and Adjustment Board.

While each of these initiatives accorded strongly with existing NDP policy, they seemed to delay the initial amendments to the Ontario Labour Relations Act (OLRA). By the beginning of the new year, the labour movement was growing restive at the delay in proceeding with this priority and over the early indications of how the business lobby would respond. They became convinced that the government would only get one opportunity to reform the OLRA and, accordingly, that the reform package should be as broad as possible. In a strong presentation to key members of the cabinet, the executive of the Ontario Federation of Labour indicated that its overriding priority was comprehensive reform of the OLRA and that it expected the government to proceed with it immediately.

Thus began what was to prove one of the NDP's most controversial and divisive policy initiatives. To sort out the elements of the eventual legislative package, the cabinet adopted a process involving two parallel teams of management and union labour lawyers under the chairmanship of Kevin Burkett, a well-known labour arbitrator. Not surprisingly, the Burkett process produced a stalemate. The union lawyers drafted an enormous wish list of reforms that proposed to rectify through legislation every arbitration case they had lost in the past decade and the management team called for no change at all. The result, as one seasoned observer noted, 'was not labour law reform, but labour lawyers' reform.'

Soon after their submission in April 1991, the labour groups' proposals to Burkett were circulating widely among the legal profession and the entire business community was up in arms. Because the business position was that no change was needed or justifiable, the government's very intention to proceed with any change was de facto wrong – an undemocratic 'payback' to union bosses for their support of the government, in the view of business lobbyists, like the Ontario Chamber of Commerce, who claimed to speak for the vast majority of Ontarians in opposing any change.

No less than three separate business coalitions were formed to combat the government's labour legislation, each one more virulent in its opposition to the government than the next. Leadership of the business community was quickly seized by well-established organizations such as the Ontario Chamber of Commerce and the Canadian Federation of Independent Business. Large firms like the auto makers were equally active in the campaign, and played a leadership role in the coalitions. Over the next year and a half, until Bill 40 was finally passed, the business lobby was relentless in its opposition, resorting in the final phases to an extensive advertising campaign to discredit the government's reforms that, even though they fell short of what the labour lawyers' committee had proposed to Burkett, still constituted the most advanced labour-relations regime in North America.

Much of the rhetoric of the various anti-government coalitions reflected a fundamental denial of the legitimacy of the government. Despite (or perhaps because of) this, the business campaign enjoyed overwhelming support in the media, especially the press, whose own labour practices would be strongly affected by some of the proposed reforms.[11] But the real disappointment was the lack of support from the labour movement for the proposed reforms. In the words of former OFL Vice-President Julie Davis, 'We didn't provide the kind of support we should have when they were getting the shit kicked out of them over Bill 40.'[12] This is a significant and disingenuous understatement. As soon as Bill 40 was introduced, the OFL organized a province-wide series of workshops for activists and rank-and-file unionists. Each session included a detailed comparison of 'Labour's' recommendations and the government bill, a process that, intentionally or not, created a widespread sense that the NDP had betrayed its union allies as a result of losing its nerve on the number-one priority of the labour movement. From the government's perspective, the result was attacks on two fronts. As Dave Cooke noted, 'Most of the calls I received against Bill 40 came from CAW members.'[13] The result was significant bitterness within the government over the extent to which some of its labour allies were willing not only to take the government for granted, but at the same time to publicly criticize and impute unsavoury motives to its members while it sustained an unrelenting pounding for its pro-labour initiatives.

There is no doubt that the extent and virulence of the business campaign against OLRA reform was profoundly damaging to the government's image and its standing in public opinion. The experience cast a pall over the rest of its agenda. For the remainder of its mandate, it was virtually impossible for any minister of the government to meet with business representatives without first listening to a torrent of complaints about Bill 40. In light of the speed with which the new Conservative government repealed Bill 40 in 1995 and replaced it with far more draconian measures, one is forced to wonder whether the benefits of OLRA reform were worth the political price that the government paid.

By the time the NDP government brought down its first budget on 29 April 1991, most of the business community was effectively mobilized in opposition. And, in the event some remained undecided, the budget brought them into the fray.

Through the winter of 1990–1, the inexperienced NDP cabinet struggled with the impossible task of reconciling its limitless policy agenda with the reality of recession finance. The task of deciding on a bottom line was undoubtedly complicated by the unreliability of one key element of its revenue mix, the personal income tax. As the bleak Ontario winter dragged on and the recession took its ever-mounting toll, beleaguered cabinet ministers were faced with steadily declining projections of personal income-tax revenues. Frustrated ministers finally took to asking Treasury officials at the end of each briefing whether the latest numbers would hold up any longer than the last set presented to them.[14] Partly as a result of this unanticipated revenue decline, the final deficit figure of $10 billion for 1991–2 was far beyond what had originally been contemplated.

Much academic attention has focused on the sources of the 1990s recession and on its depth and severity compared to the recession of the previous decade. While many factors contributed to its onset, one stands out – the unwavering commitment of the governor of the Bank of Canada to avoid an inflation spike in the wake of the federal government's new Goods and Services Tax. While many industrial countries in the 1980s followed a policy of targeting growth in the money supply to reduce the rate of inflation, few proceeded as boldly, or with such dire consequences for employment, as did the Bank of Canada in its late-1980s pursuit of its zero-inflation target.[15] According to the results of one econometric study, Ontario's GDP in 1991 would have been 3.3 per cent higher under an easier monetary policy, its unemployment rate 2.3 per cent lower, and the provincial deficit $5.58 billion lower as well.[16]

The negative impact of the federal government's monetary policy was further compounded by its fiscal policies, such as the decisions to impose an arbitrary cap on the funds transferred to Ontario under the Canada Assistance Plan and to freeze per-capita transfers for health care and post-secondary education. These actions would become heavy burdens for the NDP government to bear.

None the less, one key contributor to the dramatic increase in the deficit was the decision by the government to continue 'major transfers' to hospitals, colleges, universities, school boards, and municipalities at pre-recession rates. Noting the government's concern about the current economic environment, Treasurer Floyd Laughren apologetically announced increases in annual funding levels that 'may only be adequate to allow transfer agencies to maintain current levels of service.' That said, Laughren increased transfer funding, which amounts in any year to about 30 per cent of provincial expenditures, as follows for 1991–2: 9.5 per cent for hospitals; 7.9 per cent for school boards; 7.3 per cent for colleges and universities; and 5 per cent for unconditional grants to municipalities. Despite the fact that these increases were greater than the rate of inflation, the public reaction from the transfer agencies was immediate and negative: 'Municipalities fear cutbacks are inevitable';[17] 'provincial grants short by $240 million, hospitals say';[18] and 'Extra funding not enough, educators say.'[19]

In the preparation of the 1991 budget the NDP proceeded as if the recession would be over soon. Early in the budget speech, the Treasurer noted that 'a modest recovery is expected to begin later this year.'[20] In light of this innocent optimism, it is not surprising that many of the government's fiscal decisions reflected the heady days of the late 1980s rather than the harsh new realities of the 1990s. The problem with the budget was compounded by the fact that instead of making a clear and basic distinction between the discretionary and automatic components of the deficit, the Treasurer claimed ownership of the whole $10 billion. As he remarked, 'I think it is important for people to understand that we had a choice to make this year – to fight the deficit or fight the recession. We are proud to be fighting the recession.'[21]

Michael Mendelson was Deputy Cabinet Secretary throughout the NDP mandate and had previously been the Ministry of Finance Assistant Deputy Minister responsible for the budget. As he has noted regarding the 1991 budget, 'A budget consists of two things: the numbers and the explanation of the numbers ... In the 1991–92 Budget the explanation was naive and idealistic ... The Budget had a triumphalist tone, touting the government's willingness to spend now that the people's party was in power ... [T]he actual numbers in the 1991–92 Budget were not half so radical as the rhetoric backing them up. [But] ... the explanation ... was incendiary ... [An] alternative text would have spoken to the temporary nature of the deficit, blamed it on the spending of the previous government and developed a long term plan to get Ontario on the path of fiscal virtue. It would have spoken of fighting the deficit and the recession at the same time, not one rather than the other.'[22] The unexpected size of the deficit and the apparent relish with which the government accepted responsibility for it was the final straw for that portion of the business community not already mobilized in opposition. In the wake of the budget, Ontarians were treated to the spectacle of the first demonstration on the lawn of Queen's Park organized by Bay Street stockbrokers by cellular phone and fax machine![23] The budget's effect on public opinion was equally stunning. Support for the government dropped by 20 to 25 percentage points.[24] From there, the subsequent change was all downward.

Fear and Loathing at Honey Harbour:
'No' to Public Auto Insurance

While the events of the spring and early summer of 1991 ended the NDP's honeymoon in the public-opinion polls and mobilized business opposition against it, the government could still claim a high approval rating from its own followers. This support suffered a major setback with the reversal of its stand on public automobile insurance in September. The NDP had been committed to a policy of public auto insurance from its origins; in 1948, the leader of the Ontario CCF (Cooperative Commonwealth Federation, the forerunner of the NDP) included it in a list of first-term reforms to be undertaken by a CCF government.[25] For years, enthusiasm for the issue was sporadic. Interest picked up in the mid-1980s, as claims costs began to accelerate and court awards made liability issues serious business for individuals and many public and private organizations.

Auto insurance was a textbook example of opposition issue development. Although the policy prescribed a monopoly public provider, the insurance industry itself was ignored, except for its reported profits and the prices it charged consumers. Auto insurance was almost exclusively a pocketbook issue – a question of consumer ripoff by large, wealthy companies. In opposition, the NDP frequently used auto insurance in its membership mailings, and in other kinds of organizing and fund-raising. Always, the pitch was the same. Public auto insurance would save Ontarians money, because a public insurer would not have to return a profit to its citizen 'shareholders,' a single carrier would eliminate duplicate administrative structures maintained by each of dozens of existing auto-insurance companies, and a province-wide pool would lower costs even more. There would be little job loss, it was felt, because the agents, adjusters, and other insurance-company employees would be picked up by the new agency.

The question of tort – that is, the right to sue – became a hot issue with the Liberal government's virtual elimination of that right in 1989. At that point, and without any real analysis of the proposition, the NDP became the champion of the right of 'innocent accident victims' to sue. Because pre-existing access to the courts was being restricted by the government of the day, the NDP caucus felt no ambivalence about trumpeting the sanctity of the legal process, despite their rejection of the same argument when it came to workplace injury and disease. However, this is only one aspect of a much bigger problem inherent in the caucus and the party's handling of the public auto insurance issue. The bigger problem was that almost no work had been done beyond a fuzzy definition of a problem and the equally fuzzy identification of public auto insurance as an appropriate solution. Certainly, no one ever thought hard about how an industry involving many thousands of individuals in dozens of companies and hundreds of locations would be transformed into what amounted to a public utility.

In fact, public auto insurance had pretty much been a sleeper between 1987 and 1990. The NDP had made much of the issue during the 1987 election, to the extent that Premier David Peterson had proclaimed in the dying days of the campaign that he had 'a very specific plan to lower auto insurance rates.' Well, he didn't, and auto insurance as an issue between 1987 and 1990 became a question of successive Liberal ministers trying to control rates without controlling the industry. Because the issue had acquired almost mystical status as a symbol of NDP opposition to big, profit-gouging corporations on behalf of the Ontario Everyman, the authors of the *Agenda for People* never hesitated to include public auto insurance in what became the new government's unwitting platform.

Delivering on the promise was another matter. The public service had some, but not nearly enough, capacity to address the design of the policy, and a new auto-insurance review group was assembled. Many tricky decisions about basic policy elements had to be resolved before actuarial projections of the cost of various options could be done. Only then could decisions about benefit levels, tort thresholds, and acceptable rate increases and so on be made, and all of these considerations were logically prior to the overarching go/no-go decision and the nightmare of trying to make operational whatever scheme resulted.

Within six months, the minister responsible, Peter Kormos, knew the circle could not be squared. Years of pious pronouncements did not make the actuarial calculations come out any differently. Within the current pricing universe, you could have public delivery and improved benefits or a restored right to sue, but not both. Tort was a big problem in terms of cost. Restoring full access or even significantly greater access than the Liberal law allowed would eat up any savings that would flow from having a monopoly carrier for basic coverage.

When Kormos was dropped from cabinet in March 1991, it was surely a relief to him that he did not have to explain to his cabinet colleagues that they would have to choose between the traditional promise (better benefits delivered through a public provider), his own hobbyhorse (full tort access), and increasing the costs of auto insurance for Ontarians. Certainly, his officials were relieved that they would no longer bear the brunt of his frustration at their conclusions. In any event, the hardworking new minister, Brian Charlton, soon produced solidly grounded alternatives for discussion, and began a series of long discussions at cabinet's Policy and Priorities Board designed to secure ministerial approval for the many elements of the nascent public auto insurance scheme.

By late spring, it was clear that the issue was going to be traumatic. In essence, what had been promised could not be delivered to consumers at the current price, or even for 5 or 10 per cent more. As officials were given more options to examine and more questions to consider, a complex web of technical and political questions grew up around the basic dilemma.

For some, the benefits/public delivery/price conundrum was the end of the issue: the whole point had been financial benefits for consumers. If that could not be done, the policy ought to be rejected. For others, delivering a public auto scheme had become a political necessity; for them, the issue was what compromises would have to be made at what financial and political cost to deliver a credible plan to the people of Ontario.

Other issues arose. It was possible that the U.S. industry would sue for loss of business under the Canada-U.S. Free Trade Agreement, for hundreds of millions or even billions of dollars. It was clear that any effort to establish a public-insurance agency would be punctuated by well-orchestrated demonstrations by members of the industry's largely female workforce who would certainly be portrayed by the media as being thrown into the street by an ideology-mad government. There were those who worried about whether the government would be able to deliver on its plans if the industry decided to go to war. Here the thinking was that the opening volley would be a refusal to provide company-held information that was the only reliable basis for the new corporation's rate structure.

Still others reasoned that with 6.5 million drivers in the province, an error rate of even one-tenth of 1 per cent (an absurdly low figure in a system of this size and complexity) would mean 6500 horror stories that could be used by the opposition, the business press, and the rest of the media as constant reminders of NDP idiocy and ineptitude. And, they continued, these stories would be emerging just ahead of the next election. Did the government really want an immediate war of attrition that would continue unabated for the next three and a half years, followed by an election campaign dominated by all the arguments the government had used in opposition against previous government defenders of big, stupid, rate-gouging insurance companies?

These considerations were real. But none of them was decisive on its own; each could be addressed, more or less effectively. The more compelling fact was that (according to survey research) most people were not clamouring for public auto insurance. For the vast majority of Ontarians, it was not an issue of significant concern. And it was the government's sincere belief that because most Ontarians were not very interested in public auto insurance, they were unlikely to accept a new, billion-dollar initiative that would raise the cost of their car insurance and cost thousands of women their jobs.

At a news conference at its caucus retreat in Honey Harbour on the first anniversary of its election, the government announced that because of the cost and the job loss involved, it had decided it could not justify proceeding with public auto insurance. The dollar figure was as much as $1 billion, including one-time start-up costs; as many as 18,000 jobs were at risk. In the midst of a major recession, the premier and his ministers said, this was indefensible.

The ideological fireworks were blinding. Key party spokespersons decried the flip-flop, the timidity, the sell-out, the betrayal, the turning away from fundamental principle, the cowardly flight from confrontation with the insurance industry and from the threat of action under the

Free Trade Agreement. In some quarters of the party, the government's explanation was simply not accepted. Many supporters who were prepared to accept the decision were enraged by the premier's statement that rather than being a temporary delay in going ahead with a sound policy that had been a victim of bad timing, this was a matter that his government would not consider again, period.

In many ways, the decision not to proceed with public auto insurance exemplifies the different demands of opposition and government. The logic of opposition, at least as the NDP had defined it, was rigidly black and white. For many New Democrats, the wrenching disappointment of the government's decision was only part of a bigger, scarier, and rarely articulated concern. If it really made no sense to proceed with public auto insurance, how was one to regard the many years of organizing around the issue? If public auto insurance was a bad idea, how had it survived twenty years in opposition? No, it was easier to believe the government was lying.

What the cabinet was able to do – recognize and act on a public interest seen to have a prior claim over a deeply held desire of the party faithful – is fundamental to governing and something many in the party were unwilling to do. Privately, Premier Rae said his ministers had become a government in the process. Of course, this could not be said publicly.

The Struggle for Policy Coherence

One of the additional challenges for the NDP was coordinating its longer-term economic strategy with the more immediate crises of the recession and its fiscal constraints. In part, the government was fighting a battle on two fronts. One involved a long-term structural adjustment to the emerging, technology-intensive economy, a wrenching change that was magnified by the impact of the Canada-U.S. Free Trade Agreement. The other and more immediate challenge was responding to the devastating impact of the recession.

The government tried to proceed on both fronts at once and discovered, to its great unhappiness, that its fiscal circumstances tended to make this a lose/lose exercise. On the one hand, the gains from its longer-term initiatives were slow to develop and hard to discern among all the other economic processes at work; on the other, it was hard to show flashy counter-cyclical results in a period of declining revenues. Further, the longer-term issues were constantly overshadowed by the management of crises that preoccupied the premier and the Ministry of

Industry. Throughout 1991 and 1992, much of their attention was absorbed by a series of government-supported rescues of individual firms – Spruce Falls Pulp and Paper in Kapuskasing, Algoma Steel in Sault Ste Marie, de Havilland in Metropolitan Toronto, and the Provincial Papers Mill in Thunder Bay. As critical as each of these rescues was to the economy of the local community, and despite the thousands of jobs saved in the process, it quickly became apparent that the government could not preserve the Ontario economy one firm at a time.

The government's first attempt to set out its longer-term strategy was the budget of April 1991. Budget Paper E, 'Ontario in the 1990s,' established sustainable prosperity based on equitable structural change as the government's goal. The paper recognized that competitiveness was important to attaining this objective, but argued that it could best be realized through the creation of high-value-added, high-wage jobs and strategic partnerships. The most important adjustment challenge in the 1990s was to increase the overall productivity of Ontario's economy. The key to increased productivity did not lie in minimizing cost levels for the existing mix of product and processes, but in fostering productive systems that promote continuous improvement in products and processes across the networks of firms and sectors in the provincial economy. The budget paper also argued that any successful high-wage, high-value-added economic strategy must be based on a defence, and extension, of social equity to generate the required degree of social cohesion.[26]

These themes were reinforced and expanded in 'Investing in Tomorrow's Jobs,' a supplementary paper to the 1992 budget that outlined the series of economic policies being implemented to move towards these goals. These included enhanced measures for labour-market training and adjustment; the creation of an Ontario Training and Adjustment Board; improvements in the area of social infrastructure, especially child-care facilities and affordable housing; a strategic program of investments to upgrade the province's physical infrastructure; a regional-development strategy to ensure that communities were involved in the process; and measures to finance investments in more innovative and knowledge-based types of production, including support for worker ownership and the creation of an Ontario Lead Investment Fund.

The government adopted the phrase 'economic renewal' to describe the programs designed to foster the long-term restructuring of the provincial economy towards the creation of more well-paying, high-value-added jobs. Thus, its economic-renewal agenda aimed to promote a highly qualified labour force, strategic investments by firms in higher-value-added activities, and investment by government in the necessary social and physical infrastructure. At the centre of the economic-renewal agenda was the Industrial Policy Framework, released in July 1992 by the Minister of Industry, Trade and Technology.

By the time the government's industrial-policy framework was made public, the NDP's major challenge was generalized business hostility. This was not balanced by internal enthusiasm: the government's supporters had only limited interest in the formulation of industrial and technology policy. While they endorsed the idea of an industrial policy in principle, their primary concerns were the labour, social, and justice policy issues that affected their members most directly.

Federally and provincially, the NDP had long advocated the adoption of an industrial strategy, but was vague on specifics.[27] There was little active consideration by the ministers of the new government of the policy resolutions adopted at party conventions. The political advisers and senior bureaucrats with responsibility for economic policy were predisposed towards the arguments of the former Premier's Council in favour of shifting Ontario's economy towards high-wage, high-value-added activities, but were also sensitive to the labour movement's critique of the Premier's Council Report.[28] Some of these issues had been explored through the economic-policy review coordinated between 1988 and 1990 by the then Treasury critic, Floyd Laughren. The ideas developed in this review formed the backdrop for the evolution of the NDP's industrial and technology policies.[29]

The overall goal of the framework was to promote the transition of the Ontario economy towards those sectors and firms with the capacity to generate high-wage, high-value-added, and environmentally sustainable jobs. The framework focused on ways of developing higher-value-added activities throughout the economy. The most significant change was the emphasis placed on working with economic sectors. The approach adopted in the Industrial Policy Framework built on the argument that the institutional infrastructure of a sector can constitute an important source of competitive advantage. Through cooperation with other firms in a sector, individual firms may be able to accomplish projects that would be too large for them to contemplate individually or they may be able to create infrastructure that will potentially benefit a wide range of firms in the sector.

The Sector Partnership Fund (SPF) announced in the budget of April 1992 was a three-(later extended to six-)year initiative, budgeted at $150 million, and designed to implement the sectoral component of the

Industrial Policy Framework. The SPF provided assistance to approved cooperative projects that led to high-value-added activities. The SPF required that all labour-market partners be involved. Industry associations, labour organizations, and other stakeholders were encouraged to consult in the identification of common challenges and the development of strategies for submission to the government.[30]

Between the summer of 1992 and the election in June 1995, the Ministry of Economic Development and Trade and other ministries worked with a wide range of industry associations and trade unions to develop these strategies. In each case, the consultative efforts were broad and inclusive, drawing in as many as one hundred and fifty individuals to prepare detailed analyses of sectoral strengths and weaknesses and propose a course of action. In total, the approach involved twenty-eight different sectors and over two thousand individual participants, drawn from twenty-two different unions, ninety-three industry associations, and twenty-eight universities and colleges. This was a major accomplishment given the continuing opposition by industry to the government's key equity initiatives.

The long-term benefit of the sector strategy is less clear. While the strategy-formulation process succeeded beyond the government's expectations, it proved more difficult to launch sound initiatives that could access the Sector Partnership Fund. In the end, tangible results were too few and came too late in the government's mandate to offset the damage already done by its conflicts with the business community during the first two years.[31]

The Fiscal Challenge Continues

The NDP government continued to struggle with the level of public spending throughout its term. One of the NDP's earliest fiscal accomplishments was getting health-care costs under control. When it took office, hospital spending had been increasing by an average of 9.7 per cent a year and OHIP spending had been going up by 12 per cent annually. Overall Ministry of Health expenditures rose by 11.2 per cent a year between 1981 and 1991. In 1992–3, total ministry funding went up only 2 per cent, and by 1995, the annual OHIP increase was under 2.2 per cent.

Unwilling to cut public spending in an arbitrary, across-the-board fashion, the government tried to target its reductions more selectively using a centralized process of Corporate Expenditure Reviews coordinated by the newly created Treasury Board.[32] While these succeeded in reining in the rate at which the deficit was growing, they had little effect in actually reducing it.

Expenditure control was practised on other fronts as well. In contrast to the position of the preceding year, Floyd Laughren reluctantly announced in January 1992 that the government could not afford significant increases in major transfers. 'One of the more difficult decisions' in grappling with a decrease in provincial revenues in absolute terms was that transfer increases in the next three years would be held to 1, 2, and 2 per cent. The Treasurer's announcement coincided with a prime-time TV address by premier Rae, which did much to open up the budget process and decision making to public scrutiny. The premier noted presciently that 'we didn't get into this mess in a day, and we won't get out of it in a day either.'[33]

In late November 1992, Laughren announced that provincial transfers would rise by 2 per cent in 1993–4, as announced previously, but that this would be a one-time payment and would not become part of base funding. In addition, the final 2 per cent increase (in the earlier 1–2–2 announcement) would not occur. The reason, Laughren said, was simple. Even though 'operating expenditures for 1993–94 are on track, revenues are now projected to be $4.2 billion less than planned.'[34]

By early 1993, the government became convinced that even tougher measures were required. At a news conference on 30 March, the premier and the minister of finance announced that $1.5 billion in spending-reduction decisions already taken would lower year-over-year operating-cost increases to 3 per cent. However, 'with revenues stagnant, unless we take stronger measures, the deficit will rise from approximately $12 billion in this year, to about $17 billion in 1993–94,' Floyd Laughren said.

In addition to the alarming size of the deficit in absolute terms, continuing weak revenues meant that without action to counter it, the proportion of revenue committed to servicing the debt would rise dramatically. Worse was the possibility of a debt trap: a situation where indebtedness consumes such a large proportion of revenue that borrowing costs grow out of control and the ability to manage the economy is lost. As the premier and minister explained, Ontario was spending about 13 cents of every revenue dollar on public-debt interest. In three years, that could rise to 26 cents. Ontario was already the largest non-sovereign borrower in the world.[35]

In addition to the spending reductions totalling $1.5 billion that had already been decided on, the government announced a new three-part fiscal strategy, each element of which was targeted to achieve an additional $2 billion in expenditure savings. The first part of the deficit-reduction strategy was the Expenditure Control Plan (ECP), a month-long process conducted in March and April 1993 and coordinated by staff of the Treasury Board Secretariat and Cabinet Office. Recommendations emerging from this process were approved at a weekend-long meeting of the full cabinet and all deputy ministers. The combined savings of the earlier expenditure reductions and the ECP exercise provided total savings of $4 billion in the fiscal plan for 1993–4.[36]

The second part of the strategy involved raising additional revenue through tax and non-tax revenue measures, including asset sales. In total, the first three NDP budgets raised annual tax revenues by a cumulative $2.945 billion in 1993 – the largest three-year tax increase in the history of the province. The 1993 budget also contained $240 million in new, non-tax revenue items. Overall, the impact of the tax measures was highly progressive, with higher-income earners paying a higher proportion of their incomes in taxes than lower- and middle-income earners.[37]

None the less, it is likely that few Ontario voters felt these increases were what was meant by the pledge of 'fair taxes' made in the *Agenda for People*. Further, despite the creation of the Ontario Fair Tax Commission in 1990 and its production of a mountain of quality research, analysis, consultation, and recommendations, the NDP government failed to deliver on large-scale reform of the tax system.[38] In the end, it is likely that many taxpayers anticipating tax relief felt betrayed by the NDP. Even though a two-income family of four earning $60,000 faced tax increases totalling less than $7 per week, the bottom line for average working people in Ontario was that under the NDP their wages had continued to decline and their taxes had continued to go up.[39] Their frustration contributed substantially to the popular appeal of the Conservatives' pledge in the *Common Sense Revolution* to reduce taxes.

The Social Contract was the most innovative and volatile of the three strategic elements. It is worth noting how the government presented it to the first meeting of employer and employee representatives of the broader public sector on 5 April 1993. According to premier Rae,

Unless we reduce operating costs through restructuring and reforming government departments and programs and through agreements with public sector employers and employees, we will no longer be able to afford the level of public investment Ontario needs in jobs, training and capital to meet the economic challenges of the 1990s.

... I have been asked how we will protect jobs ... The answer is simple: if we don't do anything to get government costs under control now when we have a chance to use early retirement and voluntary exit options and retraining and other mechanisms to downsize, many, many more public service jobs will be in jeopardy down the road. They will be in jeopardy because our fiscal situation is not sustainable.

From the government's perspective, the social contract was a defensive measure. It was a way to protect jobs and services to people in a circumstance of dramatic spending cuts in the broader public sector. This was not how it was received, of course. Many of the participants, and certainly most of the unions, did not embrace the assumptions behind the government's analysis. CUPE even commissioned Informetrica, a respected Ottawa-based econometric consulting firm, to produce an 'alternative economic and fiscal forecast for Ontario.'[40] For many of the unions, whatever they felt about the technical economics, the process was flawed and, to the extent that the government had indicated its intention to proceed in the absence of a negotiated agreement, a sham.

After a tumultuous two months of bargaining, negotiations broke down when the union participants walked out on the evening of 3 June, a day ahead of the government's deadline. On 14 June, the government introduced legislation to freeze wages and benefits and impose unpaid holidays (subsequently known as 'Rae days'), unless agreements to achieve targeted savings based on the government's objectives could be negotiated sectorally or locally. If such agreements could be made, the savings target of the sector would be reduced. Whether through negotiations or legislation, the cost-savings targets had to be met, while minimizing job loss; exempting workers earning less than $30,000; not affecting pay equity; giving workers the chance to move into suitable vacancies in their own or other sectors if they were laid off; and setting up a training and adjustment plan for laid-off workers.

The Social Contract (Bill 48) became law in early July. Most sectors produced agreements before the 'fail-safe' deadline and, over the following year, the process produced the desired level of savings. The Social Contract expired on 1 April 1996. There were strong, even compelling arguments in its favour: it would save many thousands of jobs in the Ontario public service and the so-called broader public sector (hospitals, colleges, universities, school boards, municipalities, and so on); it exempted those at the low end of the income spectrum from wage cuts; it would preserve public services; it established the basis for sector-wide mechanisms that would facilitate future adjustment and restructuring. Finally, it built a notion of social solidarity into public-sector compensation issues – a most important innovation in view of other, hostile notions about the value of public-sector workers and publicly delivered services. In other circumstances, one can imagine the Ontario labour movement buying into such a set of ideas. It may be that a longer, less coercive, and more open-ended process could have produced some accommodation between the government's desire to reduce public-sector compensation costs and the raison d'être of organized labour, free collective bargaining.

According to the government's critics on the left, the passage of the Social Contract represented the nadir of the NDP's betrayal of its principles and its allies. For some, the most insidious aspect of the Social Contract was the way it tried to conceal coercion as consent. In the eyes of these critics, labelling the process a social contract was itself an act of Orwellian double-speak. 'The very fact that the term "agreements" was used, suggesting that the reopening of contracts was "freely negotiated," was a measure of the debasement of language involved in the whole process.'[41]

For many NDP supporters, the Social Contract was the last straw. Especially in the trade-union movement, it set off a firestorm. Ontario NDP President Julie Davis, Secretary-Treasurer of the OFL, resigned. The OFL convention passed a resolution condemning the government and pledging non-support for its re-election. Most of the major private-sector unions (excluding the Canadian Autoworkers) had already left the floor of the convention, rather than participate in a debate they could not win. For the remaining life of the government, a chasm persisted between the Ontario Public Sector Employees Union (OPSEU), the Canadian Union of Public Employees (CUPE), and the Autoworkers on one side, committed to non-support of the government, and most of the private-sector unions, especially the Steelworkers, Communications, Energy and Paperworkers, United Food and Commercial Workers, Machinists, and Service Employees on the other. The bottom line for the latter group, known as the 'pink' unions, after the colour of paper their statement of position had been printed on at the OFL convention, was that the NDP government's positive accomplishments and its basic progressive commitments by far outweighed the disappointment it had caused for labour supporters, and therefore it deserved continuing support, especially in view of the alternatives and what their election would mean for working people. As they expressed their position: 'It is our conviction that labour's potential as a force for real change, for fairness for workers and their families, is absolutely inseparable from its role as a key partner within social democracy as an electorally-competitive political force. The New Democratic Party must remain labour's central pivot point in the political arena. And labour in turn must re-examine its own linkages with its membership base, to rekindle, spread and strengthen the social democratic values that too few of our members recognize as their own today.'[42]

A year after the election of the Harris Conservatives, more than 10,000 civil servants had received layoff notices. It is possible that more than 10,000 teachers will face layoffs over the next year or two. Fees are increasing dramatically at colleges and universities, and municipalities are under steadily increasing pressure to cut local services. It strains understanding that for many in the labour movement the breaking point for support of the NDP government was a set of measures designed to avert exactly such a turn of events, and that one of the results of the withdrawal of labour support for the NDP government was the election of a PC government. Politically, the Social Contract was a mixed success, mostly outside NDP circles. On the one hand, it occasioned much comment expressing admiration for premier Rae's willingness to do the right thing, although this likely did little to change voting intentions among Liberal and Tory partisans. On the other, it certainly hurt morale within the party. It is also likely that 'soft' voters were not impressed by the spectacle of the government engaged in close combat with former supporters.

By the beginning of 1994, most of the government's economic agenda was in place. Indeed, there was a concerted effort throughout 1994 to limit new demands on the government's policy-development apparatus and concentrate on implementation and communication. A leaked memo, dated 15 March 1994, from Cabinet Secretary David Agnew to all ministers and deputy ministers, detailed the government's efforts to bring 'the Government's policy agenda onto a manageable and strategic footing.' The document contained four lists of policy items: those considered to be 'strategic'; those already being implemented, considered essential, or routine, business-of-government matters; a few conditional items; and a long list of 'others.' Items in this category were to be abandoned or managed in such a way that 'there are: (i) no substantive policy decisions required over the next 12–18 months; (ii) no medium- or high-profile communications; and (iii) no further fiscal resources sought.'[43]

The economic policy-development apparatus essentially shut down in

1994, and much of its resources were redeployed. Those that remained concentrated on issues of implementation and communication. Work continued in other policy areas, but it was narrowly focused as required by the Agnew memo. The government's energies clearly were being focused on the election to come in 1995. There was only an abbreviated legislative session in the fall of 1994, and the Legislative Assembly was not recalled in the spring. Instead, the government released a Budget Plan and called an election in late April for 8 June.

Conclusion

The 1995 election was a curious spectacle. The NDP government, frustrated by years of bad economic circumstances and forced to compromise, trade off, or scale back almost every item of its almost boundless agenda, ran a campaign that was almost totally 'inside' – that is, it confused its own remarkably difficult odyssey and the record of its own accomplishments in addressing difficult issues with what voters cared about. In doing so, it ignored the fact that for many people – and likely its own core supporters – the previous five years had not been a very positive experience and, to the extent that people's minds were not yet made up, the key to their hearts would be a positive vision of good times to come. The last thing recession-weary voters wanted was a cataloguing of all the tough times they had endured.

The real interest became sorting out the voter appeal of the Liberal and Tory campaigns. In fact, after floundering ineffectually, the Liberal campaign sank like a stone, and by late May it was clear that a Tory majority was in the works. From our perspective, this was not surprising. The source of NDP strength in 1990 – its ability to tap into voter anger and anxiety and portray its opponents as part of the problem – was exactly the thrust of the Tories' *Common Sense Revolution*, released more than a year before the campaign. In fact, revolution is not very accurate as a description of the outcome. Rather, June 1995 marked the beginning of a Tory Restoration, designed at root to restore the smaller, more timid, and less interventionist state of a generation before.

On the fundamental question of whether different choices could have averted the government's defeat in 1995, we are ambivalent. Even with the benefit of hindsight, it is not clear that the NDP ministers would have taken the decisions necessary to avoid the collapse of public support. This is not because of a lack of intelligence, bad advice, or the 'blinker' effects of ideology (the adherence to socialist principles to the detriment of a balanced economy, as some on the right believe, or a naïve adoption of reactionary and anti-labour views, as some on the left aver). Rather, it reflects two basic aspects of Ontario's first NDP government.

First, throughout its roller-coaster history, the government truly believed it was doing the best job possible. Certainly, a different ideological perspective would have produced a different array of choices, but very few government decisions ever were made for ideological or political, as opposed to substantively compelling policy, reasons. The other reason is that the government was in large measure a creation of its opposition-party past. The view of the world it had developed outside government was an obstacle that took almost half its mandate to overcome. In the meantime, the government missed major opportunities, took wrong directions, and pretty consistently squandered its political capital.

It would be wrong and shortsighted to view the Rae government as a failure. In the midst of a terrible recession, it demonstrated an admirable ability to ignore fashionable nostrums and, for the first time in at least a generation, account for and begin to address structural issues in the Ontario political economy. It made Ontario society fairer and more compassionate in a number of ways, including welfare support, pay equity, employment equity, advocacy for vulnerable and disabled people, child care, the minimum wage, and long-term care. It showed that there were alternatives to the 'slash and burn' approach to public fiscal management by maintaining the jobs of public-service providers and protecting services to people in need. Political winds blow from various quarters; having put these items credibly 'on the table,' the Rae government guaranteed they would return.

For the foreseeable future, the NDP government likely changed the role of opposition party, if not for others than certainly for itself. Having been in government, the NDP cannot revert to the tunnel vision of its 1980s approach. Knowing from first-hand experience the contours and constraints of power, it will not soon revert to the black-and-white world of opposition orthodoxy. For some in the party, whose frustration with the years in government turned to relief in the aftermath of the government's defeat, and for whom a new Tory government meant a resumption of comfortable, mid-1980s-style moralizing, the new realities of post-government opposition likely will be nearly as hard to face as coming to grips with political power. The task of crafting an opposition party combining passion and pragmatism will ensure a busy time for NDP leader Howard Hampton, who in June 1996 succeeded Bob Rae.

Notes

1 Stephen A. Marglin and Juliet B. Schor, eds, *The Golden Age of Capitalism, Reinterpreting the Postwar Experience* (Oxford: Clarendon Press, 1991); Jeffrey Madrick, *The End of Affluence* (New York: Random House, 1995).
2 Statistics Canada, *Income Distribution by Size in Canada, 1994,* Catalogue 13-207 (Ottawa, 1995), 18–19.
3 Economic Council of Canada, *Good Jobs, Bad Jobs: Employment in the Service Economy* (Ottawa: Supply and Services Canada, 1990), 10–13.
4 René Morissette, John Myles, and Garnett Picot, 'Earnings Polarization in Canada, 1969–1991,' in Keith G. Banting and Charles M. Beach, eds, *Labour Market Polarization and Social Policy Reform* (Kingston: School of Policy Studies, Queen's University, 1995), 43.
5 Alan Ernst, 'Towards a Progressive Competitiveness: Economic Policy and the Ontario New Democrats, 1988–1995,' paper presented to the Annual Meeting of the Canadian Political Science Association, Université du Québec à Montréal, 5 June 1995; Thomas Walkom, *Rae Days: The Rise and Follies of the NDP* (Toronto: Key Porter Books, 1994), 96–101.
6 The provincial election on 2 May 1985 gave the governing Conservatives 37 per cent of the votes and 52 of 125 seats. The Liberals got 38 per cent of the vote and 48 seats. In the weeks following election day, representatives of the NDP held discussions with the Conservatives and the Liberals. On 28 May, Liberal leader David Peterson and NDP leader Bob Rae signed 'An Agenda for Reform: Proposals for Minority Government.' The agreement, known generally as the 'Accord,' provided for two years of Liberal government, during which the Liberals would not seek and the NDP would not cause a dissolution of the legislature. It further committed the two parties to a large number of legislative reforms, on which they agreed in significant measure, 'within a framework of fiscal responsibility.' These included implementation of full funding for Roman Catholic separate secondary schools; a ban on extra billing by doctors; increased tenant protection; what became pay equity in both public and private sectors; first-contract arbitration; day-care reform; affirmative action and employment equity; workers' compensation reform; and occupational health and safety reform. It is important to understand that the Accord did not constitute a coalition: the Liberals alone

were the government. It is also important to note that the question of coalition was almost as divisive in 1985 as were the compromises the Rae government was forced to make subsequent to the 1990 election. Some in the NDP, including Bob Rae and key caucus members, supported the notion of a full-fledged coalition. For others, the idea of a coalition was anathema. It is telling that many of those who were adamantly opposed to the thinking behind the idea of a coalition with the Liberals also found the realities of NDP government extremely hard to deal with.

7 There were some unintentionally funny moments, including when one newly elected minister asked the Cabinet Secretary whether a duplicate cabinet binder could be provided to her spouse, so he could help her with some of the issues.

8 Through the 1980s the NDP had neither a program nor an election-time platform, except as defined by notions such as 'making the changes that put people first' or 'fighting for ordinary working people.' The so-called *Agenda for People* – seen after the fact as the NDP's program for governing – was mostly a compilation of demands that had been articulated in the daily Question Period over the previous year. However much the party faithful, the media, and voters saw it as a program, it was designed as little more than an election ploy. The NDP's 1990 campaign strategy was intended to be unremittingly negative. It was to focus on the shortcomings of the Peterson Liberals to the exclusion of any discussion of positive ideas. The *Agenda for People* was written solely to satisfy the demands, most of which were coming from party activists and the media, for a positive statement of party policy. Central to the decision to produce the *Agenda* was that it would be released the day before the mid-campaign party leaders' debate. The intent was two-fold: the release of the document would deflect the criticism that the party had made no statement of its intentions as a government; and, with any luck, this lone positive NDP statement would be submerged in the wake of media coverage of the debate, having served its entire intended purpose in the previous 24 hours.

9 Evert Lindquist and Graham White, 'Streams, Springs, and Stones: Ontario Public Service Reform in the 1980s and the 1990s,' *Canadian Public Administration* 37, no. 2 (Summer 1994): 279–85.

10 David A. Wolfe, 'The Policy-making System – Old and New,' in Sid Noel, ed., *Revolution at Queen's Park* (Halifax: Lorimer, 1997).

11 Walkom, *Rae Days*, 127ff.

12 Ibid., 130.

13 Ibid., 129.

14 Some historical perspective is helpful in judging the impact of the recession

on government revenues. At the bottom of the previous recession, in 1982–3, government revenue did not fall. It rose by 8.8 per cent. From 1980–5, revenues went up an average of 11.2 per cent annually. From 1985–90, the annual average increase was 12.4 per cent. The worst year for the Peterson Liberals was 1987–8: revenues rose by only 10.1 per cent. The 1990 Liberal budget predicted revenues of $44.5 billion. In fact, they were $42.9. In the NDP government's first full fiscal year, 1991–2, revenues declined by more than an additional $2 billion.

15 Pierre Fortin, 'The Unbearable Lightness of Zero-Inflation Optimism,' *Canadian Business Economics* 1, no. 3 (Spring 1993): 3–18; M.C. McCracken, 'Recent Canadian Monetary Policy: Deficit and Debt Implication,' in Lars Osberg and Pierre Fortin, eds, *Unnecessary Debts* (Toronto: James Lorimer 1996), 71–89.

16 Ernie Stokes and Odarka Koshyk, *The Provincial Economic Impact of Tight Monetary Policy* (Toronto: WEFA Canada, May 1993).

17 *Toronto Sun*, 12 February 1991.

18 *Toronto Star*, 12 February 1991.

19 *Globe and Mail*, 12 February 1991.

20 Floyd Laughren, *1991 Ontario Budget* (Toronto: Queen's Printer for Ontario), 2.

21 Ibid., 3. The automatic components include revenue losses as a result of the lower level of economic activity. The most significant elements are personal income tax, retail sales tax, corporation income tax, and land-transfer tax. On the expenditure side, there were increased costs owing to the appropriate functioning of the 'social safety net.' These included higher welfare benefits and increased costs of hospital care and Drug Benefit Plan claims. Discretionary components of the deficit refer to the costs of new initiatives, including improved welfare benefits.

22 'The "Three Horsemen" of the NDP Apocalypse,' paper presented to the Queen's University School of Policy Studies Lecture Series, Kingston, 13 October 1995.

23 Mildred A. Schwartz, *North American Social Democracy in the 1990s: The NDP in Ontario*, Canadian American Public Policy paper no. 17 (Orono, Me.: Canadian-American Center, University of Maine, April 1994), 13.

24 According to Decima Research, 60 per cent of Ontarians were satisfied with the NDP government in March 1991. This fell to 35 per cent by June. *Decima Quarterly Report: Public Affairs Trends* 12, no. 1 (Spring 1991) and no. 2 (Summer 1991). According to Environics Research, the March to June 1991 drop was from 48 to 28 per cent. *Focus Ontario Report*, 1991–1 and 1991–2.

25 Cited in George Ehring and Wayne Roberts, *Giving Away a Miracle: Lost*

Dreams, Broken Promises and the Ontario NDP (Oakville: Mosaic Press, 1993), 183.

26 Floyd Laughren, 'Ontario in the 1990s: Promoting Equitable Structural Change,' *Budget Paper E, 1991 Ontario Budget* (Toronto: Queen's Printer for Ontario), 85–101. For a fuller discussion of these themes, cf. Ernst, 'Towards a Progressive Competitiveness' (note 5, above).

27 For an elaboration of the Ontario caucus's mid-1980s view, see Chuck Rachlis and David Robertson, 'The NDP: Replying to Laxer,' *Canadian Forum* 64, no. 740 (June–July 1984): 10–14.

28 Ontario Premier's Council, *People and Skills in the New Global Economy* (Toronto: Queen's Printer, 1990); Ontario Federation of Labour, 'The Report of the Premier's Council on Education, Training and Adjustment: Comment and Review' (mimeo), July 1990; Hugh Mackenzie, 'Dealing with the New Global Economy: What the Premier's Council Overlooked,' in Daniel Drache, with John O'Grady, ed., *Getting on Track: Social Democratic Strategies for Ontario* (Montreal and Kingston: Canadian Centre for Policy Alternatives and McGill-Queen's University Press, 1992), 5–16.

29 Ernst, 'Towards a Progessive Competitiveness,' 4–14; Walkom, *Rae Days*, 92–6; Jane Jenson and Rianne Mahon, 'From "Premier Bob" to "Rae Days": The Impasse of the Ontario New Democrats,' in Jean-Pierre Beaud and Jean-Guy Prévost, eds, *La social-démocratie en cette fin de siècle* (Sainte Foy: Presses de l'Université du Québec, 1996).

30 The quasi-corporatist nature of this approach initially caused some problems. In some sectors, which were not highly unionized, employers and industry associations were initially reluctant to involve representatives of trade unions. On the other hand, some unions, particularly the Canadian Auto Workers, have traditionally been quite critical of corporatist approaches to both industrial and training policy. Despite these initial objections, both employers and labour representatives were actively involved in all the sectors where strategy development took place.

31 For a fuller discussion of the sector strategies, see David A. Wolfe, 'Negotiating Order: The Sectoral Approach to Industrial Policy in Ontario,' paper presented to annual meeting of the Canadian Political Science Association, Brock University, St Catharines, Ontario, 2 June 1996.

32 Jay Kaufman, 'Program Review in Ontario,' in Amelita Armit and Jacques Bourgault, eds, *Hard Choices or No Choices: Assessing Program Review,* Monographs on Canadian Public Administration no. 17 (Toronto: Institute of Public Administration of Canada and Regina: Canadian Plains Research Centre), 91–102.

33 Press release, 21 January 1992.

34 Press release, 26 November 1992.

35 One little-appreciated aspect of the NDP government was the skill with which its massive borrowing program was handled by the relatively small Capital Markets Branch in the Ministry of Finance. A key element in its successful management of the $50 billion it borrowed over the life of the government was the ability to make currency swaps – i.e., to borrow money in foreign currencies and then convert it back into Canadian debt instruments to protect the government against the added costs that might be incurred through fluctuations in the exchange rate of the Canadian dollar. A grave concern for finance ministry officials was that a deficit of $17 billion could cost Ontario its AA rating and thus foreclose the option of conducting these currency swaps.

36 Kaufman, 'Program Review in Ontario,' 95–6.

37 Patrick Grady, 'Ontario NDP Tax Increases,' *Canadian Business Economics* 1, no. 4 (Summer 1993): 12–23.

38 *Fair Taxation in a Changing World: Report of the Ontario Fair Tax Commission* (Toronto: University of Toronto Press and Queen's Printer, 1993).

39 Floyd Laughren, *1993 Budget* (Toronto: Queen's Printer for Ontario), 66, 15.

40 Canadian Union of Public Employees, 'A Realistic Outlook: CUPE's Alternative Economic and Fiscal Forecast for Ontario,' CUPE Research Department, Ottawa, 14 May 1993.

41 Leo Panitch and Donald Swartz, *The Assault on Trade Union Freedoms: From Wage Controls to Social Contract* (Toronto: Garamond Press, 1993), 174–5. Cf. Stephen McBride, 'The Continuing Crisis of Social Democracy: Ontario's Social Contract in Perspective,' *Studies in Political Economy*, no. 50 (Summer, 1996), 65–93.

42 'Toward the renewal of social democracy in Canada: a submission to the CLC/NDP review committee,' Toronto, 31 August 1995, 1.

43 Minutes, Cabinet Meeting of 9 March 1994, 1–2.

Further Readings

Drache, Daniel, with the assistance of John O'Grady, ed. *Getting on Track: Social Democratic Strategies for Ontario*. Montreal and Kingston: Canadian Centre for Policy Alternatives and McGill-Queen's University Press, 1992.

Ehring, George, and Wayne Roberts. *Giving Away a Miracle: Lost Dreams, Broken Promises and the Ontario NDP*. Oakville: Mosaic Press, 1993.

Monahan, Patrick. *Storming the Pink Palace: The NDP in Power: A Cautionary Tale.* Toronto: Lester Publishing, 1995.

Rae, Bob. *From Protest to Power: Personal Reflections on a Life in Politics.* Toronto: Viking, 1996.

Walkom, Thomas. *Rae Days: The Rise and Follies of the NDP.* Toronto: Key Porter Books, 1994.

FIFTEEN

Reclaiming the 'Pink Palace': The Progressive Conservative Party Comes in from the Cold

Peter Woolstencroft

In the first week of the 1985 Ontario provincial election the *Toronto Star* published a Gallup poll that put support for the Progressive Conservative Party at over 50 per cent. The Liberal Party, at 29 per cent, and the New Democratic Party, at 20 per cent, seemed to be at their traditional support levels: their respective leaders, David Peterson and Bob Rae, could be identified by roughly only one-quarter of the poll's respondents.[1] At a leadership convention earlier that year the Conservatives had chosen Frank Miller to succeed William Davis, who had been premier since 1971. The Tories, reputed to have perfected the art of rejuvenating themselves through the process of choosing a new leader every ten years or so, apparently had done it again. Few observers were betting that the election would produce anything but a majority Conservative government; but on election night it was clear that a minority government was in the cards. When the Conservatives lost a confidence motion a few weeks after the election, the Liberals formed a minority government, the first time they had held office since 1943. But there was little in the changeover to suggest that the province was on the verge of ten tumultuous years, a period in which both the Liberals and the NDP would form majority governments, the province would endure a deep recession after the booming 1980s, and, in the 1995 election, the Conservatives would return to the 'pink palace,' as the Ontario legislature is affectionately known.

Shortly after the 1985 election Frank Miller resigned as leader. At various events leading up to that fall's leadership convention, which chose Larry Grossman as leader, many Conservative partisans wore buttons proclaiming 'We'll be right back!' After forty-three years in office, perhaps the Tories could be excused for having trouble accepting their role as an opposition party and thinking that they soon would be back in government. They would, however, have had little idea that it would take ten years and three elections. That their party would undergo enormous changes in its internal structures, operating processes, and ideological orientation, so that there was little beyond their nameplate that connected the Progressive Conservative parties of 1985 and 1995, would have been beyond anyone's boldest prediction.

This chapter analyses the rebuilding of the Ontario Progressive Conservative Party in the period from 1985 to 1995.[2] Four themes dominate the discussion. The first focuses on the aftermath of the 1987 election, when the party adopted the 'one member, one vote' method of leadership selection. The second emphasis is on the period from 1990 to 1994, when the party went through a systematic, lengthy, and intensive rebuilding process, especially in policy development. The third point of discussion is how the party prepared itself in the sixteen months leading up to the 1995 election and the strategy that the party successfully implemented. The last theme is the character of Ontario's political culture in light of the victory of the Conservatives. Before these issues are discussed, it is necessary to understand the development of the Ontario party system in the period from 1943 to the 1990 election.

The Ontario Party System from 1943 to 1990

From 1943 to 1985 the Progressive Conservative Party held office as the province enjoyed unparalleled economic expansion. Under the leadership of George Drew, Leslie Frost, John Robarts, and William Davis, the party was known for its adroit management of public affairs, its skilful balancing of interests, and its ability to respond to the changing concerns of Ontarians. In a seminal piece, John Wilson described Ontario as the 'red tory' province; in effect, the Tories had established a more-or-less stable electoral coalition of free-enterprise-oriented interests and state-centred interests.[3] But the Tory hegemony wore on, signs of sustained dissatisfaction began to appear. In the 1967 election, the New Democrats surged to new levels of voter support, which in that election and those subsequent produced the numbers of seats that their predecessors, the CCF, had enjoyed only in the 1940s. But the Tories proved to be formidable in their own right as they mastered the art of macro-level political organization, well caught in the label The Big Blue Machine and their ability to use electronic media to win elections.[4]

Their domination of the province's politics was helped by the tripartite division of the vote. The twelve elections from 1943 to 1981 produced nine majority and three minority governments for the Tories. In that period, their share of the vote ranged from 36 to 49 per cent, while the Liberals had a range of 28 to 37 per cent and the NDP (and its predecessor, the CCF) garnered 17 to 32. The Tories were able to hold office because the Liberals and New Democrats each attracted a large share of the votes and, especially after the 1967 election, had sufficient strength in various regions of the province to produce enough seats that they could regard winning the next election as being within reasonable reach.[5]

The Tories' electoral mastery fell apart in the 1985 election. Frank Miller, the most right-wing of four candidates for the Conservative leadership, was unable to connect with increasingly restless voters and the Tories' commanding lead in the polls slowly weakened. David Peterson's Liberals projected a modern image and sufficiently caught the public's desire for change that no party gained a majority in the legislature.[6] For the next two years, the Liberals headed a minority government buttressed by a coalition-like arrangement with the New Democrats. The 1987 election produced a strong majority for the Liberals, their first since 1937, while both the Conservatives and the New Democrats fared poorly – especially the Conservatives, who had their lowest number of seats since the end of the First World War.

The mid-summer call of the 1990 election caught both opposition parties flatfooted. The Liberals enjoyed a commanding lead in the polls and activists in each of the parties shared the belief that the Liberals were headed to an overwhelming victory, perhaps even winning every seat. But, in the course of the campaign, the Liberals, burdened by their unfocused platform, David Peterson's lacklustre campaign, and the negativism generated by the collapse of the Meech Lake Accord, faltered. The New Democrats, buoyed by Bob Rae's sprightly debate performance and their aggressive advertising, won a majority government, a result that surely was beyond anyone's reasonable expectation at the outset of the campaign.[7] The NDP surge came late in the campaign and resulted in the winning of constituencies where previously the party had only weak roots and minuscule vote shares. For their part, the Tories managed to win a few more seats than they had in 1987 (up to twenty from sixteen) despite a slight decline in their share of the popular vote. The question was, Did 1990 mark a watershed in the province's political development?

The New Democrats entered office with euphoria and heightened expectations about what the province's first social-democratic government would do. The NDP's election manifesto, *Agenda for People*, optimistically offered a wide and expensive range of policy undertakings. However, at the very time they took office, Ontario entered the most severe recession since the Second World War. One effect of the recession was a sharp decline in the province's revenues, exacerbated by the federal government's diminished transfer payments. The immediate response of the NDP was to increase significantly its transfers to municipalities, hospitals, schools, and universities, along with increases in social-services spending. In a very short span, the NDP enormously increased the province's deficit and overall public indebtedness. Simultaneously, however, the NDP moved away from its election promises, most notably its commitment to public automobile insurance. In 1993 the government reversed the fiscal policy of its first two years by implementing spending restraints and changes to labour contracts. Its new policy, called Social Contract, alienated the NDP's traditional constituencies without attracting favour elsewhere, except for reluctant applause from the business community.[8]

Rebuilding the Progressive Conservative Party: Populism and Strategizing

A month after the devastating 1987 election, Larry Grossman, on the eve of stepping down as party leader, recommended to the party executive that the party look at the method of leadership selection as part of its rebuilding.[9] A number of leading Conservatives, many associated with the Big Blue Machine, and the party president, Tom Long, who had sought office on a reform platform, differed on the question of the rebuilding process. The 'old guard' wanted to strike a committee of high-level party members who would travel the province and report to the party about what should be done.[10] On the other side was an amalgam of populist and right-wing thinking. The perception that the two 1985 leadership conventions, especially the first, were extravagant and machine-dominated affairs, orchestrated by elite groups within the party, with the rank and file having no significant role other than for casting votes as delegates at leadership conventions, was a strong motivating force. At the 1989 meeting that approved the new method of leadership selection, the rallying cry of its proponents was 'Let the people decide.' Tom Long, for his part, wanted to undertake a root-and-branch reconstruction of the party, not filtered through the elite of the party, but through the involvement of rank-and-file members. The old form of politics, so well played by the Ontario Conservatives, in which the leaders of the party brokered interests and calculated electoral strategies on the basis of polling, had resulted in party members playing a very limited role; their ideas, interests, and values were diffusely, not explicitly, incorporated into the party platform and its electoral policies. But for Long there was an ideological element that made reconstruction imperative: the party was in a very weak position once it was out of office, because a clear gulf existed between party leaders, especially William Davis (because of his government's purchase of Suncor, mid-election [1975] commitment to rent controls, and reversal of its long-standing opposition to separate-school funding), and party members. Peter Van Loan described the mindset of the time as fearing that party members would talk about policy, 'because if they did, some reporter is going to put what they say down on tape and they'll destroy the party.'[11] Tom Long, reflecting on the evolution of the party, said that 'the grassroots of the party have always been considerably to the right of the establishment of the party. Hugh Segal and others, if they were candid, would admit that they always saw as part of their job to keep all of us under control. They needed us, but while we were necessary, they thought that we were insufficient.' Long wanted to explode the myth that the right was insufficient. The party devoid of philosophy and bereft of ideas other than those of electoral survival, especially in its last five years of office, needed to change. If it were to hold office again, the party would have to reform its basic institutions and affirm the core values of conservatism.[12]

These forces led to the conclusion that the solution to the problems of the party would be found in reforming existing institutions so that party members would have a central, rather than marginal, role in its life. The fundamental reform proposed by Tom Long and others, especially Tony Clement, was that the party leader should be elected on the basis of 'one member, one vote' rather than through the well-established convention method.[13] Adoption of the idea in 1989 by the party is seen by its proponents as foretelling the increasing populism in Canadian politics so graphically demonstrated in the defeat of the Charlottetown Accord in the 1992 referendum.[14]

The 'one member, one vote' system adopted by the Conservatives, after a long examination of a wide range of alternatives, was built on two principles: first, equality, so that every member should be directly involved in the choice of the leader; second, retention of the constituency as the fundamental unit of the party. The obvious incompatibility between these two principles, arising from the fact that constituency associations varied enormously, from the few with hundreds of members to the many with scant numbers, was resolved, somewhat unsatisfactorily, by assigning each constituency 100 points. Candidates would be apportioned their share of 100 on the basis of votes cast in their favour at the level of the constituency; and the winning candidates would have to win 50 per cent plus one of the constituency votes. One problematic consequence of the system was that it was possible for a candidate to receive over 50 per cent of the overall vote but secure less than 50 per cent of the constituency count.[15] One important consequence of the new system was the necessity to have a province-wide system of membership registration, so that members would have only one vote. Before the 'one member, one vote' system, memberships were only held at the level of the constituency, which meant that the central party had no idea about membership numbers and little ability to communicate with its supporters except those who donated directly to it.[16]

The 1990 election, coming soon after Mike Harris had won the leadership, revealed a critical problem: the party had a weak policy base. At a party meeting in Hamilton following the 1990 election, Mike Harris stressed that in the next election the party's platform would be much more detailed than what the Tories had just presented to the electorate.[17] The 'taxfighter' posture and tax-cutting language presented by Harris suffered from little explication about how the province's finances – on the revenue and expenditure sides – would be handled. Fiscal conservatism would need to be fleshed out if the party was going to be viable electorally. The Hamilton meeting also was important because of the large number of young people elected to positions on the party's executive; many continued in active roles through the 1990s.

The process of examination started with an explicit attempt to emulate what other organizations in competitive situations, especially businesses, had been doing to strengthen themselves.[18] David Lindsay, who many have identified as a driving force in the reorganization and revitalization of the party, in his account of the period referred to businesses striving to increase their market share in a competitive market place, likening a successful party to a business that very carefully positioned itself in the market place so as to be attractive to a great number of customers.[19] Instead of looking for the clever advertisement (or, indeed, the clever question in the legislature), it was necessary for the organization to go through a strategic planning exercise in which core activities would be identified, basic values elucidated, and fundamental objectives stipulated. By the fall of 1991, four deficits – intellectual, financial, strategic, and organizational – were identified as hobbling the future of the party. A 'four deficits' committee was struck to provides focused attention on eliminating them.

The financial deficit of the party was compelling. A 1991 internal party analysis of its finances showed that in every year since 1977 the party had been in a deficit situation; the financial problem had been exacerbated by the defeats in the 1985 and 1987 elections, which produced a debt of close to $6 million by 1987; various cost controls and even a profitable leadership election in 1990 reduced the debt to $4.8 million, but the party, far from office, was in a very difficult situation as interest payments encumbered its ability to rebuild.[20]

Financial problems of the party were addressed in several different ways; most – a variety of fund-raising events – were to be expected. One, however, was not. Following the financial analysis, and having rejected the possibility of declaring bankruptcy and regrouping as a new party, Mike Harris and the PC party executive shut down the party's central headquarters.[21] The effect of the decision to operate without an executive director and paid political or organization staff was to force the fate of the party upon its members and volunteers. For a party perceived to be bureaucracy-heavy and leader-dominated, this was a remarkable change and an unusual challenge.

It was not an obviously fortuitous move, though it turned out that way, reflecting the happy melding of accident and design. At the time of the decision to shut down the paid bureaucracy, the constituency base of the party was weak and demoralized. In late 1991 the PC party's organization committee presented to the executive a 'Riding Needs Assessment,' an analysis of a survey of constituency executive members, mainly presidents, in the 127 then-recognized associations. That executive members were predominantly in their forties, male, and Anglo-Celtic suggested that party activists came from a narrow slice of Ontario's society. What also was problematic was the membership base of the party. Forty-one per cent of constituencies reported having fewer than 100 members; 26 per cent said they had between 101 and 200 members; only 25 per cent had more than 201 members.[22] Respondents identified three major reasons for their party activity (ideology, 35 per cent; social contacts, 22 per cent; and community involvement, 20 per cent). Asked to identify the major problems facing their constituency associations, 35 per cent singled out 'low morale' (a variety of other problems, all cited by less than 10 per cent, trailed far behind). When asked to explain why constituencies had problems, respondents focused on two reasons: 'complacency'

(22 per cent) and 'the federal Progressive Conservative party' (21 per cent).[23]

The provincial party's difficulties with the federal party were manifested in its officials having to deal with issues arising from members of the provincial Conservative party holding membership in the federal Reform Party of Canada. Correspondence between Tony Clement and Tom Trbovich, national director of the federal party, indicated that some constituency officials were so concerned about what was happening that they sought advice on the question of whether it was unconstitutional to be a member of both the provincial PC party and the federal Reform Party. Tony Clement, recognizing the situation to be 'rather delicate,' ruled that such dual memberships were not in conflict with the PC constitution.[24] The Reform issue also reached the caucus; some MPPs, in the early 1990s, discouraged by the Ontario party's problems and burdened by the unpopularity of the federal party, wanted it to walk away from its debts and take on a new name or even merge with Reform as the route to political revival.[25] On the other wing of the party, voices called for the PCs to abandon 'the traditional right-wing core vote' and 'recapture the political centre' because, since the election of Frank Miller, the party had faced 'the prospect of becoming politically irrelevant,' as it was 'clearly out of step with the political views and aspirations of the broad mainstream of Ontario society.'[26] The provincial PCs also found their rebuilding efforts undercut by the remnants of the Big Blue Machine (mostly located in Ottawa with the federal party) who, when things were difficult for Mike Harris, were perceived to use their access to the media to raise doubts about his leadership.[27]

Given the reality of and potential for fractiousness, it was necessary for the party to learn how to be cohesive and how to think in the long term. Erasing the 'four deficits' thus became the strategic objective of the party, to be accomplished by building on the 'one member, one vote' philosophy in which every party member could participate in writing the party's mission statement and developing its strategic objectives.[28] That process, driven by volunteers and involving thousands of people, was remarkably systematic and thorough.

At three conferences (Barrie, 1991; Windsor, 1992; Richmond Hill, 1994) party members debated and fleshed out the philosophical underpinnings and programmatic details of the Tory party's approach in the next election.[29] The conference in Barrie was the first policy conference the party had held since 1983. There were no elected delegates at Barrie; rather, any party member could attend and participate.[30] Although the conference's final report indicated that 'discussions reflected the balance of the rights gained from society versus the individual's duties and responsibilities,' participants in the main spoke about 'choice,' 'co-payment' of health costs, vouchers, competitiveness and productivity, and strengthening the market economy.[31]

However, it was the Windsor conference that was much different in character from the highly managed conferences held in the Davis years. The Windsor conference's title, 'Mission '97,' was chosen to make the point that the party was thinking not just in terms of winning the next election (to be held some time before 1995), but also about how it would govern once in office. It debated a proposed mission statement that flowed out of a strategic planning exercise in which various elements of the party (caucus, executive members, rank-and-file members, and legis-lative support staff) envisioned their 'ideal party.'[32] The final document specified the party's mission statement and its strategic objectives, and it stipulated that policies developed by the PC party should be consistent with the following:

satisfy concerns of the general population rather than special interest groups (i.e. that policies meet the test of cultural/popular legitimacy; historical legitimacy; and conservative values of choice, civility, self reliance, community, entrepre-neurial spirit).[33]

Following the Windsor meeting, fourteen Policy Advisory Councils and four Regional Advisory Councils were established comprising MPPs, legislative staff, party executive members, and volunteers (who were not necessarily party members); the numbers of members in each council ranged from twenty-one to seventy-seven. The policy councils worked through 1993, and under the auspices of the PC Policy Committee re-ported to the party at its Richmond Hill conference in February 1994.[34]

Two other policy-development processes were also under way. One involved the caucus, which produced a wide range of policy papers, published as a series entitled *New Directions*. The other featured Harris himself, who undertook extensive provincial tours and meetings with five hundred of the leading chief executive officers in the Metropolitan Toronto area. The provincial tours were designed as follows: in a particu-lar community various people would be invited to attend an event with Harris where they would be invited to give their views; these meetings, which had highly variable attendance, not only introduced the Con-servative leader to people who ordinarily would not have an opportu-nity to talk at length with a politician, but also brought in several people who became involved in the policy-development process and, indeed, played an important role in the development of the *Common Sense Revolution* (*CSR*), such as economist Mark Mullins. Tom Long and David Lindsay attributed the identification of the welfare issue to the provincial tours undertaken by Harris, with the saliency of the issue later confirmed by polling research.[35]

The meetings with leading business people were intended to provide Harris with extended exposure over lunch or dinner. Five to ten people were invited to each event, at which they could talk informally about provincial affairs; at the end of the process, each business person was invited to a large dinner event at which Harris summarized their individual meetings.[36]

Another important manifestation of the systemization of the Conservative party's approach to rebuilding was the candidate-search process. Traditionally, candidate searches were constituency-based; usually the local party would nominate, following its own rules, one of its own – the central party as an organization had at best a minimal role. Latterly, parties, perhaps more so at the federal level, have become more proactive. The Ontario Conservatives developed several initiatives as a result of Harris's dissatisfaction with the chaotic nomination situation that the party endured in the 1990 election as it scrambled to find candidates. By 1995, the heart of the process was that before a constituency could hold a nomination meeting unanimous approval had to be secured from a committee comprising people from the campaign committee, the leader's office, and the party; the criteria – minimum constituency membership of 5 per cent of the PC vote in the last election or five hundred people; documented full and complete candidate search; and an active fund-raising campaign in place – had to be met before a nomination meeting could be called. One effect of the process was that it contributed to the opening up and democratization of the party.[37]

By the close of the Richmond Hill conference in February 1994 the party had erased its intellectual deficit by establishing both the broad outlines of its election manifesto and the specification of the policy directions it was prepared to propose to the electorate. At another conference later in 1994 the party formally changed in a fundamental way the policy role of party members. Its 1990 constitution simply required that 'the executive shall call a policy conference at least once every two years.'[38] After the party's 1994 meeting in London, the policy role for members required three pages of the constitution to describe. One of the standing committees of the party executive dealt with policy; it was chaired by the third vice-president.[39] Fourteen Policy Advisory Councils were established (ten for subject areas; four for regional issues), with two co-chairs, jointly appointed by the policy chair and president, with membership open to any member of the party upon approval by the Policy Committee (comprising the policy chair, leader, one co-chair of each Policy Advisory Council, and nine other individuals).[40] A policy conference must be held at least annually, with notice of the issues to be debated to be given twenty-one days before the conference. There must be a variety of ways for members to present policy resolutions, with the end result being that resolutions approved at a policy conference 'shall constitute the foundation on which Party policy and legislation is developed until the next Policy Conference.'[41]

Another important change in the operations of the party concerned the Progressive Conservative Ontario Fund (PCOF), the party's fund-raising arm. Tony Clement, referring to the situation in the early 1990s, indicated that the PCOF was more or less an independent entity, with little connection between it and the party. By 1994, the membership on the PCOF board of directors had expanded to include a wide range of individuals; and the PCOF was required to report annually to various elements of the party, including constituency associations, and to present an annual budget to the executive of the party.[42]

The party's organizational and financial deficits also had largely been addressed. Its membership was over 100,000,[43] and its financial position was greatly improved, though its deficit would not be erased until 1997.[44] The most important deficit of all – strategic – still existed: How would the party communicate its message to the voters? And were the voters listening?

War Games, the Common Sense Revolution, and the 1995 Election

In January 1994 the Conservatives, under their newly appointed campaign chairman, Tom Long, and campaign manager, Leslie Noble (who had been appointed by Harris as a full-time party employee with the title Executive Director for Election Preparedness), began their pre-election preparations.[45] While Long and Noble were pleased with the steps taken by the party, their strategy planning revealed several pressing concerns. First among them was that they had no sound reading of the party's standing in the public's mind, especially in terms of the major themes that the party had developed since the 1990 election. Two major research projects – public-opinion polling and focus groups – were undertaken.

The fundamental lesson of the research was that the public 'had no idea that we were the taxfighters, they had no idea that economic development and job creation were the things that we had been campaigning on, they didn't know what our position was on the deficit. In fact, if you asked them who was more likely to cut taxes, it was not the Conservatives.'[46] The second finding of the polling was that the Tories trailed the Liberals by 30 points. Moreover, when voters were asked to compare the parties, on every important issue the Liberals were ahead of the Tories by margins of least 20 points.[47] For the Liberals, however, there was a big problem, one that presented a clear opportunity for the Conservatives: about 60 per cent of Liberal voters were 'soft'; and a majority of Liberal voters and of those who wanted Lyn McLeod to be premier were thinking very much along the lines that the Conservatives were talking about (but were not being heard). A third point was that voters were highly cynical about politicians; they were seen as saying one thing in order to get elected and then doing something else once in office. Focus-group research indicated that 'voters who clearly held strong views on issues like spending, taxing, and workfare were in absolutely no mood to take "yes" for an answer. The more you pushed a position at them, the more vigorously they shoved it away, deeply suspicious that the whole thing was a polling-driven con game.'[48] The fourth finding that structured the Conservative election strategy was that 60 per cent of voters thought 'the province was on the wrong track' and 'seven out of ten voters believed that major change was needed to turn the situation around.'[49] The last lesson produced by the research was the electoral burden presented by the name 'Progressive Conservative,' which was described by insiders as 'radioactive,' arising from the negative after-shocks of the Mulroney governments and the provincial party's negative-positive ratio, which was two to one while the Liberals were the mirror opposite.[50]

The Tory strategists began the second phase of their pre-election preparations with the premise that they were so far behind the Liberals that it was essential that their campaign be error-free; they could afford no surprises and certainly had to avoid the kind of self-destruction experienced by their federal cousins in the 1993 federal campaign.[51] Election strategists have always wondered what their opponents are going to do, but the efforts of the Ontario Conservatives seemed to have been much more systematic than what other parties have done.[52] As had been the case in the early 1990s, the Conservatives were inspired by strategic-planning exercises undertaken by businesses to estimate what their competitors are doing. The premise of such exercises is that a business, by looking at its environment through the perspective of competitors, gains a good understanding of the range of alternatives open to competitors and their likely courses of action. Strategic planning exercises 'allow you to anticipate the attacks that may come your way, allow you to be proactive in such a fashion that you can undercut what your competition is doing, that you can remove opportunities for them, that you can shut them down earlier than otherwise would be the case.'[53] Tom Long was also conscious of two other things. Although the campaign's central participants were known to each other, this would be their first campaign to run and they had not worked together before on such a large-scale undertaking; thus, a secondary, but very important, function of the strategic planning was rapport building. Second, Long's experiences in the 1985 and 1987 campaigns, and his observations of the disastrous 1993 federal Conservative campaign, convinced him that it was imperative that the leader and the campaign team be of like mind, and that the leader be portrayed in an 'authentic' manner.[54]

War gaming was the heart of the strategic-planning exercise. A group of about fifteen people met twice in the February–March period of 1994 to construct a framework for the campaign. (A smaller group met in the summer and fall of 1994 to develop specific election plans, such as the television commercials; a similar group met on a daily basis throughout the election to review strategic issues, media reportage, and accounts from their 'bird dogs' travelling with the other parties' leaders.) Participants were divided into the groups representing the Conservatives, Liberals, and New Democrats. Having listened to a presentation by the party's pollster, John Mykytyshyn, describing in detail the results of polling commissioned by the party, and being provided with background materials on the parties and their leaders, each group was to develop a campaign strategy for its party. The task was to identify their party's 'ballot question' (that is, what do you want voters to be thinking about as they go to vote?) as well as their opponents.'[55] In a plenary session each group's presentation of its strategy (including specifying the party's approach to policy, the themes of advertisements, and the day-to-day scripting) was analysed. The first weekend of war gaming led to the conclusion that, given the situation of the party, traditional campaigning would not produce victory: the Tories needed a bold stroke.[56] The second weekend worked on the details of what was to be the CSR and election planning. Every participant in the war-gaming exercises commented on the remarkable accuracy of both the anticipated course of the election and the actions of the Liberals and New Democrats.[57]

The strategic planning led to the conclusion that the election would turn on the ability of the Conservatives to woo successfully 'soft' Liberal voters, those who thought along CSR lines but didn't know it. To do so meant stressing two things: first, the PC leader had been presenting his case consistently since the 1990 election; and, second, the PC's policy-development process had produced a platform congenial to many Liberal voters. The tactical imperative was to get the message directly to voters, since it was assumed that the mass media were not going to do it for the Tories. Moreover, the message had to be consistent, authentic (in the sense that it arose from the widespread consultations and deliberations the party had engaged in), and credible. The decision, then, was made to go for the high-risk move, the release of the party's platform within a year of the likely call of the election.[58]

The CSR, publicized through a $1 million campaign (of which $800,000 was for television) starting in May of 1994, was a marketing plan primarily designed to present the party's thinking to the 'soft' Liberal voters.[59] Its title was an explicit attempt to downplay the party's name given the imperative need to get people to listen to the message independent of the messenger. (In the election the party's usual abbreviation, 'PC,' was used, but the stress was on a 'Mike Harris government' – because voters held a positive perception of Mike Harris – rather than a 'Progressive Conservative government.')[60] The plan was to

get our mark on the ground early, so that there would be a point of reference for people. We thought that once we got into the campaign, Lyn McLeod is going to have her red book. Its going to come out in the second week of the campaign, and everybody is going to go 'ah, wow, policy' and we are going to go 'where was it two years ago' and 'conversion is great, but look at her flip flops.' We felt that we wanted to point to the day we introduced our platform, indicate that we asked people to look at our numbers, weigh what we say, and know where we stand.[61]

Marketing of the CSR included

– a province-wide press conference carried out by satellite,
– an extensive 800-number TV campaign,
– a province-wide bus tour, and
– wide distribution of copies of the CSR (by the time of the election, approximately 2,500,000).

A correlated activity was an extensive briefing of the mass media, leading business and academic economists, and the bond-rating companies in the months after the release of the *CSR*, in order to broaden their understanding of the information base and reasoning employed by the Conservatives.[62]

Tom Long, reflecting on the success of the marketing plan, used the welfare issue to illustrate what happened. A year and a half before the 1995 election, the Liberal Party was seen as being most likely to improve the system by a margin of eight points over the Conservatives (29 to 21 per cent). By the time of the election call, the Liberal lead was down to two points (26 to 24). The last tracking poll conducted by the Conservatives put the difference between the parties at 48 points (Conservatives at 58, Liberals at 10).[63]

The question of the timing of the release of the *CSR* was much debated. On one side was the view, very much the orthodox one, that a party should not make its platform the campaign issue; instead, the Tories should fight the election on the government's record. The other view said that conventional wisdom did not hold because, given the anticipated crash of the NDP, either the Conservatives or Liberals would win the election. Since the Liberals were far ahead (but many Liberal voters thought like Conservatives), the task was to differentiate the two parties.[64] Some worried about their ability to sustain interest in the party and its platform. Would the media tire of the *CSR* by the end of the summer? Others, pointing to widespread cynicism about politicians, argued that it was important to establish the 'credibility of conviction,' to be able to make the point that Harris and his party were really committed to their proposals and were not just interested in winning the election.[65]

One factor prompting the release of the *CSR* was the emergence of Reform as a viable force, federally, in the province. Leslie Noble claimed that the impact of Reform was significant, since the Conservatives were of the view that they had lost up to fourteen seats in 1990 because fringe right-wing parties had bled away potential Tory voters. If Reform entered the provincial election, it would have made the PCs' job much more difficult.[66] Tom Long was considerably less bothered by Reform because it was leaderless, resourceless, and without history in the province.[67] Tony Clement said it was no more than the 'sixth' factor in the decision-making process.[68] Every person interviewed made the point that the various policy-development processes followed by the party since 1990 had pointed in the same direction as manifested in the *CSR*: if Reform had fared poorly in the 1993 federal election, the only possible effect would have been the timing of the release of the *CSR*.

One consequence of the early release of the *CSR* was that the party in convention never ratified the document. Of course, parties ordinarily do not debate in public their manifestos, but the Ontario Conservatives, as far back as the decision to choose leaders on the basis of 'one member, one vote,' had raised expectations about the role of party members. Throughout the 1990s the ethos had been to open the doors and allow all of those who wished to participate to do so. Within and outside the party a large number of people had participated. But, in the end, the CSR was a document that reflected the thoughts of Mike Harris and his close advisers as much as the other participants in the policy-development process. The counterpoint – made in some fashion by every person asked about the timing of the CSR's release – was that it represented the coming together of every part of the policy-development process that the party had put in place. There was no doubt in their minds that the CSR reflected very deeply both the spirit and content of the policy discussions.[69]

The pressing strategic consideration was timing. Getting the message out at the right time (to federal Reform voters, to be sure, but especially to those who were supporting the Liberals without definite reasons for doing so) about what the Ontario Tories had committed themselves to do was important. While the election probably would be in the spring of 1995, it might be called for the late summer or the autumn of 1994. Given their weak standing in the polls, the fundamental consideration, then, was that it was imperative for the Conservatives to get their message out early.

The pre-election planning produced one other decision. Since the primary target was voters who thought in terms of the CSR but didn't know it, it was deemed essential, from the time of the release of CSR to the last day of the election, that all parts of the campaign – leader, candidates (who had to pass an examination testing their knowledge of the platform), and advertisements – consistently put forward the same message. The election scripting – including the leader's tours, electronic advertising, and the debate – was designed to integrate the specific iterations of the campaign themes. Most of the television commercials were purchased before the election was called; the PC plan called for a 'low buy' in the early part of the advertising and escalating frequencies in the last days of the campaign.[70] Candidates were briefed on the expected course of the campaign (especially the release of polls, the impact of the advertising campaigns, and the effect of the debate), so that they would not be put off stride by the apparent stability of voter preferences in the first month of the campaign. Further, they were introduced to the idea that the campaign was scripted (as in a film production) by being walked through how the message would be communicated every day.[71] One important organizational feature of the decision to maintain a consistent message was that in the Conservatives' provincial campaign headquarters all communication materials and issues were handled by one person.[72]

Dynamics of the 1995 Election

The Tories entered the election campaign with little public reason for optimism. Throughout the province, their federal counterparts had been thrashed in the 1993 federal election. They carried deep debt and attracted little media coverage, positive or negative, or lively public interest.[73] The CSR, because of its explicit right-wing orientation, was considered by many political commentators to be so far removed from the centre of Ontario's political culture that electoral success was unlikely. Having failed to articulate a centrist appeal, the Conservatives certainly were doomed to continue in the role of 'the third party,' and perhaps were destined to be marginalized, if not eliminated, as the Liberals swept to victory. The only virtue that observers could find in the approach taken by the Conservatives was that it left very little incentive for supporters of the federal Reform Party, emboldened by their startling showing in Ontario in the 1993 federal election, to enter the provincial political arena, a move that might have eviscerated the Tories' chances. Their best card were polls which showed that those who knew of Mike Harris thought he was the best person to be premier when compared with Lyn McLeod or Bob Rae.[74] The only other sign before the 1995 election that perhaps the media consensus about the certainty of the Liberal victory was off the mark was the 1994 by-election in Victoria-Haliburton, a seat won by the New Democrats in 1990 after being held by the Liberals since 1975. At the outset of the by-election campaign, the Tories were far behind (30 points according to internal polls), but innovative campaigning, especially the extensive use of videos and statement of the themes later elaborated in the CSR, contributed to their unexpected victory.[75]

Victoria-Haliburton aside, other than the relatively low recognition that their leader received, there was little to suggest that the Liberals were not poised to win handily the election sure to come in 1995.[76] Environics Research, which had detected a rise in Tory support to the 30 per cent level in late 1994, found in its last pre-election survey that the parties stood at 51 per cent for the Liberals, 25 per cent for the Conserva-

tives, and 21 per cent for the NDP.[77] Two weeks into the election campaign, a *Toronto Star*–Environics poll put the Liberals at 52 per cent, the
Conservatives at 26 per cent and the New Democrats at 20 per cent. Since
the poll suggested that there had been little change in the support for the
Ontario parties in the previous two years, Thomas Walkom, a leading
journalist covering Ontario politics, wrote that the election was an 'anti-
climax.'[78]

The campaign, at least from the standpoint of the public, had few
noteworthy events. Each party leader travelled across the province, generally addressing partisans at candidates' campaign headquarters or
appearing at carefully selected photo opportunities. The Liberals, imitat-
ing their federal cousins' successful *Red Book*, started the campaign bran-
dishing their version, a *Red Book* of campaign promises covering a wide
range of issues. The New Democrats appeared almost surprised by the
election call. In the early part of the campaign they issued no manifesto
and Bob Rae confined himself to attacking the federal government, especially for its cuts in transfer payments, defending his government's record,
and warning about the dangers of electing his opponents – initially, the
Liberals, and, latterly, as party preferences shifted, the Conservatives.
Mike Harris at his events focused on the major themes that had been
delineated in the *CSR*. From the standpoint of his closest advisers, this
part of the campaign was almost flawless, with only minor smudges (off-
the-cuff comments about abolishing tenure in the two university communities of Waterloo and London, and in Windsor, the site of the
province's first casino, references to it being closed) on their day-by-day
election script. That script presumed that the contest was just between
the Liberals and the Conservatives, caught in Tom Long's statement in
the second week of the campaign that 'Bob Rae was irrelevant.'[79]

The major events of the campaign were the beginning of paid political
advertising on 17 May (with television being by far the most popular
medium) and the leaders' debate, on 18 May. Both were welcomed by
media commentators, many of whom described the election with words
such as 'yawner' and 'snoozer.' The NDP's television advertisements
relied on Bob Rae talking about the difficulties of governing Ontario and
the herculean efforts his government had made to address the pressing
issues of the last five years. The Liberals ran a number of television
commercials – expensive and with high production values – in which a
great variety of themes and issues were discussed, with the centrepiece
being their leader, Lyn McLeod, talking about the *Red Book*. (Latterly,
Liberal advertisements ignored McLeod and the *Red Book* and attacked

the extremism of the Conservative party's *CSR*.) Conservative television advertising was much more focused, with only four spots being run, and being neither elaborate nor obviously expensive. The first two advertisements compared the Conservative and Liberal positions: one centred on welfare reform and employment equity; the other stressed taxes, the deficit, and balanced budgets. The third commercial – labelled 'weathervane' by party strategists – symbolically represented various policy shifts attributed to the Liberals, particularly to Lyn McLeod. The fourth spot, which ran in the last five days of the campaign, had Mike Harris speaking directly to the camera about his vision for Ontario.[80]

The leaders' debate was held three weeks before the election. It featured a series of questions from three journalists and selected videotaped questions from Ontarians. The leaders responded on an alternating basis, with brief opportunities for rebuttal. The media, following the tradition of 'horse-race journalism,' were very much interested in the question of 'who won.' The consensus in the media was that there was no clear winner, there being no knock-out blow and no collapse. Although her party was still ahead in the polls, Lyn McLeod (perceived to be the most vulnerable because she was still widely unknown) was generally conceded to have at least held her own, perhaps to have done better. Bob Rae, well regarded for his articulateness and well experienced in debates from his days at Oxford and over twenty years of elective politics, was thought to have presented himself well but also to have been unable to escape the pervasive and deep unpopularity of his government. Michael Harris was seen as having doggedly presented his case but not having lit any fires or generated any surge in support. The upshot for commentators was that the Liberals had reached the midpoint of the campaign in a position to form a majority government, even if there might be some slippage in their support.

The Conservatives, however, approached the debate in a different way than the media did. They were governed by the necessity of presenting their message in a consistent and integrated manner. The strategy was straightforward; the event was not seen as an ordinary debate, in which participants try to win points by clever demolition of their opponents' arguments, but, instead, as an opportunity for Mike Harris to speak directly to viewers; rather than engaging in debate-type interactions or deliberately confronting either of his opponents, at almost every opportunity Harris spoke directly to the camera and reiterated the major themes of the *Common Sense Revolution*. The strategy was based on research that indicated that 'people were sick and tired of politics as usual;

they were sick and tired of all the little sandbox fights. What are you going to do for me now? Tell me what you are going to do – and you had better mean it!'[81] Tom Long described the situation facing Harris as one in which his opponent was neither Lyn McLeod nor Bob Rae but the public's deep-seated scepticism about politicians and their promises. While McLeod and Rae would be addressed if they made a specific attack on Harris and the Conservatives, especially on issues of health care and education, it was essential that Harris be above the fray, that he avoid squabbles and extraneous matters, and that he emphasize the CSR, its development and the genuineness of his commitment to economic development and job creation.[82]

The efficacy of the strategy was evident in the focus groups assembled by the Conservatives to assess the effects of the debate. Participants in the focus groups were given instruments by which they could indicate their responses to the leaders' comments. Leslie Noble noted that 'when Harris talked about credibility, when he talked to the camera, and when he said how he felt about certain issues, the positives were as high as they could be.'[83]

Within a few days of the debate a poll conducted by Compas Research was published in the *Financial Post* that shattered the certain expectations about the course of the election.[84] It showed a sudden surge in support for the Conservatives paralleled by a steep drop for the Liberals. Subsequent polls showed that the Liberal fall and Conservative rise continued until the day of the vote, despite vehement attacks on the Conservatives by both the Liberals and New Democrats. The Conservatives, who had predicated their election planning on the efficacy of their advertising and the leaders' debate performance, were rewarded by the fact that 53 per cent of the electorate made their decision in the post-debate period.[85] And 59 per cent of Conservative voters made their decision in the post-debate period, compared to 51 per cent of Liberals and 45 per cent of New Democrats.[86]

The 1995 Election in Historical Perspective

Beyond the ideological character of their program, the Progressive Conservative mandate was noteworthy in four respects. First, in obtaining just under 45 per cent of the vote, the party had its best showing since 1971; and, in the seven elections since then, only the Liberals in 1987 had a higher vote share. Second, the Tories became only the third party in the province's history to form government by vaulting from either third place in the legislature or from having no legislative seats at all.[87] The third remarkable feature was the provincialization of the vote; the Tories were able to win a handsome number of seats across the various regions of the province, except for Northern Ontario, where they only managed to retain their two seats (Parry Sound–Muskoka and Nipissing, respectively held since 1981 by Ernie Eves and Michael Harris). The geographic span of the Conservative victory manifested itself in the winning of constituencies where, for many elections, the party had not been a strong competitor (especially in southwestern Ontario), even in the halcyon days of Leslie Frost, John Robarts, and William Davis. Fourth, the Conservatives attracted votes from many unionized workers and members of multicultural groups, parts of Ontario society generally hostile to them. Also, the Tories' polling suggested that, by election day, gender differences in the vote had been erased.[88]

Looking at the vote shares of the parties in the 1995 election (Progressive Conservatives, 44.97%; Liberals, 31.05%; and New Democrats, 20.54%), it would be easy to conclude that 1995 was just another iteration of the Ontario three-party system that had been in place since 1943.[89] And it is true that, in comparative terms, the Conservatives secured only a relatively weak majority government; their 63.1 per cent of legislative seats gave them the fifth-lowest showing of the twelfth majority governments from 1943 to 1995 and the fourth lowest of the nine Tory majority governments formed in the postwar period. In 'sweep' terms, there is little that is remarkable about the Conservative victory in 1995; quantitatively, it was a rather modest venture. It was, however, at least within the party, perceived to be much more than just another election.

Political Culture

Soon after their unexpected victory, the Conservatives, true to their word, moved quickly to implement central elements of their platform – abolition of photo radar; reform of labour-law legislation and employment-equity programs; cuts to welfare; drastic contractions in spending, with tax cuts scheduled to start in 1996. The province experienced a five-week strike by civil servants (followed by the provincial government issuing layoff notices to over 10,000 of their number), violent demonstrations at Queen's Park, and one-day strikes in various communities around the province. Within a short span not only had the Conservatives negated much of what previous governments had accomplished, especially the New Democrats in their five years in office, but they had proceeded in a manner far removed from the style of governance provided by previous Tory governments. Ontario, noted for the generally moderate and measured character of its political life, suddenly echoed with right-wing rhetoric; a province that for most of its history had avoided political extremes now bristled with heated political debate and, seemingly, had replaced Alberta as the leading voice of neo-conservatism. And the 1995 election, not that of 1990, seemed to have the earmarks of a watershed election.

At least part of the explanation for the Ontario election result is found in the extraordinary, lengthy, and detailed work that the Conservatives put into their election preparations. In their election post-mortems Conservative strategists concluded that the campaign was nearly perfect: few problems hobbled the leader's tour; television commercials effectively conveyed the PC message; the well-conceived and -executed debate strategy resonated positively with voters; and the election script, which required no amendment throughout the campaign, presented an integrated, consistent message. Their only disappointment was winning no seats in the north beyond the two already held.[90] Clearly, the Tories read accurately their soundings of public opinion and undercut the Liberals' huge lead by communicating effectively with the mass of Liberal voters who thought like Conservatives. But was the result merely the skilled work of highly committed technicians?

From the perspective of political science, the approach of the Ontario Conservatives in the 1995 election was highly unusual. Political science's accounts of how successful parties behave are based on the distribution of political attitudes. The argument is that, ideologically, the majority of people are located in the 'middle,' with the numbers of people decreasing as one moves to the 'left' and 'right' ends of the spectrum. Electorally successful parties practise brokerage politics: the major interests of society are addressed in their appeals to the electorate in a way that balances and harmonizes. The pressure to maximize one's electoral viability and minimize your opponent's means that parties seeking to win office locate themselves in the centre of the spectrum. Two considerations are important. First, parties can make errors, mistaking the attitudinal centre, and thus creating opportunities for their opponents. Second, parties are flexible entities, able to adopt a wide range of themes and emphases depending on circumstances and changes in their environment. The potential for error means that parties avoid specific delineation of their platforms lest they be encumbered with electorally negative appeals. Flexibility requires that parties avoid early declarations of their positions because their opponents, especially an incumbent party, may take over their policies.

The Ontario Conservatives broke the traditional rules of campaigns.

The explicit delineation of their platform made them highly vulnerable to attack. The early announcement of the CSR could have resulted in their opponents stealing parts of their manifesto (and, to some extent, the Liberals did precisely that). The Liberals, playing the traditional rules of the political game, located themselves in the centre as it has been ordinarily understood. The NDP, having learned some hard lessons in their first years of office, promised to stay the course, but from a centre-left perspective. It is difficult to conclude that the Liberals and the NDP had moved away from the traditional centre of Ontario politics, leaving many voters to find only the Conservatives holding the centre. And the Tories hardly dressed themselves in the usual political garb of ambiguity, balance, and moderation.

Donald C. MacDonald, in his review of the development of Ontario's political culture, writes that 'it is interesting to note how consistently conservatism has been the basic component of the Ontario political culture, no matter what party has been in power: equally significant, it has been conservatism with a progressive component.'[91] Such a wide prism allows MacDonald to see the various changes in government, even the NDP's victory in 1990, as reflecting the melding of the bipolarities of conservatism and progressivism.

It is hard to see how the victory in 1995 of the Conservatives, given the character of their manifesto, can be made to fit into MacDonald's interpretative framework. Does, then, the election signify that some important changes have occurred in Ontario's political culture? Does it mark a change in how Ontarians view the role of the state? the balance of individualism and collectivism? their sense of social responsibility?

The CSR begins: 'Government isn't working any more. The system is broken.' Tom Long, in his interpretation of the 1995 election in the *Fraser Forum*, described Mike Harris as fundamentally wanting 'to move the goal posts by resetting the agenda.' Long's interpretation is that the 1995 Ontario election 'represents a fundamental shift in the balance of power between the state on the one hand, and the private sector and the individual citizen on the other.'[92] Journalist John Ibbitson interprets the 1995 election and the approach of the Ontario Conservatives in highly ideological terms, reflecting the coming together of neo-conservatives inspired by Ronald Reagan, Margaret Thatcher, and Friedrich Van Hayek (especially his *The Road to Serfdom*).[93] But every person interviewed, including Tom Long, rejected the thrust of this interpretation. While a few close to the leadership of the party might follow the luminaries of new conservatism, the CSR for most of the interviewees was a home-grown attempt to deal with the perceived realities of Ontario's fiscal and economic situation. Job creation and economic growth were the litmus test, not some ideological premise or philosophical text. Several interviewees confessed to have only general awareness of political developments in the United States and had only vague impressions of European or Pacific Rim happenings; and they certainly were not immersed in dialectical debates.

Some commentators have tried to find American influences in the CSR.[94] It certainly is true that Mike Murphy, an American political consultant and a close friend of Tom Long, played a role in the development of television advertising accompanying the launch of the CSR and attended some pre-election planning sessions; but a number of interviewees, especially Tony Clement and David Lindsay, noted that Murphy's contributions, beyond stimulating discussion and thought, were limited because of differences in political cultures and the character of political competition between Canada and the United States.[95] David Frum's attribution of a primary role to Frank Luntz[96] was categorically denied by every interviewee; some had heard of Luntz because of his involvement with the Reform Party, but said he had no connection with their work either before or during the election.

For its part, the Reform Party had no independent impact on the ideological direction taken by the Ontario PCs: Reform was in the political vicinity because it was responding to the same influences that were moving the Conservatives, but its influence extended no further than to the timing of the release of the CSR. As Tony Clement pointed out, the 1990 election campaign of the Conservatives focused on spending reductions and tax cuts, the heart of the 1995 platform; and from 1990 to 1995 the party had been systematically preparing for the election with a multifaceted policy-development process that produced the CSR.[97]

A theme that emerged from the interviews was the bifurcation between the province's political elites, especially the media, and rank-and-file citizens. Media elites had not caught what many Ontarians were thinking about welfare, government spending, employment equity and affirmative action, and taxes. While the CSR was being negatively received in much of the media, the Conservatives were learning that many ordinary citizens responded positively to their message. Their confidence that they were on the right track was manifested in a campaign appearance designed to highlight their policies on affirmative action and employment equity before a multicultural audience and a campaign rally held at the General Motors plant in Oshawa.[98] In a similar vein, the media seriously misread the debate, especially in terms of the Conservative message and its effectiveness. For a number of strategists the underlying theme of the election was that it represented a victory for 'outsiders' over those who for decades had access to influence and beneficial public policies.[99]

Alongside the mass-elite divide that Conservative strategists identified as part of the dynamic of the 1995 election campaign were changes in basic political orientations in Ontario. When asked to reflect upon the evolution of fundamental political values and attitudes, the strategists – many of whom had been politically active since the 1970s – were agreed that some important shifts had occurred. They unanimously rejected the argument put forward by Hugh Segal that 1995 was just a return to 1985.[100]

Two important features were identified. First, the preceding ten years had seen a significant decline in institutional confidence: people were troubled by the increasing inability of public institutions to meet their stated purposes within reasonable cost ranges. Second, the globalization of the economy had made business people very conscious of the impact of input costs, especially labour, taxes, and government-imposed regulations, upon their ability to maintain their operations, let alone achieve growth. The processes of economic globalization have fundamentally changed the interaction between government and the economy that had traditionally been the hallmark of Ontario politics.[101] In the main, the 'common sense' political strategists would agree with Environics Research in its interpretation of the 1995 election that it represented a 'paradigm shift,' in which there has been 'a profound trend away from reliance on government and other institutions and toward greater personal control and individual responsibility.'[102]

Conclusion

The return to Queen's Park of the Conservatives was built on the combination of fundamental party reorganization and remarkably systematic and innovative preparations for the election. The glow associated with their strategic and tactical successes will be short-lived, as undoubtedly other political parties will emulate both the spirit and techniques of what the Tories did. And, while the Conservatives can pride themselves on rebuilding of their party after the debacles of 1987 and 1990, it is one thing to go to the grass roots when you are seeking office, but another to do so when you are governing. The history of parliamentary party politics reveals the cycle of increasing control by the leaders of the party when it is in office accompanied by falling membership numbers and weakening influence of the grass roots. It will not be easy for the Ontario

Conservatives to be the exception, even if they have constitutionalized the role of party members in the policy-development process.

There seems to be little doubt that the Ontario Tories will continue in the direction they set in their election platform, as contained in the words of Tom Long. Beyond their frontal attack on government spending and the cutting of taxes, the Tories have identified privatization, especially of Ontario Hydro, TVO, and the LCBO, as being on their agenda. Words in support of private universities have been heard. The character of Ontario's political culture cannot be judged, however, from the electoral success and actions of one party in a short period. The fact of the matter is that in the three elections from 1987 to 1995 Ontarians gave each of the province's major parties the chance to govern. It might be the case that many of Ontario's voters, having decided that the NDP had to go and confronted with a choice between the Liberals and Conservatives, opted for the party that presented itself in the more consistent and coherent manner and directly addressed the anxieties of the times. The failure of the Liberals to mount a well-considered and aggressive campaign was manifested in Tom Long's point that the Liberals had failed to prepare for the potential rise of the Conservatives by undercutting the credibility of Mike Harris.[103] And not only did Harris commit himself to fulfilling the CSR's promises by resigning if he failed; his party had presented a clear message about how it would achieve job growth and economic development, to the point of promising it would create 725,000 jobs by the next election. But the question remains, Did the electorate understand the details of the Conservative's platform?

Crucial insight will be gained from the interactions between Liberals, New Democrats, and Ontarians as they contemplate the changes in government effected in the years leading up to the next election. Although the Conservatives may try to soften the 'revolutionary' side of their 'common sense' agenda, the impact of their program is bound to be extensive and sharp as they simultaneously cut taxes and slash government spending. Ironically, conservatively minded people, with an instinctual aversion to massive reshaping of society by government, must contemplate the Progressive Conservative Party of Ontario engaging in a remarkable example of social engineering. Whether those who voted for the party in 1995 understood this remains highly uncertain.

Notes

1 *Toronto Star*, 29 March 1985.

2 Two earlier papers by the author have been incorporated into this chapter; see 'More than a Guard Change: Politics in the New Ontario,' paper presented to the conference Governing Ontario: Problems and Prospects, University of Western Ontario, 24 November 1995; 'The Ontario Election of 1995: The Campaign of the Progressive Conservative Party,' paper presented to the annual meeting of the Canadian Political Science Association, Brock University, June 1996. Several people associated with the election campaign of the Conservative party were interviewed. I am very grateful for their time and generous sharing of their perceptions. The interview schedule was approved by the University of Waterloo Office of Human Research and Animal Care. Robert MacDermid and Jonathan Malloy gave helpful comments, for which I am grateful.

3 John Wilson. 'Reflections on the Character of the Ontario Political Culture,' in Donald C. MacDonald, ed., *The Government and Politics of Ontario*, 2nd ed. (Toronto: Van Nostrand Reinhold, 1980), 208–26.

4 Jonathan Manthorpe, *The Power and the Tories* (Toronto: Macmillan, 1974). An interesting insight into the evolution of the Conservative party is found in Robert J. Williams and John Morris, 'Leslie M. Frost, Patronage, and "Grass-Roots" Political Work,' *Ontario History* 84, no. 2 (1992): 105–18.

5 John Wilson and David Hoffman, 'Ontario: A Three-Party System in Transition,' in Martin Robin, ed., *Canadian Provincial Politics* (Scarborough: Prentice-Hall), 198–239.

6 Rosemary Speirs, *Out of the Blue: The Fall of the Tory Dynasty in Ontario* (Toronto: Macmillan, 1986).

7 One common interpretation of the 1990 election is that it was a protest that ran amuck. Environics Research analysed the election differently: it was 'an expression of Ontarians' desire for the kind of activist, reform-minded government forged five years earlier in the Liberal-NDP Accord and, in their eyes, derailed after the majority victory of David Peterson's Liberals in 1987'; further, the vote reflected the parties' perceived commitment to governing with honesty and integrity, more openly and consultatively, and in light of the parties' positions on issues; see Environics Research, *Focus Ontario* (Toronto: 1990, no. 3), introduction and p. 47. I am especially grateful to Jane Armstrong for providing access to materials provided by Environics Research.

8 See the chapter by Chuck Rachlis and David Wolfe in this volume on the NDP in office.

9 Larry Grossman was replaced as interim leader by Andy Brandt, who did not want re-examination of the method of leadership selection; Tony Clement, interview, 30 April 1996. Mr Clement was very active in the party

in the late 1980s, especially in reference to constitutional issues; he served as president of the party from 1990 to 1992 and in the office of Mike Harris from 1992 to 1995; he was elected in 1995 in Brampton South. Mitch Patten, a long-time PC activist, and deputy principal secretary to the premier after the 1995 election, identified John Tory, long recognized as a member of the party establishment, as one of those who called for change in the party; Mitch Patten, interview, 26 April 1996.

10 Tom Long, interview, 19 April 1996. Mr Long served as president of the party from 1988 to 1990; long a friend of Mike Harris, he played a leading role on the Tories' 1995 election campaign team.

11 Peter Van Loan, interview, 17 April 1996. Mr Van Loan, a long-time party activist, served as president of the party from 1994 to 1996.

12 Long interview, 19 April 1996. Hugh Segal, a close confidant of premier Davis, leading member of the Big Blue Machine, and 'red tory,' was for many years the lightening rod for right-wing discontent.

13 Peter Woolstencroft, '"Tories kick machine to bits": Leadership Selection and the Ontario Progressive Conservative Party,' in Kenneth Carty et al., eds, *Leaders and Parties in Canadian Politics: Experiences of the Provinces* (Toronto: Harcourt Brace Jovanovich, 1992), 203–25.

14 Long, interview, 19 April; David Lindsay, interview, 26 April. Mr Lindsay's involvement in the party goes back to the mid-1970s; working in Mike Harris's office in the 1990s, he was instrumental in the rebuilding of the party and became the premier's principal secretary after the 1995 election.

15 A considerable literature paralleling the spread of the idea that party members should be involved directly in the election of party leaders is available; an important discussion is John Courtney's *Do Conventions Matter?* (Montreal: McGill-Queen's University Press, 1995).

16 Constituency party officials feared proposals for province-wide member-ship, because it would give the central party the ability to raise money directly from its supporters; the Ontario Conservatives addressed this issue by constitutionally restricting the party to one annual appeal: *Constitution*, Progressive Conservative Party of Ontario, 1994, art. 6.2.

17 Van Loan interview, 17 April 1996. Van Loan referred to an informal meeting of party activists and others in Cobourg in February 1990 at which the state of the party was discussed as being the starting point of the rebuilding process.

18 Lindsay interview, 26 April 1996. In the following discussion, it should be understood that all important decisions were made with the knowledge and consent of Mike Harris.

19 Lindsay, when it was pointed out that political scientists had used the

department-store analogy to describe the behaviour of successful political parties, expressed surprise. Apparently he and his associates thought that their conceptualization was novel.

20 '1991 Business Plan,' Progressive Conservative Party of Ontario, 5 March 1991, sect. 8; Tony Clement Papers, F 4340–1, box 1, Budget 1991 file, Archives of Ontario. I am grateful to Mr Clement for allowing access to his papers some 30 years before such materials ordinarily are available. Thanks also to Mr Jim Suderman, Senior Archivist, Archives of Ontario, and his colleagues for their kind and helpful assistance in regard to this research.

21 The party's debt not only hobbled its ability to rebuild in the 1990s; it exemplified what many in the party saw as its fundamental problem – the perceived gulf between the leaders of the party and its rank-and-file members, in which the former acted very much on their own and the latter had to carry the consequences; Long interview, 19 April 1996. One external friend of the party, writing from his perspective as a fund-raiser in a not-for-profit institution outside of Ontario, upon examination of the PC business plan commented in a letter to David Lindsay that 'the party has done a very poor job in managing expenses and ... increased success in fund raising seems to inspire the party managers to spend even more freely'; Clement papers, box 1, Budget 1991 file. It should be noted that it would be difficult for a party to maintain an intense and successful fund-raising campaign if it had a large reserve fund.

22 Peter Van Loan indicated that only to 25 to 30 constituency associations were viable entities during this period; interview 17 April 1996. Assuming that the smaller constituency organizations had close to 100 members, that those in the 100-to-200 range had close to 200 members, and that the balance averaged 300 members, the party had about 22,000 members, a drop of about 11,000 from the leadership election of 1989; Woolstencroft, '"Tories kick machine to bits,"' 215.

23 Clement papers, 'Riding Needs Assessment: Final Report,' subcommittee of the Organization Committee, pp. 2–6, box 3, Organization Committee – Riding Assessment file. The committee's call for intensive recruitment efforts was not very imaginatively constructed; while it recognized that the party did not reflect the diversity of Ontario, it recommended that the party look to the 'Junior League' and the 'Junior Chamber of Commerce' for new members; p. 3.

24 Clement papers, box 3, Reform Party of Canada file; Clement had to adjudicate between section 2 of the constitution, which listed eight 'principles' (which had no reference to a specific party) and section 3, which listed various 'objects' (one of which was to 'co-operate with and assist' Canada's

various Progressive Conservative parties, including the federal party. Clement ruled that section 2 superseded section 3.

25 Harris and the people around him leading the party were not interested (one reason being that despite their youthfulness they had deep party roots, in some cases – David Lindsay, for one – going as far back as the 1970s); Lindsay interview, 26 April 1996.

26 Harry S. Katz, 'The 1990 Ontario General Election: Results and Implications,' non-commissioned study presented to Tony Clement, 8 November 1990; Clement papers, box 2, Harry Katz's Report file.

27 Tony Clement, interview, 30 April 1996. Many of people associated with the Big Blue Machine had supported Dianne Cunningham over Mike Harris in the 1990 leadership election.

28 David L. Lindsay, 'Notes for Remarks,' presented to the Public Affairs Association of Canada, Toronto, 7 September 1995, 3.

29 There were as well several unofficial gatherings; one in February 1990 in Cobourg brought together about 100 people to discuss the future of the party; a meeting in April 1993 (the third of a series) in London attracted 150 people, including Conservative MPPs, to consider policy options; see Kimble F. Ainslie, ed., *Conservative Corrections: Democratic Conservatism from the Roots Up* (London: Springbank Publications, 1993).

30 Clement interview, 30 April 1996. There were no more than 200 people in attendance; Frank Klees, interview, 13 May 1996. Mr Klees, active in the party in the mid-1970s, was elected to the party executive in 1992 and charged with developing policy for the party; he was elected for the Conservatives in the 1995 election in the riding of York Mackenzie.

31 *Final Report: Thinking for Tomorrow Conference* (Toronto: Progressive Conservative Party of Ontario, November 1991). I am grateful to Amanda Walton for providing materials arising from this conference as the decision to shut down the headquarters of the party resulted in no records being kept of this period. Frank Klees reported that he had great difficulty after the Windsor conference finding materials pertaining to the conference; interview, 13 May 1996.

32 Clement papers, box 3, Strategic Planning Exercise file.

33 This paragraph is based on various materials considered by the convention and produced on the basis of its deliberations. The mission statement of the party read: 'We will build a safe and prosperous Ontario by adhering to shared values based on individual rights and responsibilities, fairness, and equality of opportunity; governing with responsive, competent, and principled leadership; and implementing innovative, consistent and

responsible policies.' Each word or phrase was broken down into its parts; e.g., 'equality of opportunity' was understood to mean 'that all individuals have a chance to establish and work to realize personal goals.'

34 Klees interview, 13 May 1996. The policy-development process did not cease with the Richmond Hill conference. Interim reports were prepared for the PC Policy Committee in May, September, and November 1994; and the committees continued their work into 1995.

35 Long interview, 19 April 1996; Lindsay interview, 26 April 1996.

36 The meetings with businesspeople were arranged through the efforts of Tom Long, who had little other sustained involvement in the party from 1990 to 1994; Long interview, 19 April 1996.

37 The party had been the butt of much media merriment as the result of some constituency associations placing newspaper advertisements announcing that candidates were being sought. Tony Clement thought the media did not appreciate that the advertisements reflected the efforts of weak constituency organizations to open up the party and to meet the criteria established by the central party; Clement interview, 30 April 1996.

38 *Constitution*, Progressive Conservative Party of Ontario, 1990, sect. 16.1, 'Policy Conferences.'

39 *Constitution*, Progressive Conservative Party of Ontario, 1994, art. 10.1 (f).

40 Ibid., art. 17, 'Policy Advisory Council.'

41 Ibid., art. 16, 'Policy Conferences.'

42 Ibid., art. 18, 'PC Ontario Fund.'

43 Steve Gilchrist, interview, 13 May 1996. Mr Gilchrist, long involved in the provincial party, served as party president from 1992 to 1994, and was elected to the legislature in 1995 in the riding of Scarborough East.

44 Clement interview, 30 April 1996; Long, interview, 19 April 1996.

45 Tom Long, Leslie Noble, and David Lindsay sat on a steering committee that was chaired by Elizabeth Witmer, MPP for Waterloo North. Meeting every Friday, the steering committee's purpose was twofold: to coordinate the caucus and campaign leaders; Witmer's specific task was to create a representative group of fund raisers, candidates, and local notables who would provide advice pertaining to election plans. The steering committee also met once a month with caucus. Although the steering committee did not work perfectly, one important effect was that the issues of employment equity and employment quotas were identified as a pressing concern and became one of three big issues of the election. These issues had not been highlighted in the CSR because the party's research up to May 1994 had not caught the public's unhappiness; Long interview, 19 April 1996.

46 Leslie Noble, interview, 17 April 1996. Ms Noble has been a long-time
    Conservative activist and was closely associated with Larry Grossman in
    the 1985 leadership conventions.
47 Thomas Long, 'Speech' to *Marketing Magazine*, Toronto, 30 October 1995.
48 Ibid., 2–3.
49 Ibid., 4.
50 Ibid., 5.
51 See Peter Woolstencroft, '"Doing Politics Differently": The Conservatives
    and the Campaign of 1993,' in J. Pammett, A. Frizzell, and T. Westell, eds,
    The Canadian General Election of 1993 (Ottawa: Carleton University Press,
    1994), 9–26.
52 Every person interviewed said that they were unaware of any other party
    doing what they did; Glen Wright referred to his efforts in the federal party
    to engage in strategic-planning exercises and noted that the federal associa-
    tion in the riding of Waterloo went through such an exercise after the 1984
    election. Wright, long active in the federal party, including serving as Vice-
    President (Ontario), became disillusioned in the early 1990s because of its
    unwillingness to respond to internal dissatisfaction and the movement of
    supporters to the Reform Party; he had served as Harris's tour manager in
    the 1990 election and did so again in 1995; as well, he was regularly
    involved in the strategic-planning exercises conducted by the provincial
    party; Glen Wright, interview, 30 April 1996.
53 Noble interview, 17 April 1996.
54 Long interview, 19 April 1996; Van Loan interview, 17 April 1996. One
    leading problem in the federal Conservative campaign of 1993 was that
    Kim Campbell inherited the campaign team and organization that Brian
    Mulroney had put in place; see Woolstencroft, '"Doing Politics Differently."'
55 The process produced the following ballot questions: for the Conservatives,
    'Which leader do you trust most to produce change?'; Liberals, 'Which
    party do you trust most to produce change?'; and the NDP, 'Which leader
    do you think has learned enough to bring about change?'; Lindsay inter-
    view, 26 April 1996.
56 Wright interview, 30 April 1996.
57 Many interviewees acknowledged that if the Conservatives had been in a
    competitive position in the 1994 period, their election planning probably
    would have been much more cautious.
58 The writing of the *Common Sense Revolution* required numerous drafts
    (fourteen being the common estimate); several party people, Harris aides,
    and outsiders were involved in its development, with Harris monitoring the
    process and choosing the final version. Caucus members were not directly

involved, but were apprised of its character and evolution. Neither the caucus nor the party in convention ratified the document. For an account of the writing of the CSR, see Christina Blizzard, *Right Turn: How the Tories Took Ontario* (Toronto: Dundurn Press, 1995), esp. 58–9. Blizzard's book reflects a working journalist's interpretation of the campaign; while it rightly traces change within the party after the 1987 election, it misses entirely the issue of public opinion and of change in Ontario's political culture.

59 Tom Long differentiated the 'rebranding' of the Ontario Conservatives from the ordinary advertising campaign that stresses visual differences (labels and images). 'The truth is that the rebirth of the Ontario Tories owed much less to the disciplined consumer packaged goods marketing techniques so commonly copied in politics, than it did to a new style of aggressive, focused political communications based on contrasting values and ideas'; Long, 'Speech,' 1. The $1 million cost of the launch of the CSR was money the party didn't have and had to be borrowed; Long interview, 19 April 1996.

60 The party's polling indicated 'that only 12 per cent of Ontario voters believed that there were significant differences between the federal and Ontario PC parties'; Long, 'Speech,' 1–2. 'Common sense' was a phrase that appeared regularly in the party's various policy-development processes from 1991 to 1994; Klees interview, 13 May 1996.

61 Noble interview, 17 April 1996.

62 Noble interview, 17 April 1996.

63 Tom Long, 'Speech,' 9.

64 Wright interview, 30 April 1996.

65 Mitch Patten, interview, 26 April 1996.

66 Noble interview, 17 April 1996.

67 Long interview, 19 April 1996. Perhaps Long's confidence on this point arose from the fact that some of the people (most notably Kimble Ainslie, who led a small group of 'Reform Association' candidates in the 1995 election) associated with the drive to have an Ontario Reform party had been involved in the policy-development process in the Conservative party but had left; Klees interview, 13 May 1996.

68 Clement interview, 30 April 1996.

69 Two additional policy documents were published by the party in January 1995. One 'Creating Jobs Through Small Business,' reflected consultations with and surveys of people working in small- and medium-sized businesses; the other, 'The Mike Harris Roundtable on Common Sense in Education,' summarized results of the party's policy-development processes pertaining to education (primarily elementary and secondary).

70 Summary of Leslie Noble and Tom Long interviews, transcripts, Election Broadcasting Project, a SSHRCC research grant held by Fred Fletcher, Bob MacDermid, David Taras, Edouard Cloutier, and Denis Moniere; I appreciate very much being given access to the interview transcripts.

71 Despite the confidence of the election strategists, several incumbent candidates in confidential interviews indicated that they approached the election with considerable trepidation (and some distanced themselves from the party, the leader, and the *CSR* in their early literature); part of the explanation for their fear was the youthfulness of the Tory strategists (Noble interview, 17 April 1996); another was that they perceived that their electoral success in the past was very much a reflection of their own personal standing, which may not be enough to save them if there was an anti-Tory tide. Tom Long, a strong believer in strategic planning, observed that if the Liberals had done what the Conservatives did, they would have ascertained that the only positive attribute the Tories had was their leader; a concerted campaign against Harris very well might have derailed the Conservatives; Long interview, 19 April 1996.

72 Patten, interview, April 30, 1996.

73 The Conservatives, frustrated by their inability to attract sustained media interest, announced in late December 1994 their intention to abolish photo radar at an operating photo radar site on highway 401. The election planners sometimes went outside the purported carefulness of their strategizing by countenancing a number of ill-advised pranks, most notably a video representation of Bob Rae stuttering badly that was shown at the PCs' autumn convention in 1994.

74 Even this 'positive' has to be qualified; Environics Research for most of 1994 reported that Mike Harris was the 'person best suited to be premier' for the highest proportion of voters; but by the first quarter of 1995 he was running at 18% and the other leaders at 23%; Environics Research, *Focus Ontario* (Toronto: 1995, no. 1).

75 During the 1995 election videos were distributed to voters in 65 constituencies identified as being 'volatile' on the basis of voting patterns in the 1988 and 1993 federal elections and the 1987 and 1990 provincial elections; 59 of these constituencies elected Conservatives.

76 The other four by-elections held during the 1990–5 period were only noteworthy for signalling the NDP collapse and, in one instance, the problems that the Liberals would face. In 1993 the Liberals, not at all surprisingly, retained Essex South and Brant-Haldimand; Conservatives took back Don Mills, traditionally one of their best seats; and the Liberals retained St George–St Patrick, which has a large gay population; the Liberals committed themselves to spousal rights for gays, a stance Lyn

McLeod moved away from as the 1995 general election approached; the image of waffling was never dispelled and, indeed, was reinforced in the election. The Tory win in Victoria-Haliburton was said by their opponents to be the result of homophobic electioneering, a charge vehemently denied by the Conservatives. Environics Research reported in 1995 that 7 voters out of 10 knew Bob Rae was the NDP leader; Mike Harris was known to 4 voters of 10; and Lyn McLeod, 3 of 10; Environics Research, *Focus Ontario* (Toronto: 1995, no. 3).

77 Environics Research, *Focus Ontario* (Toronto: 1995, no. 3); 34% of voters claimed they would never vote NDP; 15% Conservative; and 5% Liberal; the only positive the NDP had was that about one-third of voters thought Bob Rae was the leader best able to lead the province on constitutional and national-unity issues, with the other two leaders far behind.

78 Thomas Walkom, 'It ain't over till it's over; but latest poll says it's over,' *Toronto Star*, 11 May 1995. Walkom qualified his assertion by noting that the undecideds had doubled, from 12 to 24%, and that the increase came from the Liberal and NDP camps. The Tories suffered from low levels of support from unionized workers, visible minorities, and voters from non-European backgrounds. He also noted that the *Globe and Mail* and Canadian Press had pulled reporters from the leaders' tours.

79 Long interview, transcripts, Election Broadcasting Project.

80 This paragraph summarizes observations made by strategists for the three major parties in interviews for the Election Broadcasting Project. For a fuller discussion see chapter 8, by Drummond and MacDermid, in this volume.

81 Noble interview, 17 April 1996.

82 Long interview, 19 April 1996.

83 Noble interview, 17 April 1996; the greatest divergence in scores between Harris and McLeod occurred as they responded to the question, 'Why should I trust you?'

84 *Financial Post*, 23 May 1995.

85 Time of voting decision

	1995	1990
Before election	26	31
First three weeks	13	18
After the debate	9	6
Last week or two	36	28
Election day	8	11
Other	8	6

Source: Environics Research, *Focus Ontario* (Toronto: 1995, no. 2), 58–9.

86 Ibid., unreported data table; Leslie Noble (interview, 17 April 1996) made the point that the Conservatives planned their election strategy around the beginning of the advertising campaigns and the debate; a poll after the Victoria-Haliburton by-election had indicated that the majority of voters made their minds up in the ten days before the vote.

87 The other two cases are the United Farmers of Ontario government in 1919, which had no legislative standing before the election, and the Conservatives, who won the 1923 election after holding only 25 of 111 seats.

88 Long interview, 19 April 1996.

89 Hugh D. Segal, 'Ontario: A New Conservative Beachhead?' paper presented to the Canadian Seminar, Harvard University (12 February 1996), 2.

90 Noble interview, 17 April 1996. Several interviewees saw a mystical element in the campaign pointing to the close alignment between leader, party, and voters that had developed in the period from 1990 to 1995.

91 Donald C. MacDonald, 'Ontario's Political Culture: Conservatism with a Progressive Component,' Ontario History 86, no. 4 (December 1994), 297. MacDonald defines conservatism as 'that component of a political culture which represents contentment with the status quo and a tendency to resist change,' while progressive 'represents the component which seeks changes which initially may have limited support but which grow in public acceptance until even Conservative governments, originally opposed, become willing to accept and implement them.' Ibid., 298.

92 Thomas Long, 'What the Conservative Win in Ontario Means for All of Canada,' Fraser Forum, November 1995, 6–7.

93 John Ibbitson, 'The New Blue Machine,' Ottawa Citizen, 3 February 1996.

94 The CSR did not contain the moral and religious themes associated with much of American conservatism.

95 Mike Murphy's involvement goes as far back as 'one or two meetings' connected with the 1992 Windsor conference; Steve Gilchrist, interview, 13 May 1996. David Lindsay described the crucial difference being the three-party system in which each party has two opponents and only needs to get better than 40% to be in a position to form the government; interview, 26 April 1996.

96 David Frum, 'The Intimate State of Canada-USA Relations,' enRoute (October 1995), 17. Mr Luntz is an American pollster associated with the Republican Party.

97 Clement interview, 30 April 1996. It is worth noting that Mike Harris, in his first speeches to the legislature after the 1990 election, laid out the basic themes that were elaborated in the CSR.

98 Noble interview, 17 April 1996.

99 Long interview, 19 April 1996.

100 Segal, 'Ontario: A New Conservative Beachhead?' 3. Segal finds continuity 'between Bob Stanfield running a frugal Nova Scotia government and the economies brought in by ... Harris.' Hugh Segal, *No Surrender: Reflections of a Happy Warrior in the Tory Crusade* (Toronto: HarperCollins 1996), 227.

101 See Woolstencroft, 'More than a Guard Change' (note 2, above).

102 Environics Research, *Focus Ontario* (Toronto: 1995, no. 2), 3.

103 Long interview, 19 April 1996.

SIXTEEN

The Harris Government: Restoration or Revolution?

Thomas Walkom

I.

The election of Mike Harris as premier in 1995 has been widely viewed as the beginning of something fundamentally new for Ontario – a radical sea change in the bland, centrist politics of Canada's largest and wealthiest province. True, Ontario's political scene had already gone through changes. After forty-two years of unbroken Conservative rule, it had experienced five years of Liberal government and five more under the New Democrats. But both the Liberals under David Peterson (1985–90) and the NDP under Bob Rae (1990–5) had quickly adopted the cautious, middle-of-the-road tone of their Tory predecessors. Indeed, by the end of his mandate, Rae was describing himself as the logical successor to Bill Davis, the Tory premier whose retirement in 1985 had signalled the end of the postwar Conservative hegemony.

Harris himself has set the tone. 'The people of Ontario voted yesterday for change,' he told reporters the day after his sweeping victory. 'We intend to move.' His critics, while less complimentary, accepted the new Conservative premier's premise that his would be a revolutionary regime, vastly different from that of Bill Davis. 'Mr. Davis had a sense of proportion and balance which the right-wing zealots who have taken over the Tory party have utterly and completely lost,' Rae told the legislature. 'There is a stench of right-wing zealotry about this government.'[1]

In substantive terms, Harris moved quickly to assure voters that his government would quickly implement the raft of radical (at least for Ontario) election promises his Conservatives had listed in their campaign platform, the *Common Sense Revolution*. This document promised that Harris would do the following:

- Cut overall government spending by 11 per cent without taking money from health, classroom education, and law enforcement. As part of the spending cuts, welfare rates would be rolled back to a level set at '10 per cent above the national average of all other provinces' and all able-bodied welfare recipients under the age of sixty-five, including single mothers with children over the age of three would be required to work for their cheques.[2]
- Cut the provincial income-tax rate by 30 per cent across the board while replacing the existing employers' health tax with a new, revenue-neutral but progressive income-tax supplement. The new 'fair share health care levy' rate would kick in at 0.2 per cent ($100) for those with incomes of $50,000 and rise to a maximum 2 per cent for those earning $150,000 or more.
- Balance the provincial budget within five years.
- Create 725,000 net new jobs over five years.

Most of these jobs would come through normal economic growth independent of any government action (real growth to the year 2000 was assumed to average 4 per cent.)[3] But the Conservatives also talked of job creation through 'the removal of barriers to growth ... and ... a renewal of investor confidence.'[4]

Key to this job creation would be the repeal of the former New Democratic government's so-called Bill 40. Passed in 1992 over the vehement objections of business groups, this law had – among other things – severely restricted the use of strikebreakers by employers during legal strikes. As well, Bill 40 had broken new ground by giving employees in the agricultural sector the right to form unions. In opposition, Harris had promised to eradicate these and all other elements of the NDP law, which he called 'job-destroying legislation.'[5]

During the election campaign, Harris also spoke vaguely of reforming other, unspecified elements of Ontario labour law.[6] Although the *Common Sense Revolution* made no specific reference to this aspect, it did promise that a Harris government would 'eliminate all red tape and reduce the regulatory burden.'[7]

In fact, deregulation of the labour and other markets, while underplayed in the *Common Sense Revolution* document, was central to its strategy of job creation. There was nothing else. Contrary to later statements by the government, the architects of the Harris plan did not claim that Harris's promised tax cut would create jobs through Keynesian-style economic stimulus. In fact, they understood that the net effect of the *CSR*'s fiscal policy (spending cuts of about $6 billion offset by tax cuts of about $5 billion) would be to reduce jobs. In a background paper released to journalists before the election, the Conservatives put it bluntly: 'We do not make any claims on how the CSR will affect growth, other than by diminishing it in the short term because of deficit reduction-induced economic drag.'[8]

Nonetheless, the tax cut remained the centrepiece of the new Tory platform. In a telling line in their background paper, the Tories spelled it out, comparing their plan to Alberta Premier Ralph Klein's deficit-reduction strategy. 'It should be noted,' the paper reads, 'that the CSR, unlike the Klein plan in Alberta, takes as its starting point the measures to reduce tax rates and eliminate barriers to growth. The primary objective of the CSR is to create jobs, though eliminating the annual deficit and running an operating surplus are important outcomes.'[9]

More than anything else, this statement sums up the economic strategy of the *Common Sense Revolution*. High taxes and other unspecified 'barriers to growth' are the problem; a tax cut is the answer. To pay for this tax cut, government spending must be cut – but that should not cause undue hardship since government spending is out of control anyway. As well, certain government assets must be sold (the *Common Sense Revolution* estimates about $1 billion) to help pay for the tax cut. Finally, a little extra will be cut (about $1 billion worth) from spending to ensure that the deficit is eliminated by the end of the mandate.

Finally, Harris went beyond his Common Sense Revolution platform during the election campaign to promise that his government would repeal the NDP's new employment-equity law, an act aimed at increasing the proportion of women, non-whites, aboriginals, and disabled people in the workforce. Although not set to even begin coming into effect until September 1995, well after the June election, the employment-equity bill had become a focus of widespread resentment in a province still racked by high unemployment and job insecurity.

Still, the question remained: Once in power, how different would the new Harris Conservatives be from the old Tories of John Robarts and Bill Davis? How much of the Common Sense Revolution platform was sheer campaign bluster? Bob Rae had proved unable or unwilling to implement the moderate social-democratic platform of the NDP. Would Harris's hard-edged Common Sense Revolution suffer the same fate?

Harris himself gave off conflicting messages. On the one hand, he talked revolution. On the other, he spoke of bringing Ontario back to the position it had occupied in 1985 when his party was last in power, of eradicating what he called the ten lost years of Liberal and NDP government. Government spending, he said, had careered out of control since 1985. As for the tax cut, Harris insisted that it would merely bring tax levels back to where they were before the Liberals and New Democrats had grasped the reins of power.

This notion of restoration rather than revolution was reinforced by some of the personnel involved in the new government. True, Harris's transition team included his campaign chairman Tom Long, regarded as the party's chief neo-conservative ideologist. But it also included Tom Campbell, a seasoned politico-bureaucrat from the Davis era. Harris's principal secretary was not one of the wild-eyed young men from the campus Young Progressive Conservative clubs. Rather it was David Lindsay, a long-time political operative generally regarded as a party moderate. Indeed, Harris's office as a whole appeared to reflect a balance. The hard right was represented by Guy Giorno, a twenty-nine-year-old fresh from law school who acted as Harris's chief of policy. Bill King, a former *North Bay Nugget* reporter and long-time Harris aide represented the premier's own small-town, small-c, kick-ass brand of conservatism. Debbie Hutton, the premier's executive assistant and chief firefighter, was viewed as somewhat of a Red Tory, as, to a lesser extent, was Paul Rhodes, his top communications aide.

As for those Tories who had been attracted to Harris, they too covered a broader spectrum than many of the premier's critics liked to admit. Former MPP Susan Fish (regarded as a Red Tory) had supported him in his leadership bid. So too had fellow Red Tory and former Davis aide Janet Ecker (who ran and was elected in 1995 as the MPP from Durham West).

In short, as the government settled down to work in the summer of 1995, the nature of the new regime remained unclear. Would it indeed be revolutionary, as advertised. Or was it merely, as many of Harris's supporters argued, committed to the restoration of fiscal and social balance in Ontario?

II.

To answer this question properly requires some idea of the scope of the problems the new government faced. In opposition, the Conservatives had argued that previous Liberal and NDP governments had allowed spending to career out of control. Harris himself also routinely described Ontario as the most highly taxed jurisdiction in North America. As well, the Conservatives joined in on the chorus of disapproval over the provincial debt and deficit, both at record levels. Added in to these was the vexing problem of welfare. The rolls, after ballooning during the recession of 1990–3, were stubbornly refusing to come down, even though, technically at least, the economy was in recovery. Over all of this loomed the spectre of unemployment. Jobs lost during the recession had not come back. Ontario's official unemployment hovered around the unusually high rate of 9 per cent. Statisticians estimated that when those who had given up looking for work were added in, the real jobless rate would be significantly higher.

In the 1995 campaign, the Conservatives pulled all of these themes together masterfully to describe their vision of a province that had somehow strayed from the path. In part, this was the fault of bad stewardship under Liberal and NDP governments. But, in part, it was a systemic failure of government that had caused this overspending, overtaxation, slow growth, and general malaise. As the *Common Sense Revolution* manifesto put it, 'The political system itself stands in the way of making many of the changes we need right now. Our political system has become a captive to big special interests.' What was needed to restore the province to the right path was radical change. 'We need a revolution in this province,' the Tory manifesto rang out. 'A Common Sense Revolution.'[10] Implicit in all of this were two beliefs: first, that Ontario was worse off, particularly in the areas of spending and taxation; second, that it had slipped behind other provinces and states. In fact, this wasn't true.

Comparing tax burdens in different jurisdictions is notoriously difficult. First, the many different kinds of taxes (income, excise, sales, payroll) affect different groups differently. Second, some jurisdictions offer more public services than others. To use one obvious example: Income taxes may be higher in Canada than the United States; however, Canadians receive more benefits – particularly health benefits – from their taxes. If private-health-insurance costs are added to the average U.S. taxpayer's bill, then he becomes, in effect, worse off than his Canadian counterpart. Indeed, the major U.S. auto companies often cite the medicare advantage (which is another way of saying the tax advantage) for locating investment in Canada.

Second, even if the benefits paid for by taxation are ignored, the situation is not as simple as is commonly thought. For example, it is generally assumed that taxes are lower in the United States than in Canada. Yet the Organization for Economic Co-operation and Development points out that an average production worker in the United States actually pays more in income and social-security taxes than his Canadian counterpart.[11]

The Harris Conservatives, however, concentrated on only one tax, the personal income tax, and only one aspect of that tax – the top marginal rate. The marginal tax rate refers to the percentage that the government takes from the last dollar of income earned. While there is little empirical evidence on this issue, those on the right usually argue that high marginal rates sap the incentive of individuals to better themselves, the argument being that if someone expects most of any extra earnings to go to taxes, he won't bother doing the work to produce these earnings.

It was true that in 1995, the Ontario top marginal income-tax rate of 53.2 per cent was the second-highest in Canada. But this top rate affected only a minority of well-to-do taxpayers, those whose incomes were more than about $75,000. Indeed, for someone earning $50,000, the applicable marginal rate in Ontario was the third-lowest in the country (after British Columbia and Alberta). And for someone earning $12,500, the applicable marginal tax rate was, except for British Columbia, the country's lowest. In short, if marginal income-tax rates do affect incentive, then for low- and middle-income Ontarians, the incentive structure was quite healthy. Only the well-to-do, it appears, were being encouraged by Ontario's pre-Harris income-tax structure to wallow in their sloth.

Yet, as mentioned above, the income tax is only one of many. One way to compare the full tax burden among provinces is to look at a tax revenue as a percentage of gross provincial product. In essence, this approach shows how much of the wealth produced in each year is appropriated by the provincial government. The results, spelled out in table 1 (p. 408), are enlightening if contrary to the accepted wisdom.

During the entire period from 1981 to 1994, Ontario's own-source revenue as a percentage of gross domestic product was well below the provincial average. Ontario's tax burden was consistently lower than that of neighbouring Quebec or well-to-do British Columbia. What's more, it was lower than Alberta's throughout the period. Indeed, in 1994, the last full year of what Harris called the tax-and-spend NDP government, Ontario's provincial taxes as a percentage of GDP were not much higher than they had been thirteen years earlier when the Tories were in power – 14.2 per cent as opposed to 12.5 per cent.

In short, during the 1980s and 1990s, Ontario was not the highest-tax jurisdiction in North America or even one of the highest-tax jurisdictions. Compared to what they produced, Ontarians paid far less in provincial taxes than any other Canadians.

TABLE 1
Provincial own-source revenue as a percentage of provincial GDP

Province	1981	1982	1983	1984	1985	1986	1987
Quebec	18.7	19.2	18.7	18.1	18.7	18.8	19.0
Ontario	12.5	13.1	12.8	12.9	13.2	13.7	13.7
Alberta	19.6	20.5	20.4	20.5	18.9	15.8	18.6
BC	15.7	17.0	16.8	16.9	16.9	16.5	16.3
All	15.7	16.5	16.2	16.0	16.1	15.8	16.3

	1988	1989	1990	1991	1992	1993	1994
Quebec	18.8	18.7	19.4	20.1	20.0	20.0	19.6
Ontario	14.3	14.7	15.1	14.2	13.8	14.2	14.2
Alberta	16.8	19.9	17.6	17.0	15.6	16.5	17.5
BC	16.9	17.6	19.1	19.0	18.9	20.5	20.7
All	16.3	16.5	17.3	17.0	16.7	17.3	17.2

Source: Statistics Canada, Public Finance Historical Data 1965–66 – 1991–92 (Catalogue 68-512), 14–56; Provincial Economic Accounts, Annual Estimates, 1981–1994 (Catalogue 13-213), 2–23; 'Provincial and Territorial Government Revenue Financial Management System Basis' (15 January 1996)

Nor was government spending out of control when Harris took over. Again, one of the few ways to compare government spending is to relate it to the size of the provincial GDP. Table 2 tells the tale here. Between 1981 and 1994, Ontario government spending as a percentage of GDP remained below the provincial average. Again, it was consistently lower than that of Quebec, British Columbia and even Alberta. True, between 1981 and 1994, Ontario's spending did rise (as did that of all other provinces). But the rise was not indicative of a long-term trend. Rather it was tied to the business and, to a lesser extent, the political cycles. Thus, Ontario government spending as a percentage of GDP peaked at 17.6 per cent during the 1981–3 recession, peaked again at 18 per cent in 1985 (the first year of the Liberal-NDP accord), and fell back in 1989 to its 1981 level of 16.3 per cent. With the recession of the early 1990s, spending as a percentage of GDP took off again, peaking at 20.8 per cent in 1992 and falling back marginally to 20 per cent in 1994.

As well, Rae's government had squeezed the big health-expenditure envelope. Even the civil service in 1995 was no larger than it had been ten years earlier when the Conservatives were last in power.[12] As for debt and deficit, all the parties paid appropriate obeisance to the gods of fiscal restraint. But all implicitly believed that the deficit would be wiped out mainly by exogenous economic growth. Thus, in the 1995 election cam-

TABLE 2
Provincial government spending as a percentage of provincial GDP

Province	1981	1982	1983	1984	1985	1986	1987
Quebec	26.9	28.4	28.7	27.9	27.7	26.5	25.4
Ontario	16.3	17.6	17.5	16.8	18.0	17.0	16.7
Alberta	17.3	22.4	21.6	20.1	21.1	25.4	23.4
BC	18.1	22.1	22.5	22.1	21.5	21.1	19.6
All	20.4	22.9	22.7	22.0	22.5	22.3	21.5
	1988	1989	1990	1991	1992	1993	1994
Quebec	24.8	24.6	26.5	28.0	29.2	28.9	28.6
Ontario	16.6	16.3	18.1	20.4	20.8	20.2	20.0
Alberta	23.2	22.7	22.4	22.8	23.8	21.0	20.1
BC	19.0	19.5	21.9	23.9	23.8	24.0	23.2
All	21.1	20.8	22.6	24.5	24.9	24.2	23.4

Source: Statistics Canada, 'Provincial and Territorial Government Expenditure Financial Management System Basis' (15 January 1996); sources for table 1.

paign, all three parties confidently predicted that moderate net fiscal restraint combined with the healthy growth predicted by forecasters would eliminate the deficit sometime around the year 2000. Later, in government, the Conservatives began to play on deficit fears to justify the need for their spending cuts, pointing out that the government was spending a million dollars an hour more than it was taking in. But as noted above, in the Common Sense Revolution program itself, deficit reduction took a back seat to the tax cut.

All of this creates a bit of a puzzle around the Harris program. The Common Sense Revolution was premised on the belief that Ontario's taxes were punishingly high. Yet, as we have seen, in relative terms this was not so. The Common Sense Revolution's second premise was that Ontario government spending was unduly fat and could be cut with ease. Yet this too appears not to have been the case by 1995. Where then did these interesting ideas come from?

III.

In part, the ideas came from Harris himself. A public servant most of his working life (first as a teacher, then as a school-board trustee and chairman, latterly as an MPP), Harris none the less absorbed and reflected the small-business ethos that dominated his home city of North Bay. Indeed,

Harris's contradictions echoed those of North Bay itself. Although it is a city that defines itself primarily in terms of rugged Northern Ontario entrepreneurial individualism, North Bay's ten top employers the year Harris was elected were all public-sector agencies – including the Canadian military, the school-board empire (over which Harris had once presided), the provincially owned Ontario Northland Transportation Commission, and the provincial correctional-services ministry.[13] Although Harris appears to have had little interest in the intellectual and ideological developments in new-right thinking, he was an instinctive small-c conservative – convinced of government's inherent inefficiency, unhappy with taxes, suspicious of so-called disadvantaged groups (such as women, the poor, Indians) that the liberal welfare state of the 1970s and 1980s had busily promoted.

None of this was particularly obvious when Harris was first elected to the legislature in 1981. He was not regarded as one of the Davis government's serious right wingers. Indeed, in 1982, Harris seconded the Conservative government's throne speech, one dedicated to the Keynesian notion of spending money and increasing the provincial deficit in order to help combat the serious recession that had gripped Canada. In the legislature, Harris defended the government's decision to increase spending and in particular lauded its promise to increase grants to Northern Ontario.[14] But gradually, his politics became more definably conservative. During a rambling 1982 discussion in a legislative committee, Harris attacked the notion of union seniority rights, arguing that these allowed workers to move ahead not through merit but through the number of 'hours with a butt on a chair.'[15] But it was in a rebuttal to the Liberal budget of 1985 that Harris articulated the theme that would define his government – taxation.

In this speech, Harris compared Treasurer Bob Nixon's budget to the 1981 effort of a former federal Liberal finance minister, Alan MacEachen. The MacEachen budget of 1981, which proposed doing away with several tax loopholes, had raised a firestorm among Canadian business people and was eventually withdrawn by then prime minister Pierre Trudeau's chastened government. As well as offending the self-interest of those who profited from tax loopholes (particularly accountants), the MacEachen budget also raised a very real point of principle: to whom does potential tax revenue belong? Does it belong by right to the people as a whole? If so, then tax loopholes allow a small minority, in effect, to cheat the wider community. Or does tax revenue belong to the individual who first appropriated it? If that is the case, then a measure to close a tax loophole would be nothing less than theft. Indeed, under this logic, taxation in general was theft.

In his 1985 speech to the legislature, Harris adopted the latter position with enthusiasm. Like the ill-starred MacEachen budget, he said, Nixon's effort 'attempted to say, I think, in a very arrogant way, that government would tell these companies how to spend their money and how to create jobs and would take any surplus money that might be sitting around for small businessmen, small businessmen or large businessmen, tax the money away and then give it back to them to create jobs.

'It is an arrogant philosophy when one directly tells business people through these tax measures that one knows better than they do how to create jobs in their businesses and where they should be investing their money ... [B]usiness people themselves know in their various businesses what will create new jobs, what will allow them to expand and what will allow them to grow. That is why I do not like the term "tax holiday."'

In the same speech, Harris also – in some contradiction to his 1982 support of the Davis government's anti-recession package – gave his view on how economies come out of depression. 'We did go through a depression after the Trudeau-MacEachen budget,' he noted. 'We did have problems in those days. However, things started to turn around once governments south of the border, in Canada and in Ontario recognized that if they left the money with business people they would make things happen and create jobs.'[16]

In a nutshell, this was the core of what would become the Common Sense Revolution. Taxation was not only an affront but a danger. Taking money heedlessly from business would send an economy into recession; only by restoring this money to its rightful owners could a country or province recover.

When Davis announced his resignation as Conservative leader in 1984, Harris supported Frank Miller, the candidate of the right, as his successor. But after the short-lived Miller government fell, and following the Tories' ignominious trouncing at the polls in 1987, Harris began to consider his own leadership chances. By 1988, he had hooked up with William Farlinger, chief executive officer of one of the country's largest accounting firms, Ernst and Young, a man with impeccable corporate connections who was devoted to reducing government's role in the economy.[17] To Farlinger, whom Harris would later appoint as chairman of Ontario Hydro, the superior virtue and efficiency of private over public enterprise was a matter of deeply held faith that required no proof.

Harris's campaign for the Tory leadership centred around the twin themes of government waste and taxes. Interestingly, however, it was not a radical tax program. Harris talked merely of freezing taxes at their current levels, not cutting them. Nor had he been converted yet to the other key theme of what would become the Common Sense Revolution – deregulation. In fact, Harris pledged to increase regulation in the area of packaging, as a way to reduce waste.[18]

By the time of the 1990 provincial election, taxation had moved to the fore. While still promising to merely freeze taxes, the Tory leader presented himself as 'The Taxfighter.' In part, as his campaign manager John Laschinger later revealed, this was a cynical attempt to differentiate a struggling third party from its opponents and play to the polls.[19] But in large part, the moniker was true. Instinctively, in his heart, Harris was the tax fighter.

IV.

Still, the full Common Sense program did not come together until 1994. Following the 1990 election, the rejuvenated Tory caucus began assembling a policy platform through a series of what they called New Directions papers. Some New Directions proposals, such as a call for private universities, were, for Ontario, radical. But others were mainstream Davis conservatism. The Harris caucus warmly supported, for example, the NDP's creation of a new Ontario Training and Adjustment Board to oversee training. Only later did Harris reverse himself, criticize the new training board as yet another piece of bureaucracy, and pledge to abolish it.

What gave Harris his consistency was the publication in May 1994 of the actual *Common Sense Revolution* document. Referred to as the Bradgate Group (named for a hotel where they met), the document's authors consisted of people who would form the nucleus of the successful 1995 Harris campaign team. But the central figures were Harris, with his North Bay mistrust of taxes; Farlinger, with his faith in private enterprise; and Long, an admirer of former British Prime Minister Margaret Thatcher. The Common Sense Revolution was very much a political document. It built on polling, on focus groups, and on the remarkable gains made in Ontario by the federal Reform Party in the 1993 federal election. But it also took Harris's brand of instinctive anti-tax, anti-government conservatism and located it in the context of the more generalized and intellectually consistent conservative revival that was sweeping the Western world.

The term 'Common Sense Revolution' was in part a marketing ploy designed to demonstrate that the Mike Harris team was different – different from the poll-topping provincial Liberals and different from the discredited federal Conservatives. Yet it became a self-fufilling prophecy. Those who work closely together in politics invariably develop an esprit de corps. For the group around Harris, this spirit was accentuated by the Common Sense Revolution platform. It was clear, consistent, unusually detailed for an opposition party, and radical. With the *Common Sense Revolution* in hand, it was easy to think of oneself as a revolutionary. This sense was heightened by the outsider status of the Harris group. Most were young; few had played a major role in the party before. Harris himself was an outsider, one who had suffered the derision of the old Conservative establishment associated with Davis. But by 1995, the old Davis functionaries – the Hugh Segals and John Torys – were in bad odour themselves, discredited by their association with Brian Mulroney and the hapless federal Conservatives.

More important, Harris owed the old party little. He may have owed his financial supporters, led by Farlinger. But the great barons of the Davis years were by 1995 either retired or irrelevant. By contrast, the newly elected members of the 1995 Tory caucus – with few exceptions – owed everything to Harris and to the document all were required to treat as holy writ, the *Common Sense Revolution*.

V.

In short, the context favoured bold, radical moves. The new government possessed a clear, detailed program that all its members had endorsed. There were no significant power groupings opposing Harris either in caucus or the party. Senior Tories from the Davis era grumbled privately that their efforts to advise or temper the Harris government were roundly ignored.

In its first few months, the Harris government did move boldly to implement the Common Sense Revolution. Bill 40 and the employment-equity law were repealed as well as some other pieces of NDP legislation the Conservatives had promised to scrap. Welfare rates were cut by more than 20 per cent. A total of $8 billion in spending cuts was announced. Yet these moves, while brash, controversial, and in some measure harsh, were not revolutionary. The Liberals too had promised welfare cuts; the NDP's Rae had mused about workfare. All three parties had committed themselves to balance the budget through spending reductions (although, admittedly, the proposed Tory cuts were the deepest by far).

In two main aspects, however, the Harris Conservatives did differ

sharply from their predecessors. The first involved the style of governance. The traditional Ontario way – the way of Bill Davis, David Peterson,
and, for most of his time in office, Bob Rae – was to gain consensus from
the province's powerful and vocal interest groups, what the politicians
had come to call stakeholders. If education was the issue, teachers and
school boards would be consulted; if health, then hospitals and doctors.
Changes to labour laws were hammered out with business and the
unions (the NDP's Bill 40, which initially sidelined business, was a notorious exception). Changes to the legal system were vetted by lawyers and
judges.

Harris too consulted interest groups. The difference was, in the first
few months at least, he consulted only those that agreed with the premises
of his program. For example, the Tories wanted to deregulate the building code; only the home builders' lobby was consulted. The environmental lobby, even the insulation manufacturer's lobby, was ignored.

The new style was particularly obvious in three areas: labour, health,
and justice. The Tories not only repealed Bill 40, they rolled union organizing rights in some areas back fifty years. All was done in the face of
strident opposition from the unions. In the health field, the Tories' Bill 26
took on the province's powerful doctors. Among other things, this omnibus bill gave the minister of health unprecedented authority to determine where physicians could practise. Again, this was accomplished
without consulting the furious doctors.

One of the few areas where the government did blink in its initial cost-
cutting efforts was the legal field. Here it found its plans offended not
only the powerful lawyers' lobby but the even more powerful judges.
The judges retaliated by sending a stiff letter to the attorney general
accusing the government of undermining the legal system – and then
leaking the letter to the press.

The second radically different element of the Harris program revolved
around the tax cut. Even before it was officially unveiled, the tax cut
drove the agenda. No one – bureaucrat, aide, or politician – could ease
up on cost-cutting. For unless massive savings in the operation of government could be found, the tax cut would bump up the deficit and
create profound political embarrassment for the Conservatives, not to
mention confusion among the province's lenders. The spectre of the tax
cut provided a discipline that prevented ministers from backsliding.

In a similar vein, the tax cut demanded speedy action. On the face of it,
the omnibus Bill 26, which centralized new powers in the hands of
cabinet, seemed odd for a regime ostensibly committed to getting gov-

ernment off the backs of the citizens. Yet in terms of the tax cut, Bill 26 made absolute sense. The tax cut was due to begin coming into effect in 1996. That left no time for squeamishness; spending cuts had to be made immediately. If that meant giving government more power so that it could, ultimately, dismantle parts of itself, then so be it.

VI.

Ultimately, history will decide whether the Harris government represents a real break with Ontario's past. Even in its first year, there were some forces inside government trying to slow the revolution. Moreover, Harris was not blind to the reality of politics, a realilty which says that unpopular governments don't get re-elected. While still hostile to organized labour, by early 1996 the government appeared to be trying to mend relations with other traditional power centres such as physicians. And although Finance Minister Ernie Eves did deliver his tax cut in the government's first budget, it was not exactly as advertised. In an effort to make peace with financiers nervous about the deficit, Eves reversed the order of implementation. The Common Sense Revolution had promised a 15 per cent provincial-income-tax cut in 1996, followed by a 7.5 per cent cut in each of 1997 and 1998. Eves's budget provided a 3.4 per cent cut in 1996, followed by 12.5 per cent more in 1997 with the remaining 15 per cent to come 'between 1997 and 1999.' As a result, tax revenue was actually expected to increase marginally in 1996–7, by about $175 million from the year before. Perhaps more important, however, spending (minus public-debt interest) was projected to fall in nominal terms by $3.1 billion between 1995–6 and 1996–7, a remakarble one-year decline.[20]

Eves's minor fudging on the tax cut notwithstanding, there is an underlying dynamic to the Common Sense Revolution that promises to make the Harris government, in Ontario terms, truly radical. Again, the 30 per cent income-tax cut is central. Once in place, it will be virtually impossible to reverse. In opposition, both the Liberals and New Democrats attack the idea of a tax cut. Yet both parties know that even if they form the next government they will not have the nerve to boost provincial taxes back up to their old levels.

Given that the revenue base is being more or less irreversibly reduced, government spending will simply be unable to return in the forseeable future to past levels. Thus, the spending cuts that the Tories have implemented – to welfare, muncipalities, hospitals, and education – are also, in practical political terms, virtually irreversible.

Finally, the macroeconomic effects of the net spending cuts will put the Harris government – and future governments – under tremendous pressure to deregulate. Not only will the Common Sense Revolution's fiscal program reduce employment (as its architects openly predicted), but by slashing away at the social safety net, it will aggravate the situation of those without work. Given the parameters that the Harris cuts are imposing, the only solution to any subsequent jobs crisis will be deregulation aimed at lowering the cost of employing labour – such as reductions in safety, environmental, and employment standards. As well, under this scenario, the government will have even more incentive to follow Margaret Thatcher's lead and reduce the clout of unions. For in a world where the state has been left unwilling or unable to act, the most seductive avenue for a government interested in increasing employment will be to follow the dictum of the neoclassical economists and force down wages. In this sense, Harris's Bill 7, which dealt the first blow at organized labour, represents one of the most important pieces of legislation of the government's first year.

The Common Sense Revolution set out to solve a set of problems – unduly high spending, unduly high taxes – that, by and large, did not exist. If followed through, it will not restore the balance within Ontario to 1985 levels. Rather, it promises to fundamentally alter that balance, a balance forged over fifty years between private and public enterprise, state and market forces, business and labour, rich and poor. It is in this sense that the Common Sense Revolution is, indeed, truly revolutionary.

Notes

1 Thomas Walkom, 'Harris' evolution spawned Tory revolution,' *Toronto Star*, 10 June 1995; Legislative Assembly of Ontario, *Official Report of Debates (Hansard)*, (29 June 1996), 1630.
2 Ontario Progressive Conservative Party, *The Common Sense Revolution*, 5th printing (post–Martin budget), 3, 7, 9–10.
3 The Common Sense Revolution assumed 3 per cent real growth for its fiscal projections. But for employment projections, the assumption (not spelled out explicitly in the document) was that real growth would average 4 per cent over the period. See Thomas Walkom, 'How the Tories are juggling the numbers,' *Toronto Star*, 17 December 1994.
4 Mark Mullins, 'Common Sense Revolution,' background paper to *The Common Sense Revolution*, 25 May 1994, 1.
5 *Common Sense Revolution*, 3.

6 Thomas Walkom, 'For Harris common sense really means low wages,'
  Toronto Star, June 5, 1995.

7 *Common Sense Revolution*, 3.

8 Mullins, 'Common Sense Revolution,' 1.

9 Ibid., 2.

10 *Common Sense Revolution*, 2.

11 Cited in Ontario Fair Tax Commission, *Discussion Paper: Searching for
   Fairness* (Toronto: OFTC, 1993), 28.

12 The numbers were 81,251 full-time equivalents in March 1995 compared to
   81,008 in March 1984. Ontario, Management Board, 'Monthly Staff Strength
   Report, March 1995'; 'Public Service Strength in Ontario, 31 March 1984.'

13 'Top 100 North Bay Employers,' *North Bay Nugget*, 9 August 1995.

14 Legislative Assembly of Ontario, *Official Report of Debates (Hansard)*,
   15 March 1982, 151–5.

15 Legislative Assembly of Ontario, General Government Committee, *Hansard*,
   26 October 1983, G-282.

16 Legislative Assembly of Ontario, *Official Report of Debates (Hansard)*,
   5 November 1985, 1396–1400.

17 Daniel Girard, 'The power broker,' *Toronto Star*, 30 April 1996.

18 Mike Harris, 'Notes for the campaign kick-off, Mike Harris MPP Nipissing,
   for the leadership of the Progressive Conservative Party of Ontario, 25 Jan.
   1990 11:30 a.m.'

19 John Laschinger and Geoffrey Stevens, *Leaders and Lesser Mortals: Backroom
   Politics in Canada* (Toronto: Key Porter, 1992), 76.

20 The Fair Share Health Levy was also not exactly as advertised, although
   Eves blamed this on federal inflexibility. Ontario, Ministry of Finance, *1996
   Ontario Budget: Budget Speech*, 7 May 1996, 31; *1996 Ontario Budget: Budget
   Papers*, 7 May 1996, 6, 65, 66.

SEVENTEEN

Change in Ontario Politics

Nelson Wiseman

In the past half-century, Ontario has undergone staggering change. By 1985, the Conservatives had governed for forty-two years, having won twelve consecutive elections. This represents the longest tenure of any Canadian regime in this century. It seems paradoxical that such apparent political immobility existed against the backdrop of Ontario's profound socio-economic transformation. Wouldn't one have expected a less linear political path in a dynamically changing province? One approach to this question is comparative: how does the Ontario case contrast to other provinces or regions? Another approach is to scratch below the surface and poke at Ontario's apparent political stability and continuity.

Certainly, Ontario's Conservatives were the dominant party, between the 1940s and 1980s. However, they have not since 1929 been the majority's party, although they came reasonably close in 1951, 1955, and 1963 to winning more than half the popular vote. In the Atlantic provinces, in contrast, majority popular votes have been commonplace. Ontario's Conservatives profited from having two opponents in the quirky 'first past the post' or single-member plurality system. Compare the 1948 and 1951 elections: the Liberal vote rose from 29 per cent to 31 per cent but Liberal seats shrank from thirteen to seven. In 1985, the Conservatives actually won a thirteenth consecutive victory with a plurality of seats, but the Liberals won a plurality of votes and the Conservatives succumbed to a Liberal-NDP working alliance. The vagaries of the electoral system came to benefit the Liberals in 1987 and, even more so, the NDP in 1990, who captured 57 per cent of the seats with less than 38 per cent of the votes.

That election also revealed the influence of fourth and other parties. The votes for them and independents (totalling a robust 6.6 per cent) exceeded the winner's margin in 48 of the 130 ridings. The NDP won half those seats, representing a third of all the seats it won. The point here is not to belabour the electoral system for distorting the public will; it is merely to expose the system's masking of the relative weight of party forces during the superficial somnolence of the 1943–85 era. In brief: the Conservatives were not as hegemonic as they appeared. Ontario's politics of stability was actually a mixture: part reality and part chimera.

Examine the Ontario case in comparative perspective. Socio-economic change has been much more dramatic in Ontario than in Atlantic Canada. To be sure, regime changes occur relatively frequently in the east, but there is little about them that is mysterious. Rather, they are the predictable comings and goings of a two-party system. The Liberals and Conservatives – indistinguishable on ideological and policy grounds – play 'ins versus outs,' alternating between government and opposition. The seemingly relative calm waters of Ontario politics until 1985, in contrast, were but surface reflections. Down below much swirled. The social-democratic CCF appeared at the doorstep of power during the Second World War. Embraced by organized labour and the working class, it captured only four fewer seats than the Conservatives. The political landscape was more than shaken. More than in any other province, Ontario has come closest since the 1940s to offering up a competitive and remarkably vibrant three-party system. While the Conservatives seemed safely and semi-permanently ensconced in office, the Liberals and the CCF-NDP alternated as the official opposition, with the Liberals more often than not in the role. Ontario experienced minority governments in the 1940s, 1970s, and 1980s – something virtually unknown to the Atlantic provinces. The United Farmers of Ontario government of 1919–23 proved to be a precursor of the province's later political flux. Where in Atlantic Canada – a region relatively more rural than Ontario – has a farmers party, a social-democratic party, or any other third party so rattled the established two-party system?

Compared to Western Canada, Ontario in this century has had less socio-economic change and less political upheaval. Ontario was a product of the late eighteenth and early nineteenth centuries; the West was born in the late nineteenth and early twentieth centuries. While Ontario changed in the twentieth century – from an agricultural, traditional, and hierarchical Anglo-Celtic society into a modern, urban-industrial, and more egalitarian, multiracial one – Western Canada more than changed.

It came to life and exploded: a largely unoccupied remote hinterland became a driving engine of the national economy and the major magnet for immigrants in the first quarter of this century. Self-avowed socialists were elected in British Columbia as early as 1902 and third parties have been persistent, consistent, numerous, and relatively strong compared to the Ontario experience. The west begat two farmers' governments, the United Farmers of Alberta and the United Farmers of Manitoba, and generated the related Progressives, Social Credit, the CCF, and Reform. It also generated a host of smaller lively political fractions from the Non-Partisan League during the First World War through to the Western Canada Concept and the Confederation of Regions Party during the Cold War. Minority and coalition governments are old hat in Manitoba and British Columbia. Third-party governments throughout the west have been common, not exceptional, as in Ontario. Certainly the long reigns of Social Credit and the Conservatives in Alberta and the CCF-NDP in Saskatchewan suggest a measure of political stability. However, unlike the Conservatives' long rule in Ontario, they also connote a relatively more advanced state of ideological fermentation and class politics.

The short lesson here is that we gain insight into Ontario's political evolution by placing it in comparative perspective. We may also contrast the Ontario of yesteryear to the Ontario of today and to the Ontario in between. Lastly, we may compare Ontario politics to national politics. During their long tenancy in office, the Conservatives appeared as the province's natural 'government party,' somewhat akin to the federal Liberals, who served as Canada's 'government party' between the 1930s and 1950s.[1] Both regimes could be described as having melded party and state, to converting governance to bureaucratic management, to the grey depoliticization of politics itself by shunning ideological choices and confrontations. 'Bland works,' observed the triumphant Conservative premier Bill Davis in the aftermath of his 1981 majority victory. As the millennium draws to an end and Ontario is ruled by yet another Conservative government, its politics are hardly bland. They are decidedly ideological.

Politics both reflects society and changes it. This chapter seeks to illuminate our understanding of evolving Ontario politics over the past half-century. It casts light on three dimensions of politics: the interrelationship of state and society; the strategic and ideological predilections of parties and premiers; and culture, identity, and the very appetite for provincial politics. Hindsight should contribute to foresight as we speculate about the future contours of Ontario politics.

State and Society

In the early 1940s, Ontario's government was much smaller and less intrusive than it is today. Expectations of it were modest, as was its capacity. Ontarians were far fewer (less than four million versus over eleven million in the mid-1990s) and they made up a somewhat smaller percentage of Canadians as a whole (33 per cent versus 37 per cent). About as many were employed in agriculture as in manufacturing. Fewer than half of Ontarians lived in cities of over 100,000, and of those who lived in the countryside 87 per cent still used outdoor privies; most farm households relied on kerosene lamps.[2] Ontarians were also much less mobile, and more likely to die near their birthplaces than later generations. The federal government, in taking charge of the war effort, occupied virtually all tax fields and deprived Ontario's government of significant independent resources. Both before and for a fair time after this usurpation of fiscal power, the provincial state played a marginal role in Ontarians' welfare. Consider social assistance: in 1920 those dependent on it made up a paltry 0.37 per cent of the population. By 1950 the number was a more noticeable 5 per cent, and by 1993 about 13 per cent,[3] consuming $6 billion annually, almost as much as the government's expenditures on education. As an age of affluence took hold in the 1950s and 1960s, citizen expectations of governments and their capacities leapt.

The rise of the modern welfare state was a phenomenon common in the Western world; Canada was part of a tide, typical rather than exceptional. In other states, however, welfarism meant a strengthening of the central government; in Canada it went with the burgeoning growth of provincial governments. In welfare as well as wealth, Ontario has consistently led in measures such as per capita income and per capita gross provincial product. In 1994, its 1,379,300 social-assistance recipients exceeded the combined populations of Newfoundland and New Brunswick; they widely outnumbered the separate populations of Manitoba and Saskatchewan.[4] Oddly, the percentage of Ontarians on social assistance (one in eight people, one in five children) was higher than that in any other province, including the perennial have-nots of Confederation, the Atlantic provinces. This seemed incongruous, since the 1991 census revealed that, proportionately, Ontario had the fewest families with incomes of less than $20,000 and the most with ones over $70,000. The incongruity was in important ways a reflection of the eligibility rules for federal unemployment insurance (UI), which produced in Ontario the lowest provincial percentage of unemployed persons receiving UI payments.[5] In other words, many Ontarians who in other provinces could rely on UI were forced onto the welfare rolls.

Substantial funding for the modern welfare state came from Ottawa. In the 1960s the federal government launched a shared-cost program (Canada Assistance Plan) that paid half the cost of provincial welfare burdens. Provincial governments determined levels of assistance and, with few conditions imposed by Ottawa, eligibility. In the 1980s, Ontario's welfare regime became the most liberal in benefits paid (about 130 per cent of the national average) as well as eligibility. After the federal government unilaterally cut the rate of increase in its transfer payments to the wealthier provinces in 1990, Ontario took up the slack, so that its share of carrying social assistance went from the old shared-cost formula of 50 per cent to 72 per cent of cost. A study commissioned by the provincial government observed that 'Quebec, whose CAP budget is not constrained, is receiving from the federal government 10 per cent more federal funds than Ontario, and has 43 per cent fewer beneficiaries.'[6] De facto federal downloading, unaccompanied by provincial downsizing of its welfare and other programs, contributed to budgetary deficits hard to fathom by earlier standards. Where the total Ontario expenditure budget had been about $14 billion in 1978–9, it exploded to over $52 billion in 1991–2 and $57 billion in 1995–6.[7] Some annual budgetary deficits in the 1990s were larger than some budgets had been in the 1970s. Debt as a percentage of GPP went from 14 per cent in 1989–90 to 31 per cent in 1994–5.[8] As one part of its response to this fiscal crisis of the provincial state, Mike Harris's new Conservative government in 1995 reduced welfare benefits by nearly 22 per cent; the new rates still bettered the national average by 10 per cent. As evidence that Ontarians are no longer the deferential lot associated with their province's Tory origins, a dozen welfare recipients took the Ministry of Community and Social Services to court, arguing that the cuts were unconscionably draconian and a violation of Canada's *Charter of Rights*. Government fiat is no longer sufficient; it is compelled to legally defend its policies. Research submitted to the court showed that while real family income in the province had grown by just over 2 per cent between 1980 and 1993, real welfare rates had increased by 46 to 49 per cent.[9]

The legal/political battle over welfare reveals how embedded and meshed provincial society and the provincial state have become and how contentious and litigious the relationship can be. There is a growing popular willingness to sue the state: major suits exceeding $50 million proliferated from four in 1985 to thirteen in 1992 to twenty-six in 1995.[10] Government is no longer immune to legal sanction as it once was. In the 1940s, by contrast, when the Ontario legislature voted to extend its life to an unprecedented six years, a court challenge to that was dismissed by the bench as something it was powerless to entertain, something that could only be reversed on the basis of the royal prerogative.[11]

Beyond welfare – in health, education, and non-traditional areas of governmental activity – Ontarians have come to expect much of their government. They are paying for it: a sales tax of 3 per cent launched in 1960 escalated to 8 per cent by the mid-1980s and then to 15 per cent with the federal GST in 1990. Many see government programs as entitlements that contribute to, rather than threaten, the public weal. Governments facilitated this outlook in the postwar era by incrementalizing program spending annually and by launching ever more new programs and initiatives. As in the welfare field, Ontario's provisions tend to be rich in comparative perspective. Day care for children, long an area wholly outside the purview of government, is another example. By 1991–2, the Ontario government spent $232 per child, the highest of any province, for a total of $420 million. The Harris government budgeted even more for child care, a half-billion dollars, for 1995–6.[12] In contrast, Newfoundland spent a paltry $15 per child, wealthy British Columbia only $138, and next-door Quebec $122. In part, these discrepancies reflect the capacities, values, and priorities of provincial governments. Staff in Ontario's day-care centres receive the country's highest hourly wages for their labour, nearly double those paid in the Atlantic provinces.

It is important to note Ontario's debt burden, because in the 1990s it has come to weigh so heavily on provincial politics and public administration. In the 1980s, when the provincial economy was hyperventilated, government largesse and expansiveness appeared inexhaustible, logical, and salutary. In every year of that decade government revenues grew, twice by 15 per cent annually and in most years in excess of 10 per cent. Fortune turned, however, in the early 1990s. For the first time in decades, revenues actually declined in both 1991 and 1992. When inflation is factored in, the real decline was substantial, close to 5 per cent annually. Against this ominous backdrop, government expenditures continued to rise, exacerbating the provincial debt, which more than doubled from $42 billion to $97 billion between 1990 and 1995. For forty years, up to 1990, Ontario averaged 4.5 per cent annual economic growth. It usually paced the national economy and provincial government expanded with it. Indeed, Ontario's economy outperformed that of every G7 state in five of the seven years between 1981 and 1987 and did so again in 1994.[13] In the early 1990s, however, Ontario proved a laggard, falling into deep recession and uncharacteristically trailing the nation. One in seven industrial jobs was lost and over 250,000 jobs disappeared.

It is possible for government to cut program spending – something it did not do in the lean early 1990s – but it is impossible for it to control interest rates and the ever-rising cost of servicing the ever-accumulating debt. Thus, by 1995–6, as much was being spent (16 per cent of the budget) paying bondholders as was on education and training. For every two dollars that went to health care, one dollar went to paying interest, an unproductive, unbeneficial current expense. In the late 1970s, in contrast, almost three times as much money was devoted to education and training as to paying interest on the public debt. Whereas six provinces were projecting budgetary surpluses for 1995–6, Ontario's new Conservative regime was anticipating a deficit of $783 per person, the highest in the land.[14] The defeated NDP had the image of profligate spenders and the incoming Conservatives were painted as miserly mean-spirited scrooges, but one was hard pressed to discern a quantum difference in their bottom lines: the Conservatives reduced only marginally the NDP's last deficit of $10.1 billion to a not-much-less-astounding $9.3 billion for 1995–6. Substantial cutbacks were imposed on programs and the size of the civil service, and the government was forced to spend almost a billion dollars more on debt servicing compared to just one year earlier. The debt problem is not unique to Ontario, however. Other provinces and the federal government, to varying degrees, are also plagued by it. Where Ontario parts with most of the others, however, is in its capacity to generate public revenues.

The collective and relative wealth and prosperity of its people and economy is impressive indeed. Metropolitan Ontario, specifically greater Toronto, is in a league of its own. In some respects the province and the country serve as a hinterland to this region. It accounts for half the provincial economy and almost a fifth of the national economy. Toronto overtook Montreal as the most populous city in 1976; that was foreshadowed as early as 1934, when the value of trading on its stock exchange first exceeded Montreal's. The Toronto Stock Exchange is the tenth largest in the world, the value of its equity trading second only in North America to New York's. The Greater Toronto Area serves as the country's financial, manufacturing, communications, and cultural capital. It is home to Canada's largest concentration of educational and medical institutions and boasts that, as an English-language theatre centre, it ranks third in the world behind London and New York. Toronto's regional auto industry grew at a galloping annual rate of 11 per cent between 1986 and 1993, placing it second only to Detroit in the production of autos.[15] Greater Toronto has served as a veritable growth engine, aided by government expansion as the provincial capital and by capitalist expansion that belies provincialism. Toronto has the second-highest (after New York) share of financial employment and the third-highest (after New York and Chicago) share of head offices among the six hundred largest companies in North America. It is important to remember that the salaries paid to the city's technical and skilled labour force and the profits generated by its world-class corporations are taxable by Queen's Park. Note too that economic success and stress on overextended social services have gone hand-in-hand. In the late 1980s, as the urban economy boomed, food banks proliferated.

In stark contrast to metropolitan Ontario is remote, far-flung, sparsely populated, and relatively more francophone and aboriginal Northern Ontario. It is the area roughly north of a line running from Sault Ste Marie to Mattawa. It serves as a resource hinterland, a condition that has not changed over the decades. Of course, a metropolis-hinterland interpretation could be applied broadly to North America; in this context, Canada as a whole, including urban as well as Northern Ontario, serves as a hinterland to the U.S. American branch plants that have a long history in Ontario. From the perspective of the 1990s and the North America Free Trade Agreement, Ontario is now even more integrated into the continental economy, a development speeded up by the Canada-U.S. auto pact of three decades ago. Ontario's growth has been fed by both north-south and east-west links. Ontario's wealth is not as dependent on exploiting the markets of Quebec, Atlantic, and western Canada as residents of those regions have historically claimed; the Ontario and American markets are increasingly the power cogs of the provincial economy.

The growth of the provincial state accompanied the growth of provincial society and economy. New government ministries appeared, sometimes reflecting new initiatives, other times produced by splintering: six in the 1940s and 1950s, another three in the 1960s, followed by yet more in the 1970s and 1980s. In the half-century between 1940 and 1990, the roster of ministries or departments roughly doubled to between twenty-six and twenty-eight. Central agencies, an elaborate cabinet committee system, large omnibus departments, policy ministers, and parliamentary secretaries all made debuts. A regular stream of ministerial reorganizations and reconfigurations was designed to reinforce the top command of the political class over the apparently ever-expanding bureaucratic machine. Beyond the web of public administration at Queen's Park was an even greater proliferation of uncontrolled non-departmental agencies, boards, and commissions. A 1959 study identified eighty-four such ABCs that operate at arm's length from the government and the legislature, which extend authority to them. By 1978 the galaxy of ABCs – from the Ontario Arts Council to the Human Rights Commission to the Health Disciplines Board – had grown to nearly seven hundred. In 1992, the government advertised over 510 for which citizens could volunteer their candidacy,[16] a concession to and recognition of the growing impulse for participatory democracy. The faces of public administration changed too: in the early 1990s, half the deputy and assistant deputy ministers were drawn from non-traditional groups such as women and visible minorities, reflectors of Ontario's new diversity.

Provincial state and provincial society grew in tandem – in complexity, in diversity, and comparatively. In 1941, the population gap between Ontario and Quebec was less than a half million; in 1995 it was nearly four million. Ontarians are now also a decidedly different lot. In a once predominantly agricultural province, by 1991 there were only 100,000 farm operators.[17] Consider also religion. Anglicanism had once appeared as the official state religion. Anglicans and United Church members together made up half of Ontarians in 1941, but had shrunk to fewer than a quarter by 1991. Those claiming 'No Religion' now equal Presbyterians, Lutherans, Baptists, Pentecostals, and Jews combined (12.7 per cent). Religion is a fading factor in provincial politics, although it can still rear up as it did unexpectedly in the 1985 election when the state extended funding to Catholic high schools. Another sign of dramatic change is in Ontarians' origins. In 1941, only 9095 Ontarians reported being born outside Europe, the United States, or the Commonwealth;[18] by 1991, the United Kingdom ranked behind Asia, the Caribbean, Africa, South America, the Middle East, and even Central America as a source of immigrants; from 1988 to 1991 the number of Asian immigrants was nearly double those from Europe.[19] Since the 1940s, Ontario has received more than half of Canada's immigrants, attracting more of them between 1989 and 1995 alone than there are New Brunswickers or Newfoundlanders. The immigrants – once heavily British, then eastern and southern European – are increasingly Asian and visible. It is anticipated that soon after the turn of the century, a majority of metropolitan Torontonians will be members of racial minorities. Race and gender have become more prominent cleavages and religion now counts for less: who knew or cared in 1990 that Bob Rae is part-Jewish? His cabinet contained more women than any in Canadian history and it was sworn into office by a black lieutenant governor. David Peterson's cabinet featured the province's first Asian and black ministers. The NDP government's employment-equity initiatives, along with welfare and the debt, were the 'hot' issues in the 1995 election. As in welfare, many felt that – in setting employment targets or quotas for the private sector – the state had overreached its proper orbit. As the state legislated, reflecting the evolving and competing values of the new society, many Ontarians felt challenged and reacted.

Parties, Platforms, and Premiers

A half-century ago, Ontario's political parties were small, voluntary, and loose associations run and led by cliques. Leadership tended to be passed on rather than vigorously contested as in recent decades. The Conservatives and Liberals operated without party constitutions. Party officials and notables such as constituency presidents and candidates, rather than party members, defined what the party stood for and who would lead it. In the 1990s, and with the inexorable growth of democratic rhetoric, all three main parties are theoretically and constitutionally structured from the bottom up (the mass party) rather than from the top down (the cadre party). Ontario's Conservatives are the first party outside Quebec to give all party members a direct vote in selecting their leader, and Ontario is the first province where both Liberals and Conservatives employed such one member / one vote regimes. Changes in electoral finance laws that allow public scrutiny compel official record keeping and organizationally have transformed the parties. They are formal, legal entities operating as medium-sized businesses with offices and permanent staff outside of Queen's Park as well as substantial research and communications facilities within it.

This is not to suggest that leaders are any less important: in the 1995 election, the Conservatives projected themselves more as the Harris, rather than the Conservative, party. The relationship between leaders, MPPs, party members, and the electorate has changed slowly. Leaders are less beholden to their caucuses and more dependent on their media images. They appear simultaneously more and less secure in their tenure in an age of professionalized politics, mass party-member direct voting, and public-opinion polling. The evolving relationship of leader to party is not unique to Ontario, but is noteworthy because it means a change in the conduct of politics. For some voters, leaders are pivotal, offering a shorthand for party preference. In Ontario, perhaps more so than elsewhere, there is also strong dissonance between the consciousness and popularity of parties and their leaders. Consider the Liberals in 1985 and 1995: three months before his election as premier, fewer than one-fifth of the electorate knew who David Peterson was. Three months before the 1995 election, about half of those polled said they would vote Liberal, but only 8 per cent thought the Liberal leader would make the best premier.[20] As technology and values change, personalities with glib and telegenic features may become better positioned for leadership.

One difference between the NDP on the one hand and the Liberals and Conservatives on the other is that leadership has been more stable in the former. When Conservatives Frank Miller and Larry Grossman and Liberals David Peterson and Lyn McLeod lost elections between 1985 and 1995, they quickly resigned before their parties dispatched them. As the 'normal' third party, NDPers have had lower expectations of their leaders: they do not anticipate their winning elections. Defeat is therefore not fatal or necessarily a blow to the leader's continued prospects. When Donald MacDonald was re-elected as NDP leader in 1964, it was his eleventh consecutive victory, his uninterrupted tenure stretching back to the old CCF. As in most years, he was acclaimed. (The NDP constitutionally requires a formal leadership vote biennially unlike the other two parties.)

In contrast, the Liberal leadership has been more disputatious; in that same year, 1964, seven candidates offered themselves for it. To their chagrin, the Liberals became the 'normal' official-opposition party. Before 1985, they had won but three elections in the twentieth century, governing for only thirteen years. Since they very much want and often expect to win, running second is not good enough. Liberals are dejected in defeat. What George Perlin described as *The Tory Syndrome*[21] in federal politics – a constant questioning and therefore weakening of the leader – applies to the provincial Liberals. Where the federal Conservatives have suffered endemic weakness in Quebec, Ontario's provincial Liberals have suffered it in the greater Toronto region. The party seemed moribund for long stretches, served up six leaders between 1950 and 1967, and has had thirteen in total between the early 1940s and 1995. That is more than the CCF-NDP (5) and Conservatives (7) combined.

Conservative leadership was more stable because of repeated electoral success. When it became available – by the incumbent's resignation rather than failure, as with the Liberals – the prize was supreme: the premiership. Logically, it became highly contested as the modern leadership convention blossomed in the 1960s. John Robarts, for example, was but one of seven candidates, four of whom garnered between 332 and 352 votes on the first ballot, on which Robarts trailed. Since 1961, Ontario's Conservatives have held three conventions to select a premier, making the party the Canadian leader in this respect. It is common for regimes to fall after they replace long-serving premiers. Ontario was an exception during the 1943–85 period, changing leaders yet maintaining the reins of power. When the Conservatives stumbled in 1985, however, their leader also became more vulnerable.

Is it parties, platforms, or personalities that drive Ontario politics? The answer is all three, in varying degrees, at different times. Well into the 1970s and 1980s there were discernible partisan voting patterns that transcended policies and leaders, ones that stretched back a century and a half: the Conservatives performed relatively well in eastern Ontario's original Loyalist districts and the Liberals outperformed in southwestern Ontario's Clear Grit region where post-Revolutionary Americans and British-born Reformers had settled. The NDP, and before it the CCF and ILP, has been strongest in the urban-industrial and northern districts. These trends suggested the fidelity and constancy of partisan appeal.

Ontario's parties have old roots – both Liberals and Conservatives can trace their origins to pre-Confederation times – but what they stand for could and did change. Compare and contrast George Drew's '22 point program' of 1943 with Mike Harris's 'Common Sense Revolution' of 1995. The former catered to and the latter lambasted the welfare statism of the CCF-NDP. Such twists have reflected changing times and changing strategies. In the 1940s, in the midst of the war effort, government planning was driven by necessity, had legitimacy, and worked. In the 1990s, government appeared a burden, overextended and unsustainably expensive. In the mid-1940s, the ideological energy was on the left; the CCF was competing with Communists as well as Liberals and Conservatives for the working class and union vote. In the mid-1990s, the ideological energy was on the right; the Conservatives were competing philosophically with Reformers who were chomping at the bit of provincial politics and had overtaken the Conservatives in most of the province's ridings in the 1993 federal election. Whereas in the mid-1940s the CCF was a leading contender for office, in the mid-1990s it was the leading contender for third-party status, its customary role.

The CCF-NDP represents a constant left-wing presence on the political spectrum, while the positions of the Conservatives and Liberals have alternated. The labour movement embraced the CCF as its political arm in the 1940s and formally merged with it politically – as it did federally and in the other provinces – to launch the NDP in 1961. In every election, the CCF-NDP has relied heavily on union leaders, voters, and funds for support. In contrast, the Conservatives have had close but informal links to the business community. Where labour values were espoused by the NDP (social security, progressive taxation, workers' control, higher wages), business values were championed by the Conservatives (tax exemptions, favourable loans and outright grants, infrastructure and cheap power). For much of the period until 1985, the Liberals appeared to the right of the Drew-Frost-Roberts-Davis Conservatives. The latter positioned themselves successfully in the ideological centre as had the King-St Laurent-Pearson-Trudeau Liberals federally. When the Conservatives shifted right under Miller in 1985, they intentionally forsook their centrist bearings and permitted the Liberals to fall into the lacuna. The NDP tugged the Liberals in their direction by negotiating a legislative program, the Liberal-NDP Accord, for the Liberals' 1985–7 minority reign. After the Liberals miscalculated and squandered their good will by appearing opportunistic in calling an early election in 1990, the official-opposition NDP filled the new void as the only credible alternative. The Conservatives were still too discredited from the recent past to be resurrected.

What both the 1990 and 1995 elections had in common was a massive Liberal lead in public opinion as the campaigns were launched. In 1985, the ruling Conservatives had a similar, seemingly unassailable, lead. That the leading parties could falter so badly so quickly proved that a brief and intense six-week campaign period can be determinative of an election's outcome. What the 1990 and 1995 elections also had in common was that the winning parties were the ones that stood most clearly for change. Many who voted for them appeared more attracted to their commitment to some sort of change than to the content of the proposed changes.

In office, the NDP alienated many of its traditional labour supporters by violating collective-bargaining agreements and imposing public-sector wage cuts. At the same time, it failed to win over business support, even though it reneged on its promise to 'make the rich pay' for its social programs through higher corporate taxes. (The NDP actually collected less in such taxes than its predecessor on account of the recession). An NDP government was a startling break with the past and certainly shook up provincial politics. In totality, however, in style and content, it demonstrated how similar rather than how different it was from its competitors. The NDP represented continuity, more than revolution, in public policy. The new Conservative government of 1995, unlike its pre-1985 kin, was less keen on the state helping business directly via handouts, subsidies, or publicly funded infrastructure. It offered instead the repeal of NDP labour legislation, a smaller public sector, and a promise of lower taxes as a stimulant to economic activity.

How have Ontario's premiers changed? Symbolically, the NDP's victory represented the triumph of city over country: Bob Rae is the first and only premier to come from Toronto. He is also a lawyer, but that has been the norm: in the 128 years between Confederation and the NDP's defeat, lawyers served as premier for all but twenty-five years. All the premiers have been men, but prospects for a female first minister are bright if not immediate: Lyn McLeod served as leader of the opposition and premier-apparent for half the 1990s. All the premiers have been of Anglo-Celtic (Peterson was part Norwegian) ethnic origins. It is only a matter of time until this streak is broken too. In style, as in policy, Davis and his predecessors Frost and Robarts appeared like Mackenzie King and Louis St Laurent: conspicuously unflamboyant managers who seemed to operate like storekeepers at a time when government was relatively small. They appeared as colourless CEOs or chairmen of the boards of large, complex, and far-reaching enterprises as government became big business. In contrast, Rae and Harris, like Trudeau and Mulroney, were eager to act on programmatic agendas: 'An Agenda for People' and a 'Common Sense Revolution.' They were determined to drive the bureaucracy, whereas Peterson appeared more driven by it.

There is evidence of both growing turbulence and traces of continuity in provincial elections. At the macro level, the Liberal and NDP governments of 1987 and 1990 (along with the UFO of 1919) are the only first-term governments in provincial history not to get re-elected. (Remember: the 1985 Liberal government was not elected with the most seats, and was only subsequently installed thanks to its accord with the NDP.) Between 1985 and 1990, Ontario sported four premiers leading three different party governments. This was quite a contrast to the eight decades between 1905 and 1985, when the Conservatives governed for all but thirteen years. At the micro level, MPPs became less secure in their tenure too: the number of losing incumbents rose from 17 in 1985 to 24 in 1987 to 52 in 1990 to 61 (nearly half) in 1995. Between the 1940s and the early 1990s, however, there were also marks of stability in the party system. The three main parties have tended to have fairly persistent, relatively constant, levels of voter support. CCF-NDP support, for example, oscillated between 15 per cent and 30 per cent, never going below or above until 1990. (Federally, the CCF-NDP range in Ontario was narrower still, in a tight range of 18 to 22 per cent in the eight elections between 1965 and 1988). In terms of volatility – the readiness of voters to switch from one provincial party to another – Ontario has been more stable than any other region between 1945 and 1993.[22] In the same period, the net percentage of seats changing hands has also been lowest in Ontario.

How do the Ontario provincial and federal party systems compare? Between the 1940s and 1990s, Ontario was the province most clearly mirroring the approximate three-party system that had taken hold in Ottawa. As Robert J. Williams has demonstrated, however, such congruence was more apparent than real.[23] The provincial party system was not a microcosm of the federal one. Nor was the federal party system simply a large-scale version of the provincial one. The asymmetry of the two party systems is particularly glaring in the 1990s: after triumphing provincially at the beginning of the decade, the NDP was wiped out three years later with a pathetic 6 per cent of the Ontario vote in the federal election. Conversely, the Conservatives – similarly annihilated in 1993 – rose like a phoenix two years later provincially. The Liberals managed an unprecedented near sweep of Ontario's federal ridings (98 of 99), but twice in succession, before and after this feat, proved no better than handmaidens provincially. There may be a major realignment of federal forces occurring in Ontario currently, with the robust presence of Reform and the at least temporary eclipse of the Conservatives and the NDP. Provincially, however, the party system in the second half of the 1990s looks very much as it did during most of the past half-century: Conservatives on top, Liberals in the middle, and the NDP trailing in both seats and votes.

Culture and Identity

What values and fundamental political beliefs drive Ontarians and their politics? Is Ontario's political culture grounded in the province's traditions or is it ever changing, a product of Ontarians' wants and visions in the here and now? As we move farther from Ontario's pre-Confederation origins as a British frontier outpost of the late-eighteenth century, the distant past seems less enveloping and relevant. Historically rooted symbols, institutions, and constitutions, however, enshroud, reflect, and help to shape present-day politics: from the Union Jack that adorns the provincial flag, to the centralizing and authoritative executive-dominated Westminster model of cabinet-parliamentary government, to the special status accorded Catholics, francophones, and now aboriginals, who until recently were mere wards of the federal state. Today, Ontario politics appear propelled by public-opinion polls and by leaders whose own histories stretch back no earlier than the 1940s. In brief: is Ontario's political culture a product of past or present values? Moreover, does it reflect mass (the people's) or elite (their leaders') values?

Defining, measuring, and explaining Ontario's culture is a far more complex and challenging task than reviewing its demographic, economic, and partisan make-up. It is relatively easy to fix the size of the debt or to determine the ethnic and class composition of MPPs at Queen's Park. No similar ease applies to describing elite values and mass beliefs, their evolution, and their impact on each other. Whether we look at the past or to the present as the primary determinant of contemporary political discourse, there is no overriding consensus on what the past was or what the present is. Historical accounts of Ontario's initial Tory, hierarchical, and anti-revolutionary instincts are now countered by revisionists writing of its liberal, egalitarian, and civic-republican predilections.[24] Take your pick. Similarly, contemporary public opinion is more than divided merely on partisan grounds. Glaringly, the very same survey respondents are internally inconsistent. As evidence, let us revisit the provincial deficit: as 1995 began, 79 per cent of surveyed Ontarians disapproved of the NDP's handling of the issue, a higher disapproval rating than that for any of fourteen policy issues canvassed. Simultaneously, fewer than a quarter of these survey respondents felt that the Rae government's limiting of transfers to hospitals, municipalities, and schools should be 'tougher' while many more, 40 per cent, thought the government 'too tough.'[25] This suggests internal dissonance: people wanted a lower or no deficit, but disapproved of a freeze (let alone cuts) to accomplish it.

In an illuminating overview of Ontario's political culture, S.F. Wise cites and embraces uncritically Richard Simeon and David Elkins's analysis of the 'civic culture' questions posed and the answers extracted in John Meisel's National Election Studies of the 1960s. In this view, 'The bulk of the Ontario electorate is active in politics, confident of its role, yet positively oriented toward government and with fewer alienated or disaffected citizens than almost any other region.'[26] Subsequent surveys, employing the identical questions dealing with citizens' 'efficacy' and 'trust' in government, revealed contradictory results: yo-yo patterns, with Ontarians' alleged political activity, confidence, and positive orientations sometimes registering at or below the national averages.[27] The questions and the responses to them have proved so problematic that the designers of the more recent National Election Studies no longer pose them, having concluded that the questions dealing with 'efficacy' and 'trust' were neither efficacious nor trustworthy. Just as we thought we had discovered something precise, indeed profound, about Ontarians' political culture, we soon thereafter learned from the contradictions and inconsistencies in longitudinal and comparative data how little we actually knew.

More reliable as an indicator of Ontarians' values and identities may be their behaviour: what they do over time rather than what they say in hit-and-miss snap-shot surveys that frame responses into the preconceived categories of survey researchers. Consider voting behaviour at the most elementary level of turnout. With the exception of Albertans, Ontarians have the lowest rate of turnout in provincial elections. Since 1943, the average turnout for Ontario provincial elections has been 64 per cent. The pattern is remarkably persistent, unaffected by regime changes: in 1990 it was 64 per cent, and in 1995 63 per cent.[28] Where Albertans have consistently low turnouts in both federal and provincial elections, Ontarians reveal in federal elections how they are distinctly different: the third-highest turnout level among the provinces, at just under 74 per cent in recent decades.

This contrast establishes that Ontarians are more oriented to federal than provincial politics. The National Election Study of 1974 demonstrated that Ontarians are the most likely to think of the federal government as being more important to them than their provincial government; they are the most likely to feel closer to Canada and the federal government than their own province and their provincial government; the most likely to have an image only of federal parties and the least likely to have an image only of their provincial parties. A 1979 CBC survey reinforced these findings: Ontarians were the most likely to identify the term 'government' with Canada and the least likely to identify it with their province.[29] There is no evidence that the relatively and comparatively low salience of provincial politics has changed for Ontarians.

Ontarians possess a relative ignorance of provincial politics. This is something neither they nor their leaders may dwell on or be proud of, but it is none the less critical to understanding how Ontarians think of themselves and how they may respond to their leaders' provincialist appeals. At the beginning of 1995, only seven in ten Ontarians could name Bob Rae as the NDP leader, only four in ten could identify Mike Harris as Conservative leader, and only three in ten named Lyn McLeod, the leader of the opposition, as Liberal leader.[30] Is such ignorance of the leading provincial politicians as widespread in any other province? Consistently over the years, surveys have revealed that when asked 'Do you think of yourself as a Canadian first or as an Ontarian (Albertan, Quebecker, etc.) first?' Ontarians lead their fellow Canadians in describing themselves as Canadians first. In 1990 and 1994 surveys, an identical 90 per cent of Ontarians said so, while only 9 per cent said they thought of themselves as Ontarians first.[31] In contrast, many Quebeckers (55 per cent in 1990 and 49 per cent in 1994) and even more Newfoundlanders (53 per cent and 57 per cent) described themselves as Quebeckers and Newfoundlanders first. There are implications to Ontarians' low level of primary identification as Ontarians and their relatively high level of ignorance of provincial politics. When provincial leaders assault the federal government for allegedly short-changing Ontario – as the Rae government did – the message, irrespective of its objective merits, falls on largely deaf ears and is unlikely to succeed. In contrast, politicians in the other provinces are better positioned to benefit from 'fed-bashing.'

Changes in Ontarians' values and identities have been slow rather than sudden, evolutionary rather than sweeping, although from the perspective of the 1990s a full-blown revolution appears to have taken place since the 1940s. It has been consistent, nevertheless, with the ever-changing backdrop and interests of the province. The British connection serves as an example. Well into the 1960s, Ontario's largely Anglo-Saxon composition and Loyalist heritage was reinforced by direct British immigration, the largest single source of newcomers. Logically, Ontarians had long been in the forefront of pro-British efforts from the Boer War through two world wars. Well into the 1960s, movie theatres, television stations, and hockey arenas played 'God Save the Queen.' As provincial society became a multi-ethnic, multiracial polyglot, and as the economy and mass media became more Americanized, Britain, Britons, and British symbols slowly faded in prominence. As an example, ponder this contrast between the late 1940s and the late 1970s: in reaction to George Drew courting the anti-British mayor of Montreal in the 1949 federal election, the *Toronto Star* emblazoned its front page with the blaring headline 'Keep Canada British! God Save the King!'[32] Today such a clarion call in the mainstream media would ring absolutely archaic and is inconceivable. In the 1970s, British subjects resident in the province lost their automatic voting privileges in provincial elections; they now require Canadian citizenship on an equal footing with other immigrants.

Ontario's posture has also shifted towards the United States, but less dramatically and arguably more positively. Americans replaced Britons as the largest immigrant group during the early 1970s and the Vietnam war. That conflict was serviced militarily in small part by American subsidiaries in the province. The provincial government and majority opinion opposed free trade in both the 1911 and 1988 elections and Ontarians and Ontario-based organizations have been in the forefront of English Canadian nationalism, usually defined as opposition to Americanization. Nevertheless, Ontarians have also been receptive and eager to embrace American cultural symbols and pastimes: from Hollywood movies and television programming to fast food and sports franchises in baseball's American League and the National Basketball Association. 'No truck nor trade with the Yankees' gave way to integrated defence production in the 1940s, the auto pact in the 1960s, and the FTA in the 1980s. In contrast, the core-periphery relationship that has not changed perceptibly is the one between Northern and Southern Ontario. The north, past and present, appears as a relatively remote, dependent, passive, and alienated satellite caught in the orbit of the magnetic, dominant, affluent southern heartland.

Successive waves of immigrants since the 1940s undermined the verities associated with the provincial political culture. An overlapping panoply of diverse subcultures appeared: the long-established John Graves Simcoe Memorial Society had to compete for government funding and attention with a growing array of ethnocultural associations. Ontarians, like Canadians generally, embraced a more egalitarian constitutional and economic order. The vertical mosaic pervasive in the 1940s, still much evident in the 1960s,[33] was less recognizable in the 1990s: the presidents of General Motors of Canada and IBM Canada, both Ontarians, were a woman and an Asian respectively. Nevertheless, the vast majority of Ontario's corporate elite, whose appointments and promotions are trumpeted photographically in the financial press, are still white males of European, and especially Anglo-Celtic, extraction. Discernible disparities in the incomes and educational opportunities of some (but not all) historically disadvantaged groups persisted, but the yawning gaps narrowed and discrimination on an individual basis was less evident and legally reprehensible, something it had not been in the 1940s. Ontarians took the Charter of Rights to heart; in 1996 an alliance of organizations challenged the constitutionality of the Conservatives' repeal of the NDP's employment-equity legislation. Even when the Charter's consequences alarmed Ontarians – as when over 40,000 criminal cases were dismissed by the courts on the grounds that trials had been too long in coming – there was no talk of using the legislature to override it.

At the elite level, fiscal federalism and constitutional issues revealed more continuity than change. While Ontario's premiers and finance ministers often maligned Ottawa's taxation and spending policies, there was little uniquely Ontarian in their positions. No Ontario government has opposed equalization payments to the poorer provinces or clamoured as incessantly as Quebec or the far west for more jurisdictional clout. In CBC's 1979 survey, Ontarian public opinion was the least receptive to increasing provincial powers by constitutional change.[34] Significantly, on symbolic issues of constitutional direction and identity, Queen's Park lined up with Ottawa whatever the party in power at either level of government. Robarts endorsed federal bilingualism and was a leader in the constitutional arena, from his convening the Confederation of Tomorrow conference in the late 1960s to his co-chairmanship of the Task Force on Canadian Unity in the late 1970s. Davis was one of only two premiers endorsing Ottawa's drive for unilateral patriation of the Constitution. Peterson more than embraced the Meech Lake Accord; he offered a diminished Ontarian presence in the Senate for its ratification. And Rae was arguably the chief provincial architect in cobbling together the Charlottetown Accord. The gap between elite and mass opinion on constitutional issues (the former were united, the latter divided), came to haunt both Peterson and Rae. Situated intimately next to Quebec, Ontarians have been more sympathetic to its aspirations than those further west. Harris, in his tenure to date and in something of a change from the past, has shown less interest and passion in the national unity / Quebec dossier; it is not part of his 'Common Sense Revolution.' The Ontario legislature, like three of its Atlantic counterparts but unlike any western legislature, recognized Quebec's 'distinct' character in a symbolic resolution on the eve of Quebec's 1995 referendum. The government, however, refused the phrase 'distinct society,' claiming that would be revisiting the past and divisive.

The Future of Ontario Politics

Will Ontario politics change as much in the next half-century as they have in the past fifty years? Yes and no. Ontario society will remain and likely become even more diverse, especially if the relative rate of immigration increases. Older waves of immigrants will be socialized and come to think of themselves first and foremost as Canadians rather than as Chinese, blacks, Filipinos, Bosnians, or Ontarians. Aboriginal and gender issues, once foreign to discussions of provincial politics and of relatively recent salience, will continue to lurk and flare. Ontario's economy will probably become still more integrated with that of the behemoth to the south. It will also be more exposed to the globalization of trade, investment, and technology. In the short term, the public sector is in crisis, in relative disrepute, and shrinking. In the longer term, citizens will continue to look to government to solve perceived problems so that, paradoxically, a smaller government may come to exert greater influence in the daily affairs of provincial residents. The relations between citizens and their government will remain contentious, more so than in the past. Such generalizations are limiting, however, for none of them applies uniquely to Ontario.

In partisan politics, the established parties – the Conservatives, Liberals, and NDP – will persist. The barriers to the successful entry of new parties will remain high. In this sense, the past will continue to weigh heavily on the future. What is less certain and more significant is what these parties may come to represent and do when in office. In this sense the sheer continuity of partisan labels may not mean much. The Conservatives, once the party of the activist state, have demonstrated that they can lead the charge for a retrenched state. The Liberals, once the party of free trade, have shown they can become a foe of it. Once and still the party of organized labour, the NDP has shown it can abrogate labour's hallowed gains and lose the unions' fidelity. The Reform Party, a significant federal force in Ontario in 1993, has, at least temporarily, perhaps permanently, been trumped provincially. Smaller fringe parties are no more likely to succeed in the future than they have in the past, but, as the 1990 election demonstrated, they may play the role of spoilers and inadvertently become king-makers.

Much of Ontario's future direction will be shaped, but not wholly dictated, by developments beyond its borders and its people's capacity to determine. The decision regarding Quebec's separation will be made in Quebec, not Ontario, yet its consequences would be profound for Ontario and its place in a presumably reconstituted Canada. Similarly, there is not much Ontarians can do to keep a head-strong future U.S. Congress or president from abrogating NAFTA. It is difficult to think of the provincial interest independent of the national one, more so in Ontario than in other provinces. If Quebec *were* to separate, the status of the

French language would likely suffer in Ontario and Canada. The province would become an even more dominant region, making up half the population of a Canada without Quebec. In such a context, would provincial politics be even less important to Ontarians? Is a separate Northern Ontario province conceivable as a marginal counterweight to metropolitan Ontarian hegemony? Prospects would brighten for an Ontarian becoming a prime minister (as opposed to a premier calling himself a prime minister, as Robarts did), something rare in the past half-century.

Peering into the future is a more daunting challenge than retelling the past or describing the present. In the late 1990s, there appears to be more passion, confrontation, and ideology in the conduct of provincial politics. Will this pass or linger? The political surprises of recent years will continue and perhaps be outdone in ways that we cannot imagine. Politics in Ontario, as elsewhere, is about change. Some Ontarians will agitate for it, others will resign themselves to it, and still others will fight it as they are discomfited by it.

Notes

1 Reginald Whitaker, *The Government Party: Organizing and Financing the Liberal Party of Canada, 1930–1958* (Toronto: University of Toronto Press, 1977).

2 Robert Bothwell, *A Short History of Ontario* (Edmonton: Hurtig, 1986), 150.

3 James Struthers, *The Limits of Affluence: Welfare in Ontario, 1920–1970* (Toronto: University of Toronto Press, 1994), 5.

4 Government of Canada, *Improving Social Security in Canada* (Ottawa: 1994), 10.

5 See Leon Muszynski, 'What's in a Name? Canada's New Employment Insurance Program,' Caldeon Institute of Social Policy, March 1996.

6 Informetrica, 'Ontario and the Canada Assistance Plan,' prepared for Ministry of Intergovernmental Affairs, 1 November 1993, 8.

7 Mark McElwain, 'Ontario's Budgetary Process,' in Graham White, ed., *The Government and Politics of Ontario*, 4th ed. (Scarborough: Nelson, 1990), 359, and *Globe and Mail*, 25 November 1995.

8 *Ontario Budget, 1994,* 119.

9 Affidavit of Jack Leslie Carr, Ontario Court of Justice (General Division), Court file no. 590/95, p. 6.

10 *Globe and Mail*, 18 December 1995.

11 Eugene Forsey, *Freedom and Order* (Toronto: McClelland and Stewart, 1974), 216. The case was *Rex ex rel. Tolfree v. Clark et al.* [1943] O.W.R., p. 328.

12 Martha Friendly, *Child Care Policy in Canada* (Don Mills, Ont.: Addison-Wesley, 1994), 80, and *Globe and Mail*, 25 November 1995.

13 Floyd Laughren, Treasurer, *Ontario Fiscal Outlook: Meeting the Challenges* (January 1992), 5, and Ernie Eves, Minister of Finance, *1995 Fiscal and Economic Statement* (November 1995), tables 19 and 32.

14 *Globe and Mail*, 25 November 1995.

15 *Toronto Star*, 4 April 1995, and *Globe and Mail*, 2 December 1995.

16 J.E. Hodgetts, *From Arm's Length to Hands-On: The Formative Years of Ontario's Public Service, 1867–1940* (Toronto: University of Toronto Press, 1995), 238.

17 *Canada Year Book, 1994* (Ottawa: Statistics Canada, 1993), 476.

18 *Eighth Census of Canada, 1941* (1950), vol. 1, table III, 169–70.

19 Statistics Canada, catalogue 93-316 (data are for all of Canada, but, with a majority of immigrants settling in Ontario, doubtless capture the Ontario reality).

20 *Globe and Mail*, 21 March 1995.

21 George Perlin, *The Tory Syndrome: Leadership Politics in the Progressive Conservative Party* (Montreal: McGill-Queen's Press, 1980).

22 Peter McCormick, 'Provincial Party Systems, 1945–1993,' in A. Brian Tanguay and Alain-G. Gagnon, eds, *Canadian Parties in Transition*, 2nd ed. (Toronto: Nelson, 1996), 360, 363.

23 Robert J. Williams, 'Ontario's Provincial Party System after 1985: From Complacency to Quandary,' in Hugh G. Thorburn, ed., *Party Politics in Canada*, 7th ed. (Scarborough: Prentice-Hall, 1996), chap. 31.

24 Janet Ajzenstat and Peter J. Smith, eds, *Canada's Origins: Liberal, Tory, or Republican?* (Ottawa: Carleton University Press, 1995).

25 Environics Research Group, *Focus Ontario 1994-4* (Toronto: 1995), 5, 15.

26 S.F. Wise, 'The Ontario Political Culture: A Study in Complexities,' in White, ed., *Government and Politics of Ontario*, 54. He cites Richard Simeon and David Elkins, 'Regional Political Cultures in Canada,' *Canadian Journal of Political Science* 7 (September 1974): 397–437.

27 David V.J. Bell, 'Political Culture in Canada,' in Michael S. Whittington and Glen Williams, eds, *Canadian Politics in the 1990s*, 3rd ed. (Scarborough, Ont.: Nelson, 1990), 143.

28 Chief Election Officer, Ontario, *Election Summaries with Statistics from the Records* (1995), 34.

29 Harold D. Clarke, et al., *Political Choice in Canada* (Toronto: McGraw-Hill Ryerson, 1979), 70–1, 80, and 180, and Joel Smith and David K. Jackson,

Restructuring the Canadian State: Prospects for Three Political Scenarios (Durham, NC: Duke University Centre for International Studies, 1981), 17.

30 Environics, *Focus Ontario*, 8.

31 Rand Dyck, *Provincial Politics in Canada*, 3rd ed. (Scarborough, Ont.: Prentice-Hall, 1996), 5.

32 Norman Penner, 'Ontario: The Dominant Province,' in Martin Robin, ed. *Canadian Provincial Politics*, 2nd ed. (Scarborough, Ont.: Prentice-Hall, 1978), 210.

33 John Porter, *The Vertical Mosaic* (Toronto: University of Toronto Press, 1965).

34 Smith and Jackson, *Restructuring the Canadian State*, 18, 21.

A Guide to Sources on Ontario Government and Politics

Graham White

Students writing papers on topics relating to Ontario government and politics have available to them an enormously rich variety of sources. Often, however, they fail to take advantage of this material because they do not know where to find it. Library catalogues, periodical indices, and the bibliographic suggestions in this and other books are excellent guides to the published secondary literature of Ontario, that is, writings by academics, journalists, and others about Ontario. However, the primary sources on Ontario – government documents, interest-group submissions to government commissions, and the like – are not so easily obtained. This appendix is principally concerned with assisting students in gaining access to information about Ontario government and politics beyond that contained in books and journals.

As indicated below, the written sources – particularly about government policy and organization – are extensive. Civil servants, politicians, and others directly involved in governmental and policy processes are also valuable sources of information. Generally speaking, they are quite willing to answer questions about Ontario politics, about governmental processes, and about specific policy areas. In tapping into these sources, a little common sense and courtesy will go a long way. Identify yourself clearly and explain what it is you want to talk about, and how you will be using the information. Prepare ahead and know what you want to ask. Determine whether other students are working on similar topics and might want to interview the same person; if so, work out some means of sharing the information. Avoid having a number of people asking the same person the same questions.

Finding Your Way through Government Documents

The Ontario government (widely defined) publishes hundreds of documents every year. The trick is finding out what is available and then locating it. For best results, combine both written and oral routes. The Legislative Library produces a *Monthly Checklist* of new Ontario government publications, which is consolidated every year into Ontario Government Publications, *Annual Catalogue;* both are available at most public libraries. In addition, many libraries maintain their own catalogues for government documents. If at all possible, enlist the help of a librarian who specializes in government documents, since the ways in which government documents are organized can be very confusing for those (even general librarians) unused to dealing with them. An alternative is to seek assistance from the small specialist libraries located in each ministry; some of the more decentralized ministries have regional libraries as well. The telephone number for the ministry library can be obtained by calling the general enquiry number at the beginning of the ministry's listing in the Ontario government telephone book, which most libraries carry.

As a supplement to looking through catalogues and listings of documents, it is often beneficial to ask civil servants involved in specific policy areas to recommend documents that might be worth reviewing. This can significantly reduce the time you spend rummaging through government documents. It can also lead to documents not available in libraries. Many government documents that are not formally published (because of limited demand) are available to the public. Depending on their policy areas, civil servants would know about these sources and might even be able to send you copies. In addition, they can often tell you about other non-governmental sources you might consult, such as unpublished briefs from interest groups or publications of organizations involved in the policy area.

But how do you find the right civil servant to call? First, flip through that invaluable research tool, the Ontario government telephone book. Look for the branch or section most likely to be familiar with your topic and call it. Similarly, the *KWIC Index to Services* is very useful in ascertaining which governmental organization is responsible for which policy fields. Alternatively, each ministry has a communications branch, which will either respond to your information request or pass you along to someone in the ministry who can help. Finally, the Citizens' Inquiry Bureau of the Ministry of Government Services acts as a referral service for calls from the public about policies and services of the Ontario government. The Citizens' Inquiry Bureau can be reached as a local call in some parts of Ontario, through 800 numbers in other areas, and in other ways elsewhere; check the blue government pages in your local phone book.

Students who live outside of the Toronto area will be understandably unwilling to run up long-distance phone bills in their attempts to track down civil servants. This need not be a problem. The Citizens Inquiry Branch offers a wide range of helpful services and access to information; it can be reached at (416) 326-1234 in the Toronto area or through 800 numbers in other parts of the province (in the Ottawa area, Access Ontario performs the same functions; in Northern Ontario, assistance is available through the local Ministry of Northern Affair office). Alternatively, ministry field offices in cities outside Toronto may be able to answer questions or to pass along information requests to Toronto at no cost to the original caller. The telephone book for each city or area of Ontario includes a set of blue pages containing government telephone numbers either within the local dialing area or obtainable at no charge to the caller through an 800 number or through a zenith operator. At the end of the Ontario government listings in the blue pages there is usually a general number given for services not specified in the listings.

MPPs' offices can be called without incurring long-distance charges. They can be useful sources of advice and information, but don't expect the member's staff to do your work for you. MPPs' telephone numbers are listed in the blue pages of the telephone book.

Note that the emphasis is on calling rather than writing. Unless you have no deadline for your assignment, it is not advisable to write in search of information, because of the delays that can occur.

Once you establish which documents you require, finding them should not be difficult. As mentioned above, for unpublished government documents the principal source will be civil servants in the responsible ministry. Otherwise, almost all documents published by ministries and agencies of the Ontario government are available to depository libraries throughout the province (the relatively infrequent exceptions tend to be highly specialized and technical). Nearly four hundred libraries across Ontario are 'depository libraries,' which are eligible to receive copies of published government documents (subject to the exception noted above).

These libraries are not capable of processing the full range of government documents and thus choose materials according to local interest and intrinsic importance. More than two dozen of the larger public libraries across Ontario are 'full depository libraries,' which automatically receive copies of all published Ontario government documents. Most university libraries and a few community-college libraries are also full depository libraries. Libraries rarely permit government documents to circulate, so you will have to be prepared to use them in the library.

Reports of royal commissions, legislative committees, and similar inquiries often list (in appendices) research studies prepared for them as well as briefs and submissions made to them. These documents can be gold mines of information, but they are not always easy to obtain, especially for students outside Toronto. The difficulty is not that they are confidential, for this is rarely the case, but that they may have been produced in very small numbers and are thus hard to locate. If the organization that issued the report still exists, its office will usually be able to advise on the availability of these documents. Royal commissions, special inquiries, and other bodies that disband once their work is complete transmit their papers and background studies to the Ontario Archives in downtown Toronto, though it may take some time before this material is fully catalogued and processed. In such cases, it may be best to contact the ministry most closely associated with the policy area (the ministry libraries are probably the best places to start), which will likely have copies of all pertinent documents.

The *Debates* of the legislature ('Hansard') are widely available and are extensively indexed. In addition to setting out the parties' political slants on all manner of topics, these verbatim transcripts can provide much detailed information on policy issues. The *Debates* are not to be confused with the daily *Votes and Proceedings* (consolidated at the end of the session into the *Journals*), which record only the bare bones of House activities. The proceedings of virtually all legislative committees are transcribed in publicly available documents, which often contain extensive material on political issues and policy questions. Hard copies of committee transcripts tend to be scarce beyond the confines of Queen's Park, but they have recently become available through the Legislature's 'web site.'

The freedom of information (FOI) process is, in most cases, unlikely to be of much assistance to students because it takes a minimum of several weeks to process requests, because fees may be involved, and because the documents it handles are usually too specialized and technical for student assignments. None the less, the FOI guidebook, the *Directory of General Records* (available at most libraries) is a very useful indicator as to which components of the Ontario government maintain records on various topics: the *Directory*, however, does not give titles of documents.

The development of the 'World Wide Web' on the Internet offers greatly enhanced access to information about the Ontario government. The main government site (URL: http://www.gov.on.ca) contains extensive and up-to-date material on government policies and activities. Through its links to ministries and agencies, students can peruse and download detailed documents pertaining to every facet of the Ontario government; the nature and extent of material varies widely by ministry or agency. The legislature's site (http://www.ontla.on.ca) includes information on MPPs, legislation currently before the House, and full-text transcripts of House and committee proceedings.

Party Politics

It is more difficult to be specific about sources for topics that focus more on partisan politics than on policy or government process, since they do not relate to specific government departments or policy documents. Obviously, the politicians themselves – MPPs, defeated candidates, party officials, and the like – are prime subjects, but depending on the topic, journalists, interest-group representatives, and others may be worth interviewing.

The three major parties have all developed web sites on the Internet, where information on party policies and activities, leaders, and other political matters may be found. The URLs for the parties are as follows:

- Progressive Conservative   http://www.ontariopc.on.ca
- Liberal   http://www.interlog.com/~liberal
- NDP   http://www.web.net/~ondp

Poll-by-poll election results may be found in the report of the chief election officer, issued a few months after each general election. The annual reports of the Election Finance Commission contain valuable information about the parties' fund raising and about their spending on elections. Local party organizers are highly knowledgeable about the specific factors determining election results in particular ridings. In recent years, several province-wide polls have been published during each election campaign. These polls often break down vote intention, leadership image, policy preference, and other political variables by such demographic variables as region, sex, and socio-economic status.

Between elections, major newspapers, particularly the *Toronto Star* and the *Globe and Mail*, commission polls containing valuable data on party fortunes and public opinion on key political issues.

Legislative, Executive, and Political Records at the Archives of Ontario: A Brief Guide

Jim Suderman

Records are a by-product of interaction within the government itself, between the government and the governed, and between different levels of government. Although voluminous, government records are not homogeneous. Understanding the distinction between legislative and executive records is essential for researchers to identify records relevant to their work.

Only a tiny percentage of all government records are published and therefore widely available. The great majority of records are destroyed, at the direction of the Archives of Ontario, once they have outlived their usefulness. The Archives undertakes to identify and preserve only the most authoritative and essential records. To assist researchers to understand the recorded information in context, the Archives also strives to preserve the records in the context in which they were created.

Located in downtown Toronto, a few blocks from the Legislative Building, the Archives of Ontario, an agency of the Ministry of Citizenship, Culture and Recreation, is the official record-keeper of the Ontario government. Archival holdings are not solely very old documents of interest only to historians, although the Ontario Archives holds records dating back to the establishment of Upper Canada in the late eighteenth century. Government ministries and agencies are legally required either to deposit their records in the Archives or to check with the Archives before destroying them. Thus, for example, the Archives has already acquired the records from the Premier's Office during the Rae administration. Acquisition of both government records and records from nongovernment sources provides a comprehensive record of value to students and researchers interested in recent Ontario political history.

Legislative Records

The Archives acquires records of the Legislative Assembly and its committees via the Clerk of the Assembly's Office. These records include the videotaped proceedings of the assembly, the minutes, transcripts, submissions, and exhibits created within legislative committees as they review government bills, expenditures, and, occasionally, the conduct of cabinet members. The Archives also receives the legislature's sessional papers, which include annual reports (not all offices submit them), compendia of background information that the government tables when it introduces legislation into the House and written questions to cabinet ministers and their responses. Draft bills, created in the office of the Legislative Counsel, are also acquired.

A key tool for tracing the activities of the assembly and linking those activities with the records they generated is the published *Journal of the Legislative Assembly*. The *Journal*, essentially a daily log of each session of the assembly, is compiled from the daily *Votes and Proceedings*. It provides essential details for locating records by listing sessional papers and giving their numbers, listing public and private bills and giving their numbers, and identifying to which committee each bill was assigned for review. The *Debates and Proceedings of Ontario's Assembly*, popularly referred to as Hansard, were first recorded in 1944. Beginning in 1947 they were also published. Until 1991 the proceedings of legislative committees were not published (often not even created), with the exception of proceedings dealing with government expenditure, which were published as addenda to the *Debates and Proceedings* of the House.

Records of independent agencies responsible to the legislature rather than to the government, such as the Provincial Auditor, the Information and Privacy Commissioner, the Ombudsman, the Chief Election Officer, and the Commissioner on Election Finances, are also available at the Archives of Ontario.

Executive Records

The vast majority of government records are executive records. For the most part, the records describing a specific policy and illustrating its intent are executive records, created within the originating ministry.

Cabinet submissions, cabinet and cabinet-committee minutes and orders-in-council are acquired by the Archives of Ontario.

The execution of government policy is often illustrated by where the government allocates its fiscal resources. Each year an allocation is made by the Policy and Priorities Board of Cabinet, chaired by the premier, to each ministry and government-funded agency. Also allocated at this time are the provincial transfer payments to other levels of government and other organizations such as hospitals and school boards.

Considerable documentation on the allocations process exists at the Archives. Since 1971, Cabinet Submission 106 has been annually reserved for all the documents (including those from the Treasury and Management Board and the recommendations of the Policy and Priorities Board regarding transfer payments and allocations) necessary for cabinet to reach its decisions.

The process of assigning resources may occasionally be accompanied by competition between various ministers. Some evidence of that give and take may be found in the correspondence of the Cabinet Secretary and the Secretary of the Policy and Priorities Board. Evidence may also exist in the correspondence of the minister involved. These records are routinely acquired by the Archives of Ontario.

An invaluable tool for identifying some of the procedures and roles of various participants in the government bureaucracy, is the *Directives and Guidelines* (an administrative manual), which indicates what steps are to be followed for specific activities and identifies who is to take them. This information helps identify the best source for the most authoritative records relevant to a given topic.

The Freedom of Information and Protection of Privacy Act, 1987 governs access to executive records. Access to most government documents less than fifteen years old and held by the Archives is at the discretion of the Archives' Access Unit. Access to certain types of records, such as cabinet minutes and submissions, and certain types of information, such as personal information or third-party information, is not discretionary.

Political Records

Public inquiries form a visible and sometimes influential medium between the government and the governed. The Archives has acquired the records of most provincial public inquiries (royal commissions, judicial inquiries, and commissions of inquiry) since Confederation.

Intergovernmental forums also witness the expression of political will as different parties and policies strive to find common ground. Ontario has long had an interest in the affairs of Quebec and the future of Canada. The Confederation of Tomorrow conference organized by Premier Robarts in the late 1960s addressed issues that are still making headlines today. Evidence of Premier Rae's involvement in the recent round of constitutional talks may also be found at the Archives in the records of both the Premier's Office and those of the Ministry of Intergovernmental Affairs.

Ontario premiers and ministers often play an influential role in federal policies and areas of responsibility, such as immigration, and areas of interprovincial cooperation, such as education, trade, finances, sports, and so on. This interaction is documented in the files of the Ministry of Intergovernmental Affairs, primarily a policy and advisory body, and the lead ministry for the activity (e.g., Education), along with briefing books from a profusion of task forces and advisory committees. Many records concerning intergovernmental relations are generated in the Premier's Office and, since 1971, in the offices of the Ministry of Intergovernmental Affairs.

Sources for researching political-party activities are less concentrated than is the case for government activities. But the records are still linked to key creators, including the parties themselves and the individuals within them.

The papers of the Progressive Conservative Party of Ontario are held at the Archives. (Those of the Liberal Party and the New Democratic Party are held at Queen's University.) Also held at the Archives of Ontario are the papers of Ontario's premiers, from those of Bob Rae back to Ontario's first premier, John S. Macdonald. Many holdings of private papers of party luminaries, both un-elected and elected, are held at the Archives. Relatively recent acquisitions include the papers of Clare Westcott, a key aide to Bill Davis, of Hershell Ezrin, David Peterson's principal secretary, and Tony Clement, former president of the provincial Progressive Conservatives and now MPP for Brampton South. The Clement Papers were used by Dr Peter Woolstencroft in his essay for this book on the revitalization of the Progressive Conservative Party.

An example of the unique material available to those researching recent Ontario politics may be found in the papers of Rae and Peterson, and to a lesser extent those of Frank Miller as well, which contain considerable documentation on the striking of the 1985 Liberal-NDP Accord, which brought forty-two years of Conservative government to a close.

Access to these private papers requires written permission from the respective donors.

Logistics of Research at the Archives of Ontario

Finding the best record of government activity requires knowledge of what offices were involved, what procedures were followed, and what records those procedures generated. Of course, not all government interactions follow an identifiable procedure or necessarily result in the generation of records. And not all records are always controlled and described accurately. This can make finding files relating to specific activities difficult and time-consuming. Because of the unique nature of the records held by the Archives – most are original documents of which no copies exist – they are not allowed to leave the Archives and must be examined in the Archives' reading room at 77 Grenville Street. Professional archivists are available to assist researchers in locating material.

All researchers should contact the Archives before arriving in the reading room. A preliminary contact can help focus the record search, ensure that any relevant records are on-site, and help determine whether a formal request for information under the Freedom of Information and Protection of Privacy Act, 1987 will be necessary. Ontario residents can phone the Archives at 1-800-668-9933, or if in the Toronto area, 416-327-1600. Location, retrieval, and other information is available on the Toronto Freenet – just type 'go ao' from the main menu. At the time of publication, a preliminary contact via the web site or e-mail is not possible. The Archives' URL is http://www.gov.on.ca/MCZCR/archives. Watch the Archives' growing web page for further developments, especially the section 'Conducting Research from a Distance: Research Inquiries by Telephone, Fax, Letter or Email.'

Contributors

David Cameron, Professor of Political Science at the University of Toronto, is a former civil servant in Ottawa and at Queen's Park. In both his academic and bureaucratic roles, he has worked on federalism and intergovernmental relations, the status of Quebec in Confederation, constitutional reform, and the political and social evolution of Ontario.

Cheryl Collier holds a degree in journalism from Carleton University and is currently a Ph.D. candidate in the Department of Political Science at the University of Toronto. Her interests include women and provincial politics in Canada and political parties.

Robert Drummond is Associate Professor of Political Science, York University. His interests include Ontario politics, public opinion and voting and Canadian public policy, especially the policy issues of an aging society.

Rand Dyck is Professor of Political Science and Vice-Dean of Social Science at Laurentian University. He is author of three editions of *Provincial Politics in Canada*, two editions of *Canadian Politics: Critical Approaches*, and numerous articles on Ontario politics, political parties, and federalism.

Frederick J. Fletcher is Professor of Political Science and in Environmental Studies at York University. He has worked with several news organizations and is a former director of the Ontario Legislature Internship Programme. He has published numerous articles on Ontario politics, media and elections, and related subjects as well as *The Newspaper and*

Public Affairs: Media, Elections and Democracy and edited five volumes of research on media and elections for the Royal Commission on Electoral Reform and Party Financing.

Henry Jacek, Professor of Political Science at McMaster University, conducts research and teaches in the areas of provincial and Canadian politics, international and comparative public policy, interest groups, business-government relations, and the politics of economic policy in the OECD countries.

Richard Loreto, a former Ontario public servant and university professor, is president of RAL Consulting Limited. He holds a Ph.D. in political science from the University of Toronto and has written a number of scholarly and popular publications on government in Canada.

Robert MacDermid teaches political science at York University. His research interests include elections and campaigning, public-opinion polling, and public administration. He is currently researching the use of television advertising during Canadian election campaigns.

Desmond Morton, former Principal of Erindale College, University of Toronto, is Director of the McGill Institute for the Study of Canada.

Sid Noel is Professor of Political Science at the University of Western Ontario. He is author of *Patrons, Clients, Brokers*, a study of the origins of Ontario politics.

Chuck Rachlis, Ph.D., is a Toronto-based government-relations consultant. From 1990 to 1994 he was Director, Policy and Issues, and Economic Policy Coordinator in the Office of Premier Bob Rae. From 1983 to 1990 he was part of the NDP caucus research department and was NDP Research Director from 1986 to 1990.

David Siegel is Associate Vice-President, Academic, and an Associate Professor of Politics at Brock University. He holds degrees from the University of Toronto, Carleton University, and the University of Louisville. He is also a certified general accountant.

Richard Simeon is Professor of Political Science and Law at the University of Toronto. A long-time student of federalism and constitutional politics in Canada, his research interests have become increasingly comparative and focused on broader issues of governance in contemporary societies.

Rose Sottile has worked for CBC audience research and CBC Radio news. An honours graduate of York University in Political Science and Mass Communications, she is completing an M.A. in Communications at Carleton University. She is a former Ontario legislative intern.

Jim Suderman is Senior Archivist in the Political/Legislative Portfolio, Archives of Ontario, and is responsible for provincial agencies including the Premier's Office, the Ministry of Intergovernmental Affairs, Management Board, Cabinet Office, and the offices of the Legislative Assembly. He holds an M.A. in history.

Thomas Walkom worked as a Queen's Park columnist, first for the *Globe and Mail* and then for the *Toronto Star*. Author of *Rae Days: The Rise and Follies of the NDP*, he holds a doctorate in economics from the University of Toronto. He is currently columnist and national-affairs writer for the *Star*.

Geoffrey R. Weller is Professor in the International Studies Program at the University of Northern British Columbia. He was founding President of UNBC and was Vice-President (Academic) at Lakehead University. He has published widely in such fields as health policy, public policy in circumpolar regions, security and intelligence services, and post-secondary education.

Graham White is Professor of Political Science at Erindale College, University of Toronto, and a former Director of the Ontario Legislature Internship Programme. He has written extensively on Ontario politics, on comparative provincial politics, and on the political development of the Northwest Territories.

Robert Williams is Associate Professor of Political Science at the University of Waterloo, where he has taught courses on Ontario politics since 1971. He is Director of the Ontario Legislature Internship Programme.

Nelson Wiseman is Associate Professor of Political Science at the University of Toronto. His published work deals with Canadian provincial politics (particularly in Quebec and the Prairies), political parties, and political culture.

David Wolfe is Associate Professor of Political Science at Erindale College, University of Toronto. From 1990 to 1993, he was Executive Coordinator, Economic and Labour Policy, in the Cabinet Office of the Ontario Government.

Peter Woolstencroft is Associate Professor of Political Science and Associate Dean of Arts, University of Waterloo. He has published articles on the federal and Ontario Progressive Conservative parties, electoral geography, Canadian elections and parties, methods of selecting party leaders, education policy, and spatial aspects of urban politics.